MODERNISM IN THE STREETS

MODERNISM IN THE STREETS

A Life and Times in Essays

MARSHALL BERMAN

Edited by
David Marcus and Shellie Sclan

VERSO

London • New York

First published by Verso 2017
© Marshall Berman 2017

1 3 5 7 9 10 8 6 4 2

Verso
UK: 6 Meard Street, London W1F 0EG
US: 20 Jay Street, Suite 1010, Brooklyn, NY 11201
versobooks.com

Verso is the imprint of New Left Books

ISBN-13: 978-1-78478-498-0
ISBN-13: 978-1-78478-499-7 (UK EBK)
ISBN-13: 978-1-78478-500-0 (US EBK)

British Library Cataloguing in Publication Data
A catalogue record for this book is available from the British Library

Library of Congress Cataloging-in-Publication Data
A catalog record for this book is available from the Library of Congress

Typeset in Fournier MT by Hewer Text UK Ltd, Edinburgh
Printed in the US by Maple Press

Contents

V. The Bright Book of Life

VI. Signs in the Street

VII. The Romance of Public Space

VIII. From the Ruins

Introduction

Marxism with Soul: On the Life and Times of Marshall Berman

Marshall Berman was born in the South Bronx in 1940. Over the next three decades, he watched his lower-middle-class neighborhood turn to ruin. Between 1948 and 1972, Robert Moses—who years later became the Faustian villain of Berman's *All That Is Solid Melts into Air*—built the Cross Bronx Expressway. It ravaged the South Bronx, cutting it up into bits and pieces and bombing out other areas completely, including much of Berman's own neighborhood, Tremont. In the 1970s, the less systematic destruction began. New York City was broke and its outer boroughs were in a state of neglect and disrepair. "The Bronx finally made it into the media," as Marshall recalled in an essay about the '70s. The headline: "The Bronx Is Burning!"

The self-destructive tendencies of New York City—and, more generally, of modern urban life—were to become the central preoccupation in Berman's work. His first book, *The Politics of Authenticity* (1970), took eighteenth-century Paris and its two most brilliant thinkers, Montesquieu and Rousseau as a case study for what culminated in the revolutionary violence at the end of the century. *All That Is Solid*, which came twelve years later, was something less and something more. It marked the end of a promising, though contained, academic career in the vein of his college and early graduate school mentors—Peter Gay, Lionel Trilling, Isaiah Berlin—and the blossoming of a startling and radical new voice in social criticism. Tracing an arc of violence and destruction from Goethe's Faust to New York City's Moses, Berman argued that modernism, when coupled with the toxic tendencies of industrial capitalism, wreaked havoc on man's psychic and spiritual life as well as his social and economic conditions.

Both works and the many essays that came before and after also insisted there was another side of modern life. A figure like Robert Moses, eschewing the humanist impulses of city life and modernist aesthetics, sought to rid New York of its creative chaos. But the modern city could also be a place for human creativity and rebirth and Berman was drawn to those figures who embodied this vision. From Marx to Lukács, Baudelaire to Run-DMC, the intellectual and creative brilliance of modern urban life, fractured and chaotic as it is, could help build us anew. From alienation came freedom, and from modernity's ruins came new life. "All that is solid melts into air" was Marx and Engels's lament about what had happened to life under capital; for Berman this was also a credo for how to rebel against it.

The opening chapter of *Politics of Authenticity* is titled "The Personal is Political." I've always wondered about this title—it being, even then, somewhat of a flat-tire turn of phrase. But I think what Berman meant was something more nuanced: that the political *should* be personal. As Corey Robin and others have pointed out, Berman's historical and philosophical narratives were almost always suffused with personal trauma. This, perhaps, reached its fullest expression in *All That Is Solid*, where he moved from eighteenth-century Paris to his own midcentury New York, and also in his later essays collected in *Adventures in Marxism*. But his turn to the personal went well beyond the fact that he was now writing from his home turf; it was, rather, an attempt to make our politics more personal, more felt.

For Berman the failure of modern capitalism—in both its industrial and postindustrial phases—was as much about the emotional suffering it caused as its unequal distribution of goods and services. This was why Berman found the young Marx, who writes of alienation, and the young Lukács, who writes of a particular form of alienation (reification), so appealing. Their ideas were ways of explaining what Berman already suspected was wrong with the world he inhabited: It was not so much that his father was a failed garment-district middle-man but that his father had suffered the psychic costs of this failure.

This personalization of Marx and of social criticism more generally was what lent Berman's thinking its poignant erudition. It is what also drew him to the humanist side of the Left. "Even when capitalism was highly successful," Berman wrote, Marx helped him realize that it "could be humanly disastrous, inflicting upon people insult and injury by treating them as nothing more than a commodity." The great injustice of modern life was not just the inequalities it produced but also the high tax they placed on us: the ways in which they limited our range of expression as well as our formal freedoms, our libido as well as our workweek—the ways they helped turn whole neighbor-hoods into expressways.

One does not always practice what one preaches. But it was precisely this sensitivity to human feeling that made Berman so lovely as a person. He *cared*. His generosity came casually to him. He lent me Peter Gay's *Weimar Culture* (a reason why I went to graduate school). He read a fellow editor's four-year-old under-graduate thesis in an afternoon and then offered detailed notes and corrections. He even tried, unsuccessfully, to get Michael Walzer to listen to Bob Dylan.

A common refrain at *Dissent* meetings is, "So what do we think about this?" Berman often phrased it, "So how do we feel about this?" When I was at something of a romantic impasse several years ago, he steered our lunch conversation away from edits on a review of his to narrate a comically failed early romance.

That review—one of his late classics—told the story of Ka, Blue, and Ipek, the characters that form the sad, mostly uncon-summated love triangle that anchors Orhan Pamuk's *Snow*. For Berman, the center of the novel was not the clash between the secular and religious, the modern and the traditional. It was love: love won but also, more commonly, lost. This was our most modern of disasters: the suggestion of freedom, the age

of liberation, and yet nothing. We can speak and be heard, touch
and embrace, but something about modern life seems to stop
us from loving. Ka and Ipek, plotting to escape the religious
violence of Anatolia, never catch their train. They dream of a
place where they can overcome what keeps them apart. But the
currents of history, or at least the currents of Pamuk's novel, stop
them.

Berman wrote:

> In the history of modern culture, the archetypal couple presiding
> over Ka's and Ipek's fantasies and hopes come from the moment
> of the French Revolution: they are Papageno and Papagena, from
> Mozart's *Magic Flute*. Ka and Ipek, two centuries later, would be
> a modernist variation on Mozart's theme. Their embraces will be
> accompanied by all the latest mass media, by movies and televi-
> sion, by computer hookups and hyperlinks, and by dreams of
> America—of *undubbed* America (Pamuk highlights this), an
> America in as raw and direct a form as they can imagine. Americans
> can feel proud to be part of their dream life and their pursuit of
> happiness.

> Why shouldn't they have all this? In fact, it is only drastic last-
> minute plot intervention by the author that keeps the heroine off
> the train to freedom. Maybe Pamuk thought it would be a better
> story this way, and if he did, who knows, maybe he was right.
> Maybe stories of love crushed are more poignant than stories of
> love fulfilled. Or maybe the best story is love crushed after it's
> fulfilled.

But for Berman, this was not enough. As he ended the review,
turning back to his own life as he often did in his essays, he
wrote:

> But there's a difference between the logic of a story and the logic
> of history. At the start of the twenty-first century, our history may
> be more open than our literature. A great many people have got
> out of nightmarish situations all over the globe, and America has

given them space to breathe. On any Saturday or Sunday afternoon, at Herald Square, on Telegraph Avenue, in shopping malls in all sorts of American places I and Pamuk have never heard of, you can find couples that look a lot like Ipek and Ka (they are often of different colors), schlepping their babies around in ultramodern snugglies, overflowing with new life.

When I read these last passages of his review I was kind of surprised. It was early 2009, and not exactly a time, despite Obama's election, to be proud of the United States. A great many people had certainly escaped nightmarish situations all over the globe, and sometimes because of our beneficence. But the United States also was one of the many sources of these nightmarish situations and certainly not always a place of relief.

But what troubled me most about these last paragraphs was not that Berman still could mine a deep reserve of hope and possibility in the midst of so much disappointment. It was that he had found, in a novel about political violence, a story of unfulfilled love: a narrative, as old as Mozart's *Magic Flute*, that revealed the deeper sorrow of modern experience—our inability to connect with one another. This was, at least to me, a radically different type of criticism, a criticism that formulated not just social complaint but also psychic and spiritual pain. It was a criticism—a politics, really— of feelings.

When *All That Is Solid* was published, it was met with a wave of exuberant reviews. The *Times* called it "generous . . . and dazzling." The *Voice* insisted that it was "a visionary work which by all rights ought to have the impact of such sixties bibles as *Growing Up Absurd* and *Life Against Death*." It did, in many ways. And Berman always was grateful for the recognition it brought him, even if in later years I think he felt burdened and hemmed in by its success.

But the Left, being the Left, had a variety of responses, not all kind and perhaps none as stinging as Perry Anderson's. Writing in the *New Left Review*, Anderson argued that the book confused modernist visions of release with radical ones of liberation. "For all its exuberance, Berman's version of Marx, in its virtually exclusive emphasis on the release of the self, comes uncomfortably close—radical and decent though its accents are—to the assumptions of the culture of narcissism."

For Berman, this must have particularly stung, because the underlying argument of *All That Is Solid* was that modernism can help people come closer together: Creative expression, in the street as well as in the museum, was an effort to find communion. Modernist art, urban culture—these were ways to repair our present state of alienation. They were means to overcome loneliness.

Always generous, Berman responded this way:

I am grateful to Perry Anderson for remembering *The Politics of Authenticity*, and for pointing out the continuities between that work and what I'm doing now. Then as now, I've been trying to develop a theoretical vision of the unifying forces in modern life. I still believe that it's possible for modern men and women who share the desire to "be themselves" to come together, first to fight against the forms of class, sexual and racial oppression that force everyone's identity into rigid moulds and keep anyone's self from unfolding; and next, to create Marx's "association in which the free development of each is the condition for the free development of all." Nevertheless, *All That Is Solid*, and what I've written here, have a much thicker density and a richer atmosphere than my earlier work. This is because I've tried increasingly to situate my exploration of the modern self within the social contexts in which all modern selves come to be. I'm writing more about the environments and public spaces that are available to modern people, and the ones that they create, and the ways they act and interact in these spaces in the attempt to make themselves at home. I'm emphasizing those modes of modernism that seek to take over or to remake public space, to appropriate and transform it in the name of the people who are its public. This is why so much of *All That Is Solid* is taken up with public struggles and encounters, dialogues and confrontations in the streets; and why I've come to see the street and the demonstration as primary symbols of modern life.

Another reason that I've written so much about ordinary people and everyday life in the street, in the context of this controversy, is that Anderson's vision is so remote from them. He only has eyes for world-historical Revolutions in politics and world-class Masterpieces in culture; he stakes out his claim on heights of meta-physical perfection, and won't deign to notice anything less. This would be all right, I guess, except that he's so clearly miserable over the lack of company up there. It might be more fruitful if, instead of demanding whether modernity can still produce masterpieces and revolutions, we were to ask whether it can generate sources and spaces of meaning, of freedom, dignity, beauty, joy, solidarity. Then we would have to confront the messy actuality in which modern men and women and children live. The air might be less pure, but the atmosphere would be a lot more nourishing; we would find, in Gertrude Stein's phrase, a lot more *there* there. Who knows—it's impossible to know in advance—we might even find some masterpieces or revolutions in the making.

Marxism and modernism, for Berman, happened on the ground, in the world. In this sense, he was a "connected critic". But for Berman it was not enough to address the specific material needs of a community; the critic had to also address its spiritual and emotional ones: the subterranean desires that, when unful-filled, also limit the range and variety of our freedom. "The complaint against democratic capitalism," he argued, "was not that it was too individualistic, but rather that it wasn't individual-istic enough: It forced every individual into competitive and aggressive impasses ('zero-sum games') which prevented any individual feelings, needs, ideas, energies from being expressed." There was a need for a new moral basis for the Left's critique of what capitalism and modern life did to people. As he put it in *Politics of Authenticity*, there needed to be "a Marxism with soul."

"Marxism with soul," I think, always had a double meaning for Berman. It meant a Marxism that moved beyond the structuralist analyses and historical determinism of its more orthodox readings of the tradition. But it also meant that Marxism needed to *address* the soul. It had to be modern, carrying with it the messy energy and rhythms of our particular moment. This meant engaging with everyday culture, in all of its messiness, wherever it emerged. Berman never shied away from this, in appearance or commitment: His hair and beard sprang out in curlicues of gray and black, his shirts were almost always wrinkled tie-dyes. He had Freud and Marilyn Monroe bobble-heads on his desk at home. His body, in later years, was ailing; this was clear to many of us. But even as Berman got older, he was always full of life and surprises. At one meeting, having fallen asleep, he woke up to one of *Dissent*'s standard discussions despairing over the "state of things." Sitting up in his chair he proposed we adopt a new motto: "Keep on truckin'!"

Berman's sense of humanist exuberance, his vision of a feeling Left, offered many around *Dissent* a view of a different kind of left politics. Social criticism as psychic complaint has a long history, going back as far as Emerson, and finding its twentieth-century expression in figures like William James, Randolph Bourne, Paul Goodman, Ralph Ellison, Susan Sontag, and Ellen Willis. But Berman was our practitioner. It was not only the creative self to which he was committed. He was committed to masterpieces and revolutions, to solidarity and liberation, to utopias that exceed present imagination. He was also a master at finding meaning in the face of ruin and emptiness. He insisted that politics not only be one of feeling but also one that addressed the world as it was. It must seek out that Leibnizian imperative: the best of all possible worlds.

After a *Dissent* meeting in Soho shortly before he died, Berman and I walked up to the 1 train together. As we trod Wooster's cobblestones, Berman kept pointing at various buildings and remarking on the artists who once lived there. Everything, he said, changed in the 1980s. Art became expensive—to make, to buy, to view. The art community was replaced by a financial one. On cue, a group of young people passed: a clatter of heels, a scent of cologne. Embarrassed for my generation, I said, "It's a shame it's all gone." "No," Berman said, "it's back. Look at all the young people."

David Marcus

Part I

Origin Stories

Caught Up in the Mix:
Some Adventures in Marxism

> Once a theatregoer buttonholed [Arthur] Miller and put the ques-
> tion to him: "What's he selling? You never say what he's selling."
> Miller quipped, "Well, himself. That's what's in the valise."
>
> John Lahr, "Making Willy Loman"

Marxism has been part of me for all my life. Late in my 50s, I'm still learning and sorting out how. Until now, I think I've had only one real adventure in Marxism. Still, that one was formidable. It helped me grow up and figure out who I was going to be in the world. And it makes a good story. My father also had a Marxist adventure, one more tragic than mine. It's only by working through his life that I'll be in a position to take hold of my own. Life studies is one of the big things Marxism is for.

My father, Murray Berman, died of a heart attack in 1955, when he was just short of forty-eight, and when I wasn't quite fifteen. He grew up on New York's Lower East Side and in the Bronx, left school at twelve, and was thrown into "the business world"— that's what he and my mother called it—pushing a truck in the garment center to help support his parents and nine kids in one room. He called it "the rack" and often said he was still on it. But the garment center's friendly malevolence felt like home to him, and we would never leave that home.

Over the years, he graduated from outdoor *schlepper* to indoor *schlepper* (I guess it would be called stock clerk today) and then to various clerical and sales jobs. He was on the road a lot before I was born and when I was very young. For several years he worked, as both reporter and an advertising salesman, for *Women's Wear Daily*. All those years are vague to me. But I know that in 1948, he and a friend from the Bronx made a great leap: They founded a magazine. Its theme, announced on the mast head, was "The garment industry meets the world." My father and his friend Dave had little education and less capital but lots of foresight—the Yiddish word is *sachel*. Globalization in the garment center was an idea whose time was coming, and for two years the magazine thrived, selling ever more advertising space (my father's specialty), which in capitalist economies is what keeps newspapers and magazines alive.

But then, suddenly, in the spring of 1950, there was no money to meet the payroll, and just as suddenly his friend Dave disappeared. My father took me to the Natural History Museum one Saturday morning; Saturday afternoon, we walked around the Upper East Side, searching for Dave. In his favorite Third Avenue bars, no one had seen him for two days. His doorman said the same but he directed us to Dave's floor and said we would hear his dog barking if he was around. We didn't, and he wasn't, and while my father cursed and worked on a note to slip under his door, I looked into a half-open door in the hall and saw an open elevator shaft. As I looked down, curious, my father grabbed me and threw me against the wall—it was one of the two times he ever touched me violently. We didn't talk much as we took the subway back to the Bronx. The magazine went bankrupt overnight. The next month my father had a heart attack that nearly killed him.

We never saw Dave again, but the police tracked him down. It turned out he had a mistress on Park Avenue, another in Miami, and a gambling addiction. He had emptied the magazine's account, but when they found him there was little left, and nothing for us. My father said the whole story was such a garment center cliché (that was how I learned the meaning of the word *cliché*), he just couldn't believe his friend could do it to him. Several years later, out of the blue, Dave called again, with a new name—another garment center cliché—and a new proposition. I answered the phone, then put my mother on. She said he had ruined my father's life once, and wasn't that enough? Dave urged her to be a good sport.

My father gradually got his strength back, and my parents were now the "Betmar Tag and Label Company." They lived in the garment center's interstices as brokers or jobbers, middlemen between garment manufacturers and label-makers. This company had no capital; its only assets were my father's aptitude for schmoozing and my mother's for figuring things out. They knew their position was precarious, but they performed a real function, and they thought they had enough local knowledge to stay afloat. For a few years, it was a living. But in September 1955 my father had another heart attack, and from this one he died.

Who killed him? This question haunted me for years. "It's the wrong question," my first shrink said fifteen years later. "He had a bad heart. His system wore out." That was true; the army saw it and rejected him for service during World War Two. But I couldn't forget his last summer, when all at once he lost several big accounts. The managers and purchasing agents were all his old friends: They had played stickball on Suffolk Street, worked together and dealt with each other for years; these guys had drunk to his health at my bar mitzvah, just two years back. Now, all of a sudden, they wouldn't return his calls. He had said he could tell he'd been outbid by somebody; he just wanted a chance to make a bid and to be told what was what. All this was explained to us at the funeral (a big funeral; he was well liked) and during *shiva* week just after. Our accounts, and dozens of others, had been grabbed by a Japanese syndicate, which was doing business both on a scale and in a style new to Seventh Avenue. The syndicate had made spectacular payoffs to its American contacts. (Of course they didn't call them payoffs.) But it had imposed two conditions: It must not be identified, and there must be no counter-bidding. We pressed his friends: Why couldn't you tell Daddy—even tell him there was something you couldn't tell him? They all said they hadn't wanted to make him feel bad. Crocodile tears, I thought, yet I could see their tears were real. Much later, I thought that here was one of the first waves of the global market that Dad foresaw and understood. I think he could have lived with that better than he could live with his old friends not calling him back.

My mother carried the company on briefly, but her heart wasn't in it. She folded it and went to work as a bookkeeper. Together, one night in the summer of 1956, near the end of our year of mourning, my mother, my sister, and I threw enormous reams of paper from the lost accounts down our incinerator in the Bronx. But my mother held on to the manila folders that they had used for those accounts. ("We can still get plenty of use out of *them*," she said.) Forty years later, I'm still using those folders, containers of long-vanished entities—Puritan Sportswear, Fountain Modes, Girl Talk, Youngland—where are they now? Does it mean that, in some way, I've stayed in my father's business? (Happy Loman, at the very end of *Death of a Salesman*: "I'm staying right in this city, and I'm gonna beat this racket!") What racket? What business? My wife defined the relationship in a way I like: I've gone into my father's *unfinished* business.

"The only thing you got in this world is what you can sell." Another line from *Death of a Salesman*.[1] It was my father's favorite play. My parents saw *Salesman* at least twice on stage, starring Lee J. Cobb, and again in film form starring Fredric March. It became a primary source of material in the endless affectionate and ironic repartee they carried on till he died. I didn't know that till I got to see the movie, just a few months before his death; then all at once the meaning of years of banter became clear. I joined in the cross-talk, tried it at the dinner table, and got all smiles, though the lines were tragic, and were about to become more tragic still. One hot day in the summer of 1955 he came home drained from the garment center and said, "They don't know me any more." I said, "Dad . . . Willy Loman?" He was happy that I knew he was quoting, but he also wanted me to know it was not only a quote but the

---

1 Arthur Miller, *Death of a Salesman*, first published and produced 1949; text and criticism edited by Gerald Weales, New York: Viking, 1977. The lament "The only thing you got," by Willie's neighbor Charlie is on page 97; Happy's graveside vow, 138–9. The story about Miller cited in the epigraph is drawn from John Lahr, "Making Willy Loman," *New Yorker*, January 25, 1999, 46–7.

truth. I got him a beer, which I knew he liked in the summer heat; he hugged me and said it gave him peace to know I was going to be freer than he was, I was going to have a life of my own.

Soon after he died, scholarships and good luck propelled me to Columbia. There I could talk and read and write all night and then walk to the Hudson to see the sun at dawn. I felt like a prospector who had made a strike, discovering sources of fresh energy I never knew I had. And some of my teachers had even told me that living for ideas could be a way for me to make a living! I was happier than I had ever been, steeped in a life that really felt like *my life*. Then I realized this was exactly what my father had wanted for me. For the first time since his death, I started thinking about him. I thought about how he had struggled and lost, and my grief turned to rage. *So they don't know you?* I thought. *Let me at those bastards, I'll get them for you. They don't remember? I'll remind them.* But which bastards? Who were "they"? How could I get them? Where would I start? I made a date with Jacob Taubes, my beloved professor of religion. I said I wanted to talk about my father and Karl Marx.

Jacob and I sat in his office in Butler Library and talked and talked. He said that he sympathized with all radical desire, but revenge was a sterile form of fulfillment. Didn't Nietzsche write the book on that? Hadn't I read it in his class? He said that in the part of Europe where he came from (b. Vienna 1927), the politics of revenge had succeeded far beyond anything Americans could imagine. He told me a joke: "Capitalism is the exploitation of man by man. *Communism is the opposite.*" I had heard that joke before, maybe even from my father; it had gone round many times, for good reasons. But it was a dark joke and it hurt to laugh at it, because what followed seemed to be a total human impasse: The system is intolerable, and so is the only alternative to the system. *Oy!* So what then, I asked, we all put ourselves to sleep? No, no, said Jacob, he didn't mean to immobilize me. In fact, there was this book he had meant to tell me about: Marx wrote it "when he was still a kid, before he became Karl Marx"; it was wild, and I would like it. The Columbia Bookstore ("those fools") didn't have it, but I could get it at Barnes & Noble downtown. The book had "been kept secret for a century"—that was Jacob's primal romance, the secret book, the Kabbalah—but now at last it had been released.[2] He said some people thought it offered "an alternative vision of how man should live." Wouldn't that be better than revenge? And I could get there on the subway.

So, one lovely Saturday in November, I took the 1 train downtown, turned south at the Flatiron Building, and headed down Fifth to Barnes & Noble. B&N then was far from its 1990s monopoly incarnation, "Barnes Ignoble," scourge of small bookshops; it was only one store, just off Union Square, and it traced itself back to Abe Lincoln and Walt Whitman and "The Battle Hymn of the Republic." But before I could get there, I passed another place that I had always walked on by: the Four Continents Book Store, official distributor for all Soviet publications. Would my Marx be there? If it really was "really wild," would the USSR be bringing it out? I remembered the Soviet tanks in Budapest, killing kids on the streets. Still, the USSR in 1959 was supposed to be opening up ("the Thaw, they called it), and there was a possibility. I had to see.

The Four Continents was like a rainforest inside, walls painted deep green, giant posters of bears, pines, icebergs and icebreakers, shelves stretching back toward a vast horizon, lighting that evoked a tree cover more than a modern room. My first thought was, how can anyone read in this light? (In retrospect, I realize it resembled the lighting in certain 1950s furniture stores and romantic comedies. It was the light scheme in the bachelor flat where the hero brought home Doris Day.) The staff knew just what book I wanted: Marx's *Economic and Philosophical*

---

2   In fact, these 1844 notebooks had been published in Berlin by the Marx-Engels Institute in 1932 as part of the projected (but never completed) *Marx-Engels Gesamtausgabe*. That edition was suppressed in Germany by the Nazis but was continued for a time in Moscow, where Georg Lukács, by then a refugee, played some editorial role. Herbert Marcuse made creative use of the *1844 Manuscripts* in his *Reason and Revolution: Hegel and the Rise of Social Theory*, New York: Oxford University Press, 1941. But there was no popular edition until the Khrushchev era, when Moscow sponsored translations into many languages and sold them by the millions dirt cheap.

Manuscripts of 1844, translated by Martin Milligan, and published in 1956 by the Foreign Languages Publishing House in Moscow. It was a collection of three youthful notebooks, divided into short essays. The titles didn't seem to emanate from Marx himself; they appeared to be provided by twentieth-century editors in Moscow or Berlin. It was midnight blue, nice and compact, a perfect fit for a side pocket in a 1950s sports jacket. I opened it at random, here, there, somewhere else—and suddenly I was in a sweat, melting, shedding clothes and tears, flashing hot and cold. I rushed to the front: "I've got to have this book!" The white-haired clerk was calm. "Fifty cents, please." When I expressed amazement, he said, "We"—I guess he meant the USSR—"don't publish books for profit." He said the *Manuscripts* had become one of their best-sellers, though he himself couldn't see why, since Lenin was so much clearer.

Right there my adventure began. I realized I was carrying more than thirty dollars, mostly wages from the college library; it was probably as much as I'd ever carried in my life. I felt another flash. "Fifty cents? So for ten bucks I can get twenty?" The clerk said that, after sales taxes, twenty copies would cost about $11. I ran back to the rear, grabbed the books, and said, "You've just solved my Hanukkah problem." As I schlepped the books on the subway up to the Bronx (Four Continents tied them up in a nice parcel), I felt I was walking on air. For the next several days I walked around with a stack of books, thrilled to be giving them away to all the people in my life: my mother and sister, my girlfriend, her parents, several old and new friends, a couple of my teachers, the man from the stationery store, a union leader (the past summer, I'd worked for District 65), a doctor, a rabbi. I'd never given so many gifts before (and never did again). Nobody refused the book, but I got some weird looks from people when I breathlessly delivered my spiel. "Take this!" I said, shoving the book in their faces. "It'll knock you out. It's by Karl Marx, but before he became Karl Marx. It'll show you how our whole life's wrong, but it'll make you happy, too. If you don't get it, just call me anytime, and I'll explain it all. Soon everybody will be talking about it, and you'll be the first to know." And I was out the door, to face more puzzled people. I stopped at Jacob's office with my stack of books, told him the story; went through the spiel. We beamed at each other. "See, now," he said, "isn't this better than revenge?" I improvised a comeback: "No, it's the best revenge."

I try to imagine myself at that magic moment: *Too much, man! Was I for real?* (Those are things we used to say to each other in 1959.) How did I get to be so sure of myself? (Never again!) My intellectual impulse-buying; my neo-potlatch great giveaway of a book I hadn't even properly read; the exuberance with which I pressed myself on all those people; my certainty that I had something special, something that would both rip up their lives and make them happy; my promises of lifetime personal service; above all, my love for my great new product that would change the world: Willy Loman, meet Karl Marx. We entered the sixties together.

What was it in Marx, all those years ago, that shot me up like a rocket? Not long ago, I went through that old midnight blue Four Continents book. It was a haunting experience, with the Soviet Union dead; but Marx himself moved and lived. The book was hard to read because I'd underlined, circled, and asterisked virtually *everything*. But I know the ideas that caught me forty years ago are still part of me today, and it will help this book hold together if I can block out at least some of those ideas in a way that is brief but clear.[3]

The thing I found so striking in Marx's 1844 essays, and which I did not expect to find at all, was his feeling for the individual. Those early essays articulate the conflict between *Bildung* and alienated labor. *Bildung* is the core human value in liberal romanticism. It is a hard word to put in English, but it embraces a family of ideas like "subjectivity," "finding yourself," "growing up,"

---

3   Citations from Marx, unless I note otherwise, are drawn from the *Marx-Engels Reader* [*MER*], 2nd edition, edited by Robert C. Tucker, New York: Norton, 1978, which uses Milligan's translations of the 1844 material. The core of the *1844 Manuscripts* consists of five essays: "Alienated Labor," "Private Property and Communism," "The Meaning of Human Requirements," "The Power of Money in Bourgeois Society," and "Critique of the Hegelian Dialectic and Philosophy as a Whole."

"identity," "self-development," and "becoming who you are."
Marx situates this ideal in modern history and gives it a social
theory. He identifies with the Enlightenment and with the great
revolutions that formed its climax when he asserts the universal
right of man to be "freely active," to "affirm himself," to enjoy
"spontaneous activity," to pursue "the free development of his
physical and mental energy" (74–5). But he also denounces the
market society nourished by those revolutions, because "Money
is the overturning of all individualities" (105) and because "You
must make all that is yours *For Sale*" (96; Marx's emphasis). He
shows how modern capitalism arranges work in such a way that
the worker is "alienated from his own activity" as well as from
other workers and from nature. The worker "mortifies his body
and ruins his mind"; he "feels himself only outside his work, and
in his work . . . feels outside himself"; he "is at home only when
he is not working, and when he is working he is not at home. His
labor therefore is not free, but coerced; it is forced labor" (74).
Marx salutes the labor unions that, in the 1840s, are just beginning to emerge. But even if the unions achieve their immediate
aims—even if workers get widespread union recognition and
raise wages by force of class struggle—it will still be "nothing
but salary for a slave" unless modern society comes to recognize
"the meaning and dignity of work and of the worker" (80).
Capitalism is terrible because it promotes human energy, spontaneous feeling, human development, only to crush them, except in
the few winners at the very top. From the very start of his career
as an intellectual, Marx is a fighter for democracy. But he sees that
democracy in itself won't cure the structural misery he sees. So
long as work is organized in hierarchies and mechanical routines
and oriented to the demands of the world market, most people,
even in the freest societies, will still be enslaved—will still be,
like my father, on the rack. Marx is part of a great cultural tradition, a comrade of modern masters like Keats, Dickens, George
Eliot, Dostoevsky, James Joyce, Franz Kafka, D.H. Lawrence
(readers are free to fill in their personal favorites) in his feeling
for the suffering modern man on the rack. But Marx is unique in
his grasp of what that rack is made of. It's there in all his work.

But in the *Communist Manifesto* and *Capital,* you have to look for it. In the *1844 Manuscripts,* it's in your face.

Marx wrote most of these essays in the midst of one of his great adventures, his honeymoon in Paris with Jenny von Westphalen. The year I had my Marxian adventure, I had just fallen in love, first love, and this made me very curious whether he would have anything to say about love and sex. The Marxists I had met through the years seemed to have a collective attitude that didn't exactly hate sex and love, but regarded them with impatience, as if these feelings were to be tolerated as necessary evils, but not one iota of extra time or energy should be wasted on them, and nothing could be more foolish than to think they had human meaning or value in themselves. After I had heard that for years, to hear young Marx in his own voice was a breath of fresh air. "From this relationship, one can judge man's whole level of development" (82). He was saying just what I felt: that sexual love was the most important thing there was.

Hanging around the Left Bank in Paris, Marx seems to have met radicals who promoted sexual promiscuity as an act of liberation from bourgeois constraints. Marx agreed with them that modern love could become a problem if it drove lovers to possess their loved ones as "exclusive private property" (82). And indeed, "Private property has made us so stupid that an object is only *ours* when we have it" (91; Marx's emphasis). But their only alternative to marriage seems to have been an arrangement that made everybody the sexual property of everybody else, and Marx disparaged this as nothing but "universal prostitution."

We don't know who these "crude, mindless communists" were, but Marx's critique of them is fascinating. He uses their sexual grossness as a symbol of everything that he thinks is wrong with the Left. Their view of the world "negates the personality of man in every sphere." It entails "the abstract negation of the whole world of culture and civilization"; their idea of happiness is "leveling down proceeding from a preconceived minimum." Moreover, they embody "general *envy* constituting itself as a power" and "the disguise in which *avarice* re-establishes itself and satisfies itself, only in another way." They promote "regression to the unnatural simplicity of the poor and undemanding man who has not only failed to go beyond private property, but has not yet even attained to it" (82–3; Marx's emphasis). Marx is focusing on the human qualities of greed and crudity that makes some liberals despise and fear the Left. He would say it is stupid prejudice to think that *all* leftists are like that, but it is right to think that *some* leftists are like that though not him or anyone close to his heart. Here Marx is not only reaching out to the Tocqueville tradition but also trying to envelop it.

When Marx calls the bad communists "thoughtless," he is suggesting not just that their ideas are stupid, but that they are unconscious of what their real motives are; they think they are performing noble actions, but they are really engaged in vindictive, neurotic acting out. Marx's analysis here is stretching toward Nietzsche and Freud. But it also highlights his roots in the Enlightenment: The communism he wants must include *self-awareness*. This nightmare vision of "crude, thoughtless communism" is one of the strongest things in early Marx. Were there real-life models in the Paris of the 1840s? No biographer has come up with convincing candidates; maybe he simply imagined them himself, the way novelists create their characters. But once we have read Marx, it is hard to forget them, these vivid nightmares of all the ways the Left could go wrong.

There is another striking way in which young Marx worries about sex and conceives it as a symbol of something bigger. When workers are alienated from their own activity in their work, their sexual lives become an obsessive form of compensation. They then try to realize themselves through desperate "eating, drinking, procreating," along with "dwelling and dressing up." But desperation makes carnal pleasures less joyful than they could be, because it places more psychic weight on them than they can bear (74).

The essay "Private Property and Communism" takes a longer view and strikes a more upbeat note: "The forming of the five senses is a labor of the whole history of the world, down to the present" (89). Maybe the joy of a honeymoon enables Marx to imagine new people coming over the horizon, people less possessive and greedy, more in tune with their sensuality and vitality, inwardly better equipped to make love a vital part of human development.

Who are these "new people" who would have the power at once to represent and to liberate humanity? The answer that made Marx both famous and infamous is proclaimed to the world in the *Manifesto:* "the proletariat, the modern working class" (479). But this answer itself raises overwhelming questions. We can divide them roughly in two, the first line of questions about the membership of the working class, the second about its mission. Who are these guys, heirs and heiresses of all the ages? And, given the extent and depth of their suffering, which Marx describes so well, where are they going to get the positive energy they will need not merely to gain power, but to change the whole world? Marx's *1844 Manuscripts* don't address the "membership" questions,[4] but he has some fascinating things to say about the mission. He says that even as modern society brutalizes and maims the self, it also brings forth, dialectically, "the rich human being [*der reiche Mensch*] and rich human need" (89).

"The rich human being": Where have we seen him before? Readers of Goethe and Schiller will recognize the imagery of classical German humanism here. But those humanists believed that only a very few men and women could be capable of the inner depth that they could imagine; the vast majority of people, as seen from Weimar and Jena, were consumed by trivialities and had no soul. Marx inherited Goethe's and Schiller's and Humboldt's

---

4   Marx had offered a definition a few months earlier, in a "little magazine" called the *German-French Yearbooks*, published in Paris. That definition is mostly negative: You will know them by their multiple wounds and exclusions. They form "a class in civil society that is not a class of civil society," and "a total loss of humanity that can redeem itself only by a total redemption of humanity" ("Contribution to a Critique of Hegel's Philosophy of Right: Introduction," *MER*, 53–65). This is very different from the proletarians we will meet in the *Communist Manifesto* and *Capital*. There they are the primary source of power for the immense engine of modern production and industry. Here we come to know them by all they are *not;* they seem much more like the poor people portrayed by Dickens and Dostoevsky, or like the insulted and injured group that contemporary US social scientists have named "the underclass."

values, but he fused them with a radical and democratic social philosophy inspired by Rousseau. Rousseau's 1755 *Discourse on the Origins of Inequality* laid out the paradox that even as modern civilization alienates people from themselves, it develops and deepens those alienated selves and gives them the capacity to form a social contract and create a radically new society.[5] A century later, after one great wave of revolutions and just before another, Marx sees modern society in a similarly dialectical way. His idea is that even as bourgeois society enervates and impoverishes its workers, it spiritually enriches and inspires them. "The rich human being" is a man or woman for whom "self-realization [*seine eigene Verwirklichung*] exists as an inner necessity, a need"; he or she is "a human being in need of a totality of human activities" (91). Marx sees bourgeois society as a system that, in an infinite number of ways, stretches workers out on a rack. Here his dialectical imagination starts to work: The very social system that tortures them also teaches and transforms them, so that while they suffer, they also begin to overflow with energy and ideas. Bourgeois society treats its workers as objects, yet develops their subjectivity. Marx has a brief passage on French workers who are just (of course illegally) starting to organize: They come together instrumentally, as a means to economic and political ends; but "as a result of this association, they acquire a new need—the need for society—and what [begins] as a means becomes an end" (99). Workers may not set out to be "rich human beings," and certainly no one else wants them to be, but their development is their fate, it turns their powers of desire into a world-historical force.

"Let me get this straight," my mother said, as she took her book. "It's Marx, but not communism, right? So what is it?" Marx in 1844

---

5   Engels, in his 1880 pamphlet *Socialism: Utopian and Scientific* (derived from his polemic *Anti-Dühring*, 1878) is perceptive in judging Rousseau's *Discourse on the Origins of Inequality* and Diderot's *Rameau's Nephew* as the "two great masterpieces of dialectics" produced by the Enlightenment (*MER*, 694). My first book, *The Politics of Authenticity*, New York: Atheneum, 1970, 1972, traces some of the roots of Marxism in the radical Enlightenment.

had imagined two very different communisms. One, which he wanted, was "a genuine resolution of the conflict between man and nature, and between man and man" (84); the other, which he dreaded, "has not only failed to go beyond private property, but has not yet even attained to it" (83). Our twentieth century had produced a great surplus of the second model, but not much of the first. The problem, in short, has been that the second model, the one Marx dreaded, has had tanks, and the first, the one he dreamed of, has not. My mother and I had seen those tanks on TV; in Budapest, killing kids. We agreed, not Communism. But if not that, then what? I felt like a panelist on a TV quiz show, with time running out. I reached for a phrase I had seen in the *New York Times,* in a story about French existentialists—Sartre, de Beauvoir, Henri Lefebvre, André Gorz, and their friends—who were trying to merge their thought with Marxism and create a radical perspective that would transcend the dualisms of the Cold War. I said, "Call it *Marxist humanism.*" "Oh!" my mother said, "Marxist humanism, that sounds nice." *Zap!* My adventure in Marxism had crystallized; in an instant I had focused my identity for the next forty years.

And what happened then? I lived another forty years. I went to Oxford, then Harvard. Then I got a steady job in the public sector, as a teacher of political theory and urbanism at the ever-assailed City University of New York. I've worked mostly in Harlem, but downtown as well. I've been lucky to grow old as a citizen of New York and to bring up my kids in the fervid freedom of the city. I was part of the New Left thirty years ago, and I'm part of the Used Left today. (My generation shouldn't be embarrassed by the name. Anyone old enough to know the market's ups and downs knows that used goods often beat new models.) I don't think I've grown old yet, but I've been through plenty; and through it all I've worked to keep Marxist humanism alive.

As the twentieth century comes to an end, Marxist humanism is almost half a century old. It's never swept the country, not in any country, but it has found a place. One way to place it might be to see it as a synthesis of the culture of the fifties with that of the sixties: a feeling for complexity; irony and paradox, combined with a desire for breakthrough and ecstasy; a fusion of "Seven

Types of Ambiguity" with "We Want the World and We Want It Now." It deserves a place of honor in more recent history, in 1989 and after, in the midst of the changes that their protagonists called the Velvet Revolution.

Mikhail Gorbachev hoped to give it a place in his part of the world. He imagined a communism that could enlarge personal freedom, not crush it. But he came too late. To people who had lived their lives within the Soviet horizon, the vision didn't scan; they just couldn't see it. The Soviet people had been burned so badly for so long, they didn't know him; he called, and they didn't return his calls. But we can see Gorbachev as a Willy Loman of politics—a failure as a salesman, but a tragic hero.

Some people think Marxist humanism got its whole meaning as an alternative to Stalinism and that it died with the crumbling of the USSR. My own view is that its real dynamic force is as an alternative to the nihilistic, market-driven capitalism that envelops the whole world today. That means it will have plenty of work to do for a long time to come.

There is a wonderful image that emerged early in the 1990s—at least that is when I first heard it, at my school, City College of New York—from the street life of America's black ghettos, and particularly from today's hip-hop music scene, where music becomes itself not by being harmonized, but by being mixed. Here's the image: *caught up in the mix*. "She's all caught up in the mix"; "I got myself caught up in the mix." This image has stuck because it captures so much of so many people's lives. *My father was caught up in the mix. So were the friends who betrayed him.* I think Marx understood better than anybody else how modern life is a mix; how, although there are immense variations in it, deep down it's *one* mix—"the mix"; how we are all caught up in it; and how easy, how normal it is for the mix to go awry. He also showed how, once we grasped the way we were thrown together, we could fight for the power to remix.

Marxist humanism can help people feel at home in history, even a history that hurts them. It can show them how even those who are broken by power can have the power to fight the power; how even survivors of tragedy can make history. It can help people discover themselves as "rich human beings" with "rich human needs" (89–91), and can show them there is more to them than they thought. It can help new generations to imagine new adventures and arouse their powers of desire to change the world, so that they not only will be part of the mix, they will get to do part of the mixing.

This essay was first published in Adventures in Marxism, *Verso, 1999.*

Part II

Radical Times

The Politics of Authenticity

The idea that I have called "the politics of authenticity" is a dream of an ideal community in which individuality will not be subsumed and sacrificed, but fully developed and expressed. This dream is at once old and new. "New," first of all, in that it is *modern:* It presupposes the sort of fluid, highly mobile, urban society, and the sort of dynamic, expansive economy which we experience as distinctively modern, and which nearly everyone in the West lives in today. But it is "old" too: It has been a leitmotif in Western culture since early in the eighteenth century, when men began to feel modernization as an irreversible historical force and to think systematically about its human potentialities. This ideal was one of the deepest and most pervasive themes of the Romantic Age, the years roughly from 1789 to 1848. It is central to the work of Blake and Carlyle, of Chateaubriand and Stendhal, of Schiller and Novalis and Hegel. Marx and Engels invoke it in the *Communist Manifesto*: "In place of bourgeois society, with its classes and class conflicts, we will have an association in which the free development of each will be the condition of the free development of all."

The *Manifesto* appeared in 1848, on the eve of the revolutions that would bring to a climax a century of Romantic dreams. But this climax turned out to be a catastrophe: The defeats of 1848 to 1851 generated a disenchantment and despair so deep that the very memory of the dream was lost, wiped out, submerged; for a whole century, the politics of authenticity virtually disappeared from the Western imagination. Thus, from the start of the 1850s to the end of the 1950s, in nearly all arguments between radicals and their opponents, both parties identified the capitalist economy and the liberal state with "individualism" and equated radical aims with a "collectivism" that negated individuality. Political thought was frozen into this dualism until the cultural explosion of the 1960s redefined the terms. The New Left's complaint against democratic capitalism was not that it was too individualistic, but rather that it wasn't individualistic enough: It forced every individual into competitive and aggressive impasses ("zero-sum games") which prevented any individual feelings, needs, ideas, energies from being expressed. The moral basis of this political critique was an ideal of authenticity. This outlook was new and yet old, radical yet traditional. Thus the New Left's lasting cultural achievement—one that may outlive the New Left itself—has been to bring about a return of the repressed, to bring radicalism back to its romantic roots.

When I first thought of writing a book on "the politics of authenticity," American culture had come very close to those roots. But the road was murky and tortuous, and no one knew how close we all were. I was just coming of age then, and the 1950s were beginning to turn into the 1960s. The teachers who were teaching me most, in the fervidly genial atmosphere of Columbia College, were thinking very intensely and deeply about "the self" as an intellectual and cultural problem. They had good reasons of their own for thinking this way. They had been burned badly by the radical politics of the 1930s, a politics that had led them to the verge of a monstrous self-betrayal, or of a nightmarish self-dissolution. Now, shaken but intact, reincarnate as academic humanists and cultural critics, they were hoping to salvage whatever elements of decency and beauty they could find in a wrecked, bleak world and to put together fragmented but honest lives for themselves. Their concern with personal authenticity grew out of a loss of political faith, hope, and love. And yet, even though they had cut themselves off from all radical movements, there was some thing unmistakably radical in the way they moved. Although they denounced every Romantic hope, we could see something vividly and beautifully Romantic about the very intensity of their despair. Even as they spurned and cursed Marxism for its spiritual emptiness, they themselves embodied a different kind of Marxism, a Marxism with soul. The vibrations they unconsciously gave off were far more powerful than the ideology (or, as they would have said, anti-ideology) they tried so hard to transmit. Ironically then, so many of the great teachers of that time opened doors for their students which they had closed on themselves; they turned us on to currents of desire and hope, of feeling and thought, which they hoped to turn off forever.

Thus the same sensibility and awareness, which led them away from politics and from radicalism in the 1940s and 1950s, led us back to politics and into a new kind of radicalism in the 1960s. The upheavals of these last years have generated a bitter conflict of generations in American intellectual life. In trying to clarify the political consequences of the search for personal authenticity, I have focused on an ultimate concern, which I believe both generations share. If we all come to understand what is involved in the desire to be ourselves, it may bring us closer together than we have been.

This essay first appeared as the preface to the first edition of The Politics of Authenticity, *Cambridge: Atheneum, 1970.*

Alienation, Community, Freedom

In his attempt to define an organic "structure of feeling" in nine-teenth-century social thought, a structure capable of supporting the political Left and Right alike, Raymond Williams brings together much material that is of deepest interest to anyone who wants to rethink and refurbish socialist traditions.[1] On the other hand, the very fact that he does bring such material together is a symptom of how dangerously vague and inchoate socialist traditions have become. In Williams's view, the conservative-reactionary Wordsworth and the radical-revolutionary Blake, while pulling politically in opposite directions, are enveloped in a deeper, cultural unity of focus and insight: It is "the perception of *alienation*, even as a social fact, [which] can lead either way." But to assimilate the Blakean "structure of feeling" to the Wordsworthian, even in such a limited way, seems to me misleading. A little scrutiny will show two sharply distinct perceptions in operation here, rooted in profoundly different systems of values; the covering term "alienation" only covers up their fundamental alienation from one another.

Consider, first of all, the passages cited by Williams in which "alienation" is supposedly expressed by Blake. Blake is lamenting the absence from the world of creative energy, spontaneity, exuber-ance, sexual expression, and sensual delight. These personal quali-ties are stifled by a social system shot through with political and religious, economic, and militaristic exploitation. What makes the city, London, so fearful a place is that it reveals the general

---

1   See Raymond Williams's essay "Prelude to Alienation" in *Dissent*, Summer 1964.

exploitation ("the mind-forg'd manacles") in such a diversity and profusion of forms: a different mark on every man. But Blake never rejects urban life in itself; it is only incidental to his picture of the modern world, a world essentially defined by repression and exploitation. The city of today is a vast exhibition hall for the "arts of death"; yet its dark Satanic mills will provide the foundation for that new Jerusalem, to be built with all the "arts of life," in which Blake's visions and prophecies of liberation will be fulfilled.

If we examine Wordsworth's sense of alienation, as it is explicated by Williams from Book Seven of *The Prelude,* we will see how radically opposed to Blake's his perceptions are. Wordsworth is undertaking here to describe London—for him, the epitome of the modern world—and his first, "alienated" reaction to it. We will notice, however, that for all Wordsworth finds to deplore in the city, his vision is marked by none of the poverty, squalor, privation, and slavery that Blake was so plagued by. (Granted, there is some vague generality about the city's "low pursuits"; and the brief entrance of a beggar, who, however, is explicitly labeled as a symbol for Man and the Universe.) Not that Wordsworth is being callous: His vision of London is not really marked by anything else either. What is most striking about his response to the city—in contrast to his perennial response to the country, to nature—is its lack of *concreteness.* The doors of his perception are closed tight to what is actually going on in *this* place at *this* moment in historic time. The alibi he offers—that in fact nothing *is* going on around him, that here there are only "trivial objects, melted and reduced / To one identity"—only gives away the narrowness of his perception, the breakdown of his imagination. That he fails so dismally to grasp and evoke the contents of life in one particular city can be traced, I think, to his overriding and bitterly hostile preoccupation with the general *form* of urban life *as such.*

What is it about this urban life that upsets him so? The city is a mad rush, which, he feels, lays the "whole creative powers of man asleep." It is a wild conglomeration of "self-destroying, transitory things" from which he seeks refuge in the "composure and enno- bling Harmony," which the vision of rural nature can provide. As a primary symbol for citification and its discontents, Wordsworth uses the Fair of St. Bartholomew, which he describes ironically:

> The Wax-work, Clock-work, all the marvelous craft
> Of modern Merlins, Wild Beasts, Puppet-shows,
> All out-o'-the-way, far-fetch'd, perverted things,
> All freaks of Nature, all Promethean thoughts
> Of man.

In short, it is precisely those qualities which Blake saw as the noblest expressions of man's "Promethean" freedom and power, and with which he felt most deeply at home—energy, exuberance, diversity—which Wordsworth finds most alien in the city; he despises them as "freaks of Nature" and "perverted things" because they alienate him from the stable peace and cosmic harmony he so deeply craves. Thus Wordsworth's political and social authoritarianism is no accident: The structure of his feelings places him firmly within the metaphysical Party of Order.[2] He perceives, more clearly than Blake did, the elective affinities between the spirit of urban life and that dreadful freedom he hates and fears; that is why he is so anxious to escape it.

Williams does not recognize the conflict of values I have pointed out. Nevertheless, I would judge from his general tone, both here and in his previous works, that if forced to choose he would opt for Wordsworth against Blake, for the Country against the Town, for that tradition in English social thought which exalts and aims to recapture "a medieval unity and innocence." I am deeply disturbed by the structure of feeling that lies behind these preferences. Consider Williams's own response to the city, which—going beyond Wordsworth, who had his reservations (which Williams

---

2   And yet, as we can see in those great passages (mostly in *The Prelude*) where Wordsworth evokes nature most powerfully and beautifully, his very conception of Order explodes the premises of any such Party. The order of Nature, as Wordsworth feels it, is inherently dynamic, infused with energy and exuberance, itself "Promethean." I hope to show in a more elaborate study how Wordsworth's politics actually betray his deepest poetic insight.

mentions, but does not take seriously enough to understand)—is not so much a description, let alone an evocation, as a conceit. Thus he ascribes to city life "a new kind of display of the self: no longer individuality of the kind that is socially sustained, but singularity—the extravagance of display within the public emptiness." Wordsworth's judgment is cited, in tones of approval:

> All the strife of singularity,
> Lies to the ear, and lies to every sense.

A man's life can evidently be "true," that is, personally authentic, only with—in the context of a *community*—a small, homogeneous, face-to-face society, necessarily rural, in which his identity is clearly "recognized" (to use Hegel's term) or (in Williams's own formulation) "socially sustained." Once this idyllic community is eclipsed, individuality becomes possible only as a desperate form of overcompensation, a defense against being totally engulfed, hence in some sense a fraud, a lie. I have a feeling Williams has been influenced in these persuasive formulations by the first part of Georg Simmel's classic essay "The Metropolis and Mental Life." I only wish, however, that he had been influenced by the second part of the essay as well, in which, after presenting the thesis above, Simmel brilliantly overwhelms it with its antithesis: that personality, insofar as it is "socially sustained" within a rural *Gemeinschaft*, is jammed into a stifling system of established roles, constricted and crushed into a stereotype; and that only by breaking the bonds of community, and floating freely in the fluid anonymity of urban life, can individuality find the room it needs to breathe and to grow. This latter possibility seems never even to cross Williams's mind—yet it is the fundamental principle of modern liberalism, a liberalism which socialism claims not to abolish but to fulfill.

Again, as the litany of urban alienations runs on, we are told that "it is not only the 'ballast of familiar life' [Wordsworth's phrase] that is lost, but also all that makes one's own self human and known: the acting, thinking and speaking of man at once himself and in society." Williams's language here is depressingly loose; but if his terms "human" and "himself" and "in society" are not tautologies, the only meaning I can wring out of them is *precisely* "the ballast of familiar life": the definition of oneself in terms of some role in the stable, static, perpetually "familiar" community. In an urban milieu, this possibility indeed tends to get lost (though not at all as fast, or as inexorably, as social thinkers used to think: Neighborhoods, it has recently been noticed, live on). And yet, on the other hand, since the French and Industrial revolutions, a more open, mobile, urban social life has generated new modes of self-definition, of "making one's own self human and known": By cutting loose from the ballast of one's life, by soaring adventurously into the unfamiliar—in other words, by asserting one's *freedom.* Blake, the most radical of Romantics and the most "modern," demanded a total, anarchic freedom in aesthetic and political, sexual and moral life. Wordsworth, though politically conservative and authoritarian, nevertheless recognized and exalted this new freedom within a limited sphere: for the "highest minds," in the realm of the poetic imagination. Whether Williams, with his expressed preference for an art nourished by communal impulse and suffused with communal culture and tradition, would concede even this much—or how, by his own standards, he would justify any sort of concession—is not at all clear.

In saying all this I do not mean to cast aspersions on Raymond Williams's personal devotion to liberty, which I know is exemplary. But it is distressing to see where his sentimental need to enfold radicalism in the communal coziness of a Great Tradition has led him. Because he has resisted making sharp conceptual distinctions between the conflicting values, which any broad cultural tradition must contain, Williams has managed to avoid a clear moral choice. He has thus been drawn—unconsciously, perhaps, but steadily—into a style of social thought whose mixed indifference and hostility toward personal freedom have far less in common with socialism than with that populist mystique of "blood and soil," which has expressed itself in such sinister forms in our day.

This essay was first published in Dissent, *Winter 1965.*

Notes Toward a New Society

One of the most intense and most disturbing arguments on the Left in the late sixties has been over the possibilities of modern man creating a decent society. The New Left has put the question this way: Can a socialist revolution be made *by* Western men, or *along with* them, or *apart from* them, or only *against* them? The real question is: Is there any hope for us? Radicals of the sixties have forced this question to the surface in every advanced industrial country. It has taken on a special urgency in the USA.

The responses of the American New Left have been shaky and ambiguous; they have exposed the cracks and strains at its foundations. On the one hand, the most vital impulse of New Left activity has always been populist, driven by a characteristically American faith in everyday people, a faith that, for all the inequities in American society and the oppressive acts of the American government internationally, the American people themselves are still a source of decency and hope. This is the faith that has inspired the continuing drive for participatory democracy and community control. On the New Left itself this faith has clashed with a darker view of "the people."

The main left-wing idea of "the people" is formulated most systematically by Herbert Marcuse's *One-Dimensional Man*. "'The people,'" Marcuse argues there, "previously the ferment of social change, have 'moved up' to become the ferment of social cohesion." Thus, "The people recognize themselves in their commodities; they find their soul in their automobile, hi-fi set, split-level home, kitchen equipment . . . The political needs of society become individual needs and aspirations." The people within our society identify themselves totally, singlemindedly, with its ruling aims and values; between them and it falls no shadow. This is why it is legitimate to call them "one-dimensional." Now it is obvious that people like these will be unable, by either inclination or insight, to liberate either their slaves or themselves. If hope for human freedom and happiness depended on these one-dimensional men, it would be a lost cause. But this is not the whole story. For, according to Marcuse, even in America, there is more to the human race than is dreamt of in their dimension:

> underneath the conservative popular base is the substratum of outcasts and outsiders, the exploited and persecuted of other races and other colors, the unemployed and the unemployable. They exist outside the democratic process; [they feel] . . . the most immediate and the most real need for ending intolerable conditions and institutions. Thus their opposition is revolutionary even if their consciousness is not. Their opposition hits the system from without and is therefore not deflected by the system; it is an elementary force which violates the rules of the game, and, in doing so, reveals it as a rigged game . . . The fact that they start refusing to play the game may be the fact that marks the beginning of the end of a period.[1]

The American people, and the peoples they control, may yet become free; but the liberating force will have to come, somehow, *from outside*, that is, outside the American system.

It is clear, however, that Marcuse was using the word "outside" in a complex metaphorical way. He did not mean to deny that there could be fruitful contradictions "inside" the American system. His one example of radical action (immediately following the long passage quoted above) involves the civil rights movement: a movement which, when the book appeared in 1964, included whites as

---

1   Herbert Marcuse, *One Dimensional Man: Studies in the Ideology of Advanced Industrial Society*, Boston: Beacon Press, 1964, p. 256.

well as blacks, middle-class as much as lower-class people, students from the most prestigious universities alongside "the unemployed and the unemployable." In other words, large groups within the American system could, if they tried, get into the revolutionary "outside." One-dimensional men might yet discover—or create— new dimensions in themselves. Of course, once we grant the complexity of Marcuse's idea here, new problems arise. If it is really possible for a great many "insiders" to join the "outside" forces, without giving up their positions within the system, we might wonder whether the inside–outside dualism is a helpful way of talking about social reality. Marcuse himself, in his next work, *An Essay on Liberation* (1968), tacitly abandoned this dualistic scheme; but other men, with flatter minds, have kept it alive.

If we move forward from 1964 to 1969, and examine the first Weatherman manifesto, which came out of the great split in the Students for a Democratic Society (SDS), we will find some of the same words, but in what seems like a different world. Marcuse's language and general scheme are retained: a people that is internally monolithic is opposed by radical forces from "outside." But the Marcusean sociology has been transformed into a Manichaean cosmology. The Weathermen take the idea of "outside" force with a crude, grim literalism: The basic opposition is one of geography. "America" is condemned, root and branch, as an "oppressor nation" whose sole source of support is the life and labor of "the peoples of the world."[2] The American oppressors include not only the rich, the owners of wealth and property, the bourgeoisie, but "virtually all of the white working class," blue- and white-collar alike, who enjoy small "privileges but very real ones, which give them an edge of vested interests and tie them to the imperialists." The Weathermen judge *all* white Americans and find them wanting, totally lacking in human potential. It is wrong, they say, for radicals to concentrate on the "internal development of class struggle in this country,"

---

2   Asbley, Karin, Bill Ayers, Bernardine Dohrn, John Jacobs, Jeff Jones, Gerry Long, Home Machtinger, Jim Mellen, Terry Robbins, Mark Rudd, and Steve Tappis, "You Don't Need a Weatherman to Know Which Way the Wind Blows," *New Left Notes*, February 28, 1969.

wrong to work for better conditions in shops and factories and hospitals, wrong to fight to "reform [the schools] so that they can serve the people," for this kind of action diverts Americans from the central issue: "Imperialism is always the issue." The role American radicalism can play is thus radically restricted:

> the vanguard of the "American Revolution"—that is, the section of the people who are in the forefront of the struggle, and whose class interests and needs define the terms and tasks of the revolution—is the workers and oppressed peoples of the colonies of Asia, Africa and Latin America . . . The Vietnamese (and the Uruguayans and the Rhodesians) and the blacks and the Third World peoples in this country will continue to set the terms for class struggle in America.

The only Americans for whom there is any hope turn out not really to be Americans at all: "Black people," the statement says, "are part of the Third World and part of the international revolutionary vanguard."

Although the Weatherpeople write off all white Americans with apparent impartiality, they are especially scornful toward the group from which most of them themselves have come: the literate, educated, white-collar men and women of American metropolitan areas and university towns. This group is not easily defined. Some sociologists classify it as "new middle-class," some put it into the "new working class," some say it spans both. What everyone agrees, however, and what is important for my point, is that there is something distinctively "modern" about the group, something endemic to societies that are "advanced," highly "developed"—therefore I will refer to this group as "modern men," as "us." The Weatherpeople take great pains to disaffiliate themselves from us. When they learned "to reject the ideal career of the professional," it did not occur to them to try to create their own career models, or to connect themselves with radical traditions within their own country, their own culture, their own class. What they did was to "look for leadership to the people's war of the Vietnamese," to "look to Mao, Che, the Panthers, the Third

World, for models, for motion." The closest the Weatherpeople are willing to come to home is "the 'people's culture' of black America," which they have learned from "Chuck Berry, Elvis, The Temptations." It does not seem even to occur to them—they never mention the idea, not even to dismiss it—that anything further might be happening here. (The radical potential which they concede to "youth culture" seems to consist entirely in its capacity to identify with radical forces "outside.") If they speak to us at all, it is only to give us notice that our "television set, car and wardrobe already belong . . . to the people of the world." Until the repossessors arrive, the one worthy thing we can do is "support the blacks in moving as fast as they have to and are able to, and . . . keep up with that black movement enough so that white revolutionaries can share the cost, and the blacks don't have to do the whole thing alone." In other words, we can serve as a sort of Fifth Column for the Third World, but not for ourselves—since we're not worth saving. Our role, our historic mission, is to be overcome someday.

When the great day comes, none of us will get to share in its fruits. Liberation for the world will mean only repression for us. According to the late Ted Gold, after American imperialism is defeated abroad, "an agency of the peoples of the world" will be set up to run the American economy and society, presumably to give our television sets, cars, and clothes back to their rightful owners. Africans, Peruvians, Vietnamese will move in and take over—making every John Bircher's worst dreams come true. Indeed, said Gold, in his last published words before his tragic death, "if it will take fascism, we'll have to have fascism." Americans are so innately, irreparably, radically evil, that "it will take fascism"—the twentieth century's realest vision of hell on earth—to give us our just deserts. And the handwriting on our palace walls is just as clear as the words over the gate of the Inferno: All of us must abandon all hope for ourselves.

When the Weatherpeople burst on the scene in the summer of 1969, their manifesto stirred a storm of bitter invective on the left. What seemed most outrageous about them—even more than the terrorist tactics they were to develop a few months later—was their overwrought self-hatred, at once personal, racial, and cultural. Critics with a sense of irony were quick to pick up echoes of that old reliable "liberal guilt." But there were greater ironies which no one was ready to confront. This guilt trip, sick as it was, struck a deeper chord in a great many radicals' sensibilities than they cared to admit. For the Weatherpeople were only working out, to its absurdly logical conclusion, that idea of the American people as "one-dimensional," which most American radicals had accepted uncritically for years. By taking it seriously—dead seriously—the Weatherpeople made it plain to all of us how cruel, how antihuman an idea it was. But none of us on the Left had a clear alternative. If the mass of the American people, if "modern men" as a class, were not one–dimensionally evil, exactly what were they—or, rather, what were we? Everyone was embarrassed because no one could say. Hence, the critiques of the Weathermen, as illuminating as they are, all have a curiously hollow ring. There is an emptiness at the center, where an idea should be. What's missing is a theory of the American people—and more, a theory of "modern" people, of the men and women whom highly developed societies create; a theory of the tensions and contradictions in the life we live, of our strengths and limitations, of our hidden capacities and potentialities.

To try to fill this vacuum, we must go back to the beginning of the modern age. For the peculiar emptiness that afflicts the New Left is close to the very center of the life and experience of "modern man" as such. Ever since the first modern societies began to take on a distinctive form, and people like us emerged in their midst, one of our deepest drives has been *to get outside ourselves*. So much of the paraphernalia of the sixties—from beads to psychedelic drugs to sentimental idealizations of the "Third World"— expresses an archetypical modern impulse: a desperate longing for any world, any culture, any life but our own. This impulse has made the life of modern men and women strangely paradoxical, maybe even absurd, at its core. On the one hand, it has enlarged our sympathies and sensibilities, deepened our feelings, developed our understanding, helped us grow; on the other, it has led us, in affirming other people's lives, to turn against and deny and negate our own. It is only too typically modern that the New Left of the 1960s should gain at once a three-dimensional vision of so many other kinds of people—blacks, Indians, the Third World, women, homosexuals, schizophrenics, and on and on—and a one-dimensional view of themselves. This is only the latest punchline in a sick joke that gives some of the flavor of modern society's sickness, and yet, ironically, manages to express some of its health as well.

To understand the modern predicament, it might be useful to look at Rousseau, for he was the first truly modern radical. Living in the midst of the first great wave of modernization, he was the first radical thinker to address himself directly to the problems springing up in its wake. He was the first to get the jokes that modern men were playing on themselves. Unfortunately, some of Rousseau's radical impulses led him up a blind alley, one which prefigures and may illuminate the impasse in which the New Left is stuck today. But Rousseau also found in himself the insight and imagination to see beyond his impasse, and I believe that those of us on the Left may find in him a way to see through—and, hopefully, to break through—our own.

II

Among the many notes in Rousseau's writings that strike close to home, one of the most arresting is the uninhibited rage and violence with which he attacks the modern city, its culture and its people. A typical remark: "In this age of calculators, it's remarkable that no one should see that France would be far more powerful if Paris were annihilated." *Burn it down!* Rousseau's tone here is far more typical of the 1960s than of the 1760s. (Typical of the 1960s too, that he should be shocked and perplexed when some Parisians treat him as a menace.) But he insists that his feelings about Paris are nothing personal; he aims his malevolence at the modern city *per se*: "A big city, full of scheming, idle people, without religion or principle, whose imagination, depraved by sloth, inactivity, the love of pleasure, and great needs, engenders only monsters and inspires only crimes." Thus, "Men are not made to be crowded together in ant-heaps; they should be scattered over the earth which they have to cultivate. The more they gather together, the more they corrupt themselves." We can see here the birth of a distinctively modern apocalyptic language and one-dimensional vision—a language which we survivors of the 1960s have heard, and a vision we have seen, all too well. This language and vision borrow the rhetoric and imagery of Jewish, early Christian, and medieval apocalypse, raging against the Great Whore of Babylon (an image of which the Black Panthers and their white followers are particularly fond), hoping for its destruction. But the perspective now is secular and post-Christian: These radicals yearn not for a transcendental, purely spiritual redemption, but for a kingdom that will be immanent, material, in and of this world.

In fact, Rousseau's one-dimensional view of the city was only a small part of a much larger one-dimensional picture. He was well aware that, at the very moment he was condemning the "great cities," they were just emerging as the centers of energy in a vast social, political, and cultural evolutionary process—a process of development which is still going on today. In condemning them, Rousseau was condemning the *esprit générale* of modern society and the historical movement that was bringing this society into being.

We can find somewhere in Rousseau's work just about every objection to modern society that anyone has thought of, left, right or center, in the last two hundred years: It is too free, it is not free enough; men are too "leveled," they are too unequal; people cannot get close to each other, they are thrown into intense and indecent intimacy. But Rousseau's most concrete account of his confrontation with modern society is in his romantic and political novel, *The New Eloise*, in which Saint-Preux, the young, sensitive, intellectual hero, who is stifled by the rigid class prejudices and emotional deadness of his native petit-bourgeois provincial society, comes to Paris, in search of a place to which he and his love, Julie, can flee, a social structure into which individualistic and romantic people can be integrated, can build and live a life.

Rousseau's treatment of the trip is perhaps the first modern instance of what has since become an archetypical modern theme, both in art and in life: The Young Man from the Provinces Comes to the City. As Lionel Trilling points out, Rousseau himself—"a shiftless boy from Geneva, a starveling and a lackey, who becomes the admiration of the French aristocracy, and is permitted by Europe to manipulate its assumptions in every department of life"—is "the father of all Young Men from the Provinces, including the one from Corsica."[3] Confrontation with the great city, exposure of the self to its promises and perils, is an ultimate test of who a person is, of all that he or she can be.

Saint-Preux is immediately thrilled by the energy and vitality of Paris, the "great spectacles," the "enormous diversity of things," the "many attractions which offer so many charms to the newcomer." The most striking thing about life here is its *fluidity*. He feels himself "thrown into a torrent" that overruns all social barriers and generates an unprecedented social mobility. Everyone is approachable and accessible; thought and speech in this city lead to *action*; there is a seemingly infinite range of opportunity. "Nothing is shocking, for everyone is accustomed to everything." No society has ever been more "full of original men," because none has ever opened up so much social space for individuality to develop.

Why should anyone want to burn down a place like this, in which all human potentialities can be fulfilled? This potentiality itself turns out to be the city's greatest pitfall. In an age when individuality has become freer and more important than ever, Rousseau sees nothing more precious, more valuable, than the wholehearted *commitment* of one individual to another. Personal commitment, for him, is what gives romantic love a moral dignity. Indeed, by virtue of its power to generate commitment, romantic love acquires a political dignity as well: The romantic couple is the primary community, the nucleus of the social contract. Early in *The New Eloise*, after the young lovers have secretly slept

---

3   Lionel Trilling, *The Liberal Imagination*, New York: New York Review of Books, 1950.

together and pledged themselves to one another, Julie is racked with guilt; she considers rejecting the man she loves and marrying instead the noble lord her father is trying to force on her. But Saint-Preux insists that her guilt is misplaced: Their love springs not from immorality, but from a new morality, in which fidelity becomes the highest virtue, a political as well as sexual issue. Lovers must be steadfastly, monogamously devoted to one another, in the same way, and for the same reasons, that the true citizen must be faithfully devoted to his community. Moreover, for lovers and citizens alike, fidelity will be valuable only if it is freely given, given out of "the soul of a free man," given by a person who has the power to withhold it. For modern men and women, in the modern metropolis, at a time when a bourgeois economy and society is just coming to life—in other words, in a world of infinite options—fidelity takes on a unique, irreplaceable human value. Ironically, however, the same social conditions that make free personal commitment possible seem at the same time to make it impossible. This contradiction is what makes Saint-Preux and Rousseau feel that modernity has got to go.

"Everyone," says Saint-Preux, "constantly places himself in contradiction with himself . . . and this opposition doesn't bother anyone"—because self-contradiction is what makes this world go round. But indeed, if "nothing is shocking, because everyone is accustomed to everything," doesn't it follow that "everything is absurd"? Amid all these quick changes, what is worth hanging onto? If anything (or anyone) that is here today can be gone tomorrow, what standards can we legitimately use to decide what is right? For that matter, in the great city, do words like legitimate and right have any meaning at all? All the old moral touchstones seem to crumble in this new world. "Of all the things that strike me, none of them holds my heart, but the totality disturbs my heart, and dislocates my feelings, to the point that *I forget what I am and whom I belong to*." The modern city enables the self to expand its activity enormously; but where is the self to find a center, a core that will hold its identity together? The endless parade of possibilities which modernity presents disturbs the heart, dislocates the feelings, and forces the individual to *choose*, to *decide*, every day, every night, not only where he or she is going to go, whom he or she is going to belong to, but *what he or she is going to be*.

Paradoxically, the enormous range of possibilities destroys the possibility of a stable, integrated, indissoluble "being" which the self can securely call its own.

When one night Saint-Preux goes to bed with a girl he has met, his hysterical guilt leads him to draw reactionary political conclusions from the sexual politics of the affair—he was led astray by freedom; from now on, he will seek escapes from this ambiguous, dreadful freedom.

The impulse which Saint-Preux blames for his infidelity, and tries to reject in himself, is an impulse which he shares with all modern men, a force that animates them and drives them all, and gives modern society its distinctive form: this is what Rousseau calls *avidité*, "avidity." In the *Social Contract* it will appear as the motive force behind "the turmoil of commerce and the arts, the avid pursuit of profit"—a force which Rousseau considers absolutely incompatible with democracy. Here it appears at the heart of Parisian life, and Saint-Preux condemns it as the real motive for his crime. "They looked at me with *a violent avidity*"—and he looked back. Avidity is linked with avarice, the bourgeois desire for money and profit; but it is a great deal more than avarice. As Rousseau sees and feels it, it can express itself just as well in sexual desire or in aggressive violence. Indeed, it floats freely between one object and another. This ambiguity is a key to the deeply ambiguous character of the social system it sustains. In modern society, sex, money, and violence are hopelessly entangled with one another, need and greed are intertwined, for modern society both liberates impulses and mixes them up, with catastrophic results. What is to be done? From this point, Rousseau went off in two radically opposite directions. Sometimes, as we will see later, he tried to make distinctions, to disentangle the different kinds of avidity, to separate need from greed, creative from destructive energy. At other times, as we have seen already, he saw them all as one, condemned them all, root and branch, and tried to reject modernity as a whole.

The same logic that led Rousseau to despair of Saint-Preux's capacity for fidelity in the modern city also led him to despair of the capacity of modern men for democracy or community. What made them such bad material for democratic citizenship and participation in communal life, Rousseau believed, was their free-floating avidity. Every modern people, he said, is "noisy, brilliant and fearsome," "an ardent, avid, ambitious people . . . given to the two extremes of opulence and poverty (*misère*), of license and slavery." The basic trouble with people like this is that they *can't be counted on*: They are never fully *committed* to anyone or anything except the pursuit of their personal interests. "A prey to indolence and all the passions it excites, they plunge themselves into debauchery, and sell themselves for satisfaction; self-interest makes them servile, and idleness makes them restless; *they are either slaves or rebels, never free men.*"

III

When Rousseau turned away from the great city in search of "love, happiness and innocence," he turned toward those traditional, rural societies in the backwaters and backwoods of Europe (or beyond Europe altogether) not yet affected by the process of modernization. For it was only in undeveloped societies, he often argued, that radical democracy could take root. The impact of Rousseau's thought here has been enormous: We can see his influences on the Russian Narodniks and American Populists of the nineteenth century, and, more recently, on Mao and Fanon and many ideologues of the Third World today.

Rousseau did not think rural societies of his period were fine just as they were: He despised the fashionable pastoral conventions and saw, as clearly as anyone in his time, the starvation and oppression and misery that choked the countryside. Still, he believed that the very misery of rural life generated human qualities that were indispensable to a democratic citizenry. Peasants know how to endure, to hold on; thus they are "attached to their soil" far more tenaciously than modern men are committed to their cities. The life of the traditional peasant commune is "happy in its mediocrity"; it leaves its members "incapable of even imagining a better way of life." What is striking and disturbing about these views is that they glorify narrowness, rigidity, ignorance, even stupidity—precisely those qualities Marx later stigmatized as "the idiocy of rural life."

One of history's most compelling collective dreams has been that the last shall be first. Rousseau made the dream seem plausible. Backward people, he argued, by virtue of their very backwardness, are really able to preserve virtues which advanced peoples have had to repress in themselves in order to get ahead. Two centuries of populism, anarchism, socialism, and communism have given Rousseau's language an elaborate and complex vocabulary, which we can use to translate his ideas into ideologies of our time. The dream that the last shall be first emerges as the contemporary political theory—or, maybe, political myth—that the undeveloped societies can make the leap from feudalism or colonialism to socialism directly, without having to pass through a capitalist stage.

Rousseau's most fully realized vision of an unmodernized radical democracy occurs in *The New Eloise*, when the Swiss mountain community of the Upper Valais is experienced and evaluated for us through the eyes of Saint-Preux. In the structure of the novel, it corresponds to Saint-Preux's evocation of Paris; in the structure of Rousseau's ideas, the Upper Valais is an antithesis to Paris, an archetype of the Rousseauean alternative to modernization. This idyllic society, however, contains inner contradictions of its own, contradictions even more severely destructive than the ones they were meant to overcome; and the radical democracy of the rural commune turns out to be most inauthentic for precisely the people who need and want it most avidly.

Saint-Preux greets the new society with a rush of exaltation, which Rousseau presents to us as a sudden illumination, an ecstatic vision. For the first time in Saint-Preux's life, people are going out of their way to be nice to him. Unlike the Parisians, who constantly try to pull him into their worlds, the Valaisians, he reports, "went about their lives as if I wasn't there, and I was able to act as if I had been alone." They are totally devoid of avidity. Their hospitality flows from a "disinterested humanity," a genuine "zeal to please every stranger that chance or curiosity sends them."

Saint-Preux discovers the social foundations of these lovely qualities. The Valaisians are small independent farmers and artisans; their community is a democratic republic. The basic social units here are the extended family and the village commune. There is only the most rudimentary division of labor or exchange, and money is virtually nonexistent, for it is superfluous. The community as a whole is self-sufficient; it seeks nothing outside itself. Its economy has no luxury, but no poverty either; it is free from the economic extremes that tear the modern city apart; it produces a modest but real "abundance for all." Valaisian society is not classless, but it eliminates the inequities of feudal stratification. There is plenty of freedom here, but unlike the dreadful freedom of the metropolis, it leads to no trouble. The children seem to accept freely their parents' institutions and forms of life—forms and institutions which have brought them a freedom which they cherish deeply and use sparingly. The basic psychic fact about the Valaisians, which enables them to live at once freely and traditionally, is that their needs and desires are structurally limited. They work until certain basic needs are fulfilled, and then they stop; as a result, they have ample leisure and look upon their work as a pleasure.

Rousseau has shown us here the deep affinity between the ideal of romantic love and that of radical democracy. He has created the vision of a world—"a new world," high in the mountains, remote, serene, unknown or ignored by the world below, free from time and change—in which these two dreams, the personal and the political, can be fulfilled. Rousseau's vision prefigures the one moving so many of our young people today—up in the mountains, out in the desert, away in the undeveloped Third World, they can feel free from the pressures of modern life. And many of Saint-Preux's successors—many of my students—have done just this, dropping out of the modern world and into old yet "new" ones. And yet Saint-Preux himself doesn't. Why? Because he gradually realizes that something is wrong with the idyllic picture.

What is wrong becomes visible in the kind of sexual experience it generates. Up here, too, Saint-Preux is free and alone, surrounded by attractive women, committed to another woman who is far away. Saint-Preux is in the most provocative situation we could imagine, yet he is not in the least provoked. What is lacking, Saint-Preux comes to realize, is in fact *avidity*, that power that animates the metropolis. In the Upper Valais, nothing leads anywhere, thought and action are totally disassociated from one another—this is what makes social life so free of tension. The happiness that men pursue up here is a "peaceful tranquility" which comes to them "not through the enjoyment of pleasure, but rather through exemption from pain." Indeed, *"all our desires which are too alive are deadened here."* At the heart of the idyllic dream, Rousseau makes clear to us, is a wish for death.

For some time, we have recognized the death wish—conscious or unconscious—as an ominous undertone in the cultural mythology of romantic love, but Rousseau's vision of the Upper Valais shows us how the self-destructive impulse can animate radical politics as well. We can see it now as a longing to *turn off*. If only, as Baudelaire said, we could make a leap "anywhere out of the world"; if we could detach ourselves from body, weight, movement, time; if we could be less ardent, less avid, less passionate, less profound, less human, less alive; if we could turn off "all the desires that torment men in the world below"; if, once and for all, we could just stop being *ourselves—then* we could be happy! Rousseau's image of the Valaisian republic projects this longing onto a social and political plane. The recipe reads like a morbid parody of the *Social Contract*. It is as if the Valaisians have mutually agreed to turn off and tune out, to tranquilize themselves. When people are drained of avidity—or brought up in such a way that avidity will never develop—freedom will no longer be risky; men and women can be secure in their fidelity, and citizens will be perpetually loyal and totally committed to the state. Here, at last, a final solution to the problems of modernity. The urge to get away from it all is, in the end, a death trip.

IV

Avidity is at the heart of Rousseau's dialectic. On the one hand, avidity compels men to pursue profit and power, to compete against and exploit one another. On the other, avidity alone can infuse men with the daring to get through the masks, to feel and know themselves and each other, and to fight to fulfill their real potentialities. Avidity has liberated human energy *for* bourgeois society—it has set men and women free to develop their powers in pursuit of power over one another, ending only in death. Now, Rousseau argues, it will take avidity to liberate human energy *from* bourgeois society—so that people working together, in a genuine community, can develop themselves and each other more fully than possible before.

Rousseau persistently felt an urge to run away from modernity, and he was inexhaustibly brilliant in imagining idyllic ways out. But he saw that though idyllic rural society, untouched by modern life, could indeed generate an "equality of soul," a "perfect tranquility" that modernization would shatter forever, there was something barren here. If mankind remained fixed at this point, turned off to his desires and impulses, unaware of the freedom (and hence not possessed of any genuine freedom) to choose, "there would be no goodness in our hearts, no morality in our actions." And, "our understanding would not . . . develop itself; we would have lived without feeling anything, and we would have *died without having lived;* all our happiness would have consisted in not knowing how miserable we really were." If the great thing is to be fully and intensely alive, then we must affirm the life-giving force of modernity—even if it makes us too alive for comfort. Thus the impulses and ideas that led Rousseau away from modernity, when they are pursued most avidly, must lead him back, and back into his own life as a modern man.

For despite its decadence, the metropolis develops in its men and women "that exquisite *sensibility* which moves the heart when friendship, love and virtue are manifest, and makes us cherish in others those pure, tender and honest feelings which we no longer have ourselves." The presence of this sensibility among the

Parisians was no accident; it was integral to the character of modern men—indeed, it was a survival skill which they could not do without. The very moral imagination which enabled modern men to use ideals as screens, behind which to manipulate and exploit each other, preserved for them an inner sense of what these ideals might really mean. The insight which empowered them to see through one another today might drive them tomorrow to see through themselves.

What did Rousseau want them to see? Above all, the contradiction between the fullness of their powers and potentialities and the bourgeois imperatives which had brought these powers and potentialities into being. The necessities of the social struggle had put a premium on reason, imagination, spirit, beauty, strength—insofar as they could be used as competitive assets; beyond this one use, however, everything was excess baggage. This process had infused men and women with a newly intense sense of themselves, devotion to their personal interests, love of their individuality. But insofar as modern men defined themselves in competitive terms, they were forced "always to ask others who we are, never daring to ask ourselves"; to be "happy and satisfied with themselves on the testimony of other people, rather than on their own"; to "live constantly outside themselves," so that the individual "depends on the judgment of others for the very sense of his own existence." The *amour propre* which the bourgeoisie defined and celebrated as "self-love" was actually an inner emptiness, a total poverty and bankruptcy of self. Modernization had indeed developed the spirit to "almost the highest point of its perfection"; but the embourgeoisment which animated modernization had alienated it radically from actual human feelings and needs.

I think we can find in Rousseau a strategy that may be even more fruitful in our time than it was in his. It is to appeal to modern men on the basis of their own sensibility and awareness of life. Rousseau believed such an appeal was possible because modern society had developed in its men and women a mode of consciousness capable of transcending it. If this consciousness could be developed further, into *self*-consciousness and into *social* consciousness, then modern people—people who were intensely "ardent, avid, ambitious," who strove constantly to turn their thoughts into actions, their fantasies into realities—might be able to resolve their personal and their political problems together, to reform radically their society and themselves from within.

Rousseau's strategy was profoundly dialectical: it was to "*draw from the evil itself the remedy that can cure it.*" The first step was negative: to show modern man, "who thinks he's happy, how miserable he really is." This was the purpose of Rousseau's most probing and penetrating psychological and political writing. The next step was positive: "to illuminate his reason with new ideas, and warm his heart with new feelings, so that he'll learn that *he can best multiply his happiness and expand his being by sharing them with his fellowmen.*" Even the most avid egotist could be made to understand "how *his own personal interest demands that he submit to the general will.*" Then, "with a stout heart and a sound mind, this enemy of mankind would give up his hatred with his fallacies; *the very reason that drew him apart from humanity would lead him back to it.* Then he would become a good, virtuous, sensitive man. Instead of a vicious outlaw, he would want to be the firmest pillar of a good society."

I remember an SDS meeting at the New York Community Church on a sweltering July night in 1966. A black man spoke, from the Student Nonviolent Coordinating Committee (SNCC) I think, and told us—as Malcolm X had been telling us for a year or so before he was killed—that there was an important role for white radicals in "the Revolution," but that this role wasn't in the black ghetto. What we needed to do, he said, was to go back home, wherever we came from, and "work with our own kind." The white radicals in the audience didn't take this very well. One of the ablest and most courageous I know, a community organizer in Newark, said: "So you're telling us to go back to our parents?" In effect, said the SNCC man, yes. "But I have more in common with oppressed blacks in the ghetto than I have with my parents in Scarsdale. I have more in common with sharecroppers in Georgia, Indians on the reservation, Bolivian tin miners, Vietnamese—for Christ's sake, I have more in common with *anybody* than with my parents! That's why I'm in the movement in the first place." Most of us agreed. But the man from SNCC persisted: We had more in common with our parents than we liked to think.

For a great many of us there could be no greater insult. But the truth is that there are some very deep impulses which we and our parents share; impulses which are frighteningly ambiguous, but which are in themselves nothing to be ashamed of; impulses which have radical possibilities for fathers and sons, mothers and daughters alike. They are what Rousseau called *perfectibility* and—in its most distinctively modern expression—*avidity*. Perfectibility: the unwillingness to settle back and rest content, the need to change constantly one's life for the better. Avidity: the desire to turn thought into action, to *do it*, here and now. It is perfectibility and avidity that lead our parents, in Scarsdale or wherever they are stuck, to trade in their car for a new one every year. How to judge them? Is it absurd to think that a new car will make them happy? Of course, this is precisely the sort of absurdity that makes the American economy and our middle-class life run. But it is not at all absurd for our parents to feel that their old car and all the other things they have now do not make them happy. Indeed, it is the beginning of wisdom. And it is far from absurd for them to want to do something to change their lives! What *we* have to make clear to them is that it's not so much the car, as the system that built it, that needs changing—and that we can't trade a social system in, we must build a new one.

The perfectibility and avidity that have driven our parents in contradictory directions have been driving us too. We've demanded "Power to the people!" and we've identified with any and every people in the world—except *our people*. This drive has been genuinely liberating for many of us; it has enabled us, by getting into other people, to expand and deepen ourselves. This is what the word "psychedelic" legitimately means and what so much of the 1960s was all about. But getting into other people, identifying ourselves with them, is not enough for radicalism. Radicalism means going to the roots, and (as Marx said) the root for man is man, and if we mean to be men—*Menschen*, human beings—if we want our souls to expand authentically, we must make room for ourselves at the center. In the course of the sixties, we have learned to affirm, avidly, militantly, everyone but ourselves. Now we must affirm ourselves as well. We must move, must grow, from apocalypse to dialectic.

It is worth pointing out that the New Left began with dialectic, with a document Rousseau would have understood: the Port Huron Statement of 1962. "Some would have us believe," the statement says, "that Americans feel contentment amidst their prosperity." But the fact is, it goes on to say, most people are tormented by "deeply felt anxieties about their role in the world . . . [which] produce a yearning to believe that there is some alternative to the present, that something can be done to change the school, the bureaucracies, the work-places, the government . . . It is to this yearning, at once the spark and the engine of change, that we address our present appeal." The signers of the statement were determined to discover or to create new forms of political life and action that would express people's "unrealized potential for self-cultivation, self-direction, self-understanding and creativity"; forms that would fulfill their "unrealized capacities for reason, freedom and love." These goals can be achieved only by transforming America into a "democracy of individual participation." The New Left, at its birth, embarked on a "search for truly democratic alternatives to the present, and a commitment to social experimentation." It invited the American people as a whole to take this trip with it. Thus spoke the founders of the SDS in 1962. Where are they now? How often, since then, have we been side-tracked?

The question is, how can we start again? One thing we should have learned is not to go it alone, isolated from the "modern men"—and modern women—who share our discontents and our hopes. As Rousseau indicated, this requires an understanding of the contradictions of modern life—contradictions which Rousseau faced with remarkable clarity and courage. He was the first to explore the uncharted, perilous open sea of modernity. He left us logs and maps that we can use to learn where and who we are.

This essay originally appeared in the Partisan Review, *Winter 1971–2.*

Unchained Melody

The best story I've ever heard about *The Communist Manifesto* came from Hans Morgenthau, the great theorist of international relations who died in 1980. It was the early seventies at CUNY, and he was reminiscing about his childhood in Bavaria before the First World War. Morgenthau's father, a doctor in a working-class neighborhood of Coburg, often took his son along on house calls. Many of his patients were dying of TB; a doctor could do nothing to save their lives, but might help them die with dignity. When his father asked about last requests, many workers said they wanted to have the *Manifesto* buried with them when they died. They implored the doctor to see that the priest didn't sneak in and plant the Bible on them instead.

This spring, the *Manifesto* is 150 years old. In that century and a half, apart from the Bible, it has become the most widely read book in the world. Eric Hobsbawm, in his splendid introduction to the handsome new Verso edition,[1] gives a brief history of the book's reception. It can be summed up fast: Whenever there's trouble, anywhere in the world, the book becomes an item; when things quiet down, the book drops out of sight; when there's trouble again, the people who forgot remember. When fascist-type regimes seize power, it's always on the short list of books to burn. When people dream of resistance—even if they're not communists, even if they distrust communists—it provides music for their dreams. Get the beat of the beginning and the end. First line:

---

1   Karl Marx and Friedrich Engels, *The Communist Manifesto*, London: Verso, 1998.

"A spectre is haunting Europe—the spectre of Communism." Last lines: "The proletarians have nothing to lose but their chains. They have a world to win. WORKING MEN OF ALL COUNTRIES, UNITE!" In Rick's bar in *Casablanca*, you may or may not love France, but when the band breaks into "La Marseillaise," you've got to stand up and sing.

Yet literate people today, even people with left politics, are amazingly ignorant of what's actually in the book. For years, I've asked people what they think it consists of. The most popular answers are that it's (1) a utopian handbook on how to run a society with no money or property, or else (2) a Machiavellian handbook on how to create a communist state and keep it in power. People who were communists didn't seem to know the book any better than people who were not. (At first this amazed me; later I saw it was no accident. Classical communist education was Talmudic, based on a study of commentaries, with an underlying suspicion of sacred primary texts. Among Orthodox Jews, the Bible is a sort of adult movie—a *yeshiva-bucher* is exposed to it only after years of Talmudic training, to insure that he will respond in orthodox ways. Similarly, a trainee at a party school would begin with Stalin, until 1956; then the great indoctrinator Lenin; then, with some hesitation, Engels. Marx came in only at the very end, and then only for those with security clearance.)

Now that security is gone. In just a few years, so many statues and magnifications of Marx have vanished from public squares; so many streets and parks named for him are going under other names today. What does it all mean? For some people, like our Sunday morning princes of the air, the implosion of the USSR simply confirmed what they had believed all along, and released them from having to show respect. One of my old bosses at CCNY said it concisely: "Nineteen eighty-nine proves that courses in Marxism are obsolete." But there are other ways to read history. What happened to Marx after 1917 was a disaster: A thinker needs beatification like a hole in the head. So we should welcome his descent from the pedestal as a fortunate fall. Maybe we can learn what Marx has to teach if we confront him at ground level, the level on which we ourselves are trying to stand.

So what does he offer? First, startling when you're not prepared for it, praise for capitalism so extravagant, it skirts the edge of awe. Very early in the *Manifesto*, he describes the processes of material construction that it perpetrates and the emotions that go with them, especially the sense of being caught up in something magical and uncanny:

> The bourgeoisie has created . . . more massive and more colossal productive forces than have all preceding generations together. Subjection of nature's forces to man, machinery; application of chemistry to industry and agriculture, steam navigation, rail-ways . . . clearing of whole continents for cultivation, canalization of rivers, whole populations conjured out of the ground – what earlier century had even a presentiment that such productive powers slumbered in the lap of social labour?

Or a page before, on an innate dynamism that is spiritual as well as material:

> The bourgeoisie cannot exist without constantly revolutionizing the instruments of production, and there by the relations of production, and with them the whole relations of society . . . Constant revolutionizing of production, uninterrupted distur-bance of all social conditions, everlasting uncertainty and agita-tion distinguish the bourgeois epoch from all earlier ones. All fixed, fast-frozen relations, with their train of ancient and vener-able prejudices and opinions, are swept away, all new-formed ones become antiquated before they can ossify. All that is solid melts into air, all that is holy is profaned, and man is at last compelled to face with sober senses, his real conditions of life, and his relations with his kind.

Part 1, "Bourgeois and Proletarians," contains many passages like these, asserted in major chords with great dramatic flair. Somehow, many readers seem to miss them. But Marx's contemporaries didn't miss them, and some fellow radicals—Proudhon, Bakunin—saw his appreciation of capitalism as a betrayal of its victims. This charge is still heard today and deserves serious response. Marx hates capitalism, but he also thinks it has brought immense real benefits, spiritual as well as material, and he wants the benefits spread around and enjoyed by everybody rather than monopolized by a small ruling class. This is very different from the totalitarian rage that typifies radicals who want to blow it all away. Sometimes, as with Proudhon, it is just modern times they hate; they dream of a golden-age peasant village where everyone was happily in his place (or in her place behind him). For other radicals, from the author of the Book of Revelation to the Unabomber, it goes over the edge into something like rage against reality, against human life itself. Apocalyptic rage offers immediate, sensational cheap thrills. Marx's perspective is far more complex, nuanced, and hard to sustain if you're not grown up.

Marx is not the first communist to admire capitalism for its creativity; that attitude can be found in some of the great utopian socialists of the generation before him, like Saint-Simon and Robert Owen. But Marx is the first to invent a prose style that can bring that perilous creativity to life. His style in the *Manifesto* is a kind of expressionist lyricism. Every paragraph breaks over us like a wave that leaves us shaking from the impact and wet with thought. This prose evokes breathless momentum, plunging ahead without guides or maps, breaking all boundaries, precarious piling and layering of things, ideas, and experiences. Catalogues play a large role in Marx's style—as they do for his contemporaries Dickens and Whitman—but part of the *Manifesto*'s enchantment comes from our feeling that the lists are never exhausted, the catalogue is open to the present and the future, we are invited to pile on things, ideas, and experiences of our own, to pile ourselves on if we can. But the items in the pile often seem to clash, and it sounds like the whole vast aggregation could crash. From paragraph to paragraph, Marx makes readers feel that we are riding the fastest and grandest nineteenth-century train through the roughest and most perilous nineteenth-century terrain, and though we have splendid light, we are pressing ahead where there is no track.

*   *   *

One feature of modern capitalism that Marx most admires is its global horizon and its cosmopolitan texture. Many people today talk about the global economy as if it had only recently come into being. The *Manifesto* should help us see the extent to which it has been there all along:

> The need of a constantly expanding market chases the bourgeoisie over the whole surface of the globe. It must nestle everywhere, settle everywhere, establish connections everywhere.
>
> The bourgeoisie has through its exploitation of the world market given a cosmopolitan character to production and consumption in every country. All old established national industries have been destroyed or are being daily destroyed. They are dislodged by new industries, whose introduction becomes a life and death question for all civilized nations, by industries that no longer process indigenous raw material, but raw material drawn from remotest zones; industries whose products are consumed, not only at home, but in every quarter of the globe.
>
> The cheap prices of its commodities are heavy artillery with which [the bourgeoisie] batters down all Chinese walls, with which it forces the barbarians' intensely obstinate hatred of foreigners to capitulate. It compels all nations, on pain of extinction, to adopt the bourgeois mode of production; it compels them to introduce what is called civilization into their midst, i.e. to become bourgeois themselves. In one word, it creates a world after its own image.

This global spread offers a spectacular display of history's ironies. These bourgeois are banal in their ambitions, yet their unremitting quest for profit forces on them the same insatiable drive-structure and infinite horizon as that of any of the great Romantic heroes—as Don Giovanni, as Childe Harold, as Goethe's Faust. They may think of only one thing, but their narrow focus leads to the broadest integrations; their shallow outlook wreaks the most profound transformations; their peaceful economic activity devastates every human society like a bomb, from the most primitive tribes to the mighty USSR. Marx was appalled at the human costs of capitalist development, but he always believed that the world horizon it created was a great achievement on which socialism must build. Remember, the grand appeal to Unite with which the *Manifesto* ends is addressed to "WORKING MEN OF ALL COUNTRIES."

A crucial global drama was the unfolding of the first-ever world culture. Marx, writing when mass media were just developing, called it "world literature." I think it is legitimate at the end of this century to update the idea into "world culture." The *Manifesto* shows how this culture will evolve spontaneously from the world market:

> In place of the old wants, satisfied by the production of the coun- try, we find new wants, requiring for their satisfaction products of distant lands and climes. In place of the old local and national seclusion and self-sufficiency, we have intercourse in every direc- tion, universal interdependence of nations. And as in material, so also in intellectual [or spiritual—*geistige* can be translated either way] production. The intellectual [spiritual] creations of individ- ual nations become common property . . . and from the numerous national and local literatures, there arises a world literature.

This vision of world culture brings together several complex ideas. First, the expansion of human needs: The increasingly cosmopolitan world market at once shapes and expands every- body's desires. Marx doesn't elaborate on this in detail; but he wants us to imagine what it might mean in food, clothes, religion, music, love, and in our most intimate fantasies as well as our public presentations. Next, the idea of culture as "common property" in the world market: Anything created by anyone anywhere is open and available to everyone everywhere. Entrepreneurs publish books, produce plays and concerts, display visual art and, in our century, create hardware and software for movies, radio, TV, and computers in order to make money. Nevertheless, in this as in other ways, history slips through the owners' fingers, so that poor people get to possess culture—an idea, a poetic image, a musical sound, Plato, Shakespeare, a Negro spiritual (Marx loved them)— even if they can't own it. Culture stuffs people's heads full of ideas. As a form of "common property," modern culture helps us to imagine how people all around the world could share all the world's resources someday.

It's a vision of culture rarely discussed, but it is one of the most expansive and hopeful things Marx ever wrote. In our century, the development of movies, television and video and computers has created a global visual language that brings the idea of world culture closer to home than ever, and the world beat comes through in the best of our music and books. That's the good news. The bad news is how sour and bitter most Left writing on culture has become. Sometimes it sounds as if culture were just one more Department of Exploitation and Oppression, containing nothing luminous or valuable in itself. At other times, it sounds as if people's minds were empty vessels with nothing inside except what *Capital* put there. Read, or try to read, a few articles on "hegemonic/counterhegemonic discourse." The way these guys write, it's as if the world has passed them by.

But if capitalism is a triumph in so many ways, exactly what's wrong with it? What's worth spending your life in opposition? In the twentieth century, Marxist movements around the world have concentrated on the argument, made most elaborately in *Capital,* that workers in bourgeois society had been or were being pauperized. Now, there were times and places where it was absurd to deny that claim; in other times and places (like the United States and Western Europe in the fifties and sixties, when I was young) it was pretty tenuous, and Marxist economists went through strange dialectical twists to make the numbers come out. But the problem with that discussion was that it converted questions of human experience into questions of numbers: It led Marxism to think and talk exactly like capitalism! The *Manifesto* occasionally makes some version of this claim. But it offers what strikes me as a much more trenchant indictment, one that holds up even at the top of the business cycle, when the bourgeoisie and its apologists are drowning in complacency.

That indictment is Marx's vision of what modern bourgeois society forces people to be: They have to freeze their feelings for each other to adapt to a cold-blooded world. In the course of "pitilessly tear[ing] asunder the motley feudal ties," bourgeois society "has left remaining no other nexus between man and man than naked self-interest, than callous 'cash payment.'" It has "drowned" every form of sentimental value "in the icy water of egotistical calculation." It has "resolved personal worth into exchange-value." It has collapsed every historical tradition and norm of freedom "into that single, unconscionable freedom—free trade." The worst thing about capitalism is that it forces people to become brutal in order to survive.

For 150 years, we have seen a huge literature that dramatizes the brutalization of the bourgeoisie, a class in which those who are most comfortable with brutality are most likely to succeed. But the same social forces are pressing on the members of that immense group that Marx calls the "modern working class." This class has been afflicted with a case of mistaken identity. Many readers have always thought that "working class" meant only factory workers, or industrial workers, or manual workers, or blue-collar workers, or impoverished workers. These readers then note the changing nature of the workforce over the past half-century or so—increasingly white collar, educated, working in human services, in or near the middle class—and they infer the Death of the Subject and conclude that all hopes for the working class are doomed. Marx did not think the working class was shrinking: In all industrial countries it already was, or was in the process of becoming, "the immense majority"; its swelling numbers would enable it to "win the battle of democracy." The basis for his political arithmetic was a concept that was both simple and highly inclusive:

> The modern working class, developed . . . a class of labourers, who live only so long as they find work, and who find work only so long as their labour increases capital. These labourers, who must sell themselves piecemeal, are a commodity, like every other article of commerce, and are consequently exposed to all the vicissitudes of competition, to all the fluctuations of the market.

The crucial factor is not working in a factory, or working with your hands, or being poor. All these things can change with fluctuating supply and demand and technology and politics. The crucial reality is the need to sell your labor to capital in order to live, the need to carve up your personality for sale—to look at yourself in the mirror and think, "What have I got that I can sell?"—and an unending dread and anxiety that even if you're OK today, you won't find anyone who wants to buy what you have or what you are tomorrow, that the changing market will declare you (as it has already declared so many) worthless, that you will find yourself physically as well as metaphysically homeless and out in the cold. Arthur Miller's *Death of a Salesman,* a twentieth-century masterpiece, brings to life the consuming dread that may be the condition of most members of the working class in modern times. The whole existentialist tradition dramatizes this situation with great depth and beauty, yet its visions tend to be weirdly disembodied. Its visionaries could learn from the *Manifesto,* which gives modern anguish an address.

A great many people are in the working class but don't know it. Many are the people who fill up the huge office buildings that choke all our downtowns. They wear elegant suits and return to nice houses, because there is a great demand for their labor right now, and they are doing well. They may identify happily with the owners, and have no idea how contingent and fleeting their benefits are. They may not discover who they really are, and where they belong, until they are laid off or fired—or deskilled, outsourced, downsized. (It is fascinating how many of these crushing words are quite new.) And other workers, lacking diplomas, not dressed so nicely, working in cubicles, not offices, may not get the fact that many of the people who boss them around are really in their class. But this is what organizing and organizers are for.

One group whose working-class identity was crucial for Marx was the group to which he himself belonged: intellectuals.

> The bourgeoisie has stripped of its halo every occupation hitherto honoured and looked up to in reverent awe. It has transconverted the physician, the lawyer, the priest, the poet, the man of science, into its paid wage labourers.

Marx is not saying that in bourgeois society these activities lose their human meaning or value. If anything, they are more meaningful and valuable than ever before. But the only way people can get the freedom to make discoveries, or save lives, or poetically light up the world, is by working for capital—for drug companies, movie studios, boards of education, politicians, HMOs, etc., etc.—and using their creative skills to help capital accumulate more capital. This means that intellectuals are subject not only to the stresses that afflict all modern workers, but to a dread zone all their own. The more they care about their work and want it to mean something, the more they will find themselves in conflict with the keepers of the spreadsheets; the more they walk the line, the more they are likely to fall. This chronic pressure may give them a special insight into the need for workers to unite. But will united workers treat intellectual and artistic freedom with any more respect than capital treats it? It's an open question; sometime in the twenty-first century, the workers will get power somewhere, and then we'll start to see.

Marx sees the modern working class as an immense worldwide community waiting to happen. Such large possibilities give the story of organizing a permanent gravity and grandeur. The process of creating unions is not just an item in interest-group politics, but also a vital part of what Lessing called "the education of the human race." And it is not just educational but existential: the process of people individually and collectively discovering who they are. As they learn who they are, they will come to see that they need one another in order to be themselves. They will see, because workers are smart: Bourgeois society has forced them to be, in order to survive its constant upheavals. Marx knows they will get it by and by. (Alongside his fury as an agitator, the *Manifesto*'s author also projects a brooding, reflective, long patience.) Solidarity is not sacrifice of yourself but the self's fulfillment. Learning to give yourself to other workers, who may look and sound very different from you but are like you in depth, gives a man or woman a place in the world and delivers the self from dread.

This is a vital part of the moral vision that underlies the *Manifesto*. But there is another moral dimension, asserted in a different key but humanly just as urgent. At one of the book's many climactic moments, Marx says that the Revolution will end classes and class struggles, and this will make it possible to enjoy "an association, in which the free development of each is the condition for the free development of all." Here Marx imagines communism as a way to make people happy. The first aspect of this happiness is "development"—that is, an experience that doesn't simply repeat itself but that goes through some sort of change and growth. This model of happiness is modern and is informed by the incessantly developing bourgeois economy. But bourgeois society, although it enables people to develop, forces them to develop in accord with market demands: What can sell gets developed; what can't sell gets repressed, or never comes to life at all. Against the market model of forced and twisted development, Marx fights for "*free* development," development that the self can control.

In a time when crass cruelty calls itself liberalism (we're kicking you and your kids off welfare for your own good), it is important to see how much ground Marx shares with the best liberal of all, his contemporary John Stuart Mill. Like Marx, Mill came to see the self's "free development" as a fundamental human value; like Marx, he believed that modernization made it possible for everybody. But as he grew older, he became convinced that the capitalist form of modernization—featuring cut-throat competition, class domination, social conformity and cruelty—blocked its best potentialities. He proclaimed himself a socialist in his old age.

Ironically, the ground that socialism and liberalism share might be a big problem for both of them. What if Mr. Kurtz isn't dead after all? In other words, what if authentically "free development" brings out horrific depths in human nature? Dostoyevsky, Nietzsche, and Freud all forced us to face the horrors and warned us of their permanence. In response, both Marx and Mill might say that until we have overcome social domination and degradation, there is simply no way to tell whether the horrors are inherent in human nature or whether we could create benign conditions under which they would wither away. The process of getting to that point—a point where Raskolnikovs won't rot on Avenue D and where Svidrigailovs won't possess thousands of bodies and souls—should be enough to give us all steady work.

The nineties began with the mass destruction of Marx effigies. It was the "post modern" age: We weren't supposed to need big ideas. As the nineties end, we find ourselves in a dynamic global society ever more unified by downsizing, de-skilling, and dread—just like the old man said. All of a sudden, the iconic looks more convincing than the ironic; that classic bearded presence, the atheist as biblical prophet, is back just in time for the millennium. At the dawn of the twentieth century, there were workers who were ready to die with the *Communist Manifesto*. At the dawn of the twenty-first, there may be even more who are ready to live with it.

This essay first appeared in the Nation, *May 11, 1998.*

Part III

Living for the City

Take It to the Streets: Conflict and Community in Public Space

THE DIALECTICS OF DOUBLE LIVES

Karl Marx, writing in the 1840s, developed a perspective that can help us see why modern men and women have a special need for public space, and also why the historical forces that create this need make it especially hard to fulfill. His 1844 essay "On the Jewish Question" tries to grasp the new liberal and democratic civilization that the French and American Revolutions have produced. In all states that have had successful bourgeois democratic revolutions, Marx argues, "man leads a double life." The typical modern man or woman is "split into a public person and a private person," or into an "egoistic individual" and a "communal being," or—here Marx quotes the language of the 1789 Declaration of the Rights of Man and Citizen—"into a man and a citizen." Marx characterizes this double life as a life of "political emancipation."

It takes no special wisdom to see that this form of freedom has severe defects. Marx portrays it as only part of the way toward full "human emancipation." Nevertheless, it is "a necessary part." It is only by going through this historical split that we can integrate ourselves into fully developed "species beings." Full human emancipation will happen "only when the individual man [*Mensch*—human being] has taken back into himself the abstract citizen and, in his everyday life and his relations with other people, has recognized and organized his own powers as social powers."

It is this modern, split, fragmented individual, living a double life, that is Marx's subject—these individual people who must do the work of putting their lives together, together with their fellows. Without the experience of radical separation, modern men and women will lack the space they need to grow into people capable of full integration. This is why Marx (as opposed to some other socialists, then and now) supports civil rights, both for Jews (as he argues in the "Jewish Question") and for everybody else. It is true, civil rights for an individual or a group involve "the right of separation." But it is only by going through the most intense separation and individuation that modern men and women can develop the resources to create new forms of solidarity and community.

The paradigms that Marx developed in the 1840s can still be fruitful for understanding life in the democracies of today. We still lead double lives, split into men or women and citizens, torn between private and public; we still dream of resolving our inner contradictions and living in a more integrated way. We know, as Marx did, that this can't happen without a radical transformation of our economy, state, and society; we also know that this can't work if it's imposed from above, but only if people come together freely to do it on their own.

In this political context, the idea of public space takes on a special urgency. A society of split men and women badly needs a terrain on which people can come together to heal their inner wounds—or at least to treat them—and advance from political to human emancipation. Of course, there is no spatial form that in itself could make this happen. But we can imagine environments that could help it happen: environments open to everybody where, first of all, a society's inner contradictions could emerge freely and openly and, second, where people could begin to deal with these contradictions and try to work them out. Any society that takes the rights of man and citizen seriously has a responsibility to provide spaces where these rights can be expressed, tested, dramatized, played off against each other. Implicit in our basic democratic rights, then, is the right to public space.

Americans are faced with special difficulties in trying to secure this right. Our Republic inherited no splendid monuments and plazas, such as were built by the feudal and absolutist powers that dominated Europe's past. (I will have more to say later about those spaces.) Our built environments have been created almost entirely by private capital for private purposes and profits. Nevertheless, Americans are at least intermittently aware of what they are missing. Again and again, since the earliest days of the Republic, there have been popular demands and mobilizations for public space. Sometimes the people are lucky enough to get Central Parks and Washington Squares. But Americans haven't been so lucky for a long while.

Michael Walzer's distinction between "single-minded" and "open-minded" space is especially fruitful for understanding the politics of public space in the USA. Walzer's "single minded" metaphor can help explain what makes our post–World War Two public spaces so sterile and empty, why they have been gold mines for owners and developers but ghost towns for the public. And his "open-minded" metaphor can help us imagine what kind of spaces we really need, so that we can fight for them effectively in the generation to come.

If I have an argument with Walzer, it is that he has not adequately thought through the consequences of his own values. Specifically, his vision of open-minded space isn't open enough. I want to open it up some more, to expand our vision of what public space should be. I want to bring in all sorts of people, impulses, ideas, and modes of behavior that Walzer leaves out, to unfold dimensions of openness that he doesn't seem to see. My critique of Walzer and my own vision of open space will emerge in two parts: first, openness to modern individualism; second, openness to the urban poor. I will be promoting an ideal of open space that Montesquieu was the first to identify, and to celebrate, on the streets of Paris after the death of Louis XIV; an environment where

> Dissimulation, that art so practiced and so necessary among us, is unknown . . . Everything is said, everything is seen, everything can be heard. The heart shows itself as openly as the face.[1]

---

1 "A Persian on the Streets of Paris," in Montesquieu's *Persian Letters*, Cologne: Pierre Marteau, 1721.

A PLACE IN THE SUN: MODERN INDIVIDUALISM

There is a distinctive strain in Walzer's argument that seems to grow out of a paradoxical but persistent tradition in modern thought. This tradition professes an Olympian disdain for modern life as a whole and dreams nostalgically of a golden age of Greek or Roman antiquity. When the nostalgia takes a political form, it often focuses on idealized, magnificent public spaces where ancient men are said to have lived on a lofty plane of civic virtue. (This tradition doesn't say much about where, or how, ancient women lived.) Moderns, by contrast, are seen as petty souls mired hopelessly in trivial pursuits.

When Walzer works in this tradition, his argument shifts from an indictment of capitalism for depriving the people of public space, and turns into an indictment of people for not wanting public space or caring about it. Thus, he says, modern men and women have been deformed by "the triumph of liberal individualism—which is not merely a creed but a state of mind, a . . . characterological formation." People with this character can imagine and pursue happiness only in narrowly private forms. They seek material comfort, intimacy, love, "personal and mutual exploration."

Walzer seems to write off all these needs as exclusive private affairs. He sees his contemporaries as having fallen from the heights of "older republicanism," which left us a noble heritage of "monuments and fellow-citizens." The men of those monumental times could be at home in public space because they were supposedly free from the press of personal needs that obsess us. They understood that public life "requires impersonality and role playing; civility, not sincerity; reticence and wit, not confession." But we moderns are unable to leave our selves behind, and so public space is no place for us.

Walzer's tone is uncertain and possibly ironic here. He may not believe all this. But there are plenty of people who do believe it. The pity is that their nostalgic vision of the past blinds them to the life that is unfolding abundantly in public spaces all around them right now. If they could only learn to look, they would see private and public life coming together and interfusing in fascinating and creative new ways.

To show briefly what I have in mind, I want to describe a song and an accompanying video that appeared and became a surprise hit in the winter of 1983–84. It is called "Girls Just Want to Have Fun," featuring the previously unknown Cyndi Lauper, singing her own version of the song:

> Some boys take a beautiful girl
> and hide her away from the rest of the world.
> I want to be the one to walk in the sun.
> And girls just want to have fun. Yes, girls just want to have fun.[2]

Lauper is a singer and comedian in the mold of Fanny Brice: a flamboyant "personality" whose extravagant mannerisms often disguise the range and expressiveness of her voice; a brilliant clown who has the dramatic power to suggest underlying depth and sadness without breaking the rhythm of the clowning. "Girls Just Want to Have Fun" is remarkable for the power with which it incarnates a collective dream of what life in public space might be.

This song begins as a story set in a distinctive social space. It is a space that is central in twentieth-century popular culture, but (apart from the music of Bruce Springsteen) almost wholly absent from the popular culture of the 1980s: the tenement flat of the urban ethnic working class. In this space, shot in close-up to emphasize its claustral density and suffocating warmth, Lauper appears as a working girl in conflict with her family, fighting to break out of her parents' stifling embrace and simultaneously out of the lower class she and they are in: "Oh, mommy dear, we're not the fortunate ones, / but girls, they want to have fun." She does this by talking on the phone (her parents vainly try to stop this), and by assembling a racially and ethnically integrated group of girls, who proceed to go dancing and singing through the streets of downtown Brooklyn.

---

2   "Girls Just Want to Have Fun," music and lyrics by Robert Hazard; copyright 1979 by Heroic Music. Lyrics revised here by Cyndi Lauper.

As we follow the song and dance, we discover the distinctively public character of the fun that is at issue here. It springs from banter, flirtation, dress, theatrical display, extravagant gestures, stunning moves that are made to be seen. The heroine and her friends are not only starring in their own show, but—for a little while, at least—become their own *auteurs*. But it is only in public that such a show can go on. The protagonists must interact with strangers; some will rise to play along with them, or opposite them, while others crystallize into their audience. They must learn to depend on these reactions to give their actions a shared meaning, to incorporate them into public time.

As the girls dance through Brooklyn's streets, they find themselves suddenly thrust into a gauntlet of construction workers. This is probably one of the primal scenes that the girls' parents feared. But to our surprise and delight, the workers only smile genially and, even more surprising, some of them actually throw down their tools and join the dance. The parade descends into the underground, then emerges from the IRT in the neighborhood of Wall Street. Here they attract fellow travelers of a higher class, both aged stuffed shirts and yuppies. It appears that *everybody* can be accepted by this group and integrated into its dance. And now the video, which began as kitchen sink naturalism, metamorphoses into magic realism. These girls are not only transforming their lives, but transforming the life of the street itself, using its structural openness to break down barriers of race and class and age and sex, to bring radically different kinds of people together.

At the climax of the story, the heroine returns, along with her newly constituted popular front, to the tenement and the family that tried in vain to fence her in. She brings the street into the house, the public realm into her private space. Her parents find it horrifying, yet alluring: They are tempted to join their child, go public, and change their own drab lives.

Popular culture is worth paying attention to because of its power to dramatize collective dreams. The dream that gets acted out in "Girls Just Want to Have Fun" is a dream of bringing together our private and public lives, of uniting the rights of man and the rights of a citizen. By fulfilling the first commandment of liberal individualism—Express Yourself, Have Fun—we can create a beloved community, a community so radiant that even our parents will want to join. Karl Marx would have recognized this utopian vision: He placed it at the visionary climax of the *Communist Manifesto,* a society in which "the free development of each will be the condition for the free development of all."[3]

Let me try to approach this point from another direction. I have recently come back from Spain, where I spent several lovely afternoons in one of the world's most magnificent public spaces, Madrid's Plaza Mayor. This enormous late-Renaissance square can easily hold a couple of hundred thousand people, yet it feels comfortably contained. It is surrounded on all four sides by colonnaded arcades, and the arcades hold multitudes of shops; above the arcades a towered megastructure extends all the way around, containing a large assortment of municipal and national government offices. The visitor today sees the Plaza Mayor as a marvelously rich human mix, full of government workers, petitioners, buyers and sellers of everything legal and illegal, religious pilgrims, foreign tourists, street musicians, political agitators, performing artists, and ordinary people of Madrid seizing time out to see and be seen in the sun. It is impossible for an American not to be smitten with envy here. This plaza looks and feels like the Platonic idea of all that an open-minded public space should be. Why can't we have spaces like this at home?

The Plaza Mayor *is* all that it appears to be. But it is also a lot more. In its splendid openness, it has become something radically different from what it was meant to be. This square, built between 1590 and 1619, was designed as an arena for public spectacles that would dramatize the power and glory of an inquisitorial church

---

3   Marx would also have admired Lauper's sense of social reality. Her rendition of the Declaration of Rights at the song's end is prefaced (and modified) by a repeated refrain: "When the working, when the working, when the working day is done." Conscious of her class, she knows that the golden coach will turn into a subway train at dawn and that, whatever magic happens on the street at night, she will have to go back to work in the morning. Still, even during the working day–perhaps especially then–she is determined to dream.

and an absolutist state. The plaza's visual focus was a grand balcony from which the king and queen, along with the princes of the church, could look down. What this place was made for, above all, was the *auto-da-fé*, a ceremony for torturing and killing people, and terrorizing the populace, with all the splendor that the Spanish baroque imagination could mobilize.

One special feature of these *autos* sheds some light on our theme of private faces in public places. Among the hundreds of victims condemned in the Plaza Mayor from the early seventeenth through the middle eighteenth centuries, the most prominent and notorious seem to have been Marranos: descendants of Spanish and Portuguese Jews who had been forcibly converted after 1492 and who professed orthodox Catholic beliefs but secretly kept up fragments of Jewish law and lore, worship, and community. For more than two centuries, the Spanish church and state worked together obsessively to detect and destroy them.

Autos-da-fé were meant to show how effective the Inquisition could be in tearing these peoples' masks away, stripping them naked, exposing their most secret selves, so as to annihilate private and public selves together. The Marranos who were present at those ceremonies (to stay away would have been to court instant suspicion) were forced to witness people being publicly destroyed for being what they privately knew themselves to be. In this climate of terror, reticence and insincerity had to be absolute, role-playing a desperate imperative. Even one slip, a slight trace of one's face beneath the facade, could mean a horrible death.

This grisly scenario may be a useful antidote to the nostalgia that often overcomes Americans in the great spaces of the Old World. It can remind us that public space has a dark and checkered past. These dreadful memories should help us to see how the most expansive public space can contract into a dungeon cell and the most vibrant public life into a trial by ordeal, where people are not free to show themselves as they are. We should be able to see, too, how the liberal individualism that Walzer condemns is essential to the open-minded public space he loves. It is only when people are enjoying the rights of man that they are free to walk in the sun.

The people of Madrid are walking freely in the plaza's sun today. The breakthrough into the sunlight wasn't so long ago. Millions of Spaniards were forced to live like Marranos for forty years, all through the Franco regime. It was only at the very end of the regime that the city's planners were allowed to ban vehicles from the Plaza Mayor and let people take over. After eight years of liberal democracy, the plaza today is full of people who would have been arrested yesterday: women in T-shirts and miniskirts, children climbing all over the equestrian statue of Philip II, adolescents playing cassettes and dancing to rock and roll, young couples (including some homosexual couples) necking torridly, graffitists writing irreverent proclamations on arcade walls, agitators handing leaflets out (NO CHURCH NO STATE NO TRIBUNAL NO MISSILES NO THANKS), and God only knows how many more. Some of the people here are consciously engaging in politics (there was a huge anti-Reagan demonstration here in May, in honor of our president's state visit); others are just out to have fun. The people of Madrid love the Plaza Mayor today because it is a place were they can comfortably do both, and where both can blend and intertwine. They know that, in the realm of public space, the personal is political. The grand balcony is still there; but in a democratic Spain its meaning is purely ornamental. The people no longer focus vertically, on rulers above them, but horizontally, on each other. If they look up today, it is only to enjoy the sun.

A WALK ON THE WILD SIDE: THE URBAN POOR

The most crucial form of openness we will need, if we really mean to have open-minded public space, is openness to the urban underclass. This class of people is as old as urban life itself and a recurrent heartache to people who care about cities. Cities and metropolitan areas have frequently acted as magnets for many people whom they couldn't—or in any case didn't—assimilate. The people left out become residents of shantytowns, squatters in abandoned buildings, sleepers in the subways or the streets, dealers in illegal and dangerous commodities, victims and perpetrators of violence, potential recruits for mobs, cults, the underworld and, since the Age of Revolution, for radical movements of Left and Right. Many of them are immigrants and refugees, but others are long-time residents displaced by the city's changes. Anyone who wants to claim a share of public space in a modern city is forced to share it with some of the people of the underclass, and so to think about where he stands in relation to them.

The range of possible responses to this situation was delineated brilliantly a century ago by Baudelaire in a prose poem he wrote in the 1860s, "The Eyes of the Poor." The poem tells the story of a loving couple who are spreading their love along a newly completed Parisian boulevard and who come to rest in a glittering new outdoor cafe. Actually, the boulevard is not quite finished: there is still a pile of rubble on the street. Suddenly a family in rags steps out from behind the rubble, and walks directly up to the lovers. (Baudelaire's audience knew that the rubble in the picture was probably all that was left of the family's neighborhood, one of the dozens of ancient, impoverished neighborhoods that Baron Haussmann's gigantic urban renewal projects destroyed.) As the poet presents these people, they are not asking for anything: They are just looking around, enjoying the bright lights. But the lovers are embarrassed by the immense social gulf between them and these ragged people who, thanks to the boulevard, are physically close enough to touch. "I felt a little ashamed of our glasses and decanters," the narrator says, "too big for our thirst." Baudelaire's middle-class protagonists have got to respond, not merely to the ragged people in their midst, but also to what these people make them feel about themselves.

Baudelaire's narrator responds in a way that will come to typify the urban Left: He looks into their eyes, tries to express sympathy and empathy, conceives of them and himself as united in a human "family of eyes." His girlfriend responds in a radically different way that can be said to typify the urban Right: "These people are unbearable with their big saucer eyes. Can't you call the *maître* to send them away?"

More than a century after Baudelaire's death, urban Americans are still living inside the parameters of his poem. We are faced with a very large underclass, and the people in this class don't want to go away; they, too, want a place in the bright light. And their presence in public space forces us to think not only about their place but also about our own.

Walzer believes (as I do) that fear of the underclass is one of the main forces that has led America's urban middle class to flee the open-minded cities they have made, and to settle into (and settle for) a single-minded suburban environment that is less risky but a lot less alive. He also believes that many people who grew up in that closed world have grown sick of it and are now "ready for the pleasures and willing to pay the costs of urbanity."

I hope he is right. But once again he undermines his long-range aims by getting entangled in the very middle-class anxieties and self-deceptions that he is trying to overcome. Thus he proclaims a dualism of successful versus unsuccessful streets. "A successful street," he said, "is self-policing." Policing is meant to fend off all the elements of "an unsuccessful street," which "by contrast always seems inadequately policed, dangerous, a place to avoid." What are these bad elements? Walzer casts his net very wide, and comes up with "social, sexual, and political deviance: derelicts, criminals, political and religious sectarians, adolescent gangs." Rather than subject themselves to close encounters with these kinds, "ordinary men and women flee as soon as they can into private and controlled worlds."

Now, as an account of the way many people feel, this is undoubtedly accurate. The modern world is full of people who are terrified of other people, socially, sexually, or politically different from themselves. But Walzer seems to take their terrors at face value, to understand them as plain facts, or alternately as eternal laws of social physics, rather than as the historically relative and socially conditioned ideologies that they are.

Thus, when we encounter categories like success/failure or normal/deviant, we need to ask: By what criteria? By whose criteria? For what purposes? In whose interests? When we hear about successful public spaces, we should ask: Successful for what? Who benefits from a police definition of success, that is, success as absence of trouble? (By this definition, most of the great public spaces in history—Greek agoras, Italian piazzas, Parisian boulevards—would rate as failures, because all were turbulent places, and needed large police forces to keep the seething forces from exploding. On the other hand, some of the world's most sterile shopping malls would rate as shining successes.) Walzer himself explains who benefits from this: the upscale merchants and real estate promoters who want public space to be nothing but an unending golden shower of big spenders. But these people and their interests are, as Walzer shows, the greatest menace to free public space today; optimal success for them would mean total destruction of public life for all of us. When Walzer accepts their image of successful space, he loses hold on his own critical perspective and his deepest beliefs.

Walzer gets caught up in his enemies' values once more when he adopts the dualism of "ordinary men and women" versus "deviants." Why should he accept an ideology that stigmatizes difference as "deviance" and that considers it normal to flee from anybody different from ourselves? After all, any idea of normality is a *norm* and as such necessitates a choice of values. Why doesn't Walzer insist on standards of success and normality that square with his own values? Then he could see that the real failures in public space are not the streets full of social, sexual, and political deviants but rather the streets with no deviants at all. And he could fight for a truly open-minded idea of normality: the capacity to interact with people radically different from ourselves, to learn from them, to assimilate what they have to give, maybe even to change our lives, to grow, without ceasing to be our selves.

Walzer concedes grudgingly that his various "deviant" groups "belong, no doubt, to the urban mix." But he warns that they had better not get "too prominent within it." In other words, the people of the underclass (along with all the other deviants) can be tolerated, so long as they keep their place on the outer fringes of public space. I would argue, on the contrary, that there isn't much point in having public space, unless these problematical people are free to come to the very center of the scene. The reason for this is not that they are so lovely to look at (though some of them are, just like some of us). The reason is that they are *there*, part of the same city and the same society as ourselves, linked with us in a thousand ways that would take a lifetime to fully understand. The glory of modern public space is that it can pull together all the different sorts of people who are there. It can both compel and empower all these people to *see* each other, not through a glass darkly but face to face.

One reason I get so persistent about the urban underclass is that I have spent the last fifteen years working with students who come from that class, who have grown up looking at the life of the city through the eyes of the poor. On lucky days they were allowed to look, so long as they didn't try to touch. On unlucky days—and any young black or Latin person, along with most poor whites, will have experienced plenty of these—they encountered middle-class or upper-class people who perceived them as assailants, saw their eyes as drawn weapons and, like the woman in Baudelaire's poem, called guards to get rid of them fast. What they have had to face, in Northern cities' public space, has been not so much overt racism—though, God knows, they have felt plenty of it—as a free-floating hysterical fear. They have found themselves in the bizarre position of having to convince a multitude of strangers that they have no criminal designs on them. If they fail in this attempt—especially in encounters with police (often off-duty or in plainclothes) or, recently, with such free-lance vigilantes as Bernhard Goetz—they may well get killed.

Most of the young people I know have developed a repertory of dress and body language that manages to convince their social superiors of their innocence, and so enables them to move through the city in relative safety. On the other hand, it's hard to see how they can possibly—to return to one of Walzer's central ideas—be *urbane* in our urban space, if they are perpetually on trial in it.[4]

---

4 Sometimes the trial, judgment, sentence, and execution are all over before the defendant even knows what hit him. In September 1983, Michael Stewart, a young black man, was arrested for peaceably writing graffiti in the Union Square subway station. A few minutes later, a whole crowd of white policemen beat, stomped, and strangled him into a coma, then delivered him to Bellevue to die. (In November 1985 an all-white jury found six of those policemen innocent on all counts.)

Their lot is depressingly similar to that of the Marranos in the Plaza Mayor three hundred years ago: Now, as then, only eternal vigilance can keep the subject alive, and any slip at any moment might be his last; even in the middle of the most spacious square, he is up against the wall.

A more contemporary kindred spirit would be Ralph Ellison's *Invisible Man*. It would be no surprise if many of these young people should come to feel, like Ellison's hero, that it would make more sense to stay indoors or in a hole underground.

I hope they don't stay away. If they do, it will diminish not only their lives—which already are constricted enough—but our own. In fact, poor people have taught us so much of what we know about being fully alive in public: about how to move rhythmically and melodically down a street; about how to use color and ornamentation to say new things about our selves, and to make new connections with the world; about how to bring out the rhetorical and theatrical powers of the English language in our everyday talk.

Middle-class people often have no idea how much they have learned from underclasses, because they have picked it up second or third hand. But our serious musicians and composers, our dancers and choreographers, our designers and painters and poets can tell us, if we ask, how much inspiration they have drawn from our underclasses' overflowing life. And they have come into contact with this life, for the most part, not by making expeditions into dark ghettos (though a few adventurous spirits have done this), but simply by paying attention to the rich sounds and rhythms and images and gestures that poor men and women and boys and girls pour out on the sidewalks and in the subways of New York, and in all the rest of urban America's shared and integrated public space.

Our underclasses are mostly black and Latin today, and the rappers, graffitists, break dancers, B-boys, et al., who have done so much to animate contemporary culture, are drawn mainly from black and Latin youth. But imaginative middle-class WASPs at the turn of the century—like William Dean Howells, Hutchins Hapgood, Jane Addams—could learn similar lessons from Irish,

Italians, Slavs, and Jews. All those under-classed people, crammed together in tenements, exploited at work, oppressed in all social relationships, still overflowed with life in their teeming and violent streets, because the public space of the streets was the only place where they could come to life at all. Out in the streets, they could walk in the sun—even in streets where the sun didn't shine. One thing that has made American culture so creative in the twentieth century is that it has had the capacity to nourish itself on the life and energy that our underclasses have had to give. It would be an ominous sign for our future if we were to lose that capacity now.

THE NARROW OPEN SPACES

Late in the 1960s, a number of promoters and developers, the Rouse Corporation most prominent among them, recognized that the overwhelming suburbanization of American society was bound to generate a powerful undertow of mass nostalgia for city life. They understood that this emotion could be spectacularly profitable. The fruits of their insight have been a whole new generation of public spaces, lavishly funded (through various complex public-private mixes) and often beautifully designed, throughout America's cities. Houston's Galleria, San Francisco's Ghiradelli Square, Boston's Quincy Market, New York's South Street Seaport are only a few, and more are emerging all the time. (There have been similar movements in Europe, most strikingly in London's recycled Covent Garden.) These developments have preserved parts of our nineteenth-century cities that would otherwise surely have been destroyed, and they have interwoven modern with traditional architecture in ingenious and occasionally inspired ways. They have come to constitute the reigning model for the public spaces of the future.

Americans who care about city life should be grateful for these spaces, especially since they supplanted a model of urban development that had no appreciation of public space at all. But it is hard to spend any length of time in them without feeling that something is missing. In fact, this something is the underclass, along with all our other "social, sexual, and political deviants." The human mix in these spaces is overwhelmingly white, affluent, and clean-cut. It isn't just that hardly anybody black, Latin, or poor is here; there isn't even anybody scruffy or ragged-looking around.

These plazas are a lot less racially and socially integrated than the busy streets around them. Although their designs are meant to suggest microcosms of the cities they are part of, they are really urban-theme parks, Disney Worlds-by-the-sea; except for the skyscrapers that form their backdrop, they could almost be in the middle of the Everglades. There isn't much menace in the air, but neither is there much flash or flair; not much to embarrass people or make them want to run, but even less to hold their attention and make them think. These plazas are too diverse to be single-minded, yet far too shallow to open up the depths in anybody's mind. It would be too strong an accusation, too suggestive of conscious intent, to call them closed-minded. Maybe the word should be *absent-minded,* in memory of all that is out of sight and out of mind.

There are many ironies in this situation. The heyday of public space in recent American history was the 1960s. All over the country, in those years, streets came to life. And not just streets, but public spaces of every kind—squares, parks, malls, terminals, even highways—all filled up with people who were gathering, agitating, arguing, proclaiming, marching, stopping traffic, dancing, singing, waving flags, taking off their clothes or putting on strange new clothes, expressing themselves and making reasonable and outrageous demands on everyone else in flamboyantly theatrical but intensely serious ways; sometimes even burning things down, or getting themselves killed. Our streets were never so vibrant, so colorful, so sexy—but at the same time, and for some of the same reasons, they were never so violent or scary. By and by, more and more people began to fall prey to the pressures, including many people who had worked for years to lift those pressures. And our years of urban self-assertion and rebellion were followed by an era of wholesale de-urbanization, demographic flight beyond the suburbs to remote rural areas (which of course became suburbs overnight), and great cities on the ropes.

The masses of people who moved far away from their cities may well have found the comfort and security they sought. But many of them seem to have felt a sense of emptiness amid the flowers and the freeways, and yearned for a world they had lost. These urban refugees and their children have been among the main markets courted by the entrepreneurs of the new public space. But although many of these new spaces are pretty places, suburbanites who come in search of something missing in their lives won't find it here. This is because what they really miss is not urban forms in themselves, noble as many of these forms are, but rather a thickness and intensity of human feelings, a clash and interfusion of needs and desires and ideas. For it is this clashing and fusing of human energies—as Baudelaire said it, "their luminous explosion in space"—that fills a city's forms with life.

GROWING UP IN PUBLIC

Let me now pull together many of the strands of this argument by sketching briefly what my own vision of an open-minded space would be. It would be open, above all, to encounters between people of different classes, races, ages, religions, ideologies, cultures, and stances toward life. It would be planned to attract all these different populations, to enable them to look each other in the face, to listen, maybe to talk. It would have to be exciting enough and accessible enough (by both mass transit and car) to attract them all, spacious enough to contain them all (so they wouldn't be forced to fight each other for breathing space), with plenty of exit routes (in case encounters get too strained), and adequate police (in case there's trouble) kept well in the background (so they don't themselves become a source of trouble).

One way to develop this kind of mix will be through shopping facilities: for instance, getting another Alexander's and a Bloomingdale's to locate next door to each other. In order to maintain the mix, it will be essential to have some form of commercial rent control. Otherwise our space will be destroyed by its very success: Its attractiveness will drive rents up beyond the means of all but the classiest and most exclusive stores, and gentrification will transform a resource for the public into a reservation for the rich, as has happened in London and Paris, and is happening now in New York.

Our open-minded space must be especially open to politics. We will want to design spaces within the larger space for unlimited speech-making and assembling. (New York's Union Square used to have this sort of subspace.) But we will want our public space to be sufficiently differentiated that people who don't want to listen or join in will also have places to go. We will try to design acoustic enclaves, such as already exist in some places (for instance, Washington Square Park), which enable many kinds of discourse—speech, music, song—to go on simultaneously, without drowning each other out.

No doubt there would be all sorts of dissonance and conflict and trouble in this space, but that would be exactly what we'd be after. In a genuinely open space, all of a city's loose ends can hang out, all of a society's inner contradictions can express and unfold themselves. Just as, within the protected space of a psychoanalytic session, an individual can open himself to everything he has repressed—so, maybe, in a protective enclave of public space a whole society might begin to confront its collective repressions to call up the specters that haunt it and look them in the face.

I worry as I write this. Is this the way to sell public space to tired businessmen and harried civil servants? My estimate of "the costs of urbanity" seems to be running a lot higher than Walzer's; some of the people out there will surely conclude that the expense of spirit is too much, say thanks but no thanks, and stay home with their VCRs. Others will note darkly the echoes of the 1960s in my thinking, and argue that they have already gone through the '60s, and once was enough. I agree: I loved the '60s, but by the parade's end it was enough for me. I doubt that anybody could sustain the decade's implosive and explosive pressures—its insatiable demands for self-scrutiny and, simultaneously, for self-transformation, individual and collective, personal and political—for more than a little while. On the other hand, when an individual or a society totally represses its '60s, as Reagan's America has managed to a remarkable extent, it becomes not just politically torpid but spiritually dead. Open-minded public space can be a place where we can remember and recreate the storms and dreams of the '60s, and so bring ourselves a nourishment that, at all times, but especially now, we badly need.

I want to end this essay with Franz Kafka's help. All along, I know, I have been trying to convince people to seek out suffering, conflict, trouble. Some readers will probably find this perverse and wonder why they should bring more trouble on themselves. Kafka can suggest a reason why: "You can hold back from the suffering of this world," he writes, "you have free permission to do so, and it is in accord with your nature, but perhaps this very holding back is the one suffering you could have avoided." Open public space is a place where people can actively engage the suffering of this world together and, as they do it, transform themselves into a public.

This essay first appeared in Dissent, *Fall 1986.*

Buildings Are Judgment, or
"What Man Can Build"

The current fiction is that any overnight ersatz bagel and lox boardwalk merchant, any down to earth commentator or barfly, any busy housewife who gets her expertise from newspapers, TV, radio and telephone, is ipso facto endowed to plan in detail a huge metropolitan complex good for a century. In the absence of prompt decisions by experts, no work, no payrolls, no arts, no parks, no nothing will move.

Robert Moses, replying to Robert Caro, *The Power Broker*

I've had to save you. You are interrupting my plans now . . . Never mind. I'll carry out my ideas yet—I will return. I'll show you what can be done. You with your little peddling notions— you are interfering with me. I will return. I . . .

Mr. Kurtz, in Joseph Conrad, *Heart of Darkness*

What sphinx of cement and aluminum bashed open their skulls
and ate up their
brains and imagination?
Moloch, whose buildings are judgment!

Allen Ginsberg, "Howl"

The political and cultural storms of the sixties enabled Americans to expand their minds in a great many marvelous ways. In some ways, though, our collective consciousness seems to have contracted and shrunk. For instance, it seems virtually impossible for Americans today to feel or even imagine the joy of building, the adventure and romance and heroism of construction. The very phrases sound bizarre; you probably wonder what's the joke. Think of your gut response when you encounter something being built—a building, a road, a bridge or tunnel, a pylon or pipeline, a television tower, anything—your first impulse will almost certainly be to shrink back in fear and loathing. This impulse cuts across class, ethnic, generational, and ideological lines: Try it on your friends, your enemies, your parents, yourself; you can even try it on workers who depend on building for their bread and butter. It's true, but not really relevant, that most of what's going up today is both shoddy and brutal: Our recoil is too fast and too visceral to make discriminations; even on the rare occasions that something beautiful gets built, we cannot seem to see. We tend to think that everything around us must have been indescribably lovelier "before"—before it got "developed." We idealize the past of our whole environment, the way Scott Fitzgerald idealized his primeval Long Island—"a fresh, green breast of the new world"— paradise, till Man came and ravaged and ruined it with his parking lots.

Our contempt for construction is so immediate and instinctive today that we hardly even notice it. In fact, however, it is relatively new; at least it is new as a cultural consensus, radically different from the consensus of a generation ago. Of course, it may not last, or it may turn out to be only an undertow rather than an overthrow. Still, we need to understand where it came from, how it happened, what it means. How have we come to condemn the process and products of construction as emblems of everything we find most destructive: massive ugliness, sordid venality, outrageous windfalls of wealth, endless storms of dirt and noise, big plans laying waste little people's lives, organized viciousness without redeeming social value? How have millions of people who have never heard of Allen Ginsberg come to share his vehement judgment against the spirit "whose buildings are judgment"?

When I read Ginsberg's *Howl* at the end of the fifties, his anguished vision of "Moloch, who entered my soul early" struck close to home. When Ginsberg asked who was the "sphinx of cement and aluminum," the demon that devoured as it built, I felt

at once that, even if the poet didn't know it, Robert Moses was his
man. For Robert Moses and his public works had a very personal
resonance for me. He had come into my life just after my bar
mitzvah, and helped bring my childhood to an end, when he
rammed a highway through the heart of my neighborhood in the
heart of the Bronx. When we had first heard about the Cross-
Bronx Expressway, early in the fifties, nobody believed it, it
seemed absurd, unreal. In the first place, hardly anyone I knew
had a car: The neighborhood itself, and the subways leading
downtown, defined the flow of our lives; the very idea of an
expressway seemed to belong to some other world. Besides, even
if the government needed a road, they surely couldn't mean what
the announcements seemed to say: that the road would be blasted
directly through us—and, in fact, through a dozen solid and
settled neighborhoods very like ours; that more than 60,000
people, working and lower-middle class, mostly Jews, but with
many Irish, Italians, and blacks thrown in, would be thrown out of
their homes. It couldn't happen here, we thought: after all, this
was *our* government, America, not Russia, right?

The Bronx of those days still basked in the afterglow of the
New Deal: If we were really in trouble, we were sure our pantheon
of liberal saints and heroes—Eleanor Roosevelt, Adlai Stevenson,
Senator Lehman, Governor Harriman, our young reformist
Mayor Wagner—would come through and take care of us in the
end. And yet, before we knew it, trucks and cranes and immense
machines were there, on top of us, and people were getting notice
that they had better clear out fast, or else; they looked numbly at
the wreckers, at the disappearing streets, at each other, and they
went. Moses was coming through, and no political or spiritual
power could protect the Bronx from him. For seven years, the
center of the Bronx was pounded and blasted and smashed. When
the dust of construction finally settled, and the exhaust fumes
began to rise, our neighborhood was depopulated, economically
depleted, emotionally shattered—as bad as the physical damage
had been, the inner wounds were worse—and ripe for all the
dreaded spirals of urban blight. Thus Moses gave me, and thousands of other New Yorkers, a crash course in the dynamics of

power: what got built, and how, and for whose benefit, and what happened to the people who happened to be in the way. Moses was in the fullness of his power in those days.

Everywhere you looked, he was building something: A dozen expressways all over the state, slashed through the heart of the city and the country, leveling both; high-rise housing for literally hundreds of thousands of people, austerity barracks for the poor, opulent whited sepulchers for the richest of the rich; dozens of schools; a convention hall that loomed over Central Park; the biggest cultural center in the world at Lincoln Square; a new World's Fair rising on the ruins of the old; Shea Stadium; at the mouth of New York Harbor, the city's gateway, the world's largest suspension bridge; far upstate, along the Canadian border, reaching a climax at Niagara Falls, the world's greatest complex of dams and power plants. And all these projects were little more than beginnings for Moses, foundations on which to build more.

BIGGER THAN LIFE

What kind of man was this Moses? What made him tick? Where were the springs of his colossal energy and audacity, his monstrous pride and arrogance, his insatiable will to build up and tear down? I found myself obsessed with the man and his works. As I grew up and got a liberal education, my head filled up with a gallery of titanic builders and destroyers from literature and myth and history, in whose company Moses might belong; Gilgamesh; Ozymandias; Louis XIV, creator of Versailles; Pushkin's Bronze Horseman, the enormous statue of Peter the Great that loomed over the Imperial Capital he had built, and that, generations after his death, menaced Petersburg's citizens and drove them mad; Ibsen's Master Builder; Baron Haussmann, who razed so much of medieval—and revolutionary—Paris and created the boulevards and vistas of our romantic dreams; Bugsy Siegel, master builder of the underworld, who created Las Vegas and was killed for it; "Kingfish" Huey Long; Mr. Kurtz; Citizen Kane. It was a strange but genuine Great Tradition. The paradigm that struck me most forcefully was Goethe's *Faust*, that bible of the German bourgeoisie from which Moses sprang. Goethe's Faust is an intellectual who sells his soul to the devil in exchange for superhuman powers, but who feels fulfilled only when he gains the power to build—to irrigate and develop an arid and barren coast, to make the wasteland bloom and open it to human life—and to murderously do away with the people in his way. It was hard to think about Robert Moses without mythicizing him: Like the immense hulks he built, he looked and felt bigger than life.

Moses himself was always glad to supply the public with archetypes in case our imaginations should run dry. He could come on like a great American gangster, racing around in fleets of black limousines, going out of his way to transgress speed limits, street lights, rules of the road, boasting that "Nothing I have ever done has been tinged with legality." Or he could appear as an unreconstructed Soviet Commissar, proclaiming to the world that "You can't make an omelet without breaking eggs!"[1] He could even sound like the legendary oriental despots, serene in the totality of their power, free to let their magnificent malignity hang out. Thus, unlike most men of power, who characteristically use language as euphemism and smokescreen, Moses would bluntly say that "when you operate in an overbuilt metropolis, you have to hack your way with a meat ax." You could make no mistakes about that. But Moses could also mobilize self-images that were beneficent and benign. When he planned to turn the city dump in Flushing Meadows into an enormous park, he dressed himself as the prophet Isaiah and asserted Jehovah's mandate to "give unto them beauty for ashes." After his park was underway he would often say that he was the man who had seized Scott Fitzgerald's Valley of Ashes—the ash heaps between Long Island and New York City,

---

1 This motto, which appeared on signs along Moses's Long Island Expressway, and which was meant to explain the detours and troubles caused by the construction of his 1963 World's Fair, obligingly documented the convergence theory that American and Soviet ideologists were trying so hard to bury. The fact that Moses professed a fanatical hatred for communism—he had ruined many opponents with McCarthyite smear campaigns and often threatened, "I'll let the *Daily News* loose on you!"—only made the convergence more ironic.

which became, in *The Great Gatsby*, a brilliant symbol of our civilization's industrial waste and human hell—and transformed it into a symbol of natural beauty and human delight.

Over the years, I came across many New Yorkers who were as haunted by Moses as I was. We would watch his projects being built, trade rumors and references along with fantasies and myths. Where did his vast power come from? How had he begun? What demonic inner forces drove him on? There was one incredible story about what might be the Rosebud of this Citizen Moses. The rumor was that he had never learned to drive—and had taken his revenge by making himself Detroit's man in New York and forcing everyone around him to drive everywhere. (I never believed it but *The Power Broker* discloses that the story was true after all.) What was he going to do next? We wracked our brains to anticipate his next move, before this Great Dirt Mover (as he liked to call himself) literally grabbed the ground out from under our feet. But he kept himself miles and years ahead of us, because we never learned how to "think big." Could people be aroused to fight him? Was there any way he could be stopped? As the fifties ripened slowly into the sixties, we schemed and dreamed.

LOOKING FOR A MYTH

Now, in the stagnant seventies, with the appearance of Robert Caro's remarkable book, *The Power Broker: Robert Moses and the Fall of New York*, this builder of colossal monuments has finally gotten the monument he deserves. *The Power Broker* is, quite simply, the best biography we've had in years: the best, I believe, since Isaac Deutscher completed his life of Trotsky a decade ago. It is the most exciting American book on the city since the works of Paul and Percival Goodman, Lewis Mumford and Jane Jacobs, in the glorious sunrise of the early sixties. Caro has learned a lot from these writers; he uses their varying ideas as the foundation for a brilliant critique. I doubt that any American public figure has ever been exposed to such sustained, relentless, thoroughly devastating scrutiny. Caro piles up all the goods that anyone has ever gotten on Moses, indictments of his own, analyzes and synthesizes the evidence trenchantly, seems to leave nothing out. He dredges all the interlocked secret sources of Moses' power up from their murky depths. He shows us, in concrete and shattering personal detail, the human costs of Moses's greatest works—he has even tracked down some of the refugees from my dear, devastated Bronx, urged these long-scattered and forgotten people to tell their stories, a new dimension of history that will live alongside the highways for a long time to come.[2] He unearths old stories, rumors, and intimations of long-buried sexual, financial, and emotional betrayals. He calls up every ghost, plays back every hushed or shrill voice that might haunt Moses's nights.

Sometimes Caro gets carried away by a righteous rage and loses all sense of perspective and proportion. Does he really think that public works before Moses, or in cities other than Moses's New York, got built without plenty of payoffs to pave their way? Or that those other builders gave a damn for the feelings or lives of the people in the way? And who really cares if Moses used public funds to hold lavish banquets or to subsidize Guy Lombardo? Or who was that lady people saw him with, that winter in Florida? At times Caro sounds as obsessive and insensitive as he accuses Moses of being; and this sort of overkill will probably create a backlash of sympathy for the man in the box. Still, when Caro has put it all together, so much of the larger record is clearly appalling that even Moses's most ardent supporters will recoil. Like every Moses monument, *The Power Broker* is ruthlessly destructive—only this time it is Moses himself who is in the way. The critical insight and power of *this* book post a warning to all our leaders, a sign that those master builders "whose buildings are judgment" must themselves face judgment, probably a lot sooner than they would like to think.

_____

2   It is striking that, in what was probably Moses's cruelest and most humanly destructive project, fellow Jews were his victims. The fact that Caro, also a Jew, is telling the story now, may be a symptom of an important shift in American Jewish self-awareness. Alongside our glowing "only in America" success story, we may be slowly coming to confront a darker story that could be entitled "*even* in America."

But there is a whole other dimension of Caro's book, a dimension that accounts for much of its huge size, but also for much of its originality and dialectical complexity and emotional force. This is a dimension that reaches back into the nineteenth century, into the tradition of Balzac and Dickens and Dreiser and I.J. Singer, the masters of the great epic urban novel. Caro plunges us into the stream of Moses's historical and psychic world, immerses us in its energy and vitality and human promise. In a series of dramatic narratives—marvelous *stories,* of a kind that neither historians nor novelists today seem to want to tell—Caro makes us feel the urgency and enormity of the challenges Moses had to face, engages us in the intense pressures and thrills of his work and achievement. He forces us to recognize reluctantly that this thoroughly dreadful man is one of the authentic heroes of our time. If we take the plunge of empathy, and let ourselves be carried along on the flow of Caro's narrative, we will come to see that Moses is probably one of the greatest heroes of modern construction. We may not want to see such a thing—who needs such heroes? Who needs such complexity? But if we don't grasp his heroism, we won't understand his villainy either. We will take his story for a simple melodrama, when in fact it is a complex American tragedy that embraces not only Moses himself, but our whole society, whose most creative and most destructive impulses he has acted out so well; a tragedy in which we ourselves turn out to be implicated, a lot more deeply than we think.

The old boys (and old girls) of the New Left—the Slightly Used Left is what we should call ourselves today—will probably find it especially hard to make an empathetic leap into the world of heroic construction. Heroic destruction is a lot more up our alley: Our typical heroes are men and women who smash idols of false belief, subvert and explode corrupt institutions, overthrow murderous governments, tear down the great structures of evil in the world. We do not need to be told that, in Bakunin's words, the urge for destruction can be a creative urge—this we know only too well. To imagine that the urge for *construction* can be creative would be far more authentically radical for us—that would really shake our sense of the world to the roots! I will let Marx do a little of the shaking. Here he is, in the first part of the *Communist Manifesto*, enthusiastically praising the bourgeoisie: They have "accomplished wonders far surpassing Egyptian pyramids, Roman aqueducts and Gothic cathedrals." These bourgeoisie, as Marx exposes and explains them, are a brutal and banal ruling class. Nevertheless, he insists, they have "accomplished wonders" in construction. Not only have they built a multitude of beautiful and useful structures in a remarkably short time; what is crucial in the long run is that, by virtue of the brilliance and energy of their building, they have been "*the first to show what man's activity can bring about*" (my italics).

It is ironic that this vision, so dear to Marx, should be a lot closer in spirit to Moses, who claimed to hate everything Marx stood for, than to the New Left, which burnt endless candles at Marx's shrine. But if Karl Marx and Robert Moses can share a vision of life that we reject or ignore, we had better find out fast what we are missing. *The Power Broker* can bring the romance of construction back to life for us and show us how Moses brought that romance to its greatest flowering in American history; at the same time, by following Moses's genius where it led him, Caro can show us how and why the romance died. If we can somehow recover the radiance of this lost love, it may be the beginning of a deeper recovery. It may help us give a new life to our lost sense of larger human possibilities, to our feeling for "what man's activity can bring about." We of the Slightly Used Left know too well that radicalism without this sense of possibility is dried up at the roots and busy dying.

I want now to trace the movements and explore the meanings of Moses's life and work, to draw from this enemy of the people the elements of the master builder, a heroic myth we need so badly to rediscover. I will use Caro's narratives and analyses for my framework. However, where Caro tends to overemphasize Moses's personal biases and idiosyncrasies—this danger is inherent in the whole enterprise of biography and hard for even the best to avoid—I want to emphasize the currents of social and political and cultural change that underlie Moses's career. It was only because Moses knew instinctively and profoundly how to exploit the historical flow that he was able to build and achieve so much: to bring together within himself the most contradictory and explosive forces in American life—all our heroism and all our nihilism—and to express these contradictions and act them out in fifty years of public works.

AN AMERICAN EPIC

Robert Moses's life story is one of the great American epics of success and achievement. At the same time, like few other American success stories, it is a fulfillment of the archetypal intellectual's dream, dreamt for centuries from Plato to Mao, of a synthesis of theory and action, vision and power. Caro shows how hard Moses had to fight, again and again, for every foot of ground; still, when we look at the outlines of his life as a whole, we can see how many roads were cleared for him from the start. Moses was born in 1887, into a wealthy German-Jewish family, at precisely the moment when the upper crust of German-Jewish immigrants were making themselves felt in American life. The first generation of *Our Crowd*—the Warburgs, Guggenheims, Belmonts, Strauses, Gimbels, et al.—had made their mark by amassing immense private fortunes remarkably fast, in the early spring of America's spectacular commercial and industrial growth. The brightest and most imaginative among the second generation, growing up in the mansions of Fifth Avenue or the brownstones off Central Park— Walter Lippmann, Herbert Lehman, A. L. Kroeber, and J. Robert Oppenheimer—aspired not merely to inherit the earth (their share had already been set aside before they were born), but to civilize and humanize the rich, rough country that they had come to call home. This usually went along with ignoring or (like Moses) aggressively denying their Jewishness and striving to pass themselves off as pure Americans or Universal Men. More admirably, it meant dedicating themselves to lives of "public service."

Moses was given the very best education a young aristocrat could get: Ethical Culture, Dwight, Yale, Oxford, Berlin, Columbia, private tutors, the Grand Tour, the Mona Lisa, the Stones of Venice, the Acropolis by moonlight ("All Europe contributed to the making of Mr. Kurtz"). Everywhere he went, people were struck by his brilliance and energy, by the passion and boldness of his will to change the world. Even those who loathed him (and there were always plenty) could see that he was headed for great things. The only question seemed to be what portion of the world he would choose to change.

Moses's first choice was bureaucracy and public administration. Caro resurrects a phase in Moses's life that is generally unknown or forgotten, but important: his career as an administrative reformer. He lost his first battle, a bold plan to recast New York City's 50,000-person work force in the mold of a comprehensive "merit system." (This fierce struggle of almost sixty years ago prefigures our current intense and unresolved conflicts over standards, quotas, expertise, class, and ethnic bias.) Moses was defamed, demoralized, and driven from the city. But his intellectual power and political courage were remembered, and before long he was recruited for bigger things. Al Smith, a Tammany Hall backroom politician whom no one took very seriously, was about to embark on his career as the greatest state governor in American history. A child of the Lower East Side, Smith felt and understood the horrors of the industrial age, and he was determined that the government should do something about them. The federal environment of those pre-New Deal days lurched from gutlessness to overt reaction, so the states were America's only source of hope for social reform. But New York's state government was organized to systematically stifle these hopes. Smith saw that this system had to be changed, and he saw Moses as the man who could show him how.

As the head of Smith's State Reconstruction Commission, Moses confronted a labyrinth of 187 departments with obscure powers, overlapping jurisdictions, conflicting mandates. Policies were made behind closed doors by the upstate farmers and Wall Street bankers and businessmen who controlled (and still control) the legislature in Albany. There wasn't even a state budget, public funds were divided up in private, the government was impenetrable, and there was no way for the people to know where their money was going or what they were paying for. The governor, elected by the people, had no real power to protect or promote the public interest. Progressive laws might occasionally be passed, but the bureaucratic machine inevitably ground them into dead letters. Moses cut through the labyrinth and showed how to consolidate this Kafkaesque structure into a few big agencies whose powers and responsibilities could be clearly defined. The governor's powers were to be substantially enlarged. Most important, he would be given the power to prepare a unified state budget—which meant, in effect, the power to weigh conflicting priorities, define comprehensive public policies, and translate them into action.

Moses's plan can be attacked for making the state executive far too powerful; and it is easy for readers today to sympathize with critics of executive power. Nevertheless, we need to remember— and it is easy for a post-New Deal generation to forget—how many important pieces of social legislation in American history have had to be rammed by a strong executive down corrupt and reactionary legislators' throats. Al Smith used the powers that Moses had helped him obtain to push through a remarkable series of laws, throughout the twenties, that laid down a solid foundation and an agenda for a welfare state: minimum wage and maximum hour laws, standards for industrial safety and working conditions, equal pay for women in education and public employment, vastly enlarged facilities for public health. Moreover, once Smith was able to control the reorganized bureaucracy, he could see to it that his program was not only passed, but actually enforced. FDR, who succeeded Smith as governor of New York, would later extend his structure and his program to the nation as a whole—though the agenda of social legislation that Smith envisioned half a century ago is still far from complete. Caro is skillful in drawing our attention to this achievement and in bringing out some of its ironies. Moses always loathed the sweaty masses and never gave a damn about social welfare, yet the welfare state could never have come into being without the kind of structural reforms he worked out. Here, as throughout his career, he served the people well in spite of himself.

Having helped to lay out the structure of the welfare state, Moses went on to pioneer what would turn out to be one of its crucial functions: the building of public works. In this second phase of his career, he became famous as a creator of parks. The building of urban parks in America, which accelerated with the work of Olmsted in the middle of the nineteenth century, was submerged and lost in the flood tides of swelling population, massive immigration, breakneck urbanization, explosive and violent industrial growth that swept through the country in the generation before the First World War. Moses got interested in parks at a moment when fresh air and open space in the cities were disappearing day by day, just when a whole new multitude of people needed them most.

Early in the twenties, Moses began to explore Long Island. He fell in love with the island, which reached from the heart of New York far out into the Atlantic and contained 300 miles of spectacular shoreline. Scott Fitzgerald, too, had been drawn to Long Island and was working on the novel that would put it on the cultural map as one of the lasting symbols of the American dream. Moses dreamed of a great network of parks all along the shore, to bring the urban masses (at least those with cars) back to that nature from which the industrial city had cut them off. At first, however, Moses's dream seemed more quixotic than any fantasy of Jay Gatsby's, for Long Island had already been discovered a generation before by the richest of the rich. They had bought up all its most beautiful land and built themselves manor houses, country clubs, game preserves, palaces that made the Gatsby mansion look small. Where the millionaires had stayed away, land and water were held by isolated and fiercely isolationist villages, full of fear and hatred for the "foreigners" of the city. The villagers joined the Klan in force, burned crosses in the hills, swore to stop at nothing to keep their region pure. The picture looked bleak, the city masses seemed to be decisively fenced out. But Moses prowled up and down and around the island, by car, in boats, on foot, in search of an opening.

Some of his first openings came in surprising ways. He would cut his way through a thicket, climb an ancient stonewall, and suddenly find himself on the shore of a radiant lake, with virgin forest all around him—bought by the City of Brooklyn in the 1850s for a future water supply, but never used and long forgotten. He would be working his way through wild marshes, hidden inlets, and coves, when all at once a magnificent beach would open up before him, a strand of the whitest sand he had ever seen, stretching out unbroken to the horizon—it was not even on the maps, for it literally had not existed when the area had last been explored 20 years before, it had been formed only recently by the lashing of the wind and the sea. Moses did his exploring alone ("as a rule Kurtz wandered alone, far in the depths of the forest"), and sometimes he would be lost or stranded, and search parties would have to go out in the night and bring him back.

As Moses stumbled on that great beach, he thrilled with wild surmise. This strand could be the centerpiece of a whole system of beach and forest parks, linked with New York and with each other by a network of landscaped roads that would themselves be parks, bringing the teeming city and the isolated country together at last—"I thought of it all in a moment," he would recall. He discovered that a great deal of the land he had discovered was in public hands. But plenty of it was not, and it was far too expensive for the state to buy, and in any case the villagers and millionaires would never sell. If ever they decided to sell, it would be to private developers—who were beginning to zero in on Long Island—for suburban subdivisions. This would be especially disastrous, for it would shut the public off from the sound and the sea forever. Moses had his work cut out for him. He would have to wrest the shoreline from the robber barons, private developers, and isolationist towns, in the name of "the people" of New York State. Then he would have to build on a vast and unprecedented scale and at a staggering cost. Finally, he would have to work fast, and in virtual secrecy, because if the state government ever caught on, it would surely stop him before he could start.

But Moses had not spent years in the labyrinth of twentieth century government for nothing. In reorganizing the state bureaucracy he had blasted through walls and turned tortuous trails into straight, clear open roads. But much of what he had learned in the labyrinth he kept to himself, and now he could convert his knowledge into power. Between 1924 and 1929, he engaged in a dazzling array of legal, financial, publicistic, and political manipulations, and at the end of those five years his quixotic dream was a *fait accompli*.

First of all, Moses unearthed a long forgotten, unrepealed clause in an 1884 state conservation act that empowered the state to "appropriate" a piece of land "by simply walking on it and telling the owner he no longer owned it." He assembled crews and equipment secretly, and then when he felt the time was ripe, he sent them out into the field, citations in hand, to start appropriating. While owners rubbed their eyes in aghast amazement, and their lawyers raced frantically to the statute books—yes, that clause was really there—Moses's men went to work. For he had planned every detail in advance so that, even as opposition was organizing, the work would be going on. He understood that once a job was physically done there was no way that it could be legally or politically undone. "Once you sink that first stake," he would tell a generation of planners and builders, "they'll never make you pull it up." Moses developed this *blitzkrieg* tactic in his earliest projects; it would solidify into a systematic strategy that served him well for thirty years. Simultaneously, he learned to systematically underestimate and conceal his costs, revealing what he had spent only when it was necessary to ask for more. This might sound risky, but Moses understood the politics of inertia: Once a project was started, it would have to be finished, regardless of its cost, because to stop it in the middle would be to waste all the money that had been spent and all the work that had been done till then, and no politician would dare do that.

Moses knew, too, how to shift funds and labor power around from one public agency to another, so as to mobilize millions of dollars and thousands of workers that no one had ever given him and no one (except Governor Smith) even knew he had. Finally, he figured out fast how (in Smith's immortal phrase) "to give a bribe and call it a fee": in construction contracts, condemnation proceedings, real estate closings, insurance brokerage fees, inside dope on what land to buy cheap now and sell for a fortune to the state next year. Opposition to his plans would germinate, grow, mobilize, and then suddenly, mysteriously melt away. His work on Long Island gave him a lifelong knack for knowing what offers political men and machines would be unable to refuse.

Moses had never been to law school, but he was a wizard at manipulating the law; similarly, he was no architect or engineer, yet he displayed a talent for design. He assembled some of the best architects and engineers in the country, and drove them harder than anyone had ever driven them, to do work that would be bigger, faster, cheaper, and more beautiful than anything they (or anyone else) had ever done—and they loved him for it and gave him their best. Caro interviewed some of these men forty years later, and they looked back nostalgically on their work with Moses as the high point of their lives. "It was exciting just being around him," one engineer told Caro. "He made you feel you were part of something big . . . It was you fighting for the people against those rich estate owners and reactionary legislators . . . It was almost like a war."

Moses drove his workers as well, made them work through wind and rain, through the night, through snow and ice, living and working on floating barges all winter. But they do not seem to have resented him much, for they knew he drove himself harder than anyone. Unable to leave his job for his family, he brought his family to his job; his wife and daughters integrated themselves into the work, infused it with a sense that they were all one big family working together. Caro creates another great dramatic set-piece here, an unforgettable picture of Moses at his most creative and humanly attractive moment. It takes us back to the last act of Goethe's *Faust*, where, after a lifetime of striving and suffering, the hero feels himself fulfilled at last amidst the turmoil of men and machines building great public works. It was even better than *Faust*, for it included a family warmth and unity that Goethe's solitary hero lacked; a warmth and unity that, according to Caro, the Moses family would rarely, if ever, enjoy again.

Jones Beach, the centerpiece of Moses's plan, and the parkway that led to it, opened in the summer of 1929. "In the history of public works in America," Caro says, "it is probable that never had so much been built so fast." And Moses's early works were at least as striking in quality as in quantity. Visitors were amazed and overwhelmed, and some 325,000 came in the first month, far more than even Moses had dreamt of. The great landscape was a masterpiece, not only of natural beauty, but even more—for so much of it had been swamp and wasteland two years before, or else had not existed at all—of human design. The design was universally praised, not only for a great range of new use values, but for a hundred lovely expressions of fantasy and play. A huge water tower which could have been a gross eyesore was instead, thanks to Moses's sense of cultural history, an elegant variation on the Venice Campanile; it could be seen for miles, and it became an instant symbol of Long Island's new self-awareness and pride. And Moses's imagination worked at least as well in smaller and more personal things, such as the scattering of little rooms with adjustable tables for changing babies' diapers. The design of Jones Beach managed to be at once monumental and yet, as the *Architectural Forum* said, "scaled down to the size of a good time." This beach is still one of America's finest expressions of the romance of public works. Indeed, it helped to create a whole new form of American public space.

Moses's parkways embodied another spectacular new form of public space and expressed a romance all their own. These roads, still among the most beautiful in the world, do not (like California's Coast Highway) cross or adjoin or highlight a beautiful environment: The point about them is that they are *in themselves* a beautiful environment. Even if they adjoined nothing and led nowhere, they still would be, as we said in the sixties, a trip. Thus Moses, who never learned to drive, inspired what has since become one of the basic (and, alas, costly) American experiences: driving as an end in itself. He became a national hero.

THE MASTER BUILDER

Moses opened his career as a master builder just before the Great Crash. As the Depression hit, and cut deeper, and threw millions of people out of work, it became clear to everybody—except for the men in the White House—that the federal government was going to have to act decisively to get the country moving again. When FDR proclaimed the New Deal in 1933, one of its crucial parts was a federal program of public employment and public works on a far more massive scale than America had ever known. For a man who had just demonstrated a genius for public works, it was an ideal moment. Moses expanded the base of his power at once into New York, where he became the city parks commissioner (as well as the state's), and into Washington, where he established close and lasting ties with the energetic and innovative planners of the New Deal bureaucracy.

Moses hired a staff of first-rate planners (mostly from off the unemployment lines), mobilized a labor army—up to 68,000 men, paid with federal money—and went to work on a great crash program that would not only regenerate the city's 1,700 parks (which seem to have been even more rundown then than they are now), but also create a huge network of new ones, and hundreds of playgrounds, and a couple of zoos. Not only did Moses get the job done, but he got it done in less than a year. Caro paints more thrilling Faustian scenes of heroic construction: Central Park turned into a phantasmagoria of floodlights, earthmovers, jackhammers, sandblasters, reverberating all through the night—the work went on twenty-four hours a day, seven days a week, never stopping till the job was done; work crews, given real work to do at last, not only keeping up with the relentless pressures that Moses and his straw bosses imposed, but actually outpacing the bosses, and taking initiative, and coming up with new ideas, and working ahead of plans—so that the engineers were forced constantly to run back to their desks and redesign their plans, to take account of the progress the workers had made on their own. Here we see the romance of construction at its best: a vision that grips the men who actually do the work.[3]

Moses understood instinctively how bureaucrats thought and worked and what they wanted. Now that there was a vast, seemingly inexhaustible supply of federal money available for public works, he was first in line. His projects were always organized and planned down to the last detail, ready to start immediately, needing only money to move: There was nothing for Washington to do, except to sign the check, and it inevitably did. Manipulating men (manpower in the tens of thousands), mandates (city, state, and federal) and money (in the hundreds of millions) like a master magician, Moses repeated the "miracle" of Jones Beach on an ever larger scale. The New Deal gave him the power to build a comprehensive system of great, sweeping highways around the periphery of the city. The heart of this system was the Triborough Project, a network of bridges and approaches and parkways that would link Manhattan, the Bronx, and Westchester with Queens and Long Island, and so bring the city and the country closer than ever. Moses's projects in this period were incredibly expensive, technically brilliant—Caro gives us an unforgettable picture of one bridge being erected overnight in the Bronx, and of people discovering it, to their amazement, the next morning—and beautifully designed to the minutest details.

Through these projects, Moses took a tremendous and teeming city that had developed spontaneously and planlessly from a

---

3   This is the sort of vision that animates the great TVA and FSA documentaries of the thirties and the Soviet "tractor films" of the same era. (It may be most readily available to us through Woody Guthrie's many "dam songs" and celebrations of the man "born with a jackhammer in his hand.") It suggests that thinkers like Carlyle and Durkheim, whom the Left has always disparaged, were right to insist that workers could find meaning and fulfillment even in jobs that were physically grueling and mentally empty—jobs that would be, by many people's standards, utterly "alienated"—if they had a vision of the meaning of the work as a whole, and if they could believe in its real value to the human community. Moses was one of the first to show that it could happen even in America.

multitude of isolated villages and separate and insular neighbor-hoods and dead-end streets—took it all, as Caro says, and "tied that city together." It is one of those weird ironies of history that the "Lordly Hudson" Paul Goodman celebrated in his beautiful poem owed much of its lordliness to Moses, a man who embodied so much of what Goodman fought against all his life. Nevertheless, it was Moses who turned the uptown Hudson riverfront from a wasteland of shacks and garbage dumps into one of the most beau-tiful urban landscapes in the world.[4] You cross the George Washington Bridge, and dip down and around and slide into the gentle curve of the West Side Highway, and the lights and towers of Manhattan flash and glow before you like a vision, rising above the lush greenness of Riverside Park, and even the most embit-tered ex- and anti-New Yorker will be touched; you know you have come home again, and you can thank Robert Moses for that.

Moses was far from a New Dealer, yet most of his most beauti-ful and beloved projects belong to the age of the New Deal. The years from FDR's first inaugural to Pearl Harbor revealed the welfare state at its freshest and most imaginative, acting and build-ing on a colossal scale, yet with remarkable sensitivity to human lives and needs. Moses, despite himself, was caught up in the vision and energy of the New Deal, and it brought out the best in him.

THE DIALECTICS OF DARKNESS

Nevertheless, as Caro documents, Moses's brilliant spirit always had its darker side. At first the darkness was something that only the people who were closest to him could see. Here is the testi-mony of Frances Perkins, America's first Secretary of Labor under FDR, who worked closely with Moses during the Al Smith era and who admired him immensely all her life. She recalls the people's heartfelt love for Moses in the years of his first great

---

4   Younger New Yorkers imagine that the area was all romantic natural loveliness until Moses got there. In fact, as Caro shows, most of the romance of that riverfront was created by Moses himself.

public works. However, she says, "he doesn't love the people" for whom he worked so well:

> It used to shock me because he was doing all these things for the welfare of the people . . . He'd denounce the common people terribly. To him they were lousy, dirty people, throwing bottles all over Jones Beach. 'I'll get them! I'll teach them!' . . . He loves the public, but not as people. The public is just the public. It's a great amorphous mass to him; it needs to be bathed, it needs to be aired, it needs recreation, but not for personal reasons—just to make it a better public.

"I'll get them! I'll teach them!" Moses's expletives echo the great *cri de coeur* of that archetypal hero of modern "public service," Joseph Conrad's Mr. Kurtz. Conrad's narrator reads Kurtz's manifesto for social imperialism, and marvels at the author's intellectual power and visionary gleam, when he finds himself brought up short by a marginal note that Kurtz has scrawled in an unsteady hand at the foot of the last page: "It was very simple, and at the end of that moving appeal to every idealistic sentiment it blazed at you, luminous and terrifying, like a flash of lightning in a serene sky: 'Exterminate all the brutes!'"

Heart of Darkness helps us define the tragic contradiction that runs through the heart of Robert Moses's life and work: the contradiction between his love of "the public" and the hate he felt for actual people. The New Deal gave him immense political and economic power, yet managed to direct some of that power in the service of his—and, for the time being, America's— most radiant and generous impulses. But the spirit of the New Deal did not last long. Within less than a decade it would be eclipsed by the darker visions of the war and the Cold War years. In this new era, the governmental powers that the New Deal had so beneficently enlarged would operate in far more menacing ways. In this era, too, Moses's own inner darkness—"I'll get them! I'll teach them!"—could come to the surface and, thanks to his immense new powers, spread its blight brutally over the surfaces and into the depths of millions of people's lives.

Moses's power to build and destroy not only expanded in quantity, but also took on a radically new quality, when he plugged his activities into a device known as a public authority. This English institution had been grafted onto US public works early in the twentieth century and used in a scattered and fragmentary way in various projects. An authority would float bonds to build a particular project, a bridge or a tunnel or a highway; when its project was completed, it would charge tolls or fees for use, until the bonds were paid off; at that point it was to go out of existence and turn the public work over to the state. It occurred to Moses, however, that there was no reason for an authority to limit itself in time or space; so long as money was coming in, e.g. from tolls on the Triborough Bridge, an authority could exchange its old bonds for new ones, to raise more money, to build more works; so long as the money—all of it tax exempt—kept coming in, the banks that held the bonds would be only too glad to underwrite new ones, and the authority could go on building forever. Moreover, it would no longer be necessary to go to city, state, or federal governments, or to the people, for money to build. In fact, Moses discovered, the various elected governments did not even have the legal right to inspect an authority's books. So long as the tolls kept rolling in, there was nothing and no one that could stand in its way.

What kept the money rolling in, far faster than even Moses dared to hope, was a technological and social change that Moses only partly understood: the automobile was re-creating all America in its image. Moses's first great wave of public works, his beautiful parks and parkways just outside the city, had helped this recreation along: Now that the countryside was perfectly accessible by car, it was ripe for mass suburbanization, a commuter's dream. When Moses built his second wave of public works in the thirties, he expected that the new bridges, tunnels, and parkways would relieve the congestion of traffic on which the city was already beginning to choke. Instead, the new works generated far more traffic—more congestion, pressure, fumes, noise—than ever before. It was at this point, when America's cities needed a new imaginative leap, that Moses's vision began to reveal undertones of a nightmare. If there were more cars on the roads and bridges and in the tunnels, the only solution he could see was to build more of the same; of course, the more arteries he built, the more traffic appeared to fill them; and so the problem spiraled on viciously for another twenty years.

Caro is particularly angry at Moses for this. Perhaps it is unfair to blame him for it all: Until the end of the fifties, there were few (Louis Mumford is a notable exception) grappling with the problem any better than he. Yet Moses and his public authorities had a vested interest in lack of vision. The more they built, the more traffic they generated; the more traffic they could generate, the more money they would have to build.[5] Between the late thirties and the late fifties, Moses created or took over a dozen of these public authorities and consolidated and integrated them into an immensely powerful machine, a machine with endless wheels within wheels, turning its cogs into millionaires, drawing thousands of businessmen and politicians into its widening gyre. As Moses's creative powers sputtered and slowed down, the machine he had created picked up a blind, irresistible momentum of its own.

THE SORCERER'S APPRENTICE

With these changes, Moses came to embody some of the deepest ironies of twentieth-century American life. According to the *Communist Manifesto,* one of the crucial forces that made bourgeois society go, and that generated some of its most brilliant achievements, was its innate drive to "establish connections everywhere." However, few bourgeoisie had the imagination to think of this: The vast majority simply pursued their private profits and went wherever that pursuit might lead them, without worrying about the larger historical meanings of what they did. What made Robert Moses seem so special was the largeness of his visions and ideas, his intellectual and organizational power to grasp the whole:

---

5   It should come as no surprise that Moses fought unrelentingly—and successfully—against the diversion of public money to the alternative vision of mass public transit.

He could seize and direct the hidden historical forces that were shaping and moving the world's most vital bourgeois society; he could help the American city to utilize these explosive forces to put itself together. "It has long been a cherished ambition of mine," he wrote in 1941, "to weave together the loose strands and frayed edges of the New York metropolitan arterial tapestry." But there were wider and deeper connections that not even Moses could see. Marx had compared the bourgeoisie to "a sorcerer who is no longer able to control the powers of the underworld that he has called up by his spells." The magnificent arteries with which Moses had hoped to weave the city together had coalesced into a hangman's knot around the city's neck: squalor and suffocation at the center, space and freedom available only for those who could escape into the subdivided suburbs on the periphery. The heroic construction that had succeeded at first in bringing the city and the country together was now, after a generation of growth, succeeding at last in destroying them both.

This was the Moses of the forties and fifties, the man who built so much and devastated so many people's lives. He was at the height of his power, controlling a dozen public authorities, manipulating billions of dollars in federal funds, and using the money to bribe or break everyone in his way. His blitz could strike anywhere and no politician dared to protest, for Moses's authorities had given so much to so many that there was more than enough in his secret files to destroy them all. "I would never let Moses do anything for me in any way," Mayor Wagner warned a protégé. When Caro, in an interview with Moses, asked how he had induced an admired leader of the opposition to the Cross-Bronx road to betray his people at the last minute, Moses answered in the best gangster tradition: "After he was hit over the head with an ax." But he rarely had to hit: Public figures generally knew enough to shut up.

There was much less of the beauty and sensitivity of design that distinguished his early works. Most of what he built now was built in a brutal style, designed to overawe and overwhelm: monoliths of steel and concrete, devoid of nuance or play, sealed off from streets and people by great moats of stark empty space, stamped on the landscape with a ferocious contempt for all natural and human life. He seemed scornfully indifferent to the human quality of what he did: sheer quantity was all that drove him now—dollars spent, tons of cement, moving vehicles. "There's very little hardship in the thing," Moses had said when the Cross-Bronx Expressway was done. "More people in the way, that's all."

As the fifties dragged on, Moses's system kept up its relentless growth, but those of us who watched him began to sense something wrong with the picture: He was spreading himself too thin for his own good. The empire had become so vast, and there was simply too much business for him to take care of by himself. In the newest outposts—Urban Renewal, for one—the brilliant engineers and technocrats Moses had once attracted were staying away, and power was being grasped by hacks and crooks. These new men were not merely corrupt, but grossly stupid, blatantly inept. He must have been ashamed—not ashamed that thousands of people were being thrown out of their homes, that old and poor people were being terrorized in buildings without heat or light or water, that dozens of solid neighborhoods were being destroyed, but ashamed that, for all that, these new projects weren't even getting built. Meanwhile, however, as Moses wove his great web of public works more and more intricately through people's lives, more and more people were coming to feel that they were being strangled and eaten up, that they had to cut the web and break out. For a whole generation of New Yorkers, Moses was becoming the embodiment of all the horrible social forces that had to be stopped. And even those who had loved him most—as the *New York Times* had loved him, selflessly and even (as Caro shows) self-abasingly, for thirty years—were coming to see that he would have to go.

Caro, by putting Moses's most monstrous works in the larger context of a long and heroic career, shows just how tragic Moses's life story really is. Here was a man who had everything, whose vision and imagination and creative energy drove him to serve the people magnificently—indeed, to serve us far better than many who loved us far more—and yet, whose very genius and creative powers turned him into a danger and a nightmare to the people for whom he had done so much. Caro reveals in Moses's life a grandeur and sadness that is as old as culture itself.[6] At the same time, some of the ironies and contradictions of Moses's tragedy have a specific resonance in our collective life today. In the first twenty years of his work as a master builder, he did more than any man in American history to nourish the romance of construction and bring it to a climax; in his next twenty years of building, he would do more than any man to poison that romance and tear it down.

How was Moses finally stopped? Caro gives good accounts of some of the prologues in the late fifties and some of the epilogues in the mid-sixties, when Rockefeller and Lindsay finally wrested public works completely out of his hands. Strangely, however, Caro entirely omits the episode that seems to me most climactic and decisive: the tremendous battle over the Lower Manhattan Expressway. This was a project that Moses had dreamt of for thirty years. It would have run clear across Manhattan, from the East River to the Hudson. The cost was outrageous, even by Moses's own estimates, but the federal government was willing to pick up 90 percent of the check, and so, at one stroke, bring billions of dollars' worth of money, contracts, and jobs into New York—it seemed like an offer the city could not refuse. The highway would have cut through the heart of the West Village, Soho, Chinatown, and the Lower East Side. To Moses, and to federal and state officials at the time, there was nothing worth saving in these neighborhoods: They were "slums," filled with rotten tenements and teeming with wretched refuse.

Some protests were expected, but there had always been protests, and none of them had meant a thing. Moreover, the people in the way of this highway belonged to widely disparate

---

6 This sort of tragedy is the basis of the oldest story in the world, the Sumerian epic of Gilgamesh. King Gilgamesh destroys monsters who menace his people, but then turns on the people themselves, and turns himself from their hero into their terror. He seeks immortality, fails to find it, and dies unfulfilled. But he does attain a kind of immortality on earth by building a monumental Great Wall.

ethnic, class, age, and subcultural groups, tribes that were perpetually at each other's throats and could always be counted on to cancel each other out. However, to everybody's surprise—and the groups themselves were most surprised of all—the Chinese, Italians, blacks, Puerto Ricans, Jews, John Birchers, aristocratic WASP liberals (like Lindsay), Greenwich Village bohemians, and middle-class Reform Democrats were suddenly working together, turning public hearings from charades into real political confrontations, stopping traffic in the streets. And there was another crucial difference: Moses had always denounced his opponents as mere selfish opportunists, promoting their particular private interests against the welfare of "the Public"; this coalition was appealing to a general public on behalf of a coherent and striking public philosophy. Their basic idea, expounded most cogently and convincingly by Jane Jacobs, was that the street and the neighborhood were the very heart of city life, and that the destruction of streets and neighborhoods menaced the energy and integrity of the city as a whole. The new combination was too much even for Moses: In 1966, after a decade of desperate fighting, his plan was wiped off the map.

Moses never really knew what hit him; but the road that he had hacked through the metropolis with a meat ax for 30 years had been decisively blocked, and he could never be certain of his mission or his momentum again. The next year, when Rockefeller moved to drive him from his last and greatest fortress, the Triborough Authority, he seemed mysteriously to lose his will to power—to everyone's surprise, he let himself be blown away.

Caro captures the pathos of Moses's life in the shadows: sick at heart when his great works are abused, or forgotten, or ascribed to other men, or (like his beautiful West Side landscape) Mother Nature; but still all there, even at the age of eighty-seven, still full of wit and energy and tremendous schemes, refusing, like Mr. Kurtz, to be counted out ("I'll carry out my ideas yet . . . I'll show you what can be done . . . I will return. I . . ."). Driven restlessly up and down his Long Island beachfront in his black limousine, dreaming of a glorious 160-mile Ocean Drive to whip the waves, this old man has an undeniably tragic grandeur. What he does not have, alas, is the tragic self-awareness that is supposed to go with this grandeur. In his reply to *The Power Broker*, he asks us all: Am I not, after all, the man who blotted out the Valley of Ashes and gave mankind beauty in its place? It is true, and we all owe him homage for it. And yet, he did not really wipe out the ashes, he only moved them to another site; he created new forms of waste and blight and death to supplant the old forms that he destroyed. For the ashes are part of us, part of the inner darkness that stays with us, no matter how straight and smooth we make our freeways, no matter how fast we drive—or are driven—no matter how far out on Long Island we go.

NEIGHBORHOODS AND HISTORY

We leave Moses, then, at the edge of the sea, waiting in vain for the call to come back and make the earth move again. But where does all this leave Caro himself? This question has a special urgency for us, because Caro's ideas on the city, on planning, on government, on community, are identical with the ones that animated the New Left throughout the sixties. Unfortunately, Caro tends to treat these ideas as simple eternal truths. Had he examined the historical context in which his (and our) ideas came into being—in communal struggles like the fight against the Lower Manhattan Expressway—he would have seen that the truth-value of the ideas we share is a lot more complex and problematical than he seems to think.

Caro's lack of perspective on his own perspective leads him into tragic anachronisms. His account of the Cross-Bronx Expressway begins with a beautiful evocation of a world we have lost, the shoddy but vibrant world of a second-generation Jewish neighborhood a generation ago. This lovely vision sets us up for shock and horror when we see that world destroyed. The devastation of that world really was horrible, yet there is something wrong with Caro's picture: His appreciation of the old neighborhood is based on values that are new; they are the values of 1970, and they were nowhere in the picture in 1950, when the neighbor-hood was still in flower. The ironic fact is that the neighborhood people themselves lacked these ideas when they were most in need of them; they did not even have the vocabulary to defend their neighborhoods because, until the sixties, that vocabulary simply did not exist.

Hence the people of the Bronx were torn between our hearts, which were shattered to see our neighborhood go, and our minds, in which the neighborhood had no grounds to stand on. It was not only that, as children of the New Deal, we all believed in the ultimate beneficence of big government, centralized plan-ning, large-scale public works. Beyond that, all of us were possessed by the great American dream of mobility: To live the good life meant physically to move out, socially to move up; this was the only way to go. Not even the radicals of those days questioned the dream: Their only complaint was that it wasn't being fulfilled, that people weren't able to move fast or freely or equally enough. But when you see life this way, no neighbor-hood can be anything more than a stage along life's way, a launching pad for greater things. Even Molly Goldberg, earth goddess of the Jewish Bronx, had to move. That was just the way things were: change, progress, "improvement," the law of life (life in America, at least, for why had our parents or grand-parents come to America at all, if not to move?). This was and still is, as Leonard Michaels puts it perfectly, "the mentality of neighborhood types who, quick as possible, got the hell out of their neighborhoods." This inner contradiction has generated much of the energy that has torn so many of our neighborhoods and our people to pieces and made our economy and our culture and our country great.

The neighborhood Caro focuses on made no protest against Moses's road as a whole: They argued simply that there was no reason to build it through their neighborhood; an alternate route would leave their homes and lives intact. From Caro's description, their claim sounds plausible—though, of course, that made no difference to Moses, who crushed them like insects. But what if you had no alternate route? For most Americans in the fifties there was simply no way to argue coherently that, for human reasons, a road should not be built *at all.* All you could do in protest was to rage and weep. The people of the Bronx had no way to resist the wheels that drove the American dream—a dream that was driving us ourselves—even though we knew the wheels would break us. At the same time, the tremendous energy of the dream, the frenzied economic and psychic pressure to move up and out, was breaking down hundreds of American neighborhoods like the Bronx, even where there was no Moses to lead the exodus and no Expressways to do the work fast.

STOPPING THE MACHINE

It was only in the sixties, with the advent of the New Left and the "counter-culture," that America found ways to ask seriously: Mobility for what? These middle-class children of the dream forced our whole culture to ask: Where are we rushing, and for what human end, and at what human cost? Mario Savio of Berkeley's Free Speech Movement spoke for far more Americans than he realized when, in the winter of 1964, he said: "There is a time when the operation of the machine becomes so odious, makes you so sick at heart, that you can't take part . . . and you've got to put your bodies upon the gears and upon the wheels, upon the levers and upon all the apparatus, and you've got to make it stop."

Stop the Machine! This idea was expressed most urgently by the New Left, which spent much of the sixties trying to stop the Vietnam War and all the machines that propelled it. It is striking that two of the most stirring actions of the sixties involved sitting down on construction sites and stopping the works: a gymnasium in a park at Columbia, a parking lot on a "free space" at People's Park. But the idea reached far beyond the range of the New Left and inflamed millions of Americans who saw themselves as anything but Left or New. Suddenly, for the first time anyone could remember, America's master builders were on the defensive, publicly despised for their "public works"; there was a vast wave of free-floating popular sympathy for "the people" in the way, and this sympathy could often be utilized to block the way.[7] All through the sixties, all over America, by force or by vote, great machines and great works were stopped. In the New York version of this drama, Robert Moses played a crucial role: He was sitting on top of the world we were trying to stop, lashing his men and machines to move faster as resistance grew. Thesis and antithesis, he and we needed each other.

There was good news and there was bad news in all this. The good news is that we stopped some really dreadful things: Vietnamese as well as American neighborhoods could be grateful. The bad news is that, in the great combat between Heroic Construction and Heroic Resistance, the dialectic has fallen flat: Instead of generating some sort of higher synthesis, the two impulses and antagonists seem to have canceled each other out or eaten each other up. A decade after Mario Savio urged his fellow Americans to Stop the Machine, a great many of America's machines are stunningly silent—far more than the New Left would ever have dreamed—and (except for the rich, whom we always have with us) virtually nothing is being built at all. But the brave people who threw themselves on those wheels for a decade are now even more turned off than the machines. The ponderous Roman weight of that abstract entity, "the public," in whose supposed interest Moses built all his public works, has crumbled and disappeared; but the native American energy and vitality of "the people," the force that blocked the works, is equally remote today, equally gone with the wind.

THE SOUNDS OF SILENCE

What the Seventies have given us in place of both can be summed up in a strange slogan THINK SMALL. In other words, center yourself in the life immediately around you—your block, your

---

7   Note a crucial change in radical iconography: The arm and hammer and hammer and sickle were the most vivid and powerful symbols of the Old Left; the New Left proclaimed its presence most dramatically with a clenched fist. All these are symbols of strength, determination, and potential violence; but the icons of the Old Left also express the will and power to *build*.

neighborhood, your ethnic group, your family and friends, your loved ones, your inner life, your most intimate ways of feeling and being, and let history take care of itself for awhile. I don't want to sound smug about "thinking small," because I know it's helped me and plenty of other Americans not only to survive, but to thrive, in a dismal time. More over, it has inspired people to weave together and brighten up much of the street and neighborhood fabric of our cities, a fabric that had been terribly worn and torn by a generation of "thinking big." Still, I worry about what all this shrinking thinking is doing to America as a whole. I see our society disintegrating into a multitude of guarded enclaves and embattled camps—ethnic, class, regional, religious, racial, sexual—that are not only separated but aggressively separatist, tribal, or sectarian in our sense of life, celebrating bigotry as integrity, fierce in our fears of everything and everyone "outside"; refusing not only to melt, but even to live together in the same pot, at worst burning books and schools, and people, to keep our world pure; at best peaceably but avidly waiting for the rest of the world to go to hell. After a quarter century of manic mobility, Americans are digging themselves in for a long winter of depressive rigidity: They are freezing their souls, cloning themselves with a kind of spiritual cryogenics, as the Depression sets in. If this is the way history takes care of itself when people Think Small, it's enough to make me feel nostalgia for people with the spirit and the guts to Think Big.

So we're back with Moses again: stranded together, in a kind of spiritual Casablanca, strange bedfellows in Rick's Bar, trying to fathom each other, and ourselves, and our strange intimate enmity, as time goes by. Both he and we are entangled and intertwined in some of the deepest contradictions in bourgeois society and modern life.

Robert Moses has always claimed to be conservative, professed his faith in "law and order"—and yet, in his greatest works and acts, he has proved himself to be one of the most extravagant nihilists in modern history. There is nothing this man would not pull up by the roots, no one he would not destroy, if necessary, nothing he would not build if he had the chance. Nothing is sacred to him—he is not even interested in making money!—except the demonic compulsion to act and to organize and to build. He fulfilled Jerry Rubin's maxim "Do It!" far beyond Rubin's wildest dreams. Moses could build magnificently: His problem was that he did not know when or where to stop—and so finally he had to be stopped. Indeed, he didn't even know where to start: He seized the openings at hand and built whatever, wherever, whenever he could; he never even began to think about what kinds of buildings people might actually *need*, or about what kinds of buildings people might not need at all.

We of the old New Left had problems radically different from these. We were acutely sensitive to human feelings and needs—indeed, the New Left might be called, to its credit, a politics of sensitivity—and we understood how American institutions trampled on these feelings and needs. But although we knew what things needed to be stopped, and how to stop them, we had no idea how to *start* things. We had very little capacity to even imagine, let alone plan and organize and build, structures that could put our sensitivity into effect. Hence, for all our dreams of heroic activism, there was very little we could do, constructively, concretely, to change the world. It is true enough that we never really had much power to show what we could do; but one reason may have been that we never developed any clear ideas of what we were prepared to do. Between our visions and our plans fell a very large shadow.

Here is where our great enemy may be able to help us. In exploring Moses's works, unraveling his achievements, disentangling the beauty from the horror, we may be able to develop some sense of how to actually build things, how to put the visions and the plans and the materials and the people together. This kind of lesson may turn out to be "relevant" before long. The deeper our economy recedes into depression, the more public pressure there is going to be for massive programs of public works to get us out. Whether America's next wave of construction devastates and degrades "the people," or helps people feel and live more like human beings, may depend on us, on whether we can bring the romance of building to life again. We had better not count on a new hero of construction to put it together for us: *The Power Broker* shows what happened last time we did that. Unhappy the land that needs a hero. But we may not need a hero later on if we can confront our real needs right now. If we remember that buildings are judgment, we may be able to win a better judgment for ourselves next time around.

This essay was first published in Ramparts, *March 1975.*

Views from the Burning Bridge

I exclaimed with sadness, "Are ruins, then, already here?"
Alexis de Tocqueville, *Democracy in America*

When my friends from home come to visit, I try to show them
Central Park, the Brooklyn Bridge, the Metropolitan Museum,
but they say, "Where is the South Bronx? Take me to the burning
buildings! I want a lover from the ruins."
A Swiss art critic in conversation, early 1980s

The big thing about any New York neighborhood is its relationship to the center. The city center in Manhattan, with its spectacular cluster of big buildings and bright lights, has a magical aura. It
is the focal point of every New Yorker's primal dream. This dream
unfolds itself like a giant panorama. The picture's foreground is
the dreamer's neighborhood. This is usually across the water
(where four-fifths of the city's population comes from), but it
could just as well be on the Lower East Side or in Hell's Kitchen
or Little Italy or Chinatown or Harlem. In the dream, our eyes
reach longingly over our tenement or brownstone or rowhouse
roofs, and the smooth roofline (most New York neighborhoods
have uniform rooflines) looks like a road.

Over the roofs, over the water, at the picture's center, our eyes
meet the prize: Manhattan's skyscrapers and skyline, bathed in
sunshine or radiating electricity and neon light. The big buildings
are framed by an infinite day or night or twilight sky, which gives
the picture a vanishing point and embeds the dream in the cosmos.
This cityscape has the *chutzpah* of the biblical dream of Babel:

"Come, let us build ourselves a city, and a tower with its top in the heavens." As it reaches for the sky, this complex of buildings beckons us to a life of passionate striving, feverish intensity, and expressive fullness, and it seems to deny that there are any limits on what human beings can do. (In Genesis 11, God worries about this: If people can build and maintain such a city, then "nothing will be restrained from them, that they imagine to do.") Can it be real? Can it be as close as it looks—we could almost reach out and touch it—or is it, like Kafka's Castle, some sort of existential trap or mirage? Can we get there on the subway? Can we stay? If we go, can we come back? And if we do make the leap, if we make a life inside those buildings, if we make ourselves into authentic New Yorkers, what will it do to us as human beings? For more than a century, these have been New York's overwhelming questions. The most luminous visions of New York are views from the bridge.

In the 1950s, when I was growing up in the Bronx, the act of crossing over into Manhattan seemed like a smooth and easy flow both ways. When our relatives from Brooklyn went to a Broadway theater or Madison Square Garden, they would say they were going to "the city"; but for us, going to those same places, even to meet them there, was going "downtown": We took it for granted that we and Manhattan's wonders were part of the same town. But in the 1970s and 1980s, the Bronx's view from the bridge was radically impaired. Imagine yourself dropped into the Bronx around 1981, enjoying the familiar view downtown. You will spot the difference right away: The foreground is broken. Now many tenements and apartment houses are cracked, burnt, split apart, caved in. Whole blocks have vanished or disintegrated into wreckage and debris. On other blocks, only a single house is left, with rubble all around; the building may well be far more striking, now that it is all alone, and if you examine its curves and details, you can often see that once, maybe not long ago, this sole survivor was quite grand. Some apartment houses are split by their courtyards (the Bronx was once known for its splendid courtyards), lived-in on one side, burnt-out on the other. Some blocks that not long ago were claustrophobic, perpetually shadowed, packed too tight with people, are sun-drenched now, wide open and empty as deserts. Sometimes there is a whole new zone, a kind of a fore-foreground, that stands between you and the buildings: a blanket of cracked and burnt brick and wood and stone and tile and marble and steel and fabric and paper and plastic, shards of thousands and thousands of lives. Maybe the city has sealed it off with a steel fence or maybe it is wide open and you are welcome to take whatever fragments you want. On the horizon, you can see that the towers of Manhattan's Oz are still there, as alluring as ever; but close to the ground, the Bronx's yellow brick roads have crumbled into craters and minefields.

In the late 1970s, the *New York Times* had a little box, on page two or three of the Local Section, that listed all the buildings burned or destroyed the previous day or night. People called it the Ruins Section, and I knew many people who, like me, read the Ruins Section first of all. It was uncanny how the ruins ran on, building after building, block after block, mile after mile. On Bronx walks I met people from camera crews, sometimes from the local news—working on the latest disaster—but also from Canada, England, Italy, Sweden; I missed the one from the USSR. The people most visible on the South Bronx streets were kids, and lots of those kids looked startlingly hungry—hungry like kids in turn-of-the-century photographs by Jacob Riis and Lewis Hine, hungry like American kids weren't supposed to be any more. (I was teaching in Harlem, and the kids on the Harlem streets looked a lot better fed.) For several years, in the late 1970s and early 1980s, more than a thousand Bronx buildings each year were destroyed by fire. The Fire Department listed the great majority as "suspicious fires," which left behind traces of fire accelerants.

But there were even better accelerants at work in the social stereotyping process. "What's wrong with these people?" Howard Cosell barked on national television, during the 1976 World Series at Yankee Stadium, as the camera from the Goodyear Blimp showed a building on fire less than a mile from the field. Cosell asked, in a tone that supplied its own answer, "Don't these people have any self-respect?" What a relief it must have been to think of the fires as something "these people" were *doing to themselves*: then you wouldn't have to worry about whether the Bronx's troubles were somehow your troubles. One thing that gave this situation an especially sinister twist is how many Bronx people came to see themselves as "these people," how many victims of suspicious fires came to think of themselves as prime suspects. On the local news, you could see families weeping in front of their smoking buildings, and asking, "What did we do?" There were plenty of journalists and pseudo-social scientists (often subsidized by right-wing foundations) only too glad to tell them their character flaws. A surprising alliance of the Fire Department, the Mayor's Task Force Against Arson, the insurance companies, and the urban Left (the *Village Voice*, *City Limits*, and so on) focused instead on the character of the South Bronx's landlords. Lloyd's of London was said to have lost $20 million in the 1970s on Bronx insurance pools. Early in the 1980s, insurance companies stopped paying claims on Bronx fires, and the burning of the Bronx came to an abrupt end.

During the troubles, the Bronx lost over three hundred thousand people, and the South Bronx plummeted past census tracts in backwoods Louisiana and Mississippi to become, so the media said (I haven't been able to document this, but it could be), the poorest congressional district in the country. For people who stayed, life was hard. In the course of the 1980s, as public services kept shrinking, with gang violence and AIDS killing the young, it would get even harder. But many people found it easier to protect themselves from the flames than from the carpet bombings of invective that blamed them for the ruin of their world. (Looking for a way to evoke the full horror of this process, in 1984 I invented a word, *urbicide*, the murder of a city. I thought this word would be my contribution to the American idiom, but although I've seen it used a couple of times, it hasn't really caught on. Yet it may, down the road, because urbicide keeps happening all over.)

When the Bronx, after decades of peaceful anonymity, finally made it into the mass media as a symbol of all that could go wrong in city life, it wasn't just the buildings in the Bronx that were breaking down: It felt like a rupture in both New York's everyday reality and its archetypal dream. Our neighborhoods, including the poorest ones—maybe especially the poorest ones—were supposed to be roads and bridges leading to the city's heights. They were supposed to fuse their kids' energy and desire with the city's primal sources of energy downtown. And, to an amazing extent, they really did. For generations, they held the city together, gave it much of its distinctive flavor, and produced millions of authentic New Yorkers—wise guys and sophisticates, close to the streets but also to a global culture. What would be the wider ripples of neighborhood collapse? It was to dread.

Images change their meanings over time. The first time you see a landscape of ruins, it is terrifying but magnificent, sublime. But when you see it day after day, year after year, it gets to be a drag. Was it really true that nothing could be done? The persistence of the ruins became embarrassing to public officials, and their embarrassment produced unconscious comedy. Stanley Simon, Bronx Borough President during the worst troubles, proposed covering the miles of broken buildings along the Cross-Bronx Expressway with decals that portrayed curtains, plants, and peaceful domestic scenes. Alas, even expensive decals still looked like cartoons; the Carter Community Employment and Training Act program, which could have paid unemployed artists to camouflage broken buildings, expired under Reagan; and Bronx graffitists, violently banned from the subways, found a new life covering broken buildings with enormous inscriptions: "This is a decal," "This is a fake," "This is a ruin." Then Simon went to prison for bribery and extortion, and people laughed about the politician's new clothes and wondered what his decals would cover now.

But the Bronx did not have to hide its light under a decal. Even in its greatest misery and anguish—and in some sense, I think, *because of* its misery and anguish—the Bronx became more culturally creative than it had ever been in its life. As a Bronx character in Grace Paley's short story "Somewhere Else" put it, "The block is burning down on one side of the street, and the kids are trying to build something on the other." In the midst of dying, it was busy being born.

Anyone coming to New York for the first time in the 1970s, or returning here, had to be struck by thousands of subway cars saturated with luminous primary colors. The first wave of graffitists were at work, coming from all over the city, but from the Bronx most of all. These kids, mostly (though not entirely) black and Latin and male, were denounced and repeatedly arrested, but in the course of the 1970s their work developed a bold and adventurous visual language. They infused a drab and dilapidated transit system with adventurous graphics and youthful exuberance. Some of them showed obvious artistic talents— Revolt, Futura 2000, Daze, Crash, Sonic, Phase II, the United Artists, Fab Five Freddie, Dondi (who died this past April) and others I've long forgotten. They differed in aesthetics and sensibility: some playful and nonchalant, others existentially desperate; some projecting spontaneous overflows of powerful feeling, others tending toward elaborate patterns of design; some emphasizing pure visuals, others blending images with texts (IF ART IS A CRIME, MAY GOD FORGIVE ME); some conveying instant entertainment, usually through parodies of Disney or Warner Brothers cartoons, others more ruminative, abstract, even hieroglyphic; some addressing their audience with respect and esteem, others driven by an in-your-face punk disdain. My favorite was Lee Quinones, whose murals fused surreal landscapes with provocative texts: STOP THE BOMB, WAR IS SELFISH DEATH, MAN IS ALMOST EXTINCT. Lee was one of many who liked to incorporate "views from the bridge" in their murals, thus carrying on a dialogue and interplay between uptown and downtown. This interplay is the subject of the movie *Wild Style,* where Lee is a star.

Some of these kids developed careers as designers; some wound up with MTV; some went to Hollywood. Looking at their life stories, we can see their graffiti years as first steps up a ladder and admire their resourcefulness in finding markets for themselves. But when the graffitists of the Bronx began, they had more than self-marketing in mind: They saw themselves as *citizens* and insisted on the civic and public meaning of their work. Their shared desire to communicate with a large public all around the town, and beyond it, set the stage for a brutal, grueling, vastly expensive, materially and humanly destructive conflict with the arrogant and unresponsive bureaucracy of the Metropolitan Transit Authority (MTA). In 1980, in the midst of this conflict, Daze said:

> If the MTA really understood graffiti, they would know it's one of the best things subways have going for them. If the city would back us up and treat us as artists instead of vandals, we could contribute a lot to the beauty of New York.

"*If the MTA really understood.*" But Daze, who had worked with the relatively sympathetic school and park bureaucracies, must have known what an implacable fortress he faced in the MTA. Later on, when he and other graffitists got a chance to make money, they took it and ran. In the commercial sector, some did very well. But it's important to recall that behind the private success there was a public failure. And it wasn't the kids who failed.

Alongside these graffitists, sometimes the same people, were the Bronx rappers. In the poorest congressional district in the United States, rap was an exemplary *musica povera*. Some early rappers came from musically sophisticated families, with strong backgrounds in jazz and R&B. Others had grown up too poor to take music lessons or have their own instruments, but had strong feeling for rhythm, powerful voices, and sharp wits. In the late 1970s, at the City College of New York (CCNY), where I taught, up in Harlem, every Thursday during Club Hour somebody brought out turntables, and a DJ scratched and collaged dozens of records together while kids in the audience took turns playing MC, rapping over an open mike. I was delighted: What it meant for me was the power of the *word,* which was what I'd been trying to teach all along. At the end of the 1970s, wherever blacks lived, rap was busting out all over, but a concentration of the first great DJs came from the Bronx—Kool Herc, Afrika Bambaataa, Grandmaster Flash—and they vied with each other, in dozens of small Bronx clubs, parks, and school auditoriums, with thousands of participant young listeners, to create a distinctive rap sound of samples, beats, and rhymes.

The spirit of early raps tended toward dancehall and party music, with funny, shallow lyrics like these from "Live Connection

'82," by The Grand Wizard Theodore: "The people in the back, you ain't the wack / The people in the middle, let me see you wiggle / Young lady in the blue, I'm talking to you / but don't you stop that body rock." Rap's first great hit, when it finally came, was heavy, dark, and deep. This was "The Message," by Grandmaster Flash and the Furious Five, released by Sugar Hill in the Reagan summer of 1982. "The Message" showed that there was not only a national but an international audience for rap.

In "The Message," Melle Mel chants in a rich and intensely dramatic voice:

> Don't push me, 'cause
> I'm close to the edge,
> trying not to lose my head. *Hah!*
>
> It's like a jungle sometimes it makes me wonder
> how I keep from going under.
> (*Huhh huh huh Huhh*

Melle Mel then takes us on a Bronx neighborhood tour: Broken glass everywhere, people pissing on the streets like they just don't care; the narrator can't stand the pain, can't stand the noise, but "got no money in my pocket, so I got no choice." Myriad horrors are compressed into a couple of minutes. Rats in the rooms; junkies in the alley with baseball bats; predatory repo men; nice girls turned into addicts and whores; kids, cynical before the age of ten, who want to grow up to be drug dealers because those are the only people they know who command respect; their big brothers, who go from unemployed to killers to dead. The rapper addresses a handsome corpse, asks him how he could be so dumb: "You lived so fast and died so young."

This rapper's attitudes here are complex and hard to keep in any sort of emotional balance. He insists on the self-destructive idiocy of the people in the slum he lives in, but also on their human dignity. He, too, asks, "What's wrong with these people?" But he doesn't settle for any cliché answer—not even the answer that they are victims, though he makes it clear that they are. Moreover, his voice reveals that he sees himself as one of "these people": The story is about "us," not "them." This complex of feelings forces him to walk a thin line. His refrain warns us, "So don't push me 'cause I'm close to the edge / Trying not to lose my head." Then, once more, the concrete jungle. Then, by surprise, a burst of wishful thinking. He identifies with two people maimed by violence who get help and somehow survive:

> They pushed a girl in front of a train,
> Took her to the doctor, sewed her arm on again.
> Stabbed that man right through the heart,
> Gave him a transplant and a brand new start.

Then the chorus again. Then a collage of street sounds, culminating in a police siren, a (black) voice ordering everyone to freeze, motors taking them all away. In the end the street is empty, the rap and the rapper both disappear, only the beat goes on.

"The Message" became an instant classic, endlessly quoted, parodied, and sampled. And it made a breakthrough for the whole genre: Suddenly, all over America, South as well as North, and all over Europe as well, there were a lot of people out there who wanted to listen to rap. What was "the message"? Maybe, *We can be home in the middle of the end of the world*. Or maybe, *We come from ruins, but we are not ruined*. The meta-message is something like this: Not only social disintegration, but even existential desperation, can be sources of life and creative energy. Even as the fires and violence were wrecking the Bronx's old roads downtown, a great outpouring of cultural energy was forging new connections with downtown. The capacity for soul-making in the throes of suffering lit up the Bronx with an aura all its own.

Turn now to the visual art that was made by people from downtown who came uptown, who worked and sometimes lived in the South Bronx in its fire years, and whose work was shaped by being there. These men and women worked in very different styles, with radically different (and sometimes inwardly contradictory) imaginative visions, but there are human contexts they had in common.

They all were (and still are) part of the sixties generation: They grew up, and defined themselves as artists, during the civil rights movement and the Vietnam War. That history filled them with a high seriousness and a sense of human urgency. When they came to define themselves as artists, they were all committed to making art that would *mean* something. But in their connection to New York's downtown art scene, they were also products of a radically skeptical modernist culture that put all traditional and conventional meanings in doubt, so that, circa 1970, although they wanted to mean something, the meaning of "meaning" was not at all clear. Another theme they all absorbed from modernism was the idea that authentic art could be created only by *experiment*, constant experimentation not only on raw material (paint, canvas, plaster, bronze, paper, wood, steel, plastic, and so on), but on the artist himself, on his or her whole being.

Modern history is full of people, and groups of people, trying to find truth and meaning by going to places where life is a lot harder and more dangerous than the life they live, and trying to connect with the people who live there. These enterprises include Christian missionaries in Africa, China, and all over the world; Russian intellectuals in the 1870s "going to the people"; Gauguin going to Tahiti, and Van Gogh going to peasant sharecroppers and coal miners; the whole anthropology profession, from its beginnings in remote islands and valleys to its current embrace of inner-city neighborhoods; American civil rights workers of the 1960s, going from the North to the South; but also, in the news every day for years, the American armed forces going to "win the hearts and minds" of the Vietnamese people and destroying their villages in order to save them. Artists working in the Bronx were aware of these very mixed examples, recognized the potential for exploitation—as in, "Take me to the burning buildings! I want a lover from the ruins"—and hoped that endless self-criticism could help them avoid it. (But sometimes the self-criticism was so corrosive as to bring on paralysis.) They were united by empathy for people who, as "The Message" said, were living "close to the edge." They felt they were different from, and better than, missionaries or imperial troops, in that they were not trying to enforce a system of meanings whose truth was pre-established, but rather to work with the people of the Bronx to create new meanings that could light up the whole world. And, although different artists responded differently to graffiti and rap, they all felt inspired to be working with a generation of kids who not only knew how to be active and creative in the midst of great pain, but knew how to be citizens, seeking a public meaning for their lives. They all hoped to learn something from the people they encountered and also to give something back.

This was the context in which Stephen Eins, an artist from Vienna, established Fashion Moda, a gallery and "alternate space" in a storefront on Third Avenue, just below "the Hub" of 149th Street in the South Bronx. For a decade or more, Fashion Moda brought "downtown" artists, musicians, and writers together with "uptown" graffiti painters, rappers, breakdance crews, and curious neighborhood people. (Sculptor Rigoberto Torres is the most important artist who found his calling by walking off the street and into Fashion Moda out of sheer curiosity.) Eins was immensely resourceful at working various government bureaucracies and helping artists get space to mount innovative installations in schools and parks, in abandoned apartment buildings (there were so many), and on the streets.

One Fashion Moda artist, John Fekner, used the walls of abandoned apartment houses to create what in effect were giant billboards, with captions like BROKEN PROMISES and LAST HOPE. Fekner's billboards often dominated their environments and provided ironic commentary on some of the photo ops that various politicians grasped in front of the ruins. Jimmy Carter was there in 1976, appeared moved, and promised to rebuild the South Bronx—only, as with many Carter initiatives, it wasn't supposed to cost the federal government an extra dime. His plan turned out to be that, for several years, all of the city's share of federal community development money would be channeled here, while other city neighborhoods would get nothing at all. When City Council representatives of those other neighborhoods protested, Carter's aides said, in effect, "What's wrong with these people?" and were glad to wash their hands of the promise.

David Finn's work featured life-size figures sculpted out of garbage bags, old newspapers, and street debris, arranged and displayed provocatively in buildings or on streets, in ways that suggested political prisoners (the South Bronx was full of Latin Americans and Africans who could tell stories), massacred victims of the drug gang wars (there were plenty), or (this was the kids' favorite idea) space invaders. Finn's work was visually striking and beautifully realized: It evoked Picasso in his African mask and his "Guernica" periods. Like much exciting public art in the Bronx (and everywhere else), it elicited enthusiastic support from children and anger from many of their parents.

Many outstanding photographers appeared in the Bronx in the 1970s and 1980s, not only documenting the horrors, but portraying powerful visions of the human condition and putting together impressive bodies of work. The two I know best are Mel Rosenthal and Camilo Jose Vergara. Both of them have done serious work outside New York—Rosenthal in Puerto Rico and Central America and Vergara in Detroit and Los Angeles—but it was in the South Bronx that they came into their own. Rosenthal works in the tradition of humanist snapshots developed by Europeans like Henri Cartier-Bresson and by great war photographers like Robert Capa. An archetypal Mel Rosenthal shot is kids playing in broken buildings, or families passing by the ruins, or the last old man or woman (whose face looks centuries old) in a building that looks about to collapse, or looks like it already has collapsed. These children won't be robbed of their childhood: They don't stop playing just because their playground has been destroyed. Women dance in the street, and don't stop dancing just because there's no more street. His people use the rubble as sites for new dances and new games. Rosenthal understands how people can make themselves at home in negative spaces; they are not only survivors but pioneers.

Vergara feels a special empathy for architecture, for buildings. He especially loves the aspiration toward Renaissance and Baroque grandeur that makes Bronx apartment houses so special. He grasps one of the glories of the Bronx, for which it will go down in history: its ability to deliver real grandeur to the working classes. His serial photographs of buildings in the 1970s and 1980s dramatize, year by year, the disintegration of that glory. Because he really feels it, and makes us feel it, the process of its destruction is so heartrending. A few years ago, he displayed one of his grandest series: the gradual disintegration of an apartment house on Vyse Avenue into nothingness. It was a magnificent spectacle but, I felt, somehow too cruel: The destructive process seemed too much like cosmic entropy. (In Rosenthal's photos, it looks more like heavy artillery.) Vergara said Wait, the story wasn't over, he was sure he would be back. Indeed, his recent work shows Vyse Avenue inhabited again. The building is on a smaller scale, two-story row houses, as against yesterday's vanished palaces. But now there is a new trajectory, going upward after decades of coming down. It is as if the people of the Bronx have begun building the Tower of Babel again, reaching for Vergara's luminescent blue sky.

One of the most striking art initiatives in the recent Bronx has been Tim Rollins's studio, which he named "K.O.S.," Kids Of Survival. Rollins began in 1981 as an art teacher in Junior High School 52, working with about forty teenagers who were classified as learning disabled and at risk of dropping out. His work with these kids and his emerging love for them crystallized into a distinctive sort of art workshop. Rollins worked the system to develop a splendid art library and art studio, where kids could learn and experiment with every material and style. Then he read to his kids: some books that were in the curriculum, others that were modernist masterpieces. They would discuss the books together and try to imagine how they might be represented. I visited some of these classes on Longwood Avenue a decade ago, and I don't know what his kids' standard reading test scores were, but I can testify that they were *there*. They gradually developed a signature form, the literary mural. The mural's background was always a reproduction of the text; the foreground, exquisite variations on the common theme. For *Scarlet Letter*, it was variations

on the red letter "A"; for Franz Kafka's *Amerika,* it was variations
on a golden horn. Doing *Amerika* together at once bonded and
inspired them. In a short time, working fervidly, they created a
number of gorgeous and inspiring horn murals.

And suddenly, the whole world wanted them: Colleges wanted
K.O.S. to give a workshop; towns all over America and in Europe
wanted horn murals for their Town Halls; Charles Saatchi and
Mary Boone wanted all the work they could get; suddenly the kids
were big shots in Soho and all over town; *New York* magazine did
a headline piece that suggested Rollins was exploiting the kids'
native genius, and they should go solo and become superstars.
(The *vita* of Jean-Michel Basquiat, who could have been a character in "The Message"—an art star before he was twenty-five, dead
from a drug overdose before he was thirty—must have cast a long
shadow in their lives.) Many of these kids had hardly ever been
out of the Bronx, and they weren't ready for celebrity. For that
matter, Rollins himself, who had been out of the Bronx plenty—
he had grown up in Maine, graduated from the School of Visual
Arts, worked for Joseph Kossuth—wasn't ready for it either. (Is
any of us ready for fifteen minutes of American fame?) Some of
the kids went on to art schools and began artistic careers, and even
those who didn't stay with art learned some things about life that
have surely helped them grow up. But the company imploded.
Rollins is a great teacher of the wonder of art and the discipline of
art; he lacks the inner cynicism to be a guide through the circus of
art. K.O.S. was a splendid fusion of uptown and downtown, and it
was sad to see it mangled by its own success. But Rollins says
reports of its death are exaggerated: He is still there on Longwood
Avenue, the workshop is still open, they are still doing murals all
over the country, his senior class had 100 percent college accep-
tance last year. K.O.S. lives.

Another brilliant initiative, with a more tragic *denouement,* was
launched by the painter John Ahearn. Ahearn is a native of
Binghamton, a graduate of Cornell; his twin brother is the filmmaker Charlie Ahearn, director of *Wild Style.* John has gone
farther than any downtown artist I know in "going to the people":
He didn't just work in the South Bronx, but lived in it, all through

the 1980s and into the 1990s; like virtually everybody there, he became the victim of both random and intentional violence. Around 1980, he moved from downtown Manhattan to Walton Avenue near 171st Street, a dilapidated but lively neighborhood about a mile from Yankee Stadium. There he began to work with Walton Avenue native Rigoberto (Robert) Torres.

Together they developed what became a signature style. First they would take polaroid photos of people, to fix the details of what their subjects looked like. Then, after placing their subject on a pallet, they would pile on layer after layer of plaster, while the model breathed through a straw and prayed that it wouldn't break. (It never did.) From the cast they would make a bust or full-body sculpture, which one of them would paint. There are differences in their styles: Torres's faces are more monochromatic, Ahearn's more layered; Torres's faces suggest folk art, and (like much modern art) seem to want to look more primitive than they are; Ahearn's faces seem to want to look more archaic than they are (also a great tradition in modern art), time-travelling toward the Christian anguish of Tintoretto, Rembrandt, Van Gogh. In some ways their work evokes the Mexican muralists of the 1920s and 1930s, but the murals and frescoes of Rivera, Orozco, Siqueiros, and others tend toward aggressive flatness, while Ahearn's and Torres's works are especially striking in their exploration of depth. Together they cast and painted hundreds of figures, mostly neighborhood people, individually and in groups, posing or hanging out, talking or kissing, and many environmental friezes that adorn South Bronx walls. Among the most famous and most beautiful are *Double Dutch*, *Back to School*, and *We Are Family*. (Full disclosure: They also did me, while they were in residence at CCNY's art department in 1985. I'm part of a frieze of *CCNY People*, painted by Torres, mounted above the entrance to the college cafeteria. On bad days I go and look at my effigy, and I feel better.)

The catalogue of their 1991 Houston–Cincinnati–Honolulu show, entitled *South Bronx Hall of Fame*, contains many photographs of Ahearn and Torres working out on the street, in a festival atmosphere, caught up in creative rapture, at home at last. It's as if

Ahearn is telling us, "Behold! I went to the people, and it worked."
Look at the pieces, and the pictures, and you can see that, at least
for a while, it did. Some of the images suggest even more: There
is a series of photos of a multiple casting of what looks like a
Walton Avenue block party on a lovely summer day in 1985. Look
at the faces in the crowd, yearning to be cast or just marveling at
the work, and you could almost be in a Renaissance painting or a
movie scene where Jesus performs a miracle. Water into wine? Or
maybe loaves and fishes: The power of art creates enough for all.

In 1986, Ahearn, here working without Torres, won a city
competition for bronze sculptures to adorn a plaza in front of a
new Police Station, under the Jerome Avenue 'L' (the IRT Number
4), a couple of blocks from where he lived. The figures he chose
for this plaza, all neighborhood people he knew, were named
Corey, Raymond, and Daleesha: Corey with a boom box and a
basketball (he was configured as a homage to Radio Raheem in
Spike Lee's *Do The Right Thing*; he may have configured himself
this way), Raymond kneeling with his pit bull, and Daleesha on
her roller skates. The ensuing debacle has been vividly described
by Jane Kramer in her 1994 book *Whose Art Is It?* Ahearn didn't
seem to realize that some people wouldn't want statues of Corey,
Raymond, and Daleesha around because they didn't like *them*.
Alcina Salgado, a retired housekeeper who agitated against his
work, described Ahearn's subjects as "roof people." She offered
an arch definition: "There are people who go to school and people
who go to work, and then there are the people we find on the
roof."

Meanwhile, other people surfaced within the city bureaucracy
who had nothing to do with the neighborhood, but who attacked
Ahearn for having politically incorrect skin. Arthur Symes, an
assistant commissioner in the Department of Cultural Affairs,
delivered this verdict: "He's not of the community because he's
not black—it's simply that." On September 25, 1991, the bronze
figures were installed. Salgado, along with her daughter (B.A.,
Sarah Lawrence), stood on the plaza and denounced Ahearn, his
models, and his art. In Kramer's reconstruction of the day, Ahearn
tried to engage them in dialogue, but the more he tried to talk, the

more angrily they condemned him. Meanwhile, none of "the people" from his block stepped up to help him. (On the other hand, he didn't make any moves to mobilize defenders, though the South Bronx always was and still is full of them.) What seems to have happened next is that Ahearn decided that if "the people" could be so mad at him, then he was failing to communicate, and he must be in the wrong. He paid to have the statues taken down, and soon after he left the Bronx. Seven years later, the large pedestals are still empty.

Ahearn himself seems to have lived through this affair by framing it in starkly Christian terms: suffering, trial, ordeal, sacrifice. As he told the story to me on the phone in the early 1990s, this is the way he saw it: He believed that anyone who truly loved "the people" had to be prepared to give up everything else. His burden, but also his call, was to sacrifice something he loved nearly as much as he loved the people: his art. Now John has paid plenty of dues, and if a belief in the holiness of sacrifice helped him get over, then anybody who cares about him has to be glad. But anybody who cares about the Bronx has to see that a sacrifice of noble and dedicated people and their work is the last thing the Bronx needs.

One thing that magnifies the trouble here is misunderstanding of some big ideas: "the people," "the community." In many versions of this story, including Ahearn's own, there's a slippage between "people" and "*the* people." If even a few people are mad at Ahearn—and there's no evidence it was ever more than a few—he blames himself for trampling on a whole community. But this vision of the people's wholeness has more to do with mythology than with demography. In fact, like every modern city, the South Bronx is deeply divided within itself. In cities that have become poor and broken by urbicide, the divisions have become radical polarizations. When Salgado offers an instant analysis of the class structure that cleaves the South Bronx in two—"the people who go to school and the people who go to work" versus "the people you find on the roof"—this grim dualism rings true. You can see, from both his friezes and his Walton Avenue photos, how much John Ahearn loves the street and the people who spend much of their lives on it. So do I, and it's right to celebrate the modern city street as a primary source of creativity. But it's also true that cities today are full of people like the Salgados, who feel it's a matter of life and death to protect their children *from* the street—and they're right, too.

Another important fact of life that this sad affair reveals is the culture war among American blacks. John hoped to strike a friendly chord by casting Corey, the wannabee Raheem. He didn't grasp how terrifying a presence this large street person is to the people who live on Spike Lee's street. Arthur Symes may be able to help us see this. Symes, remember, was the black bureaucrat unearthed by Kramer who said John was the wrong man because he had the wrong color skin. But Kramer finds something else he says (she cites it on the same page) that may be more relevant here: "He saw John's pieces as monuments to everything he'd been trying to save his community from." Nobody seems to have asked Alcina Salgado her opinion of the rap music that would be the most likely sound to come out of Corey's boom box (as it came out of Radio Raheem's); but we can be pretty sure what that opinion would be. Spike Lee cuts corners a little when he has Raheem's boom box smashed by the one white man on his block; on any real block he would find plenty of black volunteers. For many black Americans, especially (though not only) kids, rap, and the street life that rap celebrates, is part of the solution; but for many others, especially their parents, it is part of the problem.

I've described this tragic conflict as a Bronx problem, a black problem, an art problem. But it's really a human problem. Are there any artists out there who can embrace both Corey–Raymond–Daleesha *and* the Salgados? Are there any *people* out there with the largeness of vision and spiritual depth to embrace them all? That would mean embracing not only the work-and-school people, and the street-and-roof people, but also the art people who try to embrace them both. Now, everybody loves Shakespeare, even four hundred years later, because we know he loved them all. After that, it's a pretty short list. (Should Jesus be on it? Karl Marx? Martin Luther King, Jr.? We could have interesting discussions about this, in the Bronx or in Manhattan.) Can we live in, can we even imagine, a city that includes them all? You can't hurry love, no, you just have to wait. But it helps if you have an idea of what you are waiting for.

If you walk or drive around the Bronx today, after a few years of being away, it looks like miracle or magic; if you didn't recognize streets and buildings, you could almost feel you were on a different planet. Many blocks are still empty and fenced off, but that expressionist dreamscape, those jagged haunting forms of ruins, are nearly gone. On block after block of the South Bronx, it is clear that Mayor Ed Koch's five-billion-dollar, ten-year plan for housing rehabilitation has been a tremendous success. (It is strange that Koch, so often a boastful man, never boasts about his housing rehabs. Has he moved so far to the right that he is embarrassed to be identified with the lives of the poor? Whatever the reason, these thousands of effective rehabs are his greatest political accomplishment, and he deserves credit, whether he wants it or not.)

The rebuilding of the Bronx has been incremental, but enormous. This overall feeling seems to be confirmed in sharply diminished crime—even those who are reluctant to admit that anything has changed finally concede that a lot fewer kids are shooting each other—and in improved public health and AIDS statistics. Political boss Raymond Velez is still bleeding the Bronx from his ever-thriving Hunts Point Multi-Service Center, just off Westchester Avenue; but, no thanks to him and his friends, the Bronx today seems to have a lot more blood than it did. Compared with the radical dualism that haunted Alcina Salgado, there seems to be a far more complex and highly differentiated social structure in place today. Almost insensibly, in barely a decade, the South Bronx has gone through a great leap, from apocalyptic horror to ordinary city life. There are no monuments of transformation; but after the nightmarish monumentality of the ruins, the absence of monuments may be a relief. Two of the short stories in "The Message"—the girl pushed in front of the train, the man stabbed through the heart—turn out, a decade later, to be stories of the Bronx itself. Like them, it has got "a brand new start," and it isn't so close to the edge anymore.

As the twentieth century ends, it looks like the South Bronx's seasons in hell are over. (We can't say for sure, but that's how it looks now.) Ironically, as the fires have abated, and the ruins have been rebuilt, it has become a less compelling subject for art. It isn't in the news very much. It doesn't signify the way it used to. You could say the Bronx has lost its aura. Should we be sad? I don't think so. For years, the Bronx existed in an urbicidal hell, over the edge. Art and artists were among the forces that helped it up and helped it get back into the flow of normal, ambiguous modern life. A great burst of creativity emerged from the Bronx's ruins, and it deserves remembrance and celebration.

What art is being created in the Bronx today? I can't say very well. It's hard to see, it's not on the street, it's not in your face. But don't doubt it's there. Although plenty of terrific art springs from desperation, I think most great art grows out of normal life. As the Bronx starts a new millennium, it will have a chance to nourish less desperate modes of creativity, and we can look forward to celebrating those.

Meanwhile, we can think about the Tower of Babel again. In Genesis 11, God is frightened by people's powers and undertakes to "confuse their language" so they won't be able to understand each other. Devoid of mutual understanding, they fight, the Tower crashes into ruins, and they "scatter . . . over the face of all the earth." But now, in the great cities of the modern world, they have come together again. What would happen if all the peoples who make up a modern city could understand each other? Then maybe, as God said, "nothing will be restrained from them, which they have imagined to do." Would it be the Garden City of Eden? That was how some people imagined the Bronx a hundred years ago. The urbicidal ruins that came to afflict American cities, the Bronx worst of all, felt like a savage destruction of that dream. And yet, its city of ruins turned out to be a place where, thanks to art, people coming from very different places started to talk together and work together and recognize each other in ways people had never quite done before. It will be a time before they can do all they imagine. But the power to imagine was itself an achievement. The ruins of the Bronx became a place where people could imagine modern life together afresh. We have to remember to celebrate that.

An earlier version of this essay was published in the exhibition catalog, Urban Mythologies: The Bronx Represented Since the 1960s, *The Bronx Museum of the Arts, 1999.*

New York Calling

Spirit is a power only by looking the negative in the face and living with it. Living with it is the magic power that converts the negative into being.

> Hegel, Preface to *The Phenomenology of Spirit*, 1807

My city of ruins / My city of ruins
Come on rise up! / Come on rise up!

> Bruce Springsteen, "My City of Ruins" from *The Rising*, 2002

When I was a child, about sixty years ago, the city's publicly owned radio station, WNYC, had a wonderful announcement that it would transmit every hour on the hour: "This is Station WNYC, New York City, where seven million people"—at some point in the early 1960s it became eight million—"live in peace and harmony, and enjoy the benefits of democracy." I was thrilled by this language; I can see now that it formed my first idea of New York.

My parents were too poor to have gone to college, but their talk was rich in ideas. We spent many weekends exploring New York's grand material structures—the Harbor (still thriving all through my childhood), the Statue of Liberty, great buildings, Times Square, Penn and Grand Central Stations, Central Park, the Brooklyn Bridge. We learned to love them, but also to see their human costs. From the deck of a ferry or a skyscraper, we would exclaim, "Wow!" Then my mother would say something like, "Isn't it beautiful? And don't forget, you can get here on the subway." And my father would say something like, "And don't forget who built this." Who? I would ask. Before long I knew the answer: "People we never heard of, who worked themselves to death." It was only later on that I realized they meant people *like them*, who worked themselves to death. But they were proud of the city that anonymous, exploited people like them had built. The bad deals they had got in their lives were mitigated by their pride in being part of "the greatest city in the world." The message on the air was a melody they could dance to. The New York they hoped to pass on to us was a real community, a place where the sadness of individual lives—and there was plenty—could be overcome by the glory and harmony of the whole.

When I left New York at the start of the 1960s to go to graduate school in England, I could hear the message till my ship, the *SS United States*, was well out on the sea. When I came back at the end of the 1960s to teach at City College and the City University of New York Graduate School, my message was gone. No one could remember when it went, or why. Nothing could bring it back.

I had no idea then how far my city of dreams had unraveled and how much more it was still going to come apart. But in fact, day after day, year after year, for thirty years and more, we were bombarded by visions of our city coming apart and falling down. "The disintegration of New York" became a media cliché, but it was rooted in real life. From 1968 till the early 1980s, literally thousands of buildings were burned down every year, and dense, lively neighborhoods all over the city morphed into enormous ruins. From the early sixties to the early nineties, the number of people killed almost quintupled, from around 500 homicides a year to more than 2,400 at the height of the crack wars. Nobody kept records of how many kids came apart, but anyone who worked with children could see. Sometime in the middle of the eighties, I invented a word, *urbicide*, "the murder of a city." Did I hope, then, that naming it would stop it? But it went on and on. The attacks on September 11, 2001, were the climax of a long wave—that's what historians call these things—that had been breaking and crashing against us for years.

For a generation, New York's ruins were its greatest spectacles. As many old, shabby buildings began to crumble, they were being

redlined by banks—"redline," a crucial word in the self-awareness of the 1970s—so that landlords on the wrong side of the line,
as most were, couldn't get bank loans to fix them up. As a result,
the buildings fell apart faster, landlords lost hope, and more and
more came to feel that their buildings were worth more dead than
alive. The result was a tremendous, protracted boom in arson,
with many people—especially kids and old people—killed in the
cross fire. All through the 1970s it happened in dozens of neighborhoods. But the biggest firestorm was in the South Bronx, not
far from where I grew up. At the start of the 1980s, I was finishing
a book on what it means to be modern. But I couldn't finish till I
had gone back to where I started. So I went back—the house I
grew up in was still there and still lived in, but the whole block
across the street had burned and crumbled and finally sunk into
the swamp that the whole neighborhood was built on. I spent
many lonely afternoons wandering through the ruins. What was I
looking for? I met fellow wanderers (and camera crews) from
countries that not so long ago had had formidable ruins of their
own: Germany, Poland, Japan. I met American photographers
and filmmakers, as obsessed as I.

These ruins went on and on, block after block, mile after mile,
year after year. Some blocks seemed almost intact, with live
people—but then look around the corner, and there was no
corner. The fire years created a new vocabulary and iconography.
Urban fires make great visuals—from horizons lit by lurid flames,
montages of buildings in different stages of disintegration, shards
of beds, tables, television sets, fragments of clothes (especially
children's clothes), the rubble and debris of people's lives. For
several years the *New York Times* carried a box that contained
addresses of buildings destroyed the previous day or night. I and
many people I knew always turned to the Building Box first, even
before the box scores: would our old homes be there?

Sometimes these images helped generate empathy and solidarity: These shattered fragments of people's lives could have been
ours. Sometimes they were used to support one of the great media
clichés of the 1970s: that the poor people of New York were inflicting this destruction on themselves. Many elected officials insisted

that the victims of the fires were also their perpetrators; hence they deserved no sympathy or emergency aid. A typical metaphor: The victims of fires are "fouling their own nests." The saddest thing about those "Blame the Victim" tirades was that so many victims—including many of my students and their parents—did blame themselves. Yet the one thing, the only thing they were to blame for, was being there.

After seeing life in New York unravel for years and years, I wasn't surprised by the near bankruptcy of 1975–1976. But the fact that I had felt it coming didn't make it any easier to be a hostage to people who prided themselves on their hate for us. For the first time since the heyday of the Vietnam War, I started watching the national news. One standard news clip then was a congressman going back to his home district and asking his constituents what should be done about New York. There was a standard tirade, and the news people were able to find plenty of people to deliver it, often while shaking their fists and grimacing for the camera: New York is a parasite, it contributes nothing to America, it is noisy and dirty, it is full of foreigners and disgusting sex, every kind of sinfulness, hippies and homos and commie degenerates, a blot upon America, and now God has given America the chance to rise up and destroy New York forever, wash it down the drain! One clip featured a congressman from a district that lived totally on federal money, with a naval base and a shipyard. He asked his constituents, "Should New York live or die?" They jumped to their feet, grinned obscenely at each other like the people in a classic lynch mob photo, and screamed, "Die! Die! Die! Die!"

Thirty years on, those screams still cut through me. Their primal power makes me wonder, did this really happen, or did I imagine or dream it? Maybe both.

That was the year of Gerald Ford's "drop dead" speech. He didn't actually say anything as honest as that. He merely said he would veto any congressional plan for aid, because "the American people" had no concern with the fate of New York. "Ford to City: Drop Dead" was the excellent paraphrase in the next day's New York *Daily News*. A photo showed Mayor Abe Beame reading the headline on the steps of City Hall. Beame displayed the page, looking both wounded and defiant. Whatever the federal government may do to us, he was telling the world, we won't go quietly. It was Beame's moment of glory: For just an instant he looked like John Garfield at the end of *Body and Soul*—or the way Garfield might have looked, had he lived—surrounded by creeps poised to crush him, blowing them off: "What are you gonna do, kill me? *Everybody dies.*"

"FORD TO CITY: DROP DEAD" is one of the all-time great newspaper headlines. It turned out to be also a superb consciousness-raiser. And it helped the city get the aid it needed. I figured that would happen: The billionaires in the GOP would get the word to the party's Sunbelt that all markets were integrated—the key word today would be "global"—and that crushing the biggest city in the country, and the biggest economy, could easily recoil against them. Those billionaires owned the GOP as well as the world, and I knew the White House would cave and sign on to the federal loans (at extortionate interest, of course) that New York needed to pay off its creditors; I knew the city would get something like what it got, an Emergency Financial Control Board, and the Board would get it back into the credit markets soon. (In fact, the Board turned out better than I thought: It was run by Felix Rohatyn, a financier who was also a liberal Democrat and who had the candor to admit, "We have balanced the budget on the backs of the poor.") I knew we would go back to something like business as usual. I even knew that Ford's "Drop Dead" speech would hurt him in the 1976 elections: There were plenty of people who shared his overall view of the world, yet who thought his nonchalance about wiping out New York showed a dangerous lack of judgment. I did my best to get this across to my students, so they could see the sky wasn't falling and relax a little. Still, it hurt to feel all that hate out there.

Sometimes, in the midst of the 1970s horror show, there were surprise happy endings. All through the 1970s, New York lost something like 2,000 buildings a year to fires; the biggest losses were in the Bronx. The fires felt like an inexorable force; year by year, they enveloped more and more respectable neighborhoods. Why would these people destroy their world? There was endless speculation, foundation grants, conferences. Nobody could quite get it right. The Left's explanation was brutally simple: The landlords did it (arson) and they did it for the money (fire insurance). An unusual alliance came into being to get this story out: the Fire Department, the insurance industry, and the New Left. The Mayor's Arson Task Force, established by John Lindsay, was the most radical agency in city government. Its reports dramatized ideas like "fire accelerants" (chemicals that New York Fire Department chemists found in about 90 percent of tenement fires) and "the ecology of fire" (which limited the damage if somebody came in ten minutes, but could wipe out a whole block if nobody came for half an hour); it made arson clear. Meanwhile, after suffering staggering losses, the insurance industry decided it had had enough, and all the major insurers resolved to stop paying claims on tenement fires. As if by magic, the fires stopped. In the last year of fire insurance, the Bronx lost about 1,300 buildings; in the first year of no fire insurance, it lost twelve. No money, no fires—the simple, crude explanation was totally right. Amazing! Moreover, the New York Left had won something. True, it was a limited, defensive victory, stopping something horrible from happening rather than starting something new. But putting fires out made real differences in many people's lives, and indeed made it possible for their lives to go on.

Meanwhile, the South Bronx, at its moment of greatest misery and anguish, and in some sense because of its misery and anguish, created the mass culture called Hip-Hop. Hip-Hop today envelops the whole world. I knew of no one in the 1970s who imagined that anything like this could happen. The kids of those neighborhoods in those days created because they had to; they couldn't help themselves, they couldn't stop. The Bronx above all became more culturally creative than it had ever been in its life. In the midst of dying, it went through rebirth.

You could say it started on the subways. The subways were probably drearier and scarier in the 1970s than at any time in their history. The stations were full of broken benches impossible to sit on, unfilled light sockets, long, dark shadows. The cars were old, painted battleship gray, and flaking away; many had been recalled from deep storage when a shipment of new cars had turned out to be dangerous and had to be withdrawn right away. Suddenly, hundreds of trains were drenched with aerosol-sprayed graffiti, saturated with luminous primary colors and exuberantly bold designs. Their graffitists, who worked mostly in crews, were happy to identify themselves and to be recognized. Most were black and Latin teenagers; most were boys, though a few of the best were girls; they came from all over the city, but from the South Bronx most of all. They were endlessly denounced by politicians and in the mass media, and repeatedly arrested. I even heard a neoconservative sociologist, a militant cold warrior, say he envied the USSR, where there was "no nonsense about the First Amendment" and where the state could simply arrest kids like these *en masse* and pack them off to labor camps. Thanks to America's nonsense about the First Amendment, New York's graffitists had room to breathe and to create an exuberant new visual language.

Two of the best died young: the painter Jean-Michel Basquiat (1960-1988), initially known for his street art under the tag SAMO, and the muralist Keith Haring (1956-1990), whose early work was done in the cavernous spaces of the Times Square subway station. But the great majority survived; they're still here. Many succeeded as serious painters; animators; and theatrical, fashion, and video designers. Looking at their life stories, we can see their graffiti years as first steps on a ladder upward and admire their resourcefulness in finding markets for themselves. But when the Bronx's graffitists began, they had more than self-marketing in mind: they saw themselves as citizens and insisted on the civic and public meaning of their work. Indeed, it was a shared desire to get out of their neighborhoods (in which many were already doing well) and to communicate with a larger public that made public transit so alluring. Civic spirit plunged them into a brutal, grueling, materially and humanly destructive conflict with an arrogant and unresponsive Metropolitan Transportation Authority. Later on, some of these kids had a chance to make money, and they made it. Within the private sector, they did fine. But it's crucial to remember that behind the private success, there was a public failure. And it wasn't the kids who failed.

Alongside New York's graffitists, and sometimes the same people, were the first generation of rappers. In the poorest congressional districts in the United States, rap was an exemplary *musica povera*. Like so much else, it started in the subway, with a single ragged and scrawny kid, backed by small speakers with a drum track, telling the story of his life. In the late seventies, at my school, City College of New York, during Club Hour on Thursday, somebody would bring out turntables, and a DJ would scratch and collage dozens of records together, while kids in the audience took turns playing MC, rapping over an open mike. (Some teachers rapped, too; I would have loved to, but I just couldn't rhyme.) I was delighted. What it meant for me was the power of the word, which was what I had been trying to teach all along. By the end of the seventies, rap was busting out all over. But a concentration of great DJs came from the South Bronx. They vied with each other in dozens of small clubs, parks, high school gyms and auditoriums, with thousands of active and participant young listeners. Together, they created a distinctive rap sound of samples, beats, and rhymes. That sound pervades, and maybe even defines, the globe today.

There will be more to say about rap as time goes by. I only want to say one thing now. "The Message" (1982), the first international rap hit, by Grandmaster Flash and the Furious Five, has a provocative quatrain that's in tune with my overall theme. People often miss this quatrain, which seems to drop from the sky:

> They pushed a girl in front of a train,
> Took her to the doctor, sewed her arm on again.
> Stabbed a man right through the heart,
> Gave him a transplant and a brand new start.

Hegel says that "spirit is a power only by looking the negative in the face and living with it." "Living with it is the magical power that converts the negative into being." Well, that's the message. In New York in the 1970s, this meant that social disintegration and existential desperation could be sources of life and creative renewal. A whole generation of kids from America's worst neighborhoods broke out of poverty, violence, and ghetto isolation, and became sophisticated New Yorkers with horizons as wide as the world. As The Clash in "London Calling" in 1979 affirmed that "London is drowning, I live by the river," these kids from the Bronx could tell the world not only that "We come from ruins, but we are not ruined," but that "We shall overcome." Their voices became the voice of New York Calling. Their capacity for soulmaking in the midst of horror gave the whole city a brand new aura.

New York feels like a very different place today. It has gone through spectacular population growth: It could reach nine million by 2010. It is more saturated with immigrants, more ethnically diverse and multicultural than it has ever been, more like a microcosm of the whole world—and thanks to New York's distinctively configured public space, you can see the whole world right out there on the street. Its mode of multiculturalism is sexy and threatening to the ultra-orthodox in every religion. Summer in New York is hot and humid—it is summer as I write—but great for bringing people together and for looking at them. Look at the colors and complexions of the men and women holding hands along Upper Broadway, on Queens Boulevard, at King's Plaza, and of the children they are pushing in their strollers: colors never seen under the sun. And today's sexiness coexists with safety. Over the last decade, not only homicide but all violent crimes have plummeted. The tremendous increase in violence that began in the late 1950s, and that for decades seemed inexorable, has been reversed. Our shared anxiety about world politics coexists with a remarkable sense of greater safety in our everyday lives. We are back to about 600 homicides a year, one-quarter of what it was in the crack-war early nineties. Who knows what made it happen or how long it will last? Nobody knows. But something is happening that I never imagined: We have a metropolitan life with a level of dread that is subsiding. Some people say they fear that a life without dread will lose its savor. I tell them not to worry. If they scrutinize their lives in any depth, they will find grounds for more than enough to keep them awake. While they're up, they should take a midnight walk.

Meanwhile, that immense expressionist dreamscape of ruin is nearly gone. I love the Bronx Zoo, but for years I didn't go, because I couldn't bear to ride the 'L' through the wreckage. Finally, early in the 2000s, I bit the bullet. My son Danny's class at P.S. 75 was making a class trip; they desperately needed parents; I wasn't teaching that spring day; and how could I say No. As we came into the Bronx, I prepared myself for the worst. I stood up, craned my neck, and—the ruins weren't there. In their place were ordinary buildings, parked cars, kids on bikes, trucks unloading, mothers with babies, people getting on and off buses, old people playing cards—the whole *shmeer* of modern city life. I turned to the teachers on the train with me, "Look, it looks like an ordinary city!" They said. "Well, isn't the Bronx an ordinary city?" They were young, still in their twenties; when the Bronx was burning, they weren't even born. Now, it looked like nothing much—and yet, a miracle.

What about the rest of the city? Downtown is more crowded, also more multinational and multicultural, more a real microcosm of the world. The big office buildings are full of workers from India, Russia, China, Japan. There is a tremendous overflow of tourists, staying in dozens of new hotels. Many New Yorkers resent their presence, but this is the greatest city in the world, so why shouldn't people want to come?

For most of my life I've enjoyed getting into conversations with strangers on the streets, especially around Times Square. I ask people where they are going and if they need help. One thing I've heard from many people recently is that they aren't going anywhere special, they're just walking around the streets—often they say they want to show the streets to their kids—and that they love the New York streets *"because they're so real."* I agree with them, and I'm glad they can see this and appreciate it. They are like all the Americans who after September 11, 2001, expressed such generous feeling and let their congressional representatives know they cared. But all this appreciation and friendliness are so different from the bad vibes that surrounded us only thirty years ago. Have we changed? I don't think so. Have they changed? I think they've changed a lot more. America has been steadily filling up with immigrants for the last forty years (after being closed for the forty years before), and people around the country are far less frightened than they used to be by human diversity: Demographically, the rest of America has become more and more like New York. At the same time, environmentally, America has become more and more of a suburban car culture, without streets, without places where people can walk around and have random experiences and interact with strangers. New York is a different environment: If you look up to the top of the buildings, it is brand new, but at the level of the street, it is a couple of hundred years old, rooted in the Paris and London of the Enlightenment. It keeps alive and nourishes the intensely interactive aura of the modern street—a place where people could experiment with their being, being both themselves and each other, and where a walk around the block could feel like both a brothel and a holy communion. Even the rich and famous today are likely to go through their lives starved of vital energies that any ordinary New Yorker on the street can enjoy. Compared with New York, the environments where most Americans grow up feel unreal. In the past generation, many more Americans have come to feel this and to love our city for what it is and what their suburbs are not. Do New Yorkers know how rare and precious it is to be loved for what you are? We should enjoy it while it lasts.

But the ironies keep on rising with the buildings. There is the price of love—just because the whole world wants to be in New York, New York has become impossibly expensive to be in. This seems to go with being a "global city," along with London, Paris, Tokyo, Rio, L.A., D.C., and a few more—it's a small club; and for a global city, the word is that New York is cheap. The papers feature articles on the frantic construction of luxury housing in Manhattan: So many churches have generated modern miracles, transforming "air rights" into gold mines. Twice as many corporate headquarters are here today as were here in 1990. So many neighborhoods have accelerated from abandonment to gentrification in what feels like ten seconds or less. People who worked through the darkest years are crushed by their own success. As they see their streets on the front page of the real estate section, they feel both swollen with pride and stabbed with dread.

One of New York's primary sources of pride, for at least a century, has been its superabundance of small book, music, and art shops, which have done so much to keep the city's cultural life close to the street. These little palaces of culture have nourished and enriched the city's sense of place, empowered New Yorkers to feel like citizens of both the street and the world. But in a rising real estate market, they are all under fire. Their very success in bringing people together often encourages landlords to demand rent increases that will doom them. Every month, it seems, another beloved culture shop is forced to close, and thousands of New Yorkers feel more vulnerable and alone. You could even argue that, for any New Yorker in the 2000s, the sense of being under fire is central to the sense of being at home.

Two or three years ago I saw the headline, "The Bowery Lives Again," and I knew at once that my favorite Bowery life sign, the punk rock club CBGB, was doomed. CBs was one of New York's freest voices in the city's worst days. It had nurtured a great generation of rockers and a great audience. It had come proudly through the crash; but could it survive the boom? On October 16, 2006, the news said it was gone. The landlord was no real estate shark, but an agency that helped homeless people. Patti Smith played its last set. She said the closing was "a symptom of our city's empty new prosperity." But she added, "There's new kids with new ideas all over the world. They'll make their own places, here or wherever." She told the *New York Times*, "The Internet will be their CBGB." Is Smith ready to resign from real places, in favor of cyberspace? Can she, or anybody, make the Net "their own"? We'll have to see.

If I were forty years younger and yearning to come to New York, high on brains and imagination but low on capital, could I come here? Well, yes and no. There would be no way I could afford the Upper West Side—or anywhere else in Manhattan. Very few of us could afford the West Side if we had to pay market prices to be here now. That's the bad news. The good news is that today's younger generation has learned to explore the city as a whole with a zeal and energy and resourcefulness that my generation, obsessed with Manhattan alone, never even dreamed of. They've missed the delightful experience of living in Manhattan in their youth, and I can't blame them if they are mad; I'd be mad in their place. Still, they can get here on the subway, and they do. Meanwhile, their New York is a lot fuller than ours; they have opened up a city horizon far wider than anything we could imagine. It's amazing, in their New York, there's so much more there.

In the spring of 2006, I gave a reading at a Hispanic Cultural Center in Mott Haven, in the South Bronx, in a small brownstone, just behind the giant neon "H" sign of the History Channel. In the 1970s and 1980s, this house had been just about reduced to rubble; in the 2000s, it was still in the midst of rebuilding. The generation of kids who create new centers like this is making small-"h" history, and making the city's post-1898 official name, "Greater New York," mean something real. They are reinventing New York's immense horizon, its capacity to include the whole world. But they are also facing the city's vulnerability and inner destructiveness. They are "looking the negative in the face and living with it." They are converting the negative into being. By affirming the ruins, they are making the rising possible. Theirs is the most authentic voice of "New York Calling" now.

This essay was the introduction to New York Calling, *edited by Marshall Berman and Brian Berger, Reaktion Books, 2007. This version appeared in* Dissent, *Fall 2007.*

Part IV

Jay Talking

The Dancer and the Dance

An apparition floated by me on Upper Broadway not long ago: a girl in a red T-shirt that displayed, on and around her breasts, a group of Karl Marxes, about four or five of them, in a semicircle, arms linked, smiling broadly, kicking their legs high in a rousing dance. This delightful vision turned out to be real: After I'd backtracked a block and caught up with the girl, she told me that it was the emblem of U.R.P.E., the Union for Radical Political Economics. That shirt can tell us something about what has happened to Marx in the America of the 1970s. First of all, everybody seems to have accepted the existence of many Marxes: No party, movement, or country has a monopoly on his thought. Second, these many Marxes seem to be coexisting rather well—a nice surprise, for weren't they only yesterday at one another's throats, each insisting that the others weren't really Karl Marx at all? Finally, they are coming together in an activity that's expressive, playful, even a little vulgar—an activity that would have been considered most un-Marxian not long ago. Today's Marxes have kept in touch with their youthful romantic visions of politics as dancing.

The cultural leap that made this dance possible was first assayed on a mass scale about twenty years ago, when Marx's unpublished essays and notes of 1844 were translated into all major European languages—they are generally known in English as the *Economic and Philosophical Manuscripts*—and published by Moscow in cheap editions for a large public. The central idea of these youthful essays was "alienation." The trouble with capitalism, it said here, was that it alienated people from one another, from nature, and—here is where Marx was most original—from themselves: from their senses, their emotions, their imaginative powers, from "the free development of their physical and spiritual energies." Marx focused on work as a primary source of meaning, dignity and self-development for modern man; the bourgeois organization of labor was a crime against these human needs. But Marx also wrote lyrically about sexual love and about its perversion by the power of money; about history as the unfolding education of the five senses and the ways in which that education had gone awry; about the material roots of the widespread modern sense of spiritual rootlessness. These essays, coming out in the midst of the greatest capitalist boom in history (1959 in the United States), provided a searing indictment of capitalism even at its most triumphant. At the same time, Marx's critique cut just as deeply into Stalinist communism—there was even a model of a "crude, mindless communism" that Marx feared as a regression from capitalism—from the perspective of communism's own ultimate values.

The young Marx was condemned, of course, by the ideological commissars of the various communist parties, and by their right-wing equivalents in the United States. But Marxism had gained, or regained, a sensual warmth and a spiritual depth that all the Sidney Hooks and all the Althussers could not take away. The spirit of the young Marx animated the radical initiatives of the 1960s, from Berkeley to Prague; and even when political energy was crushed, as in the East, or when it dissipated itself, as in the West, this spirit survived. Even after a barren decade, today's Marxes can dance.

If Marx's early writings are no longer so central to his reputation as they were, say, a decade ago, this is mostly because their lessons have been learned, their themes and energies assimilated into our sense of his work as a whole. But there is one vital area in which our perspective on Marx has not deepened at all: the study of his life. Many works have appeared over the years that have examined his life with increased political acuteness and philosophical sophistication. Almost without exception, however, these biographies have been emotionally flat, spiritually arid, psychologically remote. If we compare the current state of Marx studies with Edmund Wilson's magnificent *To the Finland Station* (1940), we will find that we have a far deeper understanding of Marx's ideas, and yet, if anything, rather less of a feeling for the emotions at the heart of those ideas.

In this context, Jerrold Seigel's new book, *Marx's Fate: The Shape of a Life*, should be welcomed very warmly. Seigel brings us, in many crucial ways, closer to Marx than we have ever been. He captures the desperate intensity and volatility of Marx's inner life, the exhausting anxieties that kept his mind inexhaustibly alive. I should say at once that the book has its problems: Seigel never makes up his mind whether he is writing a psychoanalytical "Young Man Marx" or a full-scale intellectual and political biography; hence he lurches uneasily between genres, changes gears at high speeds, frequently loses touch with his overall aims, gets lost in endless exposition and paraphrase, and writes a book that is twice too long. In other ways, though, the book is too short: It omits crucial aspects of Marx's life, even at the moments that concern Seigel most; it circles obsessively around a very limited number of themes and wholly omits other motifs that are at least as urgent and fruitful; it gives little sense of the expansiveness of Marx's mind. Nevertheless, *Marx's Fate* puts us in touch with much of Marx's deepest thought and feeling, and reveals the history of his ideas as a history of the most radical self-contradiction, as one of the great inner dramas of modern times.

Seigel thrashes around for the first couple of chapters, and it isn't clear for a while what the book's focus is going to be. He is clearly frustrated in writing about Marx's childhood: Neither he nor anyone else has found much solid material to build on here. Seigel takes off at the point where Marx begins to take off, in his late teens, when he is getting ready to leave home for the first time to attend university and choose a vocation. Now, suddenly, Seigel and his readers find themselves flooded with material. Marx at this point was just beginning to overwhelm people with his volcanic intellectual power and frightening himself and his loved ones as to what was going to become of that power.

Like many highly gifted adolescents whose brilliance at once amazes and frightens those around them (today we should have to include their therapists), Marx overflowed with endless fantasies and myths, models, and conceptualizations about himself: Prometheus, of course; but also Faust, and his demonic pact; the philosopher Democritus, who supposedly put out his eyes so he could see ideas in their full clarity; Karl Moor, Schiller's robber-hero, who tears down half the world but yearns only for his father's blessing; Hölderlin's Hyperion, racked with inner darkness amid Greek sunlight; Rameau's nephew, with what Hegel called "the disintegrated consciousness"; specters of suicide (on which Seigel has unearthed an early essay) and madness. Part of the problem for Seigel, as for any therapist working with gifted adolescents today, is to figure out which of the subject's marvelous imaginative constructs are essentially screens and which are for real; the more brilliant the subject, the more ingenious the disguises are apt to be, and the harder and more elusive will be the analyst's work.

What Seigel considers real for Marx is, above all, his relationship with Hegel. This relationship is familiar enough as an organizing principle in Marx studies. But Seigel isn't really interested in Marx's criticism or transformation of Hegelian ideas. Instead, he wants to look at the history of social thought in much the same way that Harold Bloom, in *The Anxiety of Influence* (1973) and *A Map of Misreading* (1975), has approached the history of modern poetry: as an arena in which primal emotions, for the most part Oedipal ones, can be expressed, fought out, and sometimes worked through. Thus Seigel's Marx confronts Hegel more as a demon than a doctrine, a totemic figure that must be fought and overcome: this Marx strives incessantly to expel the demonic force, both from his own mind and from Western culture, only to find himself again and again in need of its sustenance, or else to have it creep up on him unawares, like Freud's return of the repressed.

Marx's relation to Hegel is so complex and agonized, Seigel argues, because it is infused with all the energy and agony of Marx's relationship with his father. The Marxes, like many an intellectual family then and now, seem to have mythicized their emotions and fought out their deepest emotional conflicts in intellectual and ideological terms; then as now, the intellectual language may both articulate and conceal what is really going on. In any case, both Marx and his father Heinrich twisted Hegel into a mythical figure that had less to do with Hegel's works than with the Marx family's desires and fears. For both father and son, in the 1830s, Hegel seems to have symbolized a life of narcissistic ecstasy: the thinker's temptation to build up a self-subsistent world of inner life and activity, cut off from the material world, from people and human feeling, but radiant with joy and a sense of magical power that no reality could give.

In fact, this temptation and danger, inherent in the activity of contemplation, are as old as the history of ideas. Plato's version—the visionary philosopher who dreads returning to the cave of normal human life—is already a relatively late one. Meditative and mystical circles, like the Jewish cabalists, have always sought to guard against the allure of disembodiment. The Romantics were especially tempted and endangered by it, as readers of Coleridge and Hölderlin know well. Seigel does nothing to put this strange longing in historical or psychological perspective—its full history has never even been attempted—but he does a great deal to show how crucial it was for Marx. For the adolescent Marx, Seigel argues (and illustrates abundantly), there was something intensely seductive about this vision of life; his reason and conscience condemned it as sterile and empty—if not, indeed, insane—but his desire to submerge himself in pure thought was too deep for mere reason or conscience or sanity to erase.

This temptation, and the guilt it provoked, form the context for a fascinating and crucial exchange of letters between Marx and his father in 1837, when he was nineteen years old and studying in Berlin. Marx's father, who has always been warm and affectionate toward his son, suddenly turns on him with a torrent of hysterical fears. "Sometimes," Heinrich Marx writes, "my heart revels in thoughts of you and your future. And yet, I cannot rid myself of ideas that raise a presentiment of fear, when like lightning the thought closes in: does your heart correspond to your head . . .?" He fears that his son's heart does not "beat in a purely human way," and that instead Karl is possessed by a "demonic spirit" that "estranges your heart from finer feelings." Should his son take the dark road that looms ahead of him, he would see "the finest aim of my life in ruins."

What was eating this normally loving and supportive father? What possessed this Voltairian rationalist to start raving about demon possession? What did Marx do to deserve this? Nothing so far as we can tell; and this may have been the trouble: he wasn't doing anything to choose a profession, to settle down to work for family (he had just proclaimed his love for Jenny von Westphalen, the girl who would be his wife) and humanity; all he wanted to do at this point was to read, to speculate, to develop his mind as an end in itself. An innocent pursuit, most of us would think, for a youth of nineteen. In the terms of the family mythology, however, innocence equals temptation—indeed, in a sense, equals guilt: The young thinker enjoying his mind's powers is in fact being tempted by inner demons—the specter of Hegel first among them—that would spirit him forever away. Heinrich must have seen his curses as desperate attempts to drive them out.

This must have been unbearably painful for Marx, not only because he loved his father and felt endlessly obligated to him but also, as we will see, because he wholly shared the mythology from which his father's fears sprang. We see this in a long letter of a few months later, in which, alternately proud and abject, lyrical, explosive, and semi-delirious, Marx substantiates his father's worst fears: he has gone over to Hegel. This famous letter (November 10, 1837) reads, in its central narrative, like a conventional account of religious conversion: dejection, melancholy, physical and mental wasting away; then, at the nadir of negativity, a sudden infusion of light, a renewal of life and energy, a rededication of all the self's powers; finally, a plea for understanding and sympathy from the loved one, an affirmation of faith that everything can be made clear and the two of them can live in harmony once again. This drama, enacted by so many of us in our own adolescent years (or later), is deeply moving when we watch Marx go through it. And yet, interwoven with this archetypal experience of human growth, we find strands of stranger feeling, permeated with the Marx family's peculiar mystique.

Karl's conversion took place, he says, in the midst of a lovely but anguished moonlit night. He had begun a dialogue on nature and God, and given himself up to the inner movements of his mind, when suddenly an unconscious current carried him away: "This darling child of mine [his dialogue?], nurtured in moonlight, bears me like a false-hearted siren into the clutches of the enemy." There are so many dimensions of meaning here: the language of sexual temptation and infidelity, seduction and betrayal, with Marx as a not wholly unwilling victim; the erotically charged radiance of ideas, intensely alluring but, like the sirens, lethal; the equivalence of woman (siren) and child, and the strong ambivalence toward them both, and toward their almost supernatural pull (the moon) on Marx's self; finally, Marx's way of placing himself in the same relationship to his father—beautiful but weird and dangerous child—that his uncontrollable thoughts bear to himself. In this remarkable sentence, Marx sees himself simultaneously as seducer and seduced, guilty and innocent, male and female, parent and child. He then pleads for his father's understanding—at a point where it is not at all clear that he understands himself—and guiltily affirms his undying love. He begs for a chance to come home—had his father forbidden him to come, or is he merely asking for carfare?—so that "I can clasp you in my arms and tell you all I feel"; then, maybe, "the clouds that hang over our family will lift." Finally, foreshadowing the most famous image of Marx's mature years, "I shall not be able to lay aside the spectre that haunts me until I am in your dear presence." Six months later, Heinrich Marx was dead.

Seigel's treatment of this crucial episode shows both the strength and the weakness of *Marx's Fate*. Its strength lies in its feeling for the emotional intensity, conflict, and anguish that underlie Marx's ideas; its weakness, in its inability to keep these searing emotions in focus. Seigel surmises, plausibly enough, that Marx must have been deeply haunted by guilt when his father died. But he tells us nothing about how Heinrich actually died; about where Karl was when he died; about what transpired between them in the interval between the letter and the death—did Karl ever make it home, did he get his chance to clasp his father to his breast and share his

deepest feelings?; about how Karl responded concretely to
Heinrich's death—what he said, what he did—for surely he must
have expressed something to somebody. Given the psychological
intensity of the book up to now, this is a great disappointment:
Seigel's Marx becomes vague and recedes from our vision at
exactly the moment when he should be coming really close. Seigel
has gotten caught up in the language and mythology of Marx's
self-constructions, just where he should be deconstructing the
myths and showing us the man himself.

Although Seigel remains excessively entangled in Marx's many
webs, he is perceptive and often brilliant in penetrating their intri-
cacies and depths. He argues that, emotionally (unconsciously),
Marx equated the solid material world with his father, and with his
own sense of filial obligation; his desire to immerse himself in a
world of pure thought expressed a kind of Oedipal will-to-power,
the power to create a world of ideal freedom beyond his father's
reach. Thus, even though Marx would criticize German Idealism
as a conservative ideology, Idealism remained his own mode and
symbol of personal rebellion. Materialism, though he portrayed it
as politically radical, was for him emotionally conservative, a way
back to the father he had denied. The dialectical fusion of materialism and idealism, which Marx first imagined in his "Theses on
Feuerbach" (1845, when he was 27), was also a symbolic emotional
reconciliation between father and son, between his adolescent
desire for total freedom and his father's insistence on the ties that
bound him to this world. This psychological synthesis enabled
Marx to come into his own—in the language of Erik Erikson, it
enabled him to resolve the problem of his identity. His genius
enabled him to sublimate his personal dialectic to a world perspective—a perspective that sheds brilliant light on the mixtures of
autonomy and constraint that define our lives and that dramatizes
our need for a world in which we can fulfill ourselves with and
through one another—and so, to become the world-historical
man we know.

  One of the primary powers in Marx's synthesis seems to have
been sexual love. Biographers have noted, as even police agents

noted, that Karl and Jenny Marx had, despite much turbulence and suffering, a passionate and joyous marriage, sustained for forty years, ending only in death. Indeed, Marx is one of the very few great thinkers in all history to have enjoyed a happy marriage and family life. Seigel shows how sexual love played a vital part in the formation of his identity, helping to liberate Marx from psychic isolation and center him in the real world. Marx thought and wrote a great deal about sexual love in the mid-1840s, just after his marriage, when he was trying to fulfill his father's ideal of a life with people. Note the basis on which, in 1845, he would reject German Idealism: He remarks derisively that this philosophy and "the study of actuality" have "the same relation to each other as masturbation and sexual love." This is the image of a man self-confident in his newly fulfilled adult sexuality. He passes the same cruel judgment on a rejected mode of thought as on a discarded mode of sexual life: Both are masturbatory, outgrowths of a solitary, barren self-absorption; he has outgrown them both, he feels, and grown into a healthier and more mature mode of thought— "the study of actuality"—which, like sexual love, reaches out and embraces other people.

And yet, even here, specters haunt him. We can faintly see the shadow in another remark about love from this period: It is love, Marx says, that "first teaches man to believe in the objective world outside himself." A lovely image; and yet, imagine how deep a man's inner isolation must be for him to need such a proof! It should be easy to understand why, under the pressures of this psychic undertow, Marx should need an inner ballast to hold him to this world.

Sexual love could fulfill a vital part of this need. But materialist thought, which Marx also embraced in the mid-1840s, seems to have served the same purpose. Hence the sense of intense exhilaration and relief that animates Marx's first materialist manifestoes: "One has to leap out of philosophy, and devote oneself like an ordinary man to the study of actuality"; "as history moves forward, [intellectuals] . . . have only to take note of what is happening before their eyes, and to become its mouthpiece"; and, of course, "the philosophers have only interpreted the world, in various ways; the point, however, is to change it." It is as if a crushing burden had been lifted from Marx's soul, so that he might live in the real world "like an ordinary man" at last. But there is also something unsaid and disturbing beneath the surface. Marx's project sounds remarkably like Kierkegaard's "leap of faith," with which it is exactly contemporaneous. There is an aura of religious renunciation here: Marx seems to be hoping that he will never have to think another thought; the forward movement of history, he thinks, will do his thinking for him, and he will need only to speak for it.

Seigel argues that Marx's leap, rooted in his inner need for ballast, made a certain kind of sense in the Eastern Europe of the late 1840s. This was a time when everyone, regardless of philosophy or politics, believed that material forces were moving toward a final polarization and confrontation that, whatever the outcome, would decisively resolve everyone's fate. Not only the *Communist Manifesto*, but equally the 1848 writings of Tocqueville, Herzen, Baudelaire, and a hundred lesser figures—indeed, everyone who lived through these years—are full of the imagery of veils and masks being stripped away and of social forces revealing themselves in their naked truth. What made the defeats of 1848–51 so dreadful for Marx and his generation was not merely the repression and mass murder—this was to be expected from the Party of Order—but the mysterious, even bizarre character of the new social formations. The mystery seemed deepest in France, where reality had once seemed so clear: the Second Empire, a strong centralist state that repressed bourgeois liberalism as much as proletarian socialism, that stood above all classes and exploited them all.

The defeats of 1848–51 shattered Marx's life, not only politically and economically but psychologically as well. In exile, unconnected, unemployed (except for intermittent journalism, often brilliant and original, but often underpaid or not paid at all), hounded by the police, Marx was more than ever thrown back on himself and the dangerous dynamisms of his inner life. And yet, Seigel argues, in the depths of his solitude, Marx was saved by a return of the repressed. He rediscovered the power of pure thought: His conceptual and theoretical powers, which he had dreamed of putting to sleep, now came marvelously awake and brought him a new and fruitful life. He renewed his inner links with his Hegel and his strengths as a philosophical thinker. He accepted the mysterious nature of post-1848 capitalism and the mystery of his (and so many other people's) isolation in its midst, and he concentrated all his inner resources on penetrating beneath its surfaces and plumbing its depths. In searching out the hidden structures and dynamics of capitalism, Marx came into touch with buried sources of energy and dynamism within himself. Thus a traumatic isolation prepared the ground for a series of new syntheses and triumphs, from *The 18th Brumaire of Louis Bonaparte* to *Das Kapital*.

The Hegelian conceptual structure of *Capital* has been known since the 1920s, when it was unveiled by Lukacs and Korsch. Seigel is original in showing that structure's psychological foundations—and in showing, too, its terrible human costs. First of all, just as Heinrich Marx had feared in the 1830s, the part of Karl's nature that pulled him toward Hegelian pure thought also pulled him away from the material world, from human feelings, from the people who loved and needed him most. Thus, while Jenny and the children starved and suffered dreadfully for fifteen years (circumstances eased up only in the late 1860s), Marx largely withdrew from responsibility for their material and human needs, to wrestle in solitude with ultimate ideal truths. ("When you, poor little devil, have to go through the bitter reality"—he writes this to Jenny as she is fighting off landlords, grocers, bailiffs—"it is no less than just that I live through the torture at least ideally." Thus he complacently cordons off his wife to deal with reality on her own while he floats freely, though perhaps not happily, in the sphere of the ideal.)

Second, his flight from material reality led him cruelly and systematically to wreck his own health: As much damage as he did to his loved ones, he probably did even more to himself. (Maybe, unconsciously, he was punishing himself for punishing them.) Third, his immersion in thought often alienated him from the human realities that his thought was meant to grasp; hence, Seigel argues, especially in the later parts of *Capital*, Marx's thought turned increasingly in on itself and became hopelessly uncommunicative; the deeper he delved, the closer he came to drowning in his own material. Fourth, especially in his last years, Marx drove himself and everyone around him crazy by his refusal to finish *Capital*. "I had to use every moment in which I was capable of working in order to complete my book, to which I have sacrificed my health, my happiness and my family." Marx wrote this in 1867, just as volume one was about to appear; but he would keep making these sacrifices for another sixteen years, indeed till the moment he died. Engels, Jenny, their daughters, all Marx's friends, urged him to let the work go, accept its imperfections and incompleteness, let it take its chances and do its work in the world; but he held on for dear life, plunging ever deeper into its dialectics, refusing to give it up until, somehow, its ideas would resolve and realize themselves.

Seigel is inexhaustible in generating ideas about Marx's life and his work and the connections between them. Sometimes his conjectures seem arbitrary and forced, and occasionally—as in dealing with Marx's mother, the most elusive figure in the story—gratuitously bitchy. But the overall level of his intuitions and speculations is impressively high, and *Marx's Fate* is full of fruitful suggestions for future working through. Sometimes, however, even where Seigel is doing well, we wish he would stop. He tends to do what he shows Marx doing: drown in his material. It is a measure of the book's peculiar power that this reviewer, too, feels himself pulled under with them.

This is a pity, because *Marx's Fate* would have twice its impact if it were half its size. Instead of trying to cover everything and prove everything, Seigel should have presented his vision as clearly and vividly as possible, and let it run on its own power. It would have gone far, because as an intellectual vision it is very impressive. It reveals the isolation and anguish that were interfused with Marx's most radical creativity. It explains why Marx so often tried to represent this thought—and, indeed, thought in general—as a passive mouthpiece for material forces; but it also makes clear what a desperate and pathetic piece of wishful thinking this was. It shows Marx as one of the great tormented giants of the nineteenth century—alongside Beethoven, Goya, Tolstoy, Dostoevsky, Ibsen, Nietzsche, Van Gogh—who drive us crazy, as they drove themselves, but whose agony generated so much of the spiritual capital on which we all still live.

Seigel is brilliant, then, in illuminating Marx's shadows. In at least one place, however, he sees more shadows than are really there. For Seigel, the great tragedy of Marx's life was his inability to finish *Capital*. He likens Marx to the hero of a Balzac story that Marx loved, "The Unknown Masterpiece." Balzac's hero, recognized universally as one of the great painters of his age, buries himself in his studio for thirty years to create a work that will not only be surpassingly beautiful—that, for him, would be nothing new—but will revolutionize all art. Finally, his peers win admission to his studio—and are horrified by what they see: The canvas has been so endlessly reworked, and overlaid with so many layers of paint, and so many different ideas, that it is utterly unintelligible. In one corner of the canvas a human foot is visible, a vestige of the original inspiration, radiantly beautiful, but enveloped and overwhelmed by chaos. This, Seigel seems to say, is Marx's own story. (He doesn't take us to the end of the story, in which the old painter, finding his vision meaningless to others, burns all his works and perishes in the flames.)

But there is a whole other layer of meaning in "The Unknown Masterpiece," ignored by Seigel, but profoundly relevant to Marx. Balzac's description of the old man's great work is in fact a perfect description of a twentieth-century abstract painting. The fact that Balzac could not have known this only gives it a deeper resonance. The point is that, where one age sees only chaos and incoherence, a later or more modern age may discover meaning and beauty. Thus the very open-endedness of Marx's later work can make contact with our time in ways that more "finished" nineteenth-century writing cannot; *Capital* reaches beyond the well-made

works of Marx's century into the discontinuous modernism of our
own.[1]

It is worth noting that, in volume one of *Capital*, Marx plays
with the idea of an ending, makes us think he's bringing us to an
ending, only to shift and surprise us at the last moment. The
would-be ending comes in Chapter 33, "The Historical Tendency
of Capitalist Accumulation." Here we find, in its most compressed
and dramatic form, a scenario for the developing inner contradictions of capitalism, leading to proletarian revolution and bourgeois collapse. Increasingly, "the monopoly of capital becomes a
fetter" on the modern forces of production that capital has brought
into being. "The centralization of production and the socializa-
tion of labor reach a point at which they become incompatible
with their capitalist husk. The husk is burst asunder. The knell of
capitalist property sounds. The expropriators are expropriated."
A fine dramatic climax, and a perfect moment, we might think, at
which to end the book. And yet, although the end is a mere ten
pages off, Marx suddenly takes us off into a whole new metamorphosis of capital: Chapter 33, "The Modern Theory of
Colonization," or how capitalism transplants itself into virgin soil
and envelops the whole undeveloped world. As we fade out, we
see capital, having torn the American continent to pieces, girding
itself to do the same to Australia. The dramatic impact is stunning:
It brings us down from the apocalyptic heights of Chapter 33,
back into the real world in which, while we were out fantasizing
about its end, capital was busy accumulating more capital.

---

1   Even within the terms of the nineteenth century, we can ask—as men of
the nineteenth century themselves asked—whether many conventional
endings didn't hurt more than they helped. Think of that Radio City Music
Hall chorus at the end of *Faust*, dissipating all its human intensity; of
Raskolnikov sitting on a Siberian river bank and suddenly seeing the light—
but don't ask, dear reader, what that light was; of the mountains of junk/shit/
money that dominate the world of *Our Mutual Friend* getting simply carted
away—but don't ask where they went; of Tolstoy at the end of *War and Peace*
doing his best to obliterate not only our experience but his own achievement.
If we think of works and endings like these—and it would be easy to think of
many more—the absence of an ending might not be such a bad idea after all.

We should be able to see, now, how absurd it would have been for Marx to finish his great work: How can *Capital* end while capital lives on? To stop simply and abruptly, rather than create an ending, preserves far more of the truth that *Capital* has to tell; Circling, spiraling, plunging one way and another, turning in upon himself, seeking endlessly for new axes to turn on, Marx kept his thought and his work as open-ended, and hence as resilient and long-lived, as the capitalist system itself. This is why we are still only beginning to explore the depths of Marx's thought; why he speaks to us in a voice fresher than ever today; why he will be dancing up Broadway when we are all dead.

Seigel does not see all this, but he sees so much that his work deserves our warmest admiration. *Marx's Fate* helps us understand how modern social thought, as much as modern poetry and art, is at once an expression of personal loneliness and an attempt to overcome that loneliness. Once we can feel the depths of Marx's solitude and his need for connections with people and life, we will appreciate his achievement in creating real bonds between man and man. In the depths of Marx's spirit, we can nourish our own.

This essay first appeared as "Marx: The Dancer and the Dance" in the Nation, *Janurary 27, 1979.*

Still Waiting at the Station

None of the eulogies for Edmund Wilson has mentioned what seems to me his most splendid achievement: to have written the last great nineteenth-century novel. *To the Finland Station: A Study in the Writing and Acting of History* originally appeared in 1940, and it was hailed generally as a sensitive, exciting history of the modern radical movement that reached its climax (or, at least, one of its climaxes) in the Bolshevik Revolution. Now, a generation after, we have a new edition, and an occasion to reappraise the book in the context of a new age, and I want to argue that it is far more original and more powerful than its first generation of readers could have known. Its virtues are so striking now because they are virtues that are not merely absent, but virtually forgotten, in both the fictional and the nonfictional writing of today.

The first thing that strikes us about *To the Finland Station* today, as soon as we are a little way into the book, is the breathtaking vastness of its scope. It takes in the whole of Europe and America, over the course of a century and a half. It cuts back and forth, effortlessly, from Vico's Naples to Babeuf's Paris to Brook Farm to Marx's London to Trotsky's Petersburg. It is easily, equally at home in the philosopher's study, in the prisoner's cell, on the steppes, in the streets, melancholy in great country houses, choking in fetid industrial slums—and it brings all these worlds vividly home to us. It interweaves philosophy, sociology, psychobiography, literary criticism, economic analysis, political history and theory, always in complex and sophisticated ways—and yet, for all this, the human narrative hardly ever flags, but sweeps us breathlessly along.

And the characters! An inexhaustible cast of brilliant, exciting, driven, beautiful, heroic, demonic people—Marx and Engels, Babeuf, Michelet, Proudhon, Bakunin, Saint-Simon, Fourier, Robert Owen, Lassalle, Lenin and Trotsky, and many more—at first they seem larger than life, but by and by we learn to live on their scale. And not only the great figures, but minor characters as well—dozens of them, wives and children, friends, enemies, lovers, rivals—nearly every one a real individual, drawn with exquisite sensitivity and care. As Wilson leads us, dizzily, on extended wings, we realize that we are back in the world of the great international novels, a world at once more concretely real and more marvelously romantic than any world we know. And we recognize *To the Finland Station* as a legitimate child of *War and Peace*.

The idea that binds all these people in all these times and places together, that animates this book and gives it an organic unity, is the great romantic dream of Revolution. Since 1789, Wilson makes clear, this dream has been absolutely central to Western imagination (increasingly of course, to non-Western imagination as well, but that is another story); what we understand today as the main traditions of modern culture could never have taken shape without it. It is a dream of people taking their lives into their own hands, coming together to forge a common destiny, to create a wholly new kind of society: a community based on liberty and equality, in which men and women can express themselves as individuals more freely, and love one another more intensely and deeply, than human beings have ever done before. It is "humanity creating itself."

Wilson starts his story in the reactionary torpor of the 1820s—the bleak years when Stendhal's Julien Sorel was coming of age. He explores the life and work of Jules Michelet, the Revolution's first great historian, to show us how the revolutionary dream could light up the lives of lonely men in dark times. In the pages of Michelet's *History of France*, Wilson writes, "The centuries leading up to the Revolution are like a long and solitary youth, waiting year after year for self-expression, release, the assertion of unacknowledged rights, free association with others." At last, in the great days of 1789–91, the release comes, the vision lives. "At no other time, I believe," wrote Michelet, "has the heart of man been more spacious." Poor and alone, Wilson says, Michelet "derived from the Revolution just behind him a sense of solidarity with others engaged in a great human undertaking, and through history he succeeded in making himself part of the human world." He brought the vision beautifully to life and made its power available for generations to come.

The tragic hero of Wilson's story, filling the center of the stage, looming over all the rest even long after he is gone, is Karl Marx. For Marx grasped the vision more forcefully and thoroughly than anyone; he struggled unremittingly with its deepest contradictions in all his work—and acted out, as Wilson shows, some of its darkest ambiguities in the course of his life.

For Marx understood, better than any bourgeois thinker, the revolutionary potential inherent in bourgeois society: its infinite productivity; its ability to break through the ice of entrenched prejudice, stupidity, and inertia; its largeness of vision, embracing the whole world, appraising every human relationship and form of life; its will to grow and develop, its openness to the future. At the same time, he saw—and explained definitively in *Capital*—the human horror that all this progress brings in its wake: The bourgeoisie can liberate human energy only by destroying human beings, using them as raw materials, resources to exploit, throwing them on the slag-heap when they are used up, grinding them to pieces when they get in the way.

Marx's life, as Wilson interprets it, incarnates the conflicting forces at the heart of the society he understood so well. We see him in London, desperately poor, helpless as his children die of starvation, withering with rage against countless enemies, capitalist and socialist, visible and invisible, unable to work cooperatively with anyone—Wilson brings out the darker sides of his "partnership" with Engels—exploiting cruelly the people he loves most (his wife and children above all) in order to produce his great work and help end exploitation forever, wracked with guilt for the way he lives, but powerless to stop the inner engine or demon that drives him insatiably on. Wilson's characterization of Marx is brilliant and probably unsurpassable, almost Shakespearean in its tragic grandeur and anguish. Forced to wound in order to create, Marx, the supreme enemy of the bourgeoisie, stands forth as one of the authentic heroes of the bourgeois age.

The last section of the book traces the rise of the revolutionary movement in Russia, starting in the middle of the nineteenth century, and leading up to Lenin at the Finland Station, in April 1917, returning triumphantly from exile abroad to lead the Revolution and bring the Bolsheviks to power. The book ends with Lenin borne from the train on the shoulders of the masses, carried through Petersburg in the middle of the night, waving to the crowds under the spotlights—a new kind of light, remember, only just invented—while in the background the band plays the "Marseillaise." It is a sublime moment in history, and Wilson evokes and orchestrates it with marvelous dramatic power.

And yet, somehow, we find ourselves putting up more resistance than Wilson—or even we ourselves—might expect. And if we do, Wilson has no one but himself to blame. He wants us to see the scene at the Finland Station as the fulfillment of the great collective revolutionary dream. But his own concrete portraits of the Bolsheviks, and in particular of Lenin, come across sounding more like savage indictments—all the more effective because unintended—than like the uncritical adorations he seems to be trying to write.

Lenin, as Wilson interprets and celebrates him here, is utterly devoid of any sort of human feeling. He totally avoids personal arguments, personal conflicts, personal expressions of anything— for anything might interfere with Party business. He fears, envies, needs, loves—nobody. He refuses to listen to Beethoven, because he fears the music will touch him, and make him soft, and so more vulnerable, and less effective. He "is the most male of reformers because he never weeps: his attitude begins with impatience." Wilson's Lenin incarnates a grim, heartless masculine mystique and founds his revolution on this hard rock.

But for those of us who were inspired by the original romantic revolutionary dream, as Wilson himself seized and expressed it, and who have followed him so far to see the vision unfold and develop, the sudden cold depersonalization of this Finland Station is the last place we will want to go—far better even to jump off the train! The real mystery is what a romantic and a tragedian like Wilson is doing in a place like this.

We can find a clue in the title of his last chapter on Marx: "Karl Marx Dies at His Desk." It is as if Wilson has felt a great surge of anger toward the people he most loves, all the passionate, complex, radiant, tragic people who fill his book. It is as if he has said to himself: Of course, people like this are bound to die at their desks, stooped over, shut in, closed off from the life and action of the world outside. As if he thought that the only way to arise from the misery of his desk was to cut the emotional cords that bound him to these beautiful losers, and try instead to enlist himself in a corps of indomitable precision machines. Our hearts and souls offend us—they make us vulnerable, lead us in contradictory ways, generate tragic conflicts that hold us back—therefore let us pluck them out. And so, it seems, Wilson arose from the desk of his despair, to make a desperate leap into a one-dimensional faith.

Wilson's Leninist faith and hope do not seem to have lasted long. Barely a year after *To the Finland Station* first appeared, he was definitively back at his desk, grappling with human complexities and tragedies again, bitter toward the false god that had led him briefly astray. He lived at his desk for thirty years more and produced many illuminating and beautiful books. But he was never able to recover the world-historical breadth and expanse, the visionary intensity and power, that make *To the Finland Station* so great. It may be that faith, even the grossest bad faith, acts as a kind of crude fuel, which the inner flame of genius must feed on in order to burn bright.

The most common form of bad faith thirty years ago was to identify oneself totally with History, to act as if it presented us with ready-made final solutions, that we did not have to decide what to do or how to live on our own. The commonest bad faith today is to act as if we were born yesterday, to believe that by simply ignoring history we can conjure away its power to shape and define what we do and who we are. In an age of historical amnesia, *To the Finland Station* can remind us that our history is alive and open and rich with excitement and promise. It can remind today's radicals of their own roots, and so put them in touch with sources of life and nourishment that they badly need to keep their vision and energy from drying up. And it can remind today's defenders of "tradition" how radical our cultural traditions really are.

The historical imagination, Wilson says, not only "makes us feel . . . that we have lived through and known so many generations of men," but "makes us feel something more: that we ourselves are the last chapter of the story, and that the next chapter is for us to create." *To the Finland Station*, a work of the historical imagination at its most creative, puts us in touch with the revolutionary dreams and visions of our past. If we read it well, we can use it to teach ourselves how to keep the dreams alive in the present, and maybe even, in the future, how to make the visions real. It can help us learn to create ourselves.

This essay was first published in the New York Times, *August 20, 1972.*

Angel in the City

Walter Benjamin is said to have been a shy and awkward man, yet there was something about him that made people want to take his picture. One of the nicest things about Momme Brodersen's lavishly illustrated biography is that, more than half a century after Benjamin's death, American readers can finally get a good look at his face. His mop of floating hair; his glasses-framed, heavy-lidded, soulful eyes, looking down or aimed into the middle distance (looking not into but past the camera); the hand that forms a V under his chin and gives his face a point; the dangling cigarette that seems to be there not so much to be smoked as to be crushed out—it all makes us feel that we are in the presence of the most serious man who ever lived.

Some of the most radiant visions of Benjamin emerged late in his life, in his beloved Paris at the end of the thirties, the age of Renoir's *Grand Illusion,* after the Popular Front broke down, before (but not long before) the Nazis came. In 1937 Gisele Freund photographed Benjamin at work in the Bibliothèque Nationale. She is one of European culture's *grandes dames* today, but then she was a fellow German–Jewish refugee, only twenty years younger than Benjamin and living even more precariously. In one shot Benjamin searches through a bookshelf, in another he is writing at a table. As usual, his gaze occludes the camera, though clearly he knows it is there. These library shots are visions of a man wholly absorbed in his work and at one with himself. His aura of total concentration can make the rest of us feel like bumbling fools. Or it can remind us why God gave us these big brains and taught us to read and write.

What was he working on that day? Probably his immense *Arcades* manuscript, the exploration of nineteenth-century Paris that enveloped his life all through the thirties. (When he crossed the Pyrenees on foot in 1940 to escape from France, he carried it with him and wouldn't let go. Lisa Fittko, his guide, later said she felt the manuscript was worth more to him than his life.) But it might have been one of his great late essays in that distinctively modern genre, Theology Without God. Here is a bit from "Theses on the Philosophy of History":

> A Klee painting named "Angelus Novus" shows an angel looking as though he is about to move away from something he is fixedly contemplating. His eyes are staring, his mouth is open, his wings are spread. This is how one pictures the angel of history. His face is turned toward the past. Where we perceive a chain of events, he sees one single catastrophe which keeps piling wreckage upon wreckage and hurls it in front of his feet. The angel would like to stay, awaken the dead, and make whole what has been smashed. But a storm is blowing from Paradise; it has got caught in his wings with such violence that the angel can no longer close them. This storm irresistibly propels him into the future to which his back is turned, while the pile of debris before him grows skyward. This storm is what we call progress.

Benjamin's very modern angel is prey to every anxiety and inner contradiction that haunts our history. And yet, here in the library, he is as perfectly at home in the modern world as any of us is ever going to be.

Maybe even too much at home for his own good. For years, his friends urged him to get out of Europe. But he insisted he was going to hang in there, "like one who keeps afloat on a shipwreck by climbing to the top of a mast that is already crumbling. But from there he has a chance to give a signal leading to his rescue." As poetry this is stunning. But as reality—signal to whom? Rescue by whom? It's insane. After Hitler started the war, Brodersen tells us, "twice at the turn of 1939–40 he met up with his ex-wife Dora, but he did not yield to her entreaties to leave Paris [as she did with their son Stefan] and bring himself into safety. Instead, he had his reader's card at the Bibliothèque Nationale renewed so that he could proceed with his work."

He couldn't work long. Brodersen and Jay Parini tell this grim and absurd story well. After he was arrested by the helpful French police and interned in a camp for enemy aliens—he edited the camp paper!—Benjamin saw he had to go. But the gates were closing fast. He headed for Marseilles, where he met Arthur Koestler and had the amazing good luck (thanks to Max Horkheimer) to get an entry visa to the United States. But he couldn't use it without escaping from France, where Nazi armies were closing in. In a small group of refugees, he made a heroic trek across the Pyrenees to Spain. Hobbled by a heart condition, he had to stop constantly for breath. At last he and his group got across. But they were stopped that night in the village of Portbou, where the local authorities refused their papers and threatened to send them back the next day to France and the Gestapo. The other refugees decided to wait and see: Maybe the local police could be cajoled or bribed. Benjamin didn't wait: A longtime serious drug user, he was carrying morphine. He took an overdose; in the morning he died. After his death the police abruptly changed their minds and let all the others through. In 1994, with Spain a democracy once more, the townspeople of Portbou erected a monument in his memory.

It's one of the classic heart-rending stories of the twentieth century. And it's important, especially for people who admire Benjamin and revere his memory, to notice his participation in the story: He was a victim of the most murderous regime in history, but he also killed himself. Underappreciated for his writing, he hit the charts with his death. The monument in Portbou is engraved with a single sentence from the essay "On the Concept of History," one of his last works: "It is more arduous to honour the memory of the nameless than that of the renowned. Historical construction is devoted to the memory of the nameless." Brodersen offers a gloss:

It is hard not to ask whether . . . Benjamin's death was "preventable," "unnecessary," though these are unanswerable, pointless questions. Hundreds of others were dying, unnecessarily, anonymously, on other borders; millions were to die with no border in sight.

I'm sure both Benjamin and Brodersen are right, yet both sound a little complacent. Humphrey Bogart at the end of *Casablanca* nobly effaces himself and his happiness, but he knows and we know the camera is on him; he's the star. Benjamin, insulted and injured for much of his life, found a way to be a star in death. His essay, his monument, Brodersen and I trying to write about them, are all in some basic way off-key. It may be impossible to talk about the murders and the victims of Nazism without false notes. But not to talk about them would be even falser.

Benjamin's death overshadows his life; it's a hard act to follow. But we need to fight to bring him back to life because he had so much to say. One problem is that so many people who loved him—Brecht, Adorno, Gershom Scholem, Hannah Arendt—all wrote moving testaments that he was really just like them. In the 1970s, Benjamin became the focus of a Sylvia Plath-like death cult. It has magnified everything eccentric and impenetrable in his work. Happily, the authors and editors of these books see him and love him as a man speaking to men.

Brodersen has done impressive research and excavates a great deal of fascinating material. His book is indispensable for unraveling Benjamin's life and work. Alas, he tends not to know what to do with what he digs up. For instance, when Brodersen discusses Walter's father, Emil, he takes at face value the son's Oedipal picture of the old man as a stupid, conventional German philistine. Then he mentions the fact that Emil had lived for many years in Paris and made his money in the art business. These are startling facts. They suggest that, though father and son did not treat each other very well, there may have been some deep "elective affinities" between them. For Brodersen, these are throwaway lines—as is the detail that Walter grew up with a French governess.

Brodersen shows how much of Benjamin's spirit and energy went into the pre–World War One German Youth Movement, in which hundreds of thousands of teenage boys (in the big cities there were girls as well) went into the countryside, in highly organized groups, to commune with nature, hike in the mountains, sleep in haylofts, bathe in streams, play guitars, sing folk songs, and celebrate a "simple life" they considered "authentic"—so radically different from the business, professional, and military careers their parents had raised them for. In some ways "Young Germany" evokes the sixties counterculture; in others, it sounds like a prep school for fascism. Benjamin knew that, as a Jew, he would always be an outsider there. But he persisted, encouraged by his friendship and intimacy with Gustav Wyneken, a follower of Nietzsche and the movement's charismatic guru. (This friendship might have shaded into a teacher–pupil love affair. But it is hard to know what Brodersen thinks, because his writing, never vivid, grows especially opaque where human emotions are in play.) Benjamin worked on several movement papers and was often reproved for "going too far"; alas, we aren't told what "too far" meant. When the First World War began, Wyneken urged the boys on to patriotic gore—keeping himself and the movement in the state's good graces, but losing many of his most devoted disciples, including Benjamin. Benjamin never got over the lost dream of a "free youth" that could renew the world.

Benjamin's own scene, the Berlin Free Students' Union, must have been weird. We are told by Brodersen how, a week into the war, one of Benjamin's dearest friends, the young poet Fritz Heinle, and his fiancée, Rika Seligson, turned on the gas in the Union kitchen and killed themselves. Benjamin would mourn this boy all his life, yet would also—ominous leitmotif—admire his suicidal act. The whole crowd then seems to have urged Heinle's younger brother, Wolf, and Rika's younger sister, Traute, to go and do likewise. The girl did in 1915; the boy lingered until 1923. What should we make of these murderous fusions of the personal and the political? (It might help to know if other European kids were killing themselves in that dreadful time.) Brodersen shows nice boys and girls in the grip of wild and lethal emotions; but apart from remarking on "the confusion that war and death created in these young people's minds," he doesn't try to read them.

Brodersen's Weimar chapters are full of interesting material, but they tell the same tale again and again. Benjamin is encouraged to work in a university department, but then the one professor who understands him abruptly retires, and the new one can't stand him. He becomes an editor of a national magazine, only to see it fail before he can start. He makes what looks like a lucrative book deal, but the publisher goes bankrupt while his book is in press. *Oy*! Is this an I.B. Singer story called "Benjamin Shlimazl" or a cantata on the Stations of the Cross?

Benjamin's troubles were real. He was disliked by some because he was a Jew, a cosmopolitan and, though never a communist, always a fellow traveler of revolution. He was disliked by others—starting with the Communist Party—because he thrived on irony, paradox, and dialectical play, and nobody could predict, much less control, what he was going to think or say. But he earned this trouble because of the man and the writer he was proud to be.

Much of the material Brodersen has gathered can be read much less gloomily than he reads it. It's impressive that, even in daunting circumstances, Benjamin kept on writing. (Nor was he ever forgotten; publishers kept calling and he was always making deals.) And that so many of Weimar's great writers—Hesse, von Hofmannsthal, Rilke, Brecht, Thomas and Heinrich Mann—thought the world of him, even though they couldn't stand one another. And that not only was he one of the first serious writers in any language to grasp the possibilities of radio—no surprise to readers of his masterpiece, "The Work of Art in the Age of Mechanical Reproduction" (1936)—but he actually made more than a hundred broadcasts, and built a devoted audience, turned off only by the Nazis in 1933.

Then there is the parade of fascinating women who passed through his life: his wife, Dora Kellner, thriller writer and feminist editor; his lover, communist dramaturge Asja Lacis; psychoanalyst and sexologist Charlotte Wolff; Hannah Arendt; Gisele Freund; and more. There was always at least one very special woman around. With Benjamin himself, they are the stars of Brodersen's great store of illustrations. But he won't talk about them. He digs up luminous images, but sometimes seems to want to bury them again. Who is that woman with hair in her eyes? How close did she and Benjamin get? What did she mean to him? Brodersen's own policy seems to be, Don't ask, don't tell. His women are sisters from another planet. Too bad: Women helped Benjamin feel at home on this one.

A poet in his youth, Benjamin began in gladness. This is the ambience of the first of three volumes of his *Selected Writings*. The editors must have debated whether to organize the set chronologically or thematically; they made the right choice. Time progression helps us see how his mind developed in passages from Berlin to Paris, from youth to middle age, from gentility to marginality, from Weimar's springtime to Hitler's. (My own feeling is that the best stuff came last.)

A glance at the Table of Contents of *Selected Writings*—he writes on language, time, colors, children's books, love, violence, messianism—shows us at once Benjamin's provocativeness and his infinite variety. The two longest pieces, both from the early twenties and neither translated till now, are his doctoral thesis, "The Concept of Criticism in German Romanticism," and his long essay on Goethe's late novel, *Elective Affinities*.

His thesis on Romanticism, emphasizing the Schlegels and Novalis, develops an idea of "universal progressive poetry." Benjamin explodes the reactionary canon of German culture that is pulling like an undertow against democracy. He is trying to capture the army of right-wing culture heroes for the French— and implicitly, the German—Revolution. His Goethe essay shows how the great man at the height of his fame was really of the devil's party; how much he hated the straight German world that had made him a national monument. It is an exemplary piece of lit crit, brilliantly analyzing the book's layers, motifs, symbols, and subtexts. It is also an in-your-face, eat-your-heart-out gesture to the German universities, showing them what they lost when they passed him by. Benjamin's reverent feeling for tradition gives weight to his radical readings of tradition. Both essays could be an inspiration to people doing cultural studies today.

Jay Parini's novel *Benjamin's Crossing* offers something that all the biographies lack: a clear vision of what the man might actually have been like. Parini makes us see and feel his sweetness and nobility; his mood swings and volatility, which could make him a commanding presence one moment and a pile of broken glass the next; his quick changes from empathy and generosity to narcissism and back; his sexiness (look at those pictures), which tends to get airbrushed out of the commentary, maybe because critics don't think it's noble enough.

I have two problems with *Benjamin's Crossing*. First, while it's a great idea to tell the story in different voices, Parini allows Gershom Scholem (and his Jewish mystical agenda) to increasingly muscle out the other voices without letting us know why. Second, while Parini concentrates entirely on the end of Benjamin's life, he is strangely distant and opaque about his death. The book seems to be moving toward a climactic set piece where Parini will try to get inside his mind on his last night, as he tosses in his bed and waits for the morphine to kill him. But it doesn't happen. Any reader who has bonded with Parini's hero is bound to be overwhelmed by anguished questions of the kind survivors always ask. What drove him over the edge? Why should a man who had faced the Gestapo be daunted by some crummy village police? Was he determined to die in his beloved Europe and never board the ship to the promised land? If someone had knocked on the door that last night, might they have saved him? As he lay in bed, would he have had any regrets? Would he have felt complete? In real life, questions like these are not just unbearable but Unanswerable. But isn't that why we have novels? Why Parini takes us so far along, and then pulls back, I wish I knew.

There is a profound problem with much of the literature on Benjamin, and on Central European culture. The young men and women who came of age in that culture—from the Age of Goethe way up to the 1930s—grew up on German Romanticism, with its cosmic nostalgia, soulful, heavy-laden yearning for dark forests and isolation from the modern world, suicide pacts and love of death. This is Brodersen's culture; his heart leaps up when he hears those tragic chords.

This is surely part of Benjamin's story. But in the culture of Central Europe's Jews, from Mahler to Freud to Kafka to Benjamin himself to Ernst Lubitsch, Max Ophüls, and Billy Wilder, Romantic doom always coexists with a comic and ironic spirit, cosmopolitan and urbane, seeking light on the modern city's boulevards and in its music halls and cafes. Benjamin thrived on the contradiction between the joy on the street and the doom in his soul. Remember Gene Kelly dancing in the streets in *An American in Paris?* As a young Kelly flew over the boulevards with his body, so the middle aged Benjamin, with equal flair and finesse, whirled and soared with his mind. He did it in the brilliant 1935 essay "Paris, Capital of the Nineteenth Century" and in essays on Naples, Marseilles, Moscow, and Berlin. He did it in "The Work of Art in the Age of Mechanical Reproduction," where he unveiled a dialectical optics enabling us to see movies and psychoanalysis as part of the same historical long wave. He was dancing that day in 1937 when Gisele Freund took his picture in the Bibliothèque, and all through the *Arcades* manuscript that he carried till he died. (At last a complete text has come out in German, and Harvard will publish an English translation soon.) Even as the Nazis and his own sense of doom pulled him down toward death, he showed his readers how to dance in the streets and make themselves at home in the modern world.

All these books grasp Benjamin and help bring him back. But now that he's back, we should revere him not for his death but for his overflowing life. File him under Eros, not Thanatos: Auden's "Eros, builder of cities." Enjoy his largeness of vision, his imaginative fertility, his openness to the future, his grasp of the comedy along with the tragedy of modern times. Be glad. The Angel of History is back on the streets.

This essay first appeared in the Nation, *May 12, 1997.*

Cosmic *Chutzpah*

. . . was that *your* "calling" or whatever?

        Max Weber to Georg Lukács in prison, March 1920

Georg Lukács, one of the remarkable men of the twentieth century, began life in the age of Disraeli and Nietzsche and carried on into the age of the Beatles and walks on the moon. He is the author of two world-class masterpieces, *History and Class Consciousness* and *Theory of the Novel,* and of dozens of other books and thousands of articles, pamphlets, manifestos, and other writings of nearly every genre on nearly every subject we can imagine. His ideas are central to the history of Marxism (this is widely recognized), but also of existentialism (which is hardly recognized at all). He spent the last half-century of his life as a committed communist, participating in the revolutions of 1918–19, living through the horrors of Stalinism, emerging into political life again in the Hungarian revolution of 1956, suffering imprisonment by a wide assortment of jailers but surviving his jailers, and being there to denounce the bombs over Hanoi and the tanks in Prague.

Record of a Life is a series of sketches and interviews that Lukács hastily put together shortly before his death in 1971, when he realized that he would never live to write his autobiography. There is a wonderful grandeur about Lukács as he emerges here. He is physically frail but intellectually powerful and spiritually intense, striving to grasp the meaning of his life and work. He radiates the aura of those old men of Greek mythology: Philoctetes with his wound and his bow, Oedipus at Colonus, the androgynous prophet Tiresias who has foresuffered all. These comparisons are meant only to show what a problematical figure he was: His intellectual and visionary powers were always intertwined with blindness, wounds, and guilt.

I first encountered Lukács in Washington Square Park in the spring of 1958. I was a freshman at Columbia, out of the Bronx for the first time in my life, enthralled by the sights and sounds of Manhattan and the books and ideas of the world. As I wandered through the park one lovely afternoon, I saw, among the singers and players and hustlers and kibitzers, a fellow I had known in high school, standing under the arch, declaiming and handing out leaflets to the crowd. He had been a Communist Party stalwart all through school, but 1956 had hit him hard, and after Budapest he seemed to drop out of sight. Now here he was again, testifying that capitalism was on its last legs, and that the international working class and its vanguard party were alive and well. I greeted him and got him to take a break; we walked around the park, gossiped about old school friends, looked longingly at the girls, and started to worry about the world.

He remarked on the books I was carrying—Kierkegaard, Dostoevsky, Martin Buber—and wondered if I was becoming a junkie on that old opium of the people. I in turn wondered if he was still recruiting people to join the Red Army and see the world. Suddenly he turned dead serious: "Are you asking if I'm still a communist?" All right, I said: Was he, could he be, even now? He replied that he was more of a communist than ever. I must have looked dubious, or maybe just disgusted. He reached into his briefcase and pulled out a text, poorly mimeographed and heavily underlined. It was called "What Is Orthodox Marxism?" by a Georg Lukács. "Here," he ordered, "read this!" The text began with the proclamation that even if every single one of Marx's theses about the world were to be proved wrong, an orthodox Marxist could simply discard them "without having to renounce his orthodoxy for a single moment." I was instantly stunned: Who was this guy and what was he saying? I fell back on a reality I was sure of: "And those tanks in Budapest? Don't they prove something?" My friend hesitated for a moment, then drew himself up and answered decisively. "They prove," he said, "that the USSR is not orthodox."

I can still remember the way that first page of Lukács made my head spin. The cosmic *chutzpah* of the man was staggering. I'd known plenty of Marxists who were willing to admit that Marx might be wrong about many things; in spite of this, they said, he was right about the essential things, and that was why they were Marxists. Now here was a Marxist saying that Marx might be wrong about *everything,* and he couldn't care less; that the truth of Marxism was independent of anything that Marx said about the world, and hence that nothing in the world could ever refute it; and that this was the essence not merely of Marxist truth, but of Marxist orthodoxy—even if it was the orthodoxy of a single believer, shut out from the communion of the ecclesiastic party, keeping the faith alone in the park. When I thought about it later, it struck me that the Marxism of Lukács's "What Is Orthodox Marxism?" had more in common with the existential flights of the religious writers whose books I was carrying that day— Kierkegaard, Dostoevsky, Buber—than with the Stalinist dogmatics on which my friend had grown up. As I thought of Lukács in their company, it flashed on me that what I had just read was a Marxist *credo quia absurdum.* Could it be that communism had found its St. Augustine at last?

I asked my teachers about Lukács and found out all I could. No one knew too much in those years, but everyone found him fascinating. He was a Hungarian Jew, son of a banker, born in Budapest in 1885. He had studied in Heidelberg with Max Weber and in Berlin with Georg Simmel; both considered him, though still in his twenties, one of the most brilliant and original minds of the age. He had begun his career as a writer on art and culture, a founder of magazines and a theater—he brought Ibsen and Strindberg to Budapest but then, horrified and radicalized by the First World War, became a militant member of the Hungarian Communist Party. In 1919, during the brief life of the Soviet Republic of Hungary, he served as commissar of education and culture. After its overthrow, he escaped to Vienna and then to Berlin, where he became active and prominent in the Communist

International. When Hitler came to power he found himself a refugee again, this time in Moscow, where he helped to discover, excavate, and publish some of the buried writings of the young Marx. At the end of the Second World War he returned to Budapest, where he wrote and taught philosophy for the rest of his life.

Lukács's reputation rested above all on a work of philosophy, politics, and social theory that he published in German in 1923, *History and Class Consciousness*.[1] This book had been long out of print and very hard to get—and therein lies a tale. It began with the essay I had read that day in the park, "What Is Orthodox Marxism?" Ironically, although Lukács had been constantly preoccupied with establishing a Marxist orthodoxy, he became a prime victim once the communist movement began to persecute internal heresy. In the Comintern in 1924 and 1928, in Moscow in 1934, in Budapest in 1949, he was subjected to campaigns of the crudest vilification; three generations of Stalinist hacks had stigmatized him as a symbol of all the dangers of "deviation." In all these cases (Morris Watnick chronicled them in *Soviet Survey* in 1958,[2] the first discussion of Lukács in English), he had submitted to his persecutors, repudiated his ideas, and begged forgiveness rather than be isolated from the world communist movement. In 1928 he was condemned by the Comintern for "premature antifascism" (he was vindicated later, but too late for him). He then withdrew from political activity and hoped for a quieter life, writing literary and cultural history. But it was not to be.

In 1934, *History and Class Consciousness* was condemned for the heresy of philosophical idealism. At this point, Lukács seemed to enlist actively in the fight against his life and thought. He confessed "not only the theoretical falsity of my book, but its practical danger." The diatribes against him "all the more strengthened my

---

1   *History and Class Consciousness*, trans. Rodney Livingstone, Cambridge, MA: MIT Press, 1968.

2   See Morris Watnick, "Georg Lukács: An Intellectual Biography," *Soviet Survey*, January–March, April–June, and July–September 1958, and January-March 1959.

conviction that, in the intellectual sphere, the front of Idealism is the front of Fascist counter-revolution." He ended by praising Comrade Stalin and his henchmen for their "iron implacability and refusal to compromise with all deviations from Marxism-Leninism." He did not offer to burn *History and Class Consciousness* (or himself) in Red Square, but he did swear to do everything in his power to ensure that his masterpiece would never be reprinted anywhere again. ("In the fight between you and the world," Kafka once wrote, "back the world.")

When I read this, I felt confirmed in my sense of Lukács as a religious figure. His capacity for abjection and repentance, his drive to punish and mortify himself for the sake of sanctity, had more in common with the inner world of Augustine's *Confessions* than with the sensibility of Karl Marx. But this was a very modern Augustine, as he might have been imagined by Dostoevsky or Freud: endlessly reinventing himself, hoping to obliterate his past once and for all, only to trip over it or maybe dig it up again and again; persecuting and purging himself in a quest for pure ortho-doxy, only to find himself inventing new modes of heresy, leading to new orgies of guilt, confession, and self-recrimination.

In 1956, Lukács went through a stunning metamorphosis. That year, as the Stalinist system shook and crumbled, the Hungarian people rose up against their Soviet masters. Lukács participated enthusiastically in this revolution, and once again, after thirty-seven years, served as minister of education and culture in a Hungarian revolutionary government. When the USSR moved in, Lukács, as a member of Prime Minister Imré Nagy's cabinet, was one of the first to be arrested. Imprisoned in Count Dracula's old Transylvanian castle, he was interrogated by the Soviet secret police and put under pressure to submit, confess, recant, inform, denounce. Lukács had gone through these motions many times before over the previous thirty years. This time, however, he refused to betray his comrades, his people, or himself. Pressed to denounce Imré Nagy, Lukács said that he would be glad to air his opinions about Nagy once the two of them were free men in the streets of Budapest, but he would never break solidarity with a fellow prisoner. After six months in prison, Lukács was released and allowed to return to Budapest. It was understood that he would not agitate actively against the new government; neither, however, would he endorse it. At the age of seventy, this lifelong seeker after orthodoxy found himself an authentic heretical hero.

History and Class Consciousness appeared in French translation in 1960. Lukács protested its publication, but his objections only made the book more notorious and intriguing. My friends and I, and many intellectuals like us—members of the generation that would soon be called the New Left—opened the book with breathless anticipation and found that it lived up to its advance notices. Whatever we might think about its many theories and arguments, *History and Class Consciousness* convinced us that socialist thought in our time could be carried on at the highest pitch of intellectual power, fused with the most passionate feeling, transformed into an inspired vision. Lukács gave us both a standard that challenges and a specter that haunts any radical who sits down to write today.

The heart of *History and Class Consciousness,* and the primary source of its power, is a 140-page essay, situated at the book's center, entitled "Reification and the Consciousness of the Proletariat." *Reification* is a poor Latinized equivalent for *Verdinglichung,* a German word that means "thingification," the process by which a person is transformed into a thing. The basic trouble with capitalism, Lukács argues, is that it treats people as if they were things, and treats human relationships as if they were between things. The particular sort of thing that people in modern capitalist societies get turned into is the *commodity.* Lukács takes Marx's idea of the "Fetishism of Commodities" (*Capital*, Volume 1, Chapter 1), and extends it into a total vision of what capitalism does to human life.

He begins with an exploration of work, carrying Marx's discussion of "alienated labor" into the age of immense bureaucracies (private and public), efficiency experts, systems analysis and long-range planning. The process of labor is "progressively broken down into abstract, rational, specialized operations." Workers lose contact not only with the products or services they create, but with their own thoughts and feelings and actions. "Even the worker's psychological attributes are separated from his total personality, and placed in opposition to it, so as to facilitate their integration into specialized rational systems and their reduction to statistical units." This fragmentation of activity tends to generate a "fragmentation of the subject," so that a worker's personal qualities, talents or idiosyncrasies "appear as sources of error."

The worker is meant to be "a mechanical part incorporated into a mechanical system. He finds it already pre-existing and self-sufficient, it functions independently of him, and he has to conform to its laws whether he likes it or not . . . Here, too, the personality can do no more than look on helplessly while its own existence is reduced to an isolated particle and fed into an alien system." In such a system we feel passive and contemplative; we experience ourselves as spectators in processes that happen to us, rather than active participants shaping our lives.

Most of Marx's successors focused almost exclusively on the oppression of manual and industrial workers. Lukács shows how the force of Marx's analysis and indictment goes far beyond them. In fact, capitalism treats all men and women as interchangeable parts, as commodities exchangeable for other commodities. Administrators, soldiers, scientists, even entrepreneurs—everybody in modern society is forced into the Procrustean bed of reification and systematically deprived of the freedom that everyone is supposed to enjoy. Even the modern capitalist "experiences the same doubling of personality, the same splitting up of man into an element of the movement of commodities and an objective and impotent observer of that movement." Capitalists are rewarded for their inner passivity and lack of integration; but it is urgent to see the human costs of this system, even to its ruling class. Lukács deepens the case against capitalism by showing us how, even in its mansions on the hill, no one is at home.

He puts much energy into a critique of early twentieth-century forms of discourse that passed for social science. He attacks the attempt to formulate laws of human behavior that will have the static, timeless quality of physical laws about the behavior of matter and energy. Such an aim assumes that human realities and social relationships are unchangeable, inexorable as gravitational force, impervious to human will, beyond any kind of social or political control. This paradigm masks the enormous diversity of human relationships in different times and places—indeed, even within the same time and place—and the capacity of human beings, acting collectively, to change the world. Something is fundamentally wrong with modes of thought (whether they are called philosophy, history or science) whose main force is to convince people that there is no alternative to the way they live now. One of the most insidious powers of modern capitalism, Lukács believes, is its capacity to mobilize the energy of our intellects and of our intellectuals to blur our minds and paralyze our will, to reduce us to passive spectators of whatever fate the market inflicts on us.

The young Lukács often writes as a kind of Left neo-Kantian: In the face of the world we live in, to revolt is a categorical imperative. It is the only way to seize control of our fate, to assert ourselves as subjects, as people, against a social structure that treats us as things. In his model of Marxism, the crucial issue isn't one class oppressing another class, but one total *system* oppressing everybody: The ultimate end isn't economic justice, but personal *authenticity*. Lukács insists on the crucial importance of consciousness and self-awareness in political life. Capitalism may be breaking down, but there is no reason to think that it will give way to something better, unless the people are conscious that things *can be* better, that they have the power to transform and renew the world. If the workers can come to know themselves—to grasp the sources of their present weakness and self-alienation, of their potential freedom and power—then capitalism is doomed. Lukács connects the 1900 Marxist ideal of "revolutionary class-consciousness" with the ancient Socratic demand to "know thyself." But these aims require an arduous process of education and self-education, of struggle (both in theory and practice), of continual self-criticism and self-overcoming. One of the main reasons for having a communist party, Lukács argues, is to focus and organize the work of self-knowledge, to transform it into a collective project. Equally important is the creation of a vibrant, dynamic, self-critical and self-renewing radical culture. Without culture and consciousness, the workers will not be able to grow up. If they don't grow, the reification-machine will go on running, and its victims won't ever know what's hit them or why they feel like hollow men inside.

If they do learn and grow, the *soviet* or worker's council will be an ideal expression of their new life. Government and politics won't be obscure processes enacted on behalf of remote or invisible interests, but activities that men and women do, on their own, in their everyday lives. The economy won't be a machine running on its own momentum toward its own goals, but a structure of concrete decisions that men and women freely make about how they want to live and fulfill their needs. Culture, instead of being a veil of mystification thrown over everyday life, will be created by ordinary people out of their real desires and needs and hopes. In a workers' democracy, the constraints of the exploitive economy, of the repressive state, of the culture of mystification, will all wither away. Then "the life of man as man in relation to himself, to his fellow men and to nature, can now become the authentic content of human life. Socially, man is now born as man."

History and Class Consciousness appeared in English at an ideal moment for an emerging generation of radical intellectuals. It helped us in the West to see how, even where capitalism was highly successful in economic terms (the 1960s, remember, was the climax of the greatest capitalist boom in history), it could still be humanly disastrous, inflicting insult and injury on the people in it by treating them as nothing more than commodities. Simultaneously, Lukács's book enabled intellectuals in the Soviet bloc to understand how the so-called workers' states had developed their own distinctive forms of reification. The 1960s spawned an amazing variety of eruptions and rebellions by people who were sick and tired of being treated as things, who fought to end reification and to assert themselves as subjects, as active participants in their everyday lives. For those of us who were trying to think this through, *History and Class Consciousness* was a rich source of ideas and energy. Moreover, for a generation accustomed to a Marxism of sterile formulas and rigid dogmas enforced by party hacks, this book brought Marxism back to its deepest sources as a vision and a theory of human liberation.

One of the most striking things about *History and Class Consciousness* was the religious language in it. First there was the theme of "orthodoxy" with which the book began; then the revolutionary party was supposed to bring "total absorption of the personality" of its members; then the goal of socialism was said to be "the redemption of man"; the transition from capitalism to socialism would be "a leap into the realm of freedom," after which "man is now born as man." No one knew enough about Lukács, back in the 1960s, to sort out these ideas and drives. But it was clear that one of his most important achievements was to bring together the body of Marxist theory and practice with the stream of *Innerlichkeit* and spiritual yearning, which, more than any economic analysis or attachment to the working class, has led countless men and women to "prove their ideas by action, by living and dying for the revolution."

This fusion was the primary source of Lukács's power and originality. But it had its dark side as well. One of the most disturbing of his religious ideas—an idea that has been deeply problematical whenever it has occurred in the history of religion—is the idea of *incarnation*. Thus, in the course of expounding on the Leninist idea of a "vanguard" Communist Party, Lukács gives it a twist that would have been unimaginable to a secular and pragmatic mind like Lenin's: "The Party," he says, "is the historical embodiment and active incarnation of revolutionary class consciousness," and, again, a little later, "the incarnation of the ethics of the fighting proletariat."

Lukács's doctrine of incarnation is as profound a mystery as anything ever proclaimed by any Christian church. But it poses special dangers all its own. If the Communist Party, in some mysterious way, "is" the revolutionary working class, then it becomes impossible to imagine that, say, the party might betray the working class, or even to ask whether the party is serving the working class as well as it should: The party stands not only beyond doubt, but also beyond question or scrutiny.

Similar problems arise around Lukács's notion of Marxist orthodoxy, equally impervious to any facts or events that might cast doubt on its truth. Finally, there is the idea of *totality*, according to which the question of freedom becomes "purely tactical," because "freedom cannot represent a value in itself": The only real issue is whether the Communist Party, incarnation of the working class, holds the "totality of power." If these ideas were brought together—the trinity of totality, orthodoxy and incarnation—they could generate a theology of total submission, a metaphysical undertow that might well be strong enough to drown all Lukács's dreams of liberation.

The radical contradictions that animate this book, and the strength and depth with which its contradictory ideas are expressed, mark *History and Class Consciousness* as one of the great modernist works of the century. To young readers who discovered Lukács in the 1960s, he seemed to belong in the company of great modern thinkers at war with themselves: Rousseau, Dostoevsky, Nietzsche—theorists and exponents of both liberation and of domination. Although Lukács was in some obvious way a Marxist, his kindred spirits were all a lot weirder than Marx.

We were just getting used to seeing Lukács as a great modernist when he came out with a scurrilous, hysterical attack on modernism. This essay, "The Ideology of Modernism," reads like an indictment at a Stalinist trial.[3] It puts together an amalgam in the defendant's box, consisting of great twentieth-century writers (Kafka, Proust, Joyce, Faulkner, Musil, Freud), utterly mediocre writers (Steinbeck, Thomas Wolfe), and assorted Nazi ideologues and hacks. It then assaults these "modernist" subjects. In "their" writings, the personality is dissolved, the objective world is inexplicable, there is no past and no history; perversity and idiocy are the essence of the human condition. Modernism has no

---

3   "The Ideology of Modernism," in *The Meaning of Contemporary Realism*, trans. John and Necke Mander, London: Merlin, 1962, 17–47. The essays before and after "Modernism" are blows in the same culture war, and just as bad.

perspectives, furthers the dissolution of the personality, destroys
the complex tissue of humanity's relations with the environment.
Kierkegaard says that the self is opaque to itself, and this furnishes
a convenient alibi for Nazi murderers. Kafka "substitutes his
Angst-ridden view of the world for objective reality." Freud is
"obsessed with pathology" and sickens an otherwise healthy audience; he lacks the sane wisdom of Pavlov, "who takes the
Hippocratic view that mental abnormality is a deviation from a
norm." So it goes.

"The Ideology of Modernism" is colossally, willfully ignorant.
Or maybe it is not exactly ignorance, but rather what Veblen
called "trained incapacity" to see what is there. This learning
disability is a special embarrassment for those who like to think of
themselves as Marxists. Marxists are supposed to be able to understand art in relation to historical and material reality. Instead,
Lukács speaks as if it were writers who autonomously *create* reality: as if Freud had created the twentieth century's pathologies
and Kafka its police states. (After his imprisonment in Dracula's
castle, Lukács was reported to have said, "I was wrong, Kafka was
a realist after all." But he never put this insight into print or
thought it through.)

Lukács says that he is fighting in the name of "realism," whose
basic idea is that "reality can be known." What he really means,
we see as we read on, is that reality *is* known, and he knows it,
and he doesn't want to read any writing that doesn't tell him
what he already knows. He totally identifies with the aggressors,
assaulting Kafka and Joyce and Freud in exactly the language
that Nazi and Stalinist hacks and thugs used to assault them. It's
as if he is hoping to destroy their masterworks in just the way
that his Soviet masters destroyed his own. Luckily, they were
beyond his power—though his diatribes probably kept some
great writers from being read. The one great modernist within
his reach, whom he violated and brutalized shamefully, was
himself.

I remembered hearing that in *The Magic Mountain* Thomas
Mann had used Lukács as a model for Leo Naphta, one of his most
luminous characters, a Jewish-Jesuit communist who kills himself

on the verge of the First World War.[4] I was glad that, unlike Naphta, Lukács was living on (and on). But if Mann was suggesting something about Lukács's need for rough trade with himself, this was hard to deny. Works like "The Ideology of Modernism" read like a kind of ritual self-murder. Why did Lukács keep throwing himself off the bridge? What crime or sin was he atoning for, and how long would *his* trial by ordeal last?

By the early 1970s, you could find people in American (and European and Australian) universities who had actually worked with Lukács. They were a pretty smart bunch; philosopher Agnes Heller is probably the most illustrious. I remember asking some *Lukácsniki* how one of the best minds of the century could sink so low. They said that I had to understand the political context: Even as he assaulted modernism, Lukács also denounced socialist realism, the one form of literature that Stalin condoned. In fact, Lukács was the only writer in the Soviet bloc who had ever been able to get away with this. Did I think it had been easy, or without risks? By attacking the "Western orthodoxy" of modernism, Lukács was clearing space in which he would be free to attack the "Eastern orthodoxy" of socialist realism. Couldn't I see how, within the immense constraints of life in the Soviet bloc, Lukács had created space for literary and cultural freedom? Yes, I could see it. Still, I feared that the force of Lukács's cultural politics might well be to open the door for the free spirits of the 1860s, while keeping those of the 1960s locked out.

More of Lukács's writings were reissued and translated in the course of the 1960s. There were the works of literary criticism and cultural history written in the 1930s and 1940s: *Studies in European Realism, Goethe and His Age, The Historical Novel, The Young Hegel.* These books lacked the brilliance and originality of *History and Class Consciousness,* but moved on a level far above the antimodernist diatribes of the 1950s. The books were full of marvelous connections and insights, and full of nostalgia for the

---

4   On Lukács and Naphta, and Lukács and Mann, see Judith Marcus [Tar], *Georg Lukács and Thomas Mann: A Study in the Sociology of Literature,* Amherst: University of Massachusetts Press, 1987.

sweetness of life before the First World War. They showed Lukács as a conservative thinker: conservative in the best sense, striving to embrace, nourish, and protect the heritage of bourgeois humanism even as the twin menaces of Nazism and Stalinism were closing in. Lukács's comrades in this preservationist enterprise were a generation of gifted Jewish scholars, scattered to the winds by Nazis—among them Ernst Cassirer, Erich Auerbach, Arnold Hauser, and Erwin Panofsky. In these works, Lukács's communism often faded into the background. But he was surely right to say that any socialist movement that abandoned this heritage or let it die would be surrendering its soul.

As Lukács's historical works were being reissued, a number of his post-Stalin political essays were coming out, hot off the presses. (The *New Left Review* played a crucial role in getting this material to British and American readers.) These articles made it clear how thrilled Lukács was to see Stalinism unmasked, and how eagerly he embraced Khrushchev's promises of domestic liberalization and international détente. Some of this writing showed an unprecedented emotional openness, and readers could not help sharing the old man's unmediated joy that he had come through and outlived his jailers.

But even here shadows of ambiguity begin to close on the pure daylight. Lukács's invectives against Stalin cite many disastrous flaws but make only the briefest, most cryptic reference to his mass murders. And it is disturbing that, in his essays on Stalin, Lukács spends so much space and energy denouncing Trotsky as if, just as in his attacks on modernism, he needs to prove his own orthodoxy; lest the force of his criticism place his loyalty in doubt. Often in this period, Lukács seems to be going out of his way to protest too much, to suggest inexhaustible ironic depths. This systematic ambiguity pervades the process of the republication of his early works, complete with recantations, official bans, and underground printing. The wheels within wheels turned more frantically than ever in a 1967 preface to a new edition of *History and Class Consciousness,* an edition that Lukács had apparently fought to suppress. He testified it was a mistake for him to write the book, and advised readers it would be a mistake for them to read it—but in a language of enticement that ensured his advice would fail.

Lukács's death in 1971 was far from the end of his story. In the years since, an amazing array of his early writings has come to light, including much that Lukács himself believed lost; some of his most brilliant and original writing is just beginning to appear in print.[5] We are still in the process of discovering Lukács, running the movie backwards, and getting the first things last. In fact, we are discovering parts of the movie that Lukács clearly hoped to censor, faces he left on the cutting-room floor, the return of the repressed.

The most fascinating of Lukács's early works is *Theory of the Novel,* written in the midst of the horrors of the First World War, long suppressed by the author, finally republished (with another of those famous seductively self-denying prefaces) shortly before his death. *Theory of the Novel* argues that every literary form expresses a particular "metaphysical dissonance," which springs from the inner contradictions of its historical and social milieu. It goes on to evoke, with great lyrical brilliance, the dissonances that were tearing the modern world apart in 1915. It tries to imagine, and indeed to call into being, a true modernist art in which "all the fissures and rents inherent in the historical situation [will] be drawn into the form-giving process." *Theory of the Novel* is one of the great works of romantic criticism, in the class of Wordsworth's Preface to the *Lyrical Ballads* and Schiller's *Letters on the Aesthetic Education of Man.* It concludes with a ringing declaration that the inner dialectic of the modern novel leads beyond the novel and, indeed, beyond the wretched and alienated world whose spirit the novel expresses. The emergence of Tolstoy and Dostoevsky are distinctive "signs of the world to come." Their interpretations of the modern world mark the start of a great wave of change in this world, a "breakthrough into a new epoch," the dawn of a "new unity" of soul and social institutions. Moreover, even before the

---

5 *Theory of the Novel,* trans. Anna Bostock, Cambridge, MA: MIT Press, 1971.

Russian Revolution and Lukács's conversion to communism, he insisted that backward, grungy Russia was fated to be the salvation of the corrupt and decadent West.

Theory of the Novel is also fascinating in its religious anguish and longing. Lukács describes the modern novel as "an expression of transcendental homelessness"; the novel's typical environment as "a universe abandoned by God"; the epoch in which he writes as "an age of absolute sinfulness"; the modern hero's predicament as "the torment of a creature condemned to solitude and devoured by a longing for communion." Here, and throughout the book, Lukács makes clear the sort of inner needs that his commitment to communism, for a time at least, would fulfill.

Recent scholarship has unearthed the way in which Lukács became a communist. In fact, it was a religious conversion, an upheaval of the mind and heart, a second birth. It seems to have happened very suddenly in the last days of 1918. According to one of his intimate friends, it happened "between one Sunday and the next, like Saul turning into Paul." [6]

Even as he was turning, Lukács wrote two remarkable brief essays, perhaps the clearest and most candid things he ever wrote: "Bolshevism as a Moral Problem," a few days before his conversion, and "Tactics and Ethics," a few days after. [7] The "Bolshevism" essay, which was long believed lost and rediscovered shortly before Lukács's death, makes it clear that he saw himself as making an existential "leap of faith" into Bolshevism, and moreover considered this revolutionary faith to be utterly absurd. The

---

6   Said by Lukács's friend Anna Lesznai; quoted in Michael Lowy, *Georg Lukács: From Romanticism to Bolshevism*, trans. Patrick Camiller, London: Verso, 1979, 128.

7   "Bolshevism as a Moral Problem," trans. and introduced by Judith Marcus Tar, *Social Research* 44.3, Autumn 1977, 416–24. This was written in Hungarian in December 1918 for the journal of the Galileo Circle, a group of radical intellectuals at the University of Budapest. Editor Karl Polanyi had asked Lukács for a contribution. "Tactics and Ethics" was written a couple of weeks later, directly after his conversion. It is reprinted in Lukács, *Political Writings, 1919–1929*, trans. Michael McColgan, ed. Rodney Livingstone, London: New Left Books, 1972.

question at hand was whether the Bolshevik revolution would really "mean the end of *all* class domination" or "simply entail the reshuffling of classes" in which "the previous oppressors will become the new oppressed class"; whether the emerging socialist regime would in fact "bring about the salvation of humanity" or merely create "an ideological shell for class interests." Anywhere a Bolshevik regime comes to power, "the existing class oppression will . . . be replaced by that of the proletariat." The Bolshevik regime will aim "to drive out Satan so to speak, with the help of Beelzebub—in the hope that this last and therefore most open and cruel of class oppression will finally destroy itself, and in so doing put an end to class oppression forever." "In order to become a Bolshevik," Lukács says,

> We have to believe true *credo quia absurdum est*—that no new class struggle will emerge out of this class struggle (resulting in the quest for a new oppression), which would provide continuance to the old sequence of meaningless and aimless struggles—but that oppression will effect the elements of its own destruction. It is, therefore, a question of belief—as it is in the case of any ethical question—of what the choice will be. Let me emphasize again: Bolshevism rests on the metaphysical assumption that the bad can engender the good, or, as Razumikhin says, in Dostoevsky's *Crime and Punishment,* that it is possible to lie our way through to the truth.
>
> This author is unable to share this belief.

And yet, within a few days of this essay, Lukács had decided to make the leap. What changed his mind? It's hard to say for sure. "Tactics and Ethics" offers a pragmatic argument that in East Central Europe in 1919, the likely political alternatives are either a communist revolution or a fascist dictatorship; at this time, in this place, liberal democracy is simply not in the cards. This argument is plausible but has a limited force. It justifies participating in a communist movement on the grounds that it is the lesser of two available evils. But Lukács invests far more emotion in communism, and expects far more from it, than his pragmatic argumentation could ever comprehend. We need to look between the lines of his text and search out the emotional subtext. The most intense emotion in the inner world of "Tactics and Ethics" is Lukács's sense of guilt. The ethical rhetoric he speaks in at first sounds Kantian; we should act as if we were universal legislators, ethically responsible for the whole world. But if we listen for the feeling, it is less Kant than Dostoevsky, or Kant as he might have been remembered by Raskolnikov.[8]

Thus, for Lukács, we really are responsible for all the oppression, violence, and murder in the world. If we become communists, we are guilty of all the murders committed in the name of communism, not only now but in the indefinite future, *just as if we had killed them all* (my emphasis). If we refuse to commit ourselves to communism, and fascism triumphs instead, we are guilty of all fascist murders, now and to come. No matter what happens, whatever we do or don't do, we are all murderers, there is no way to escape the blood on our hands. What can a murderer do? Is there any way to atone? These were the sorts of questions that were tormenting Lukács at the end of 1918. He seems to have concluded that if the criminal were to lean to the left, his crimes might actually accomplish something, his murders might help to end (or at least diminish) murders, his lies might open the way to some sort of truth.

In his later years, Lukács disparaged the thinking that led to his conversion as "utopian," "messianic," "sectarian." It wasn't till

---

8   Although it is indeed Razumikhin, in *Crime and Punishment*, who gives this formulation—to lie one's way through to the truth—it is not his own lies and truths that he is talking about, but Raskolnikov's; and he offers the formulation as a caricature, hoping (in vain) that Raskolnikov will disavow it. Razumikhin is a delightfully un-Dostoevskian character, poor and radical like Raskolnikov—he has been kicked out of the university for punching a policeman—but sane, emotionally sunny and unproblematic in all the ways Raskolnikov is not. (When Raskolnikov is sentenced to Siberia, Razumikhin gets to marry Raskolnikov's sister, and readers are happy to throw rice.) But Raskolnikov is the one with whom Lukács identifies, and the prime model for his various betrayals and regenerations, from youth to old age.

later on, he said, that he became a "realist" and "materialist" and learned true Marxism. After digging deep into his early work, I would argue the exact opposite: that at the high tide of his messianic hopes, Lukács's moral and political thinking was clear, honest, and deeply attuned to material realities, in the finest Marxist tradition. He said repeatedly, in 1919, that it was impossible to know how history was going to turn out, that all political choices would have to be continually reappraised, that the ethical subject would have to weigh the violence and evil he helped to perpetrate against the actual freedom and happiness that he was helping to create.

It was only afterward, when it became clear that his hopes were not being fulfilled in the real world, that his leap of faith froze into a form of bad faith. We can see this happening even in the last sections of *History and Class Consciousness,* where Lukács's religious and moral hopes are gradually reified into a theological system of beliefs. His concept of incarnation, orthodoxy, and totality become a trinity in a secular political theology. Lukács's *credo quia absurdum est,* and his real bad faith, lay not in his 1919 hope that oppression today might help to end oppression tomorrow, but in his post-1921 doctrine that through the Party's power, oppression had ended already. He clung to this doctrine all through the Stalin era, even as it undermined and slowly poisoned his thought and his life.

There is one more big clue to Lukács's life that came to light after his death. In 1973 a Heidelberg bank released a safe deposit box full of long-lost Lukács letters, diaries, and manuscripts.[9] This material uncovered the story of his first love. Late in 1907, Lukács

---

9   See Georg Lukács, *Selected Correspondence, 1902-1920.* Lukács's tragic romance is one of the focuses of this fine volume (the others are Lukács's intimacy with Max Weber, Georg Simmel, and other great thinkers old enough to be his father). After Seidler's suicide, Lukács published a heartrending dialogue, "On Poverty of Spirit." It has been translated by Jane and John Sanders, and reprinted in *Philosophical Forum* 3, 1971–72, 360–83, with an introduction by Agnes Heller. Cf. Heller's longer essay "Gyorgy Lukács and Irma Seidler," in *Lukács Reappraised,* edited by Agnes Heller, New York: Columbia University Press, 1983, 27–62.

and Irma Seidler, a young Hungarian Jewish painter, met and fell in love. She wanted marriage and a normal life with him. He seems to have genuinely loved her but, like many men before and since, feared commitment. "What I wish to accomplish," he wrote her, "only an unattached man can accomplish." For three years, even as he idealized and mythicized her ("Irma is Life," etc.), he fought her off. In the spring of 1911, she killed herself. Lukács was devastated and racked with guilt. "I could have saved her if I'd taken her hand . . . I have lost my right to life." It would be foolish to reduce Lukács's (or anybody's) ideology to psychology. Still, this heartbreaking affair, and Lukács's self-lacerating judgment on his role in it, may help to clarify some of the mysteries of his thought and action in years to come. It gives us an idea why he felt so guilty—guilty, as he repeatedly said, of murder—and why he had such a deep need for confession, repentance, mortification, atonement. It gives a personal urgency and emotional depth to the idea, advanced in *Theory of the Novel* in 1915, that modern humanity's basic problem is "the torment of a creature condemned to solitude and devoured by the longing for community." And it suggests why it was Ernő Seidler, Irma's brother, who—along with Party leader and (for a little while) Prime Minister Béla Kun—recruited Lukács into the Hungarian Communist Party at the end of 1918.[10]

Lukács himself, for most of his career, treated the whole medium of cinema with learned ignorance; his throwaway dismissals through the years make him sound like one more park-bench *alte kocker* who can't accept that he's living in the twentieth century. That wouldn't be a problem if so much of his writing

---

10 What a great Hungarian movie this sad story would have made! And there were two generations of fine Hungarian directors—Miklos Jansco, Marta Mezaros, Pal Gabor, Istvan Szabo, Karoly Makk, and others I've forgotten or never knew—who could really have grasped it, who knew how to situate a phenomenon like communism and an emotion like love in the same frame, and knew there was a rich variety of possible ways for them to play out. Alas, *Irma and György* will never be made. It is too late now: the memory is gone. Eastern Europe in the 1990s has lost its tragic sense of communist life, lost it as inexorably as Western Europe once lost the art of medieval stained glass.

weren't framed as a demand for "realism." But then, in the glorious month of May 1968, Lukács not only supported the troubles, but gave the cinema special credit for starting them: "In Hungary," he said, in an interview with the cinema magazine *Filmkultura*, "or at least in Hungarian culture, film nowadays plays the role of the *avant-garde*."[11] This sentence isn't only about movies, or about Hungary. It is about *being there:* about an old realist who wants to make whatever imaginative leaps he must to be part of the real world around him; about an old modernist who remembers that to seize the day is to be alive; about an old man who isn't ready to go gentle into the good night. It is the reason you can't ever give up on Lukács: just when you are ready to close the books on him—as he so often yearns to close the books on himself—he makes a spurt of new life and growth.

So where does Lukács leave us in the end? The sketches and interviews that make up *Record of a Life* offer no final epiphany, but only more layers under layers and wheels within wheels, more of Lukács's enticing and infuriating blend of blindness and insight, of bad faith and transcendent inspiration. He says, with an apparently straight face, "I am perhaps not a very contemporary man. I have never felt frustration or any kind of complex in my life. I know what these mean, of course, from the literature of the twentieth century and from having read Freud. But I have not experienced them myself." Yet even as he says this, he recognizes, fugitively, how much of his life's energy has gone into repudiating his thoughts and burying his feelings. When he says, "It has cost me nothing," he reveals to us how much it really has cost.

---

11   This interview was reported in the *New York Times*, whose Central and Eastern European correspondents discovered Lukács's importance in 1956. It is discussed in detail in J. Hoberman, *The Red Atlantis: Communist Culture in the Absence of Communism*, Philadelphia: Temple University Press, 1998, 48–51, 276–8. Hoberman writes elegiacally of the Kádár era, the age of "frigidaire socialism," when, he says, "Hungarian pop offered a way to criticise Hungarian socialism," and "the worker's state incubated its own revolutionary opposition." In Hoberman's fine essays on Polish, Hungarian, and Czech cinema yesterday and today, Eastern European culture converges surprisingly with North American in a shared nostalgia for radicalism born of abundance.

Lukács is still intermittently swallowed up by the totalities he created for himself in the 1920s. When asked what he said to himself during the monstrous excesses of Stalinism, he replies that "the worst form of socialism was better to live in than the best form of capitalism." And yet, just a few pages before and after, he shows a bitter clarity about the so-called socialism he has served for so long. When the Warsaw Pact armies invaded Prague in 1968, he told István Eörsi, "I suppose that the whole experiment that began in 1917 has now failed, and has to be tried again at some other time and place." Lukács comes to believe, in his last years, that only a "complete rupture" with Stalinism will enable the communist movement to reclaim its creative powers; but he sees no "objective forces" that might fulfill this hope. In the end, he condemns all communist regimes for betraying the original promise of communist revolutions, "genuine socialist democracy . . . democracy of everyday life." He sees capitalist and communist powers at home in a detente of domination, oppressing both their own and foreign people. He hopes—not in his lifetime, he knows, but someday—for a convergence of freedom. "Both great systems in crisis. Authentic Marxism the only solution." These were virtually the last words he wrote before he died.

Georg Lukács is one of the real tragic heroes of the twentieth century. Tragic in the price he had to pay—indeed, the price he fought to pay. Heroic in the demands he made on modern art, on modern politics, on the whole of modern life—demands he affirmed to his life's end. It seems uncanny that he was here, in our midst, only yesterday. He seems too big for these times, times when people in both capitalist and socialist countries are demanding so little: big cars, villas in the country, trips abroad, pension plans. These are updated models of the things Lukács grew up with and learned to see through. Maybe after more of the people who haven't grown up with these things have had a crack at them they, too, will learn to see through the many forms of comfortable reification that pass for life. Maybe we will live to see the day when the people who don't want to be commodities in a market, even luxury commodities, and the people who don't want to be items in a plan, even top-priority items, will discover each other and struggle together for what Lukács called "democracy of everyday life."

This essay first appeared as "Georg Lukács's Cosmic Chutzpah*" in the* Village Voice Literary Supplement, *July 1985.*

Part V

The Bright Book of Life

The Jewish Patient

When I first encountered Franz Kafka, as a high school student in the mid-1950s, there was a real romance of Kafka in the air. People talked about him with hushed reverence then, as some sort of modern saint: His books were infernos—but sorry, no paradise, because in the modern world God Is Dead, haven't you noticed, stupid?—allegories of sin and grace, sublime but doomed quests for the Holy Grail. Allegory was the correct way to read him, because although his fiction was full of realistic detail, it existed on a plane of pure spirituality far beyond the crude world of readers like us, teenagers worried about getting into college and getting laid. We were told Kafka had no politics at all, he was Above or Beyond Politics. Yet his works in those Cold War days were also weapons against communism, because all his visions of tortured and mutilated people were accurate prophecies of the Evil Empire. As for his bio, the fifties Kafka was a neo-Sebastian born out of his time, stretched on the rack of this rough world, crushed by his cruel family, by his enslavement in a bureaucracy, by banal women who wanted him to have not only sex but children; no wonder the poor man died young! This romance actually says less about Kafka than about the grim life of the fifties—and about why we needed the sixties.

Since the sixties, new dimensions of Kafka have opened up. Writers of the Prague Spring era (Milan Kundera, Jiří Gruša, Josef Škvorecký, Ivan Klíma, Václav Havel, and others) gave him a political identity as a socialist humanist, a precursor of 1956 and 1968, a fighter for human dignity against the perpetrators of Trials and the residents of Castles. They also showed how *funny* he was, how he saw that futility and absurdity could be comic as well as tragic facts of life. American Jews like Philip Roth, Morris Dickstein, Leonard Michaels, and Woody Allen placed Kafkaesque comedy in an Eastern European Jewish tradition, the "low" comedy of *shlemiels*, *shlimazls*, *luftmenshen*, and other chronic victims of power.

In 1984, Ernst Pawel published *The Nightmare of Reason: A Life of Franz Kafka*, one of the great biographies of recent years. Pawel, a Jewish refugee who worked for insurance companies on both sides of the Atlantic, may have been the first student of Kafka who actually understood his work. He showed that although Kafka described himself as a helpless *shlemiel* on the job, in fact he was a superachiever: He used bureaucratic procedures to trans-form the Czech system of workmen's compensation into a system of accident prevention; he learned how mines and factories worked from the inside, fought the bosses, forced big changes, helped save thousands of workers' lives; he was probably the inventor of OSHA, and one of the most creative bureaucrats of the century. He worked through the night not because he was enslaved by routines but because he *mastered* the routines in a way that could change the world.

Pawel also showed how Kafka, who grew up surrounded by pogroms, was engaged with Judaism all his life, running with Yiddishists in the 1910s (he made a speech, addressed to Germans, "On the Yiddish Language," which ended with the admonition, "You understand Yiddish much better than you suppose") and with Socialist Zionists in the twenties (one of his last fantasies was to end his life as a waiter in a cafe in Tel Aviv). He was involved with Martin Buber, writing some brilliant existentialist Jewish parables. And, while the fifties romance of Kafka had portrayed him as somehow too pure for sex, Pawel showed him and his friends getting it on, down and dirty, in the Prague cabarets and whorehouses where West End boys met East End girls. There is a marvelous photo in *The Nightmare of Reason* of Kafka as a student, in a high collar and a derby, "with Hansi, the 'Trocadéro Valkyrie,'" putting on the ritz. What a thrill to discover that this man who portrayed himself as a walking shadow was really *there*, that he was active, resourceful, and admired in the world, that he even (sometimes) could have a good time. The post-sixties Kafka stank of profane vitality like you and me.

But if Kafka was so healthy, why was he so obsessed with sickness? In fact, you can't read three pages of his collected letters or diaries without encountering riffs on somebody's dread disease, usually the author's own. Like Webster, he was "much possessed by death." Whoever knew him knew his hypochondria, which he always joked about but never shed. He vacationed at health spas and lived with the dying. He was a connoisseur of disease long before he got sick. (He came down with tuberculosis in 1917 and died from it in 1924.) It's likely he spent most of his adult life convinced he was dying and likely, too, that this belief somehow gave him strength to live. Sander Gilman tries to untie these knots in his provocative and fascinating new book, *Franz Kafka: The Jewish Patient*. Gilman, who teaches at the University of Chicago, is a historian of medicine as well as a critic of Central European, especially Jewish, literature and life. He is fluent in many languages, at home in many cultural genres, overflowing with energy. Sometimes it seems he writes a book a year, including *Jewish Self-Hatred* (1986), *The Jew's Body* (1991), and *Freud, Race and Gender* (1993). He sounds proud to be a Jew, yet uncertain what Jewishness ultimately means. And he is a child (born in 1944) of the romantic sixties.

The particular sixties and post-sixties romance that Gilman's readers should recognize is the romance of *paranoia*. This romance thrived abundantly in the endless speculations about President Kennedy's assassination, but also in the music of the Velvet Underground, Talking Heads Steely Dan; in movies like *Blow-Up*, *The Passenger*, and *The Conversation*; in the fiction of William Burroughs, Norman Mailer, Thomas Pynchon, and Don DeLillo. Paranoid social science flourished in the circles around Erving Goffman and Michel Foucault. Much in Gilman reminds us of Foucault: He thinks language is the essence of being; he believes doctors and their diagnostic debates are the key to history; he is a brilliant excavator of obscure texts, which he invests with vast, dire meanings; he often threatens to crush the reader with metaphysical gravity, to submerge us in ontological gloom. But he does not press a metaphysico-political agenda upon us; indeed, his

writing is driven by wheels within wheels of irony, so that it is
often hard to know what Gilman is up to. He is a distinctively
weird writer, which makes him and his subject a perfect match.

In *The Jewish Patient,* Gilman argues that "Kafka's illness(es)
came to define his sense of self" and that illness furthermore was
"the axis on which he and his world turned." In fact, says Gilman,
Kafka's "discourse of illness" is actually talk about "specific differences among human beings." Kafka leans unconsciously on a
structure of stereotypes that were created or transformed by the
virulent and growing anti-Semitism of his time. "These stereotypes shaped Kafka's sense of himself so intensely that he . . . may
well have been unaware of their historical specificity." So much *fin
de siècle* talk about health and disease was racialized, and Kafka,
usually far beyond the awareness of his contemporaries, often
falls back on "the discourses of his time." When he talks about
health and disease, his own or other people's, he is talking in code,
and the code is usually about *Jews.*

Gilman locates Kafka within a number of *fin de siècle* controver-
sies about Jews: the cliché dualism of "Eastern" and "Western"
(Western Jews strong, healthy, Enlightened, but empty within;
Eastern Jews dirty, ragged, illiterate, diseased, but "authentic");
arguments about kosher laws, Jewish ritual slaughter and circum-
cision (were they healthy or harmful, meaningful or meaningless
in modern times); arguments about syphilis and TB (whether
Jews were more or less susceptible, and what had they done to
deserve this); arguments about whether Jews could speak or write
"authentically" in German (or French, English, Russian, etc.);
racist theories of "degeneration," in which Jewish brains, beauty,
strength, and creativity were all interpreted as symptoms of
degeneracy; accusations of ritual murder, often the first act in
massacres and pogroms; the Dreyfus Affair, that rehearsal for
Nazism, which brought together and acted out every Jewish fear.
Kafka read the papers closely and had plenty to say on all these
topics, and some of what he said was luminous and visionary.

Gilman is very well read in the history and literature of anti-
Semitism, and brilliant at taking language apart. He shows the

amazing extent to which racist anti-Semitism dominated European—and, incidentally, American—public discourse in Kafka's lifetime. Anti-Semitic images and themes seem to have been embraced uncritically by nearly everybody. Gilman walks us through this talk and highlights its *plasticity*: Jews were condemned for being more sickly than "normal" Europeans, but also condemned when they appeared healthier (e.g. immune to TB), and condemned again when their health stats were identical with those of the goyim. With sadly few exceptions, the most "advanced" physical and social scientists of the *fin de siècle* not only joined the chorus but even took the lead.

Ironically, as Gilman shows, many Jews themselves, including those who fought heroically against various oppressors, shared their enemies' belief that there was something basically wrong with them. Max Nordau, medical doctor, Zionist pioneer, and author of the landmark book *Degeneration* (1895), is an outstanding example. Gilman finds a similar affinity at many points in Kafka's work. On the other hand, much of Kafka's writing radiates Jewish pride. He only sometimes believed that there was something basically wrong with the Jewish people; what he never doubted was that there was something basically wrong with *him*.

One part of himself that Kafka always hated, and punished, was his body. He was about six feet tall and weighed around 130 pounds, with black hair and piercing eyes. "I am the thinnest person I know," he wrote. Calvin Klein, another scrawny Jewish boy, would have loved Kafka's body (can't you see him in black-and whites on a bus billboard?), but Kafka himself didn't get much *naches* from it:

> Nothing can be accomplished with such a body . . . My body is too long for its weakness, it hasn't the least bit of fat to engender a blessed warmth, to preserve an inner fire . . . Everything is pulled apart.

Gilman shows how Kafka regularly put his body on trial, convicted and condemned it. This anorexic's life sentence was a dread series of increasingly spartan diets: no meat or fish or sugar or spice, and every morsel of food to be chewed a dozen times (known as "Fletcherizing"). Such a diet not only kept him thin and thinner but insured that whoever sat down to eat with him ate their hearts out.

Pawel was the first to catalogue Kafka's eating disorders and to locate his strange diets in the context of his obsessions about his health. Kafka's food taboos were a grim parody of the *kashrut* laws—his father's father had been a kosher butcher—except that *kashrut* diets bound Jews together and created solidarity among them, while Kafka's diets served to isolate him ever more. Gilman argues that as lonely as Kafka may have felt, or made himself, it was always a *Jewish* loneliness. A brilliant graphics researcher, he reproduces some turn-of-the-century racist catalogues of "Jewish types," where Kafka is a perfect fit for "the diseased." (Another type in one of the racist picture galleries uncannily resembles Marcel Proust.) The acme of the "diseased Jew" was the anorexic, tubercular Sarah Bernhardt, a heroine of Kafka's, and Proust's, and my grandmother's, and probably millions of Jews—always ill, obsessed with her health, looking as if she were sinking from week to week, yet knocking people out with an uncanny vitality, and destined to live into her late seventies.

Many Jews, especially young ones, were sick of these types. They feared not only that Jewish sickliness kept them from being accepted as healthy "normal" Europeans but also that they, too, could get sick someday. (As it turned out, Hitler would save them the trouble of growing old.) Gilman, ever ingenious in his scholarship, excavates a 1914 article, "The Jewish Patient"—this is where he gets his subtitle—from the Prague Zionist Journal *Self-Defense*. The article, a petulant complaint against Jewish hypochondria, features scenes of vaudeville-*shtick*-like encounters between Jewish patients and their doctors. Specimens:

DOCTOR: How long have you been sick?
PATIENT: My friend, I came into this world with my illness.
DOCTOR: How is your stomach?
PATIENT: Since I eat, how should my stomach be?

When Kafka laughed, this is the sort of thing he laughed at. Gilman understands, as did Kafka and Freud, but as the impatient young Jews of 1914 did not, how Jewish hypochondria could be a vital means of self-defense.

One of Gilman's best chapters is an essay on the Dreyfus Affair, the event "which more than any other focuses the anxiety of assimilated Jews about their physical integration into the world where they find themselves." Frederick Karl, in his recent study of Kafka, sees the affair as "the archetypal court case in the background of *The Trial*." This is so obvious, how come nobody said it before? Gilman focuses on Dreyfus's body and its disintegration under torture. He mounts Dreyfus on the grid of the stereotypical dualism between "Western" and "Eastern" Jews. Thus Dreyfus metamorphosed from what people saw as the strong, healthy body of a "Western" Jew into what they saw as a bent, twisted, ragged, diseased body, the alleged body of an "Eastern" (or a "Wandering") Jew. Anti-Semites had always said the integration of Jews into Western European life was shallow and phony, and that they were really all Polish beggars and ragmen "underneath"; the torture machines of Devil's Island were supposed to prove their point. (Gilman reproduces Dreyfus's own diagram of the one used on him.) In the short run, the cruelties backfired. News photographs of Dreyfus in prison horrified even people who had thought he was guilty, but who now compared his suffering to Jesus Christ's. We can imagine how this incident might have stirred Kafka's imagination and helped lay the foundations for the death machine of "In the Penal Colony." At the same time, we can imagine how it might also have stirred other Europeans, who dreamed of mass murder by machine. Who knows? Where Gilman is at his best, lack of hard evidence doesn't seem to matter. He isn't doing forensics, it isn't the O.J. trial; we already know everybody's guilty, including of course people who weren't born. He's presenting a luminous poetic vision of the twentieth century, and it doesn't hurt if some of the garden paths are imaginary, because we know the toads are real.

One of Gilman's most provocative themes, but a deeply problematical one, is the Jew's allegedly "stolen" language. Anti-Semites everywhere have always disparaged Jewish writers on the ground that "they" have no right to "our" language and that what passes for their creativity is actually a form of cancer or murder. In French, this was the theme of a flood of virulent polemics aimed at Proust. In his lifetime Kafka was not a special target in German, but we know he felt guilty of everything, and he was especially susceptible to the tirades of the great Viennese critic and Jewish anti-Semite Karl Kraus, self-appointed defender of the "purity" of the German language against Jewish "pollution." Kafka often agreed: He should be writing in some language more "authentic," more "his own." But what? At different moments in his life, Kafka was both a Yiddishist and a Hebraist. Yiddishism and Hebraism shared the metaphysical belief that it was "authentic" for Jews to talk only with one another, and somehow "inauthentic" to talk with anybody else.

Gilman seems to express a curious sympathy for this belief. Now I can understand it as a defense mechanism—just like hysteria and hypochondria—in a world where, God knows, Jews have so often been horribly attacked. But as an *idea,* as something to be taken at face value, it strikes me as not only a great mistake but a moral outrage. If the great modern revolutions mean anything, and I believe they do, then everybody has the right to speak to the whole world, and the only thing "authenticity" can mean is putting your thoughts and feelings across in ways the world can understand. Kafka always knew that, in German, he was one of the great writers in one of the world's great literatures, and that his voice was getting across to plenty of total strangers. He was proud of this, and there's no way on earth he would have given it up.

Gilman clearly loves the German language, yet seems willing, even eager, to see Jews give it up. What drives him to this? It's hard to know. But at the book's very end he makes a great leap from a paranoiac vision to an apocalyptic one, where all modern history leads up to the moment of total polarization of Germans and Jews, the *Shoah,* the Holocaust.

His last chapter, "Kafka Goes to Camp," starts with a glimpse of Kafka at a Jewish vacation camp in Germany in July 1923. It is a heart-rending moment: Now that he knows nothing can save him, he realizes how much he really wants to live. He sees some poor Polish-Jewish children singing and dancing, and his heart leaps up. Then—jump-cut—we are suddenly thrown from health camps to death camps, where, Gilman says, Nazi doctors will infect people with TB to study their pain. There, any of those twenties children still alive will be tortured and killed, along with Kafka's sisters and his lover Milena Jesenská, and there Kafka too would have been killed, if only he had lived long enough. Through unnamed inexorable processes,

> camps set up to protect Jewish children are replaced by camps set up to infect them. Thus the fantasies about the Jewish body in the medicine of the *fin de siècle* become the horror of the *Shoah*.

Gilman ends his book with the view from the crematoriums. From there, any attempts by Jews to seize life—those poor kids dancing, Kafka falling in love or writing words—are judged with a heavy irony that is very close to contempt: The *Shoah* has, and is, the last word.

In the years after World War Two, some impressive people— Elie Wiesel, Theodor Adorno, George Steiner—took that view. They spoke as if the Nazis had won the war; they were the last to leave a sane world, and they were turning out the light. At least we knew the dark places they were coming from. But what's Gilman's excuse? He was born in the United States just when his dread story ends. He has grown into middle age, as I have, in an America filled with horrors, but with no death camps, and some nice stuff mixed in. He starts the book with a page of epigraphs: Kafka was too Jewish, or not Jewish enough, or Christian. Then he asserts, in bold type, "and then comes me." But then *he doesn't come*. There's a total absence of presence, of subjectivity; over three-hundred pages the author remains a missing person. The ontological gloom that haunts *The Jewish Patient* is one of its unsolved mysteries.

It is clear that Gilman loves Kafka, but he thinks Kafka did something terribly wrong. What was his original sin? Apparently it was Modernism:

> [Kafka] moved from a language marked by the discourses of his
> time to one that he and his contemporaries saw as "modern," and
> therefore, they hoped, universal, transnational, and infinitely
> interpretable in the ideological strife of their age.

Again,

> Kafka . . . needs to efface any reference to an external world [the
> world of anti-Semites] that questions his control over his language
> and his body. And the high modern . . . encourages this efface-
> ment in its striving for seeming universals and its reduction of its
> characters to types.

So Kafka's modernism was a shrinking ("reduction") of literary
values, a form of repression ("effacement"), of bad faith, of the
whole pathology of "Jewish self-hatred." Gilman writes as if he
knows how Kafka should have written, but alas, he doesn't tell. In
treating Kafka's language as something degenerate, Gilman ironically proves one of his larger points: that it's desperately hard for
Jews to talk about themselves without sounding like
anti-Semites.

Gilman uses one more sinister-sounding word for Kafka's original sin: to *deterritorialize*. He gets this clunky word from the
French critics Gilles Deleuze and Felix Guattari, but he uses it in
his own special way:

> I use the term "deterritorialization" to mean the creation of a
> seemingly universal discourse . . . This discourse replaces and
> represses those discourses that demean or denigrate one's ability
> to command the language of the high culture with which one
> identifies.

Once more, Gilman deploys loaded words—"represses," "seemingly universal"—to disparage Kafka's modernism without ever
confronting him directly. If he did, he would have to say why he
thinks Kafka's vocabulary is only "seemingly," not authentically,
universal; why his language "represses" rather than (say)

"surpasses" the racist discourse that Gilman knows so well; why Kafka was merely "replacing," and not, as he thought, *creating;* why Gilman uses the verb to "deterritorialize," which implies that only the territorial is real, in place of a more familiar verb, to "universalize," a key word in the liberal socialism that Kafka believed in all his life. Even when he felt that he was guilty, Kafka believed that *other people* were innocent, and his greatest works were affirmations of their rights.

I see where I am going now: toward a new romance of Kafka. This is the Kafka of 1989, who works at his respectable job to tear down the walls. Gilman himself observes that "the adjective 'kafkaesque' now exists in all the languages of Europe and the Americas." I bet so able a linguist could find it in Asian and African languages as well. Kafkaesque experiences are what happen to people who claim their human rights and are referred to departments that can't be found. Some people were making those claims, and running into that trouble, in Kafka's lifetime. A lot more people around the world are confronting their Castles, including their interior ones, today. The fact that they do so, and recognize Kafka as a guide, shows not only that twentieth-century modernism has plenty to be proud of, but that Franz Kafka, the Jewish Patient, was healthier than he thought.

This essay originally appeared as "Kafka Family Values" in the Nation, *November 20, 1995.*

Waiting for the Barbarians

I continued on my way, imploring fate to grant me the simplest of proficiencies—the ability to kill my fellow man . . .

We are the vanguard, but of what?

Isaac Babel, *1920 Diary*

"Where are the barbarians of the twentieth century?" Friedrich Nietzsche wrote, longingly, a bit more than a century ago. He was writing near the end of a hundred years of peace in Europe, and he was convinced that peace had made Europeans sick. With their highly developed Christian conscience (even for agnostics and atheists) and their acute sense of guilt, modern men and women had crippled themselves: They were "broken" like their horses, "fixed" like their cats, of no more consequence than their domestic pets. But just across the frontier, Nietzsche imagined, there were prides of wild beasts, untamed, ferocious, but *fully alive*. He also imagined a "fully alive" pre-Christian pride of men whom he called "blond beasts": men who could sweep the borders and margins of their homelands and come rolling home "from orgies of murder, arson, rape, torture, jubilant and at peace with themselves." Maybe the time was ripe for post-Christian men to "re-barbarize" themselves and their world, to somehow be born again as beasts. "Where are the barbarians?" 1914 was near; Europe wouldn't have to wait long.

At such a rich historical moment, Nietzsche thought, there was a great new mission for intellectuals: to "live dangerously." They should spring from their studies and build their houses under volcanoes; they should live through every day as if it were their last. In a re-barbarized world, the dangers in living dangerously would be intensely physical, but inward and psychic as well: "He who fights with monsters should be careful lest he thereby become a monster. If you look too long into the abyss, the abyss will look back into you." Long after their abysses ate them up (Nietzsche's mind snapped in 1889), their lives and works would stand as monuments to how far a human being could go.

I haven't been able to find out whether Isaac Babel (1894–1940) read Nietzsche; but it may be that he didn't have to—Freud once said something like this about himself—because, in turn-of-the-century culture, there was so much of Nietzsche in the air. In any case, Babel abundantly fulfilled Nietzsche's prophecies and hopes: He lived more dangerously, made himself at home under more volcanoes, looked deeper into more abysses, than any intellectual of the century. It's interesting that he did this as a citizen and life-long supporter of the USSR. "Lifelong" is just the sort of gallows humor that Babel, murdered by the NKVD in 1940, would have liked. As horrible as life in the USSR could be, and Babel got as close to the horror as anybody, it had a spiritual depth that its enemies never knew.

Babel came up as a protegé of Maxim Gorky, who told him he couldn't develop as a writer until he knew more of life. The date of this advice was 1916, a fine time for a young man to learn about life in death and death in life. Babel volunteered and fought in assorted campaigns with the Russian Army, and then, after 1917, with the Red Army. He fought to defend Petrograd under siege. He joined an expedition to the countryside to extort grain for starving cities. He joined the Cheka, the first incarnation of the Soviet secret police. (How long did he last? What did he do? We still don't know. Even with millions of files opened, it's still the secret police!)

Writing for soldiers' papers, Babel gradually convinced people he might have talent as a war correspondent. The breakthrough event in his life occurred in 1920, at the height of the Civil War: He was assigned to cover the First Cavalry, the one band of Cossacks that supported the Reds, in their campaign against the Polish Army. (Poland had support from British and American

armies, along with artillery and air power.) The Cossacks, a privi-
leged estate under the tsars, whose borders they guarded, were
world-famous for their anti-Semitic frenzies. In 1905, as a boy in
Odessa, Babel had seen one of their pogroms and was lucky not to
have been killed. Did this assignment come down from above
(maybe some bureaucratic joker thought his experience in 1905
made him a Cossack expert), or, as some people say, did he
perversely seek it out? Something else we'll never know. But his
superiors (party? press? police?) clearly felt he was in danger,
because they prepared papers for him that dropped his Jewishness
along with his name, and converted him to a Russian Orthodox
man named Lyutov, "ferocious." (All this is explained in Carol
Avins's excellent introduction to the *Diary.*) So he went forth, a
spy in the enemy camp, only his supposed enemies were also
supposed to be his comrades.

Babel's year with the Cossacks generated a remarkable series of
stories, published individually through the 1920s and then as a
book, *Red Cavalry*, in 1926. *Red Cavalry* is a *Bildungsroman*, one
of the most powerful and persistent forms in modern literature. It
thrives not only in written fiction and drama but in movies, TV
series, rock and roll. (Bruce Springsteen is a genius of the
Bildungsroman.) One of its central themes is that in order to
become himself, the hero must learn not only to face but somehow to internalize his anti-self. Both Babel's self and his anti-self
turn on an axis of violence. He sees violence/non-violence as a
crucial issue for any modern man trying to answer the question
"Who am I?" to create what Erik Erikson calls an ego-identity.

Babel's self and anti-self evoke Nietzsche, or E.M. Forster, or
D.H. Lawrence. The self is a learned, rational, critical intellectual,
tending toward melancholy, "a man with spectacles on your nose
and autumn in your heart." The anti-self is a man of action, rarely
literate, but innocently "physical," "animal," "primitive," unre-
flectively cruel and glamorously sexual. Here, for instance, is the
Cossack general whom Babel calls "captivating Savitsky":

Savitsky, Commander of the VI Division, rose when he saw me,
and I wondered at the beauty of his giant's body. He rose, the

purple of his riding breeches and the crimson little tilted cap and the decorations stuck on his chest, cleaving the hut as a standard cleaves the sky. A smell of scent and the sickly sweet freshness of soap emanated from him. His long legs were like girls sheathed to the neck in shining riding-boots.

He smiled at me, struck his riding-whip on the table, and . . .

("My First Goose")

"Where are the barbarians?" asked Nietzsche. Babel could have given him some good addresses.

Cynthia Ozick, in the May 8 *New Republic*, puts Babel up against the wall. He should have known all that she knows about the USSR.[1] He should have known that all collective attempts to create a better life are fated to turn monstrous. (Including Zionism?) He should have been smart enough to go to America. (I've often thought this myself: He would have made a terrific Hollywood screenwriter of *films noirs* and a terrific victim of the anti-communist blacklist; he would have given cryptic and provocative answers to the FBI, just as he did to the NKVD; he would have done time, but at least he would have survived; people would have pointed him out in the L.A. Farmer's Market or on Central Park West; he would have walked up and down Broadway with I.B. Singer, translated him into Russian, become a character in his stories . . . Wouldn't it have been a wonderful life? Be still, my heart, be still.) Ozick's lack of generosity is surprising because Babel's romance of violence and *shtarkers*, "tough guys," is identical with that of her hero, Babel's fellow Odessan, Vladimir Jabotinsky.

In *Red Cavalry*, Babel's hero is forced to face the existential question of whether he, too, can become a barbarian. The typical plot goes like this: The hero is dissed by the Cossacks for being the person he is; in order to be accepted, he must do something vicious, preferably to a woman; he does something (it isn't rape);

---

1   Cynthia Ozick, "The Year of Writing Dangerously," *New Republic*, May 8, 1995.

he has passed the test and the men do accept him—for the time being. He is thrilled and happy to be with them—almost. Thus, in "My First Goose":

> We slept, all six of us, beneath a wooden roof that let in the stars, warming one another, our legs intermingled. I dreamed; and in my dreams saw women. But my heart, stained with bloodshed, grated and brimmed over.

In the story "After the Battle," he fails. He has been in the thick of the fighting and exposed himself to heavy fire, but it turns out he hasn't loaded his own gun. A Cossack bawls him out and beats him up, and he "implores fate to grant me the simplest of proficiencies, the ability to kill my fellow man." But we suspect Babel's heroes will keep flunking the Cossack initiation; in this Mafia, they will never get "made."

What inner force holds them back? Maybe the intellectual power and honesty that made them special in the first place. Alongside Babel's rhapsodic celebration of the anti-self, *Red Cavalry* features a powerful assertion of the self. It turned out that the man "with spectacles on your nose and autumn in your heart" could write about combat and the battlefront in a way that was remarkably compelling: clear, terse, penetrating, stripped down, emptied of all the grand sentimental words—homeland, civilization, courage, sacrifice, hallowed, etc., etc.—that have been used forever to justify killing and getting killed. Paul Fussell, in *The Great War and Modern Memory*, argues that, ironically, the horrors of World War One drove people to create more honest ways of seeing war.[2] Ernest Hemingway, who set a standard for honest war writing, thought Babel did it even better than he did.

At the climax of many a *Bildungsroman*, the hero, who has expanded and deepened himself (or herself) through love, grows disenchanted and learns to see through the one he loves. In *Red Cavalry*, the self cuts in on the anti-self: Babel's smart military

---

2   Paul Fussell, *The Great War and Modern Memory*, New York: Oxford University Press, 1975.

analyst interrupts his reverent groupie and shows that the Cossacks may look glamorous, but in the real conditions of twentieth-century war, they are inept, they can't fight. Against an army that has artillery and airplanes for support, the Cossacks' M.O., the gallant charge with horses and swords in open country, is a recipe for disaster. In the battle of Czesniki (the battle in "After the Battle"), in Galicia in September 1920, the disaster finally happens. Just like Pickett's charge at Gettysburg, wave after wave of men on horseback rush up a hill into an emplacement of machine guns and get blown away. Inside an hour, the magnificent Red Cavalry disintegrates. Now everybody starts screaming at everybody else. This is where Lyutov gets beaten up for refusing to shoot, and silently prays for the power to kill. (Whom would he like to kill, the Poles or the man who hit him?) But Babel's writing is always driven by wheels within wheels of irony. He has shown us that even if the hero could shoot to kill, and even if he did kill, it would be for nothing, because the barbaric ignorance and arrogance of the Cossack leaders have doomed their barbarian army from the start and imperiled the civilized civilians whose lives they were supposed to protect.

The peril of civilians, the vulnerable people caught in the Russian Civil War's crossfire, turns out to be a central theme in Babel's *1920 Diary*. I imagined that this would be a rehearsal (with outtakes) for *Red Cavalry*, and in many ways it is. There is the same pathos of the sensitive intellectual in the midst of an army he despises, trying to protect people he instinctively loves, but power-less to help these people unless he is accepted as a comrade in arms by the army. There is a similar dialectic of enchantment and disen-chantment: initial polarization between *shtetl* Jews who appear withered and dying and Cossacks who seem to be overflowing with life; the same sense of revelation when the Red Cavalry disintegrates and Babel comes to see that the Cossacks themselves may be *schlemiels*, and the Jews may be stronger and more resourceful than he initially thought.

What's new and startling here is, first, the directness, the turbu-lence, the sloppiness, the repetitiveness, the unmediated,

anguished, implosive tone of the writer's voice. It's amazing to hear Babel without composure, without smoothness of surface, without apparent irony. It makes us appreciate anew the intricacy and craftsmanship and constructivist complexity in *Red Cavalry* and the *Odessa Stones*. At the same time, it makes us wonder if maybe they aren't a little *too* brilliantly constructed. To get the perfect Rothkoesque symmetry and luminosity of Babel's great stories, maybe he left too much out, paid too high an emotional price? (Maybe he did, but it would have been perverse to expect Rothko to paint like Pollock, say, or Picasso; artists create as best they can, and art consumers like ourselves should be damned grateful for all we get to eat.)

The second surprise in this *Diary* is the depth and complexity of Jewish life in it: the Jewishness of the *shtetls* that Babel's cavalry passes through; the more assimilated Jewishness of Odessa, where Babel was a child; and Babel's own personal adult post-Revolution Jewishness, which is very intense but volatile and uncertain in its meaning, and which, in his mid-20s (he was 26 in 1920), he seems to be making up as he goes along. "What a mighty and marvelous life of a nation existed here," he says in wonderment as he explores the ancient synagogues and markets of Komarów. He is more deeply Jewish than he thought.

The Soviet-Polish campaign of 1920 cut directly through the heart of Galicia, the densest and culturally richest settlement of Jews in Europe. The names of the towns Babel passed through— Zhitomir, Brody, Dubno, Chernobyl, Demidovka, Kovel—are rich in resonance in Jewish history. (Hemingway said that in war writing, the names of towns and dates were the only honest things you could say.) Editor Carol Avins has provided excellent maps, photographs, and demographic data. The four years of the Russian Civil War set off dreadful massacres, with dozens of Jewish towns totally destroyed, and something like 100,000 Jews killed. Historians (even the professional anti-communists of the Hoover Institution, who have done a standard casebook on the Civil War) agree that nearly all the mass murder, arson, rape, and torture of Jews was done by the Whites—the Polish Army, Ukrainian peasant bands, and the Cossack majority fighting for

the Tsar. Still, the Cossack minority did some, and Babel was close to the knives. He was forced to play the role of a sensitive *goy,* fighting to protect his people from his comrades, knowing that any minute they could turn on him:

> The little girl: aren't you a Jew? Uchenik sits watching me eat, the little girl on his lap, trembling. "She's frightened—cellars, shooting, then your side." I tell them everything will be all right, explain what the Revolution means, I talk on and on. "Things look bad for us, they mean to rob us, don't go to bed."

Think of Queen Esther under fire, without the happy ending.

One dramatic incident that most upsets Babel happens on July 24, 1920, in the small Jewish town of Demidovka. Lyutov is billeted with a Jewish family, along with Prishchepa, a dashing young Cossack, a deserter from the Whites who has committed at least one mass murder (see "Prishchepa's Revenge" in *Red Cavalry*). Today is the Sabbath, tomorrow the fast day of Tisha B'Av, anniversary of the destruction of the first Temple. Prishchepa decides he wants fried potatoes and orders the family to dig and cook them. The head of the household, a woman dentist, "pale with pride and a sense of her own dignity, declares that no one is going to dig potatoes because it is a holiday." But "Prishchepa, restrained by me for quite a while, finally breaks out—fucking Yids, whole arsenal of abuse," and a clear threat that he will kill them all. Terrified, "hating us and me," they go and dig. A little later, "We eat like oxen." (In Jewish idiom, "ox" always signifies a beast without a soul.) Lyutov is ashamed, yet enjoys it: "I tell them fairy tales about Bolshevism—the blossoming, the express trains, Moscow's textile mills, universities, free meals . . . and I captivate all these tormented people." Does he feel like "captivating Savitsky"?

A little later that night, an old woman sobs, and her son begins to sing, from the Book of Lamentations, about the aftermath of the Temple's destruction:

> The terrible words of the prophet—they eat dung, their maidens are ravished, their menfolk killed, Israel subjugated, words of

wrath and sorrow. The lamp smokes, the old woman wails, the young man sings melodiously . . . Demidovka, night, Cossacks, just as it was when the Temple was destroyed.

"Just as it was." Is progress nothing but a dream? Later still, Prishchepa makes a sexual advance to one of the young women in the house. This time the aggressor is charming and mellow, but everyone knows his shadow.

> She blushes prettily. Prishchepa is easy to talk to, she blossoms and behaves coquettishly, what can they be talking about . . . he wants to go to bed, to pass the time, she is in agonies, who understands her soul better than I?

It is Babel's genius to show us, from this poor girl's perspective, the dashing young murderer's charm.

The overall perspective of this *Diary* is pretty bleak. Sometimes Babel sees the situation in dialectically tragic terms: "We're striving for light, but we have no lighting"; "people everywhere trying to rebuild . . . but they have no building materials, no cement." At other times, the note is one of total betrayal and despair: "I ask a Red Army man for bread, he says, 'I don't have anything to do with Jews.' I'm an outsider, I don't belong, I'm all alone"; "This isn't a Marxist revolution, it's a Cossack rebellion"; "how is it different from the times of Bogdan Khmelnitsky?"; "Grief for the future of the Revolution." *We are the vanguard, but of what?*

> Why can't I get over my sadness? Because I'm far from home, because we are destroyers, because we move like a whirlwind, like a stream of lava, hated by everyone, life shatters, I am at a huge, never-ending service for the dead.

It's hard to imagine how the author of this *Diary* could have stayed in the USSR. Indeed, it's even hard to imagine how he could have got out of bed in the morning. But sometime in the early 1920s, we know Babel made his peace, or at least made a truce. It was then, too, that he developed his signature style of poetic prose, the terse luminosity that would astonish the world in *Red Cavalry*. This idiosyncratic but visionary work is probably the best one book ever written about the Russian Revolution. The book's most inspired characters are two Jews, the elderly "Gedali" and the youthful but mortally wounded "Rabbi's Son." In barely a couple of pages, they mark the spiritual hopes of the Bolshevik Revolution and the spiritual poverty of what that Revolution soon became. Here is Gedali, keeper of Zhitomir's old curiosity shop:

> Where is the joy-giving Revolution? I want an International of good people . . . I would like every soul to be listed and given first-category rations . . . There, soul, please eat and enjoy life's pleasures.

The Prishchepas of today have long since left communism behind, and they are happily "ethnic cleansing." Gedali, guardian of Babel's vision, reminds us why there had to be a Russian Revolution—not just another coup d'état—and why that revolution was something to be proud of, at least at first, but also why it couldn't last.

So, to come back to where we began, where are the barbarians of the twentieth century? They're *everywhere*. We can turn on CNN and see a pile of dead bodies from a different part of the world every night. Some are from places we've never heard of—be honest, how many of us had ever heard of Kigali?—others are menacingly familiar and close to home. If we stay tuned, we get to see the killer militias, too, and a wonderfully multicultural lot they are (heralded by Elvis Costello's "Oliver's Army" and Leon Golub's *Mercenaries and Interrogations*). Most are young men, and they look like they have seen many pictures of young men who look like them, so they know how to pose—cigarettes are as vital a prop as rifles. (Other props: high mountains, parched prairies, burnt towns.) There are usually old men behind them, but patriarchs aren't so eager to get in front of cameras. Now, because the world really *is* changing, there are also women in the cast—often with a baby on one shoulder, a cartridge belt on the other—even in places where the repression of women is one of the militia's basic aims. And children! It isn't only in Doonesbury comics that young Raoul Dukes are growing up too fast. You can see the 12-year-olds in the militia team photos, flaunting their hardware, telling the world it's never too early to start to shoot. (Maybe you can see them on the streets of your hometown.) Democracy may be in trouble today, but the democratization of violence lives and thrives on trouble. In the 1920s they said, with Ford Madox Ford, "No More Parades." At the end of the twentieth century, the parade looks bigger, more ecumenical and more triumphal than ever.

Isaac Babel lived and died at the start of this long wave. In his youth he had a great romance with the idea of violence. For a little while, his romance of violence converged with a romance of revolution. Both possibilities thrilled him because they seemed to offer a chance to leap "beyond good and evil" and become "fully alive." He staked his life on them in the thick of a real mega-lethal civil war—and then he recoiled with disgust and dread. What's the verdict? Babel tried but failed to become a barbarian; he succeeded, maybe against his will, in being a *mensch*. His writing brings to life both the daring and the dread, the failure and the success. We need to know both when the next band of captivating Savitskys comes over the rise.

This essay first appeared in the Nation, *June 26, 1995.*

In the Night Kitchen

As the twentieth century ends, New York Jewish intellectuals are finally getting some *goyishe naches*: great prizes, triumphal banquets and conferences while they live, splendid memorial services when they die, page-one obits and reviews. I've been to many of these banquets. The guest of honor says he's being misunderstood, he's a much more difficult character than people think. They know it's true, it only makes them cheer more. Another thing about these tributes: They nearly always come too late. People like Alfred Kazin, Irving Howe, Meyer Schapiro, Henry Roth, and Grace Paley are celebrated in old age or after death by mass media that ignored or denounced them at the height of their powers. That's the sort of irony you learn on the sidewalks of New York, where people wear more Brooklyn Dodgers gear today than they ever did when the Dodgers were in town. (It could be worse: Think of Delmore Schwarz, Harold Rosenberg, Paul Goodman, Kate Simon, and all the others who died lonely, without irony, before the banquets could begin.)

These banquet years present contradictions. Any demand that the world remember *him* or remember *her* is also a demand that it remember *us*. Jews, of course, are used to days of remembrance; we live and die by them. On the other hand, the churning momentum of New York condemns us all as obsolete, often before we get old—remember the beautiful Jewish Grand Concourse?—and blows us away. It will be fascinating to see how this contradiction plays out, though not many of us will be here to see it.

Everyone agrees that Alfred Kazin, as much as anyone who ever lived, typifies the New York Jewish Intellectual (NYJI). But what does this incarnation mean? What's so special about these people? And why should the rest of us need them, anyhow? I think it's the way they're both smart and vulgar: They are full of Plato and Marx and Freud and everybody else on the Great Books list, but they also think ideas are there to be used, and they want to use the best ideas they can lay their hands on to change the world. They love intellectual play, but they play loud and rough, like they once played stickball or double-dutch in the streets. No matter how much they learn or how far they go, they never leave these streets, never forget the poor immigrant neighborhoods they came from: the stoops and subways, the shops and school-yards, the pushcarts and libraries. Their vision of life is always colored with childhood memory and desire and always cleft in two: the grimy vibrant streets in the foreground, the bridges and skyscrapers of the golden city in the distance, the cosmic rupture that Kazin once called "The Block and Beyond." America needs its NYJIs because until it can learn to know both, and be both, it can't even start to be true to itself.

Much of the talk about NYJIs asserts, or simply assumes, that they're a thing of the past. This nostalgic discourse actually tells us nothing about NYJIs, but it shows that our town needs better census takers. In fact, there are plenty of NYJIs, and they are doing fine, but they come in funny places and you have to know where and how to look. Has anybody checked out children's liter-ature? Maurice Sendak is a writer and illustrator of genius. Many of his stories are perfect models of NYJI sensibility: They raise the grungy everyday routines of Jewish families and neighbor-hoods to a poetic and metaphysical intensity. I am bringing him up here because there are deep affinities between him and Kazin. Both know the romance and the terror and the yearning for transcend-ence that saturate a Jewish child's everyday life. His *Where the Wild Things Are* (1963) presented Max, a child as sixties existential hero, a boy who dares to look into the eyes of all the monsters he can dream of. (With one stroke, Sendak not only revived the name "Max" but transformed it from "old world" to avant-garde.)

Sendak's masterpiece, *In the Night Kitchen* (1970), is another, far deeper quest romance. It imagines a little boy separating from his mother, discovering his body, and also discovering his capacity to act and make things happen. In darkest night, Mickey falls into free fall "out of his clothes" (he was naked; he had a penis; in many American towns and school districts the book was instantly banned), "into the light of the night kitchen." The kitchen is a claustrophobic chamber where three giant bakers, all replicas of Oliver Hardy, mix him into their batter. But just as the bakers are about to throw him in the oven, he thrusts through the dough, escapes and becomes who he is: "I'm not the milk and the milk's not me. *I'm Mickey.*" Then Mickey shapes the dough that clings to him into a soft, Oldenburgesque piper cub, and takes off in it, transforming what was his prison into a medium of freedom. In a grand, centerfold set-piece, he flies over the neighborhood: The packages of food from the kitchen become urban buildings, saltshakers become church domes, loaves of white bread become subway cars, a table full of loaves becomes the local 'L', and a bottle of milk metamorphoses into a skyscraper that looms over the whole scene.

At the top of the skyscraper Mickey shakes off the dough and, naked again, dives in, swims to the top and pours milk down, giving the bakers what they need. Now it's almost tomorrow; our hero crows like a rooster and goes back into nude free fall, "straight into bed, carefree and dried." The last page is a curtain call: Mickey clasps a milk bottle happily, surrounded by a rainbow. Look, he has come through! "And that's why, thanks to Mickey, we have cake every morning." A Brooklyn Jewish boy's journey to the end of the night brings identity for him and sweetness for us. The NYJI's imaginative power can transform a child's nightmare into a *Bildungsroman*, a story of growing up.

Alfred Kazin has been criticizing books, and criticizing life, since the early 1930s. All his books are interesting, but his first two, *On Native Grounds* (1942) and *A Walker in the City* (1954), are masterpieces. *On Native Grounds* offers an expansive vision of the America of Theodore Dreiser, Stephen Crane, Edith Wharton, Jack London, Alfred Stieglitz, et al. Kazin has always been adamant in his anti-communism, but in fact *On Native Grounds* is a perfect Popular Front book, immense in horizon, scathing in criticism of big business, but visionary in its hope for America. (Popular Front: the years when the slogan "Communism is Twentieth-Century Americanism" appeared every day on the masthead of the *Daily Worker*.) *A Walker in the City* is a memoir of growing up poor in Jewish Brownsville. Its portrayals of family and neighborhood are heart-rending but lyrically beautiful, in a vein reminiscent of D.H. Lawrence, Henry Roth, and (just a bridge away) Betty Smith. If you can get through this book without tears, you aren't reading hard enough. But even in its deepest sadness, *A Walker in the City* is written with total self-assurance.

Kazin would bring out several collections of critical essays, culminating in *An American Procession: The Major American Writers From 1830 to 1930: The Crucial Years* (1984), and two more autobiographical volumes, *Starting Out in the Thirties* (1965) and *New York Jew* (1978). All these books offer brilliant literary analyses and marvelous novelistic accounts of people and scenes. But they lack the aura of enchantment that those first two books had and that put Kazin on our cultural map forever. Still, like the Wordsworth character who has lost the "visionary gleam," Kazin has kept striving for the insights of the "philosophic mind." (Or like a pitcher who has lost his youthful fastball, he has taught himself a whole new array of pitches and built a new career on his brains.) He has kept working, decade after decade, with an awesome persistence and unrelenting energy. And he has worked not only on other writers and their books—hundreds of writers, thousands of books—but on himself and on his life.

The title of Kazin's new book, *A Lifetime Burning in Every Moment,* may give us the hope that we are going to get closer to his life, to get to know him in a depth we haven't seen before. Alas, no such luck! The book tells us plenty of fascinating things, some of them pretty intimate, yet in the end *A Lifetime Burning* contains more mysteries than revelations. The mysteries strike us right away: What were these 341 pages of journals "Selected and Edited by the Author" selected from? Was it 600 pages or 50,000? (Kazin has told interviewers that he has kept a journal continuously since the age of 10, but he tells readers of this book nothing.) What was his principle of selection? None of these entries are dated, except within intervals of two to twenty-eight years, and none are framed in ways that might help us see where he is coming from. (Some people will have fun guessing the dates from their contexts; this assumes they are in strict chronological order, but in fact Kazin offers no guarantees.) Some of the entries are highly polished essays that have been published before, so that we think, "Wait, where have I met this woman before? And why am I seeing her again now?" Some are sharply revised accounts of tales earlier told—so that some of us will say, "I knew he and Hannah Arendt weren't 'just friends'!" Some are polemical attempts to settle scores with ex-wives or fellow intellectuals (Allen Tate, Susan Sontag, Norman Mailer, Henry Kissinger, Norman Podhoretz, et al.). Some are simply clippings from the day's news, reprinted without comment, though they are usually items about which plenty could be said. Some read like graffiti in a jail cell, or what NYJI Paul Simon would call "the words of the prophets . . . written on the subway walls." Kazin knows how to read city wall: *Un poco de luz y no mas sangre* [A little light and no more blood]—Cervantes." His shortest entry, reprinted completely here, is this: "Black night! Black night!"

How do we sort all these voices out? In fact, this book's polyphonic form, its confusing abundance of authorial voices, is the most fascinating thing about it. With all these voices inside him (and maybe more that we haven't heard yet), it must have been frustrating to go through all those years speaking in one voice alone. It must have required great discipline, especially since so much of Kazin's work has been with modernist writers whose genius is to let it all hang out. Now, in his 80s, he is being more like them, letting the voices resound and interact, not demanding resolution, just letting go. It is a courageous attempt to grow (the NYJI word is *chutzpah*) and to fulfill the romantic promise he proclaims in his title, *A Lifetime Burning in Every Moment*. This title is something like a favorite image of mine, from one of my generation's great NYJIs, Bob Dylan: "He not busy being born is busy dying." In Kazin's new polyphony, he is busy being born.

We have to admire Kazin's guts, but that doesn't tell us what to do next. In the hundreds of critical essays he's written—and in his life studies as well—it was possible for us to act as judges of whether or not he was *right*. (Of course, there was no guarantee that *we* would be right.) Now, in *A Lifetime Burning*, it isn't even clear who "he" is, let alone how we're supposed to read him. It's as if he is presenting "Alfred Kazin" to us, like a protagonist in one of those modernist novels: how about, say, the latest hot novel from Barcelona or Sao Paulo, *The Journals of Alfredo K——?* We have to become detectives to read him right, and we don't even know was there a crime? We better get busy being born ourselves.

We first meet "Alfredo" in his youth, where he is on the verge of, and then in the midst of, spectacular success, but tormented with guilt. "The age was with me," he says, describing the reception of *On Native Grounds* in and after 1942. He had been rejected by the army for health reasons (unspecified), but "in the midst of the war . . . my wildest hopes [are] amazingly realized." Overnight, it seems, he is drenched with adulation, money pours in, magazines beg him to write and work for them, women throw themselves at him,

> women in the morning light, the proud beautiful women of New York, the breasts and hot purple mouths of the Bergdorf women, the fantastic sexiness of New York in certain cool restaurants, all of it hot and cold at once.

Yet everything in his new life reminds him of his dear mother, "Mama in her eternal housedress." And: "Looking back is opening myself to everything out of childhood I've wanted desperately to lose." Alfredo K. lies awake in a cold sweat and nauseated, awaiting "the invisible hostile stranger who has never actually met me but has condemned me in advance." He keeps track of the Holocaust as it unfolds, and occasionally manages to get it into the *New Republic*, where he edits the back of the book. But when the war ends, he notes that "I did nothing to beat Hitler. I saved no one"; not only that, but, after being put on 4-F, he thrived all through the war; and now he feels guilty as hell.

Then we see him through a long middle age when he is success-ful and highly esteemed, but unable to sustain the love and crea-tivity of his dreams. He takes pride in identifying himself as a Jew, but rejects the Jewish forms of chauvinism that flower after 1967. He defends liberal democracy against both Left (such as it is) and Right. He is especially outraged by the crew we now call neocons, some of whom he grew up with, who have come to pride them-selves on their lack of human feeling. In these conflicts we are likely to feel he is in the right, though his eternal self-righteous-ness grates. But being right doesn't make him happy. At last he falls in love with a woman who sounds stable and devoted: Judith, to whom the book is dedicated. Even then, "I writhe sleepless in a bed that is like a raft in a devouring ocean . . . Black night! Black night!" At some point after 1978 (remember, nothing is dated), Alfredo K. begins to connect his melancholy with God:

> Stop indulging yourself, Kazin, in anything except work! But don't forget to pray, for God *is* the only continuity and by pray-ing, even by trying to pray, miserable schismatic that you are, you are in the vicinity of His duration, the very hope and sign of the Everlasting.

Alfredo's God sounds very abstract and metaphysical, in the post Bergson vein, à la Simone Weil, a symbol of *durée*. On the other hand, this God has the power to put him through a very concrete personal hell. Note the strange word Alfredo uses against himself: "schismatic." This is the language of the Spanish Inquisition, often used as a preface to murder—of Jews, Protestants, Muslims, hundreds of thousands of Others. For Alfredo to condemn himself with this word is especially weird, since it was the followers of Jesus who schismatized Judaism. Why is Alfredo forgetting the history he learned in those Brownsville libraries, identifying with the aggressor, and drowning himself in guilt? We never find out. In an adoring entry/essay about Simone Weil, he says she said that the most important thing about a person is, "What are you *going through*?" But we never learn what Alfredo himself was going through, what brought him to this pass.

Alfredo tries to reinvent "the argument for Jesus, not Christ the Lord," apparently unaware how many twentieth-century Jews have been there before. (Could Kazin have forgotten Sholem Asch?) He rediscovers sin and evil: "The wish to obliterate our 'brother' is as strong as the need for sex"—which means, for Kazin, very strong indeed. "In the middle of the night . . . I feel up against the ropes . . . I pray to get beyond myself." Reading page after page of inner torment, any normally decent reader will want to hold Kazin's hand; probably not even his ex-wives wish him such hell. But forget it, it's not our hands he wants. In his "Black night! Black night!" he is so "desperate for grace" that only God will do. Maybe because he's so desperate, he feels no leverage to ask this God any tough questions about the Holocaust or about any of the other public horrors that, for most of this book, he remembers so well.

Does Alfredo K. ever resolve his religious crisis? Kazin keeps us in the dark: In the last fifty pages, the proto-Christian vocabulary simply disappears. And yet, the splendid final "old age" section, which starts with radiation treatment for cancer in 1991, sounds as if he outgrows both his terror and his need for grace. Waiting for radiation, he sounds more humanly centered than anywhere else in the book:

> Every day there are new faces. The young girls make me shudder, it seems so unjust. There is a men's group of my generation, all in their seventies, *alte kockers* who sit around recalling old radio shows . . . It gives me a pang to hear again the best lines of Fred Allen, my favorite satirist from a time when anyone named J. Danforth Quayle would have been straight man to Groucho and not so near the presidency of the United States . . . Once these men would have met to play pinochle around the pool at Grossinger's. Now they wait, still all good humor with each other, for the machine that is going to postpone our death.

Is it the sense of imminent death, "our death," that gives him a connection with people and with life that he's never felt? We can't say for sure, but it's delicious to see this man so relaxed, so glad to be part of a community. The twenty-five pages that follow are familiar subjects—cameos of the living and the dead, of childhood and maturity in Kazin's life, climaxing (as always) with his parents—and yet written with a *mellowness* that's so new. When his parents come onstage (as we know they will), and the story of their lifelong misery and sadness is told for what seems like the hundredth time, it's in a new key: They're not so alone this time; now they join in the company of a bunch of *alter kockers* that—thanks to Kazin's new Magic Realism—includes their son, opening doors for them, laughing at the past, loving life.

What a long night Kazin has gone through! It's a thrill to see him return to a new morning, like Mickey, "carefree and dried," with new powers and new gifts and new joy. Does it mean we, too, can go through the night kitchen and emerge more alive than ever? New York had better love a man who can show us how to make it through the night and be busy being born in the morning. If we forget, then those who remember will have to start doing something New York Jews know how to do well: make noise.

This essay first appeared in the Nation, *May 6, 1996.*

The Bright Book of Life

Is there is a global culture today? I think there is. Its images come from movies, old and new, and from television; its sounds are rock-and-roll, rap, and heavy traffic on the street. But only the novel has the Faustian *chutzpah* to try to connect all the dots, to put this immense world together. Orhan Pamuk, one of the world's great novelists, lives and works within shouting distance of *Dissent*. The least we can do is shout to our readers that he's here. I don't know him, but it's a thrill to know he's nearby. He spends half the year in New York, where he teaches comparative literature at Columbia, the other half in his hometown, Istanbul, where he speaks truth and gets in trouble.

Even if Pamuk weren't this physically close, he would be easy to connect with. Most of his books are easy to get and remarkably easy to get into. They are at once brilliant debates and psychedelic trips. All are set in Turkey, last year or five hundred years ago. Pamuk country is weirdly *other*, yet he makes us feel we've known it all our lives. Now in his fifties, he is working at the height of his powers. People worried not so long ago about "the Death of the Novel." Pamuk's books, along with Roberto Bolaño's, reassure us that this is not true. The novel is still what D.H. Lawrence said it was a century ago: "The one bright book of life." Only now the light and the life are coming not just from a few centers, but from all over the world.

Pamuk's novel *Snow* appeared in the West amid widespread anxiety triggered by the attacks of September 11, 2001. It was easy for reviewers and readers to frame it in the context of what one author (Daniel Benjamin) called "the age of sacred terror." Pamuk turned out to be a terrific writer of melodrama, and his melodrama got incorporated into our collective melodrama. *Snow* became an instant bestseller. Now, living in a saner time, we can read it again and see more and find more between the lines. One thing we can find is first-rate dialogue on the question of what it means to be modern.

"Don't be afraid, these people are modern." Sunay Zaim, a cultural bureaucrat of the Turkish Republic, says this just before the end. He says it to Ka, a self-consciously "modern" poet. Ka has been in exile in the West for years. He has come back to this miserable border town to write an investigative article on a wave of religious—or pseudo-religious—suicides among teenage girls. We never do learn what is driving these girls; but we learn that, in Turkey at the end of the twentieth century, out-of-control violence is erupting in everybody's everyday life. Sunay says that if people have faith in the republic, it will all work out. But in Pamuk country, the primary crop is *irony*. It grows all year round, even when all other crops fail. The Turkish people live on it, but there is plenty left for export. So when any Pamuk character tells any other not to be afraid, we can see the author ringing alarms. When a character says being modern will make the Turkish people stable and happy, we can hear the author's ironic laugh, even when we're not sure we get the joke. The one thing that seems to resist irony here is the snow itself, layer piling on primal layer, smothering history, freezing life, blotting out the sun. Yet we know it's *Pamuk's* snow, as artificial and as modern as everything else in his work. This snow falls on the beach and in the jungle as much as it falls at the poles; global warming offers no protection against it; it envelops the world.

Sunay offers his reassurance at the start of one of Pamuk's most brilliant scenes, which forms *Snow*'s dramatic climax. He is a veteran actor, producer, show-biz *tummeler*, and overall wise guy who somehow has found a niche working for the Republic as a provincial cultural bureaucrat. He is a broadly comic character, as if on loan from some road production of *Pal Joey* or *Guys and Dolls*; it is surprising to meet him in the solemn world of *Snow*. His job in Kars is to be a kind of public relations man for modernity, for the Enlightenment, for secular humanism. Sunay overflows with cliché versions of ideas that most readers of *Dissent* believe in and that some of us would die for. (Probably so would Pamuk.) This makes his presence truly grueling. We listen to his spiels, and we think, Is *that* what I believe in? *Oy!* But once we read to the end, we see we have to feel for him, because of what he goes through—or rather what Pamuk puts him through. He transforms his comedy into tragedy.

Sunay tells his friends not to be afraid. In Pamuk country, this message sets off every alarm. What disaster lies ahead for this poor man? *Snow* is almost over, so at least we know we won't have long to wait. But in another way we'll have to wait forever. Pamuk's answer will only raise more questions and will open up a Moebius strip of what he calls "secret meanings." It is typical Pamukian irony that this PR man for clarity and openness is about to become a mystery case that will never be closed.

Snow is set in a time of troubles that culminate in a military coup d'état. Some of my Turkish students think Pamuk means the coup of 1980; others deny a precise date and say his point is to create a "typical post-1970s coup." But first, Sunay wants to put on a theater piece that will rally the people of Kars to the republic. He thinks it can overcome their troubles—economic depression and mass unemployment are the worst—if they will only believe in it. He has faith that in the end they will. When he says the people are modern, he means they are self-aware, they are willing to fight for the right to think for themselves, for the right to love, for the right to be happy. Even if conflicts arise between modern people or between modern values, "Don't be afraid." This is a classical humanistic vision of modernity; it could have been embraced by Stendhal, by Ralph Waldo Emerson, by Victor Hugo, by George Eliot, by John Dewey, by Margaret Mead. Sunay sees the pre-coup Turkish Republic as a realization of this classic vision.

Sunay says not to be afraid, and at once we worry. There is trouble with Kedife, his leading lady and old friend. He has composed a weird, disturbing script where his character urges her character to throw off her Islamic headscarf, in the name of human freedom. She resists, then hesitates, then gives way, and then after she does it, she turns on him and shoots him to death. For the curtain call, the actors will appear hand in hand, the best of friends.

Kedife is reluctant to take the role. There are nasty and belligerent people in the house, and she is worried about provoking them. But Sunay bullies her and she lets him and, at last, she agrees to go on. Everything goes smoothly until the climactic moment: Then it turns out that the gun is loaded, the bullets are live, the blood that drenches the stage isn't stage blood, and Sunay really dies. People start screaming. Soldiers come in, a little late. The house is in a state of chaos and pandemonium. We know that if anything like this were to really happen, Pamuk the man and citizen would be horrified. But in a dramatic scene where ordinary life morphs into bloody horror, Pamuk the author is happily at home.

Many of Pamuk's readers will find themselves as mystified by this climax as the people on the spot, or as the authorities trying to piece the case together later on. How could Sunay not have known about the gun? Are we meant to think he arranged to be killed? If he did, he didn't let the killer in on it. Pamuk makes it clear that once Kedife sees what she has done, she is distraught. But even if she didn't mean to kill him, the fact that she did will destroy her life more effectively than any religious veil.

What was he thinking? What inner demons drove this man who denied the demonic? In this mystery one thing is clear: These shots have blown to pieces Sunay's sunny vision of modern life. The night has turned out to be, as he planned, a display of the modern. But it is a nightmarishly twisted modern, largely unconscious of itself, dense with psychic reversals and existential traps like landmines, where people become suicide bombs and destroy people they love as they destroy themselves. Sunay meant to show the glories of modern life; but somehow modern death steals the show. In fact, that irony haunts much of twentieth-century history. (Will it be better in the twenty-first? It's too soon to know.)

As Sunay's vital powers ebb away, his visionary power grows. He gets only one line before he dies: "They'll never be modern," he says, "they know nothing about modern art." This is a great piece of black humor, dead serious. But why should a people want to know modern art? What can it give them? Pamuk doesn't offer a single ringing answer, but here's a start: A global horizon and an expansive flow of empathy, a feeling for irony and complexity, a capacity to embrace contradictory ideas and believe and love them both. The poet John Keats, as he lay dying, called this power "negative capability." The anguished last sentence in Sunay's life is also his first work of art. The heavy changes that Pamuk puts him through can help us see how modern art could be something to die for—or to live for.

In *Snow*, and in all his best writing, Pamuk creates a drama of modern life in the process of moving toward radical polarization. Modern men and women are *under pressure*, and they know it. What is to be done? There are two radically different roads people can take: (1) They may reach out toward the most open and generous inclusiveness; this, for Pamuk, is the meaning of modern art, the reason it has flourished and still lives. Or else (2) they may plunge into the most rigid and violent exclusions; among the first to go will be modern writers and artists, whose love for modern life is greater than anyone's. Pamuk makes it clear that he is rooting for Plan (1), but he worries about the raw demagogic power of Plan (2). He identifies with (1) because he thinks it is morally right, but also because, in the real modern world, it can bring us a happiness that is not only more intense and "hot," but more solid and lasting. However, he thinks, in order to fulfill its human promise, (1) has to find a way to envelop (2). In other words, modernism has an existential task, to somehow assimilate the people and the powers that want to destroy it.

One thing that will magnify this task—but also make it more profound and absorbing—is that the prime enemy of modernism is not, as people used to say when I was young, "tradition," but something much weirder and more complex, which we might call modernist anti-modernism. (For short, I'll call it MAM.) More than any writer since Thomas Mann, Pamuk grasps the world-historical importance of MAM.

In the triumphs of the Third Reich, MAM shook the world.

When the Nazis were defeated in 1945, liberals like my parents thought that it was gone for good and that an age of honesty and openness had dawned. Alas, it didn't work out that way. MAM has had a continuing enormous human appeal, and despite many defeats it keeps coming back. It fits comfortably into the most diverse political cultures; it unites parts of the Left—not my part, and not Pamuk's—with parts of the classical right. It haunted the whole second half of the twentieth century, and it is still alive and well.

MAM both frightens and fascinates Pamuk. It inspires one of his most brilliant characterizations, the handsome womanizer and charismatic demagogue Blue. The main voice of modern art in *Snow* is the poet Ka. The conflict between Ka and Blue is one of the book's driving forces. Much of their conflict is focused on Kedife's sister, Ipek, an impressive and independent woman, and one of Pamuk's best characters. She loves them both, she sleeps with them both, and they fight for her soul. Will Ipek embrace the poet of modernism or the genius of MAM? Pamuk gives her an inner radiance that makes us really care; for a little while, we feel that the fate of the world is riding on the outcome of this love triangle. (Pamuk has said he doesn't think people appreciate his women and his writing about love. I hope there's a way to let him know he's wrong!)

Ka and Blue spend lots of time talking. Or rather, Ka talks. He tries to converse and argue. Blue rants; he talks to one person in exactly the same language he would use before a jammed football stadium. "Democracy, freedom, human rights, don't matter" in the West, Blue says; "all the West wants is for the rest of the world to imitate them like monkeys." Ka tries to explain that the West, at the end of the twentieth century, places value on human diversity. Blue just waves him aside. "There is . . . only one West and one Western point of view. And we take the opposite view." Who are "we" in this sentence? Is Blue using the royal "we"? Is he trying to claim the whole non-Western world as his own? Whatever this is, it is a perspective from which people are interchangeable. This is how he treats women, and he finds plenty of women (including some pretty strong ones) who are glad to be treated that way. It's also how he treats innocent militant kids: He manipulates his youthful followers into provoking the army and getting themselves killed—but "please don't tell our mothers," they say from their hospital beds before they die.

Blue is a leader of a militant Islamic movement, but he shows not the slightest trace of religious feeling. He is cold, detached, cynical, opportunistic, manipulative. If there's one word for him, it's a word that the great Russian novelists of the nineteenth century put on the map. The word is *nihilist*. Ka's first encounters with him reduce the poet to despair. He feels like the helpless suckers in W.B. Yeats's poem "The Second Coming":

> *The best lack all conviction, while the worst*
> *Are full of passionate intensity.*

Blue denounces the sexual license of the West, but, nihilist that he is, he is utterly blasé about conducting simultaneous love affairs in Turkey. His girlfriends include both Ipek and Kedife. There are more, and they all seem to know it. They throw themselves at him like groupies at a rock star; they regard him with total devotion, and eagerly offer up their whole being. (Ipek and Kedife would be a perfect sister duet for a classic torch song—say, "My Man" or "All of Me.") Blue's sex life is a kind of travesty of the vanished Ottoman sultans and pashas with their harems. But his power over women is *postmodern*; what turns him on is *submission of the free*. Pamuk puts arrows on the sidewalk that point us back to Dostoevsky's Grand Inquisitor. What do women see in Blue, anyway? When they try to explain, the one thing they come up with is Blue's unwavering total certainty, which throws some of them into a kind of hypnotic trance.

Ka realizes he needs to sort out what his convictions are and to offer Ipek some sort of happiness that she can't get in Kars. Having been an exile in the West, mostly in West Germany, for more than a decade, he needs to remember what he has learned there:

They don't live that way in the West. It's not as it is here; they
don't want everyone thinking alike. Everyone, even the most
ordinary grocer, boasts of having his own personal views.

Ka comes to realize that the freedom of "the most ordinary
grocer" in a Western city in 2000 is a tremendous historical achievement; a modern poet can be proud to affirm it. (Any of Kafka's Ks
would have been glad to shop in this grocer's *bodega*.) More good
things go with these: honesty, complexity, respect, real love, a lifetime of intimate dialogue, communication with other people, exposure to relatively free and open mass media, and a ticket to a place
where Ipek's individuality will be recognized, where she will enjoy
freedom of the city, and where she won't be totally dependent on a
family or a man. Ka develops a vision of them as a couple who
would not only have a great time, but who would stand for something. The thing they would stand for could be called *Modernist
Liberalism*. The biggest problem for this vision is that, as Pamuk
sees it, it can't be realized at home. They've got to get out.

Ipek is thrilled by this vision. For a while she wrenches herself
out of Blue's grip; she and Ka have several love scenes, at once hot
and tender; and she comes to yearn for a new life with him, in
Germany, right now.

> "When we get to Germany, we're going to be very happy," said
> Ipek, with her arms around Ka's neck. "Tell me about the cinema
> you'll take me to."

> "There's a cinema in the [Frankfurt] Film Museum that shows
> undubbed American art films late on Saturday nights," said Ka.
> "We'll stop in one of the restaurants around the station and have
> *doner* and sweet pickles. After we come home, we can relax in
> front of the television set. Then we'll make love. We can live on
> my political exile allowance and the money I'll make doing read-
> ings of this new poetry book of mine—and neither of us has to do
> anything more than make love."

> "That's beautiful," she said.

This fantasy is so sweet! One thing that makes their love so hot is our knowledge that they have had to build the bed themselves. If sexual love means, as John Donne says, that a couple "make this little room an everywhere," we get to see this couple construct their room, create the existential space they share. Before they could be there, they have had to fight both others and themselves: he, to break out of his inner isolation and focus on another person; she, to break away both from a loving but enveloping family and from a domineering lover to whom she still yearns to submit. In order for modernism to deliver on its human promise, it has to be shared. To reach that point of mutuality takes tremendous struggles, struggles that good people can easily lose through no fault of their own.

Ipek's line, "When we get to Germany we're going to be very happy," is so poignant and heartbreaking that it deserves scrutiny on its own. I know the German-Turkish connection goes back centuries, to a time when Germany was provincial and Ottoman Turkey was perhaps the most powerful country in the world. What does it mean today, that a smart and soulful Turkish woman should dream of Germany? Turkey and Germany have a deep darkness in common: Both nations have been *perpetrators of genocide*. The darkness goes even deeper. In 1942, when some of Hitler's intimates worried about the long-term scandalous impact of the Nazis' "extreme measures" against the Jews, the Führer is said to have exclaimed, "Who remembers the Armenians?" So, Turkey's mass murder of Armenians during the First World War was not only monstrous in itself, but served as a precedent for an even greater mass murder. Moreover, genocidal policy stemmed from a belief that it was feasible to extinguish not only people's lives, but even the memory of their lives; so that genocide, if done "right," would never be criticized, because the victims would never be remembered.

But in fact, post-Nazi German governments have made extraordinary efforts to remember— the people who were killed, the ways in which the state killed them, the people who participated in the crime, and the mechanisms with which the whole thing was covered up and denied. Genocide is so humanly inexplicable that we still don't really grasp how it could happen; the struggle for memory and understanding has to go on and on. But this struggle has helped to make Germany a more open and humanly caring society than it ever was before.

Meanwhile, it seems, Turkey has worked equally hard to forget. About half a century ago, Alcoholics Anonymous coined a phrase that fits Turkey very well: in denial. Both Ipek and her creator seem to believe that a country in denial is poisoning its springs of life and inviting more darkness. This is why Ipek is thrilled at the chance to get out, and why many Turks today see Germany and German culture as sources of light, against the background of their shared darkness. Germany has made a commitment to being open and honest about its genocidal past. This has to be one reason why, half a century after the first Turks began going to Germany for work, many Turkish intellectuals still see Germany as their promised land.

It may take heroism for Ka and Ipek to get there. But the life they look forward to, once they do get there, will be unheroic, ordinary, "normal." When I was growing up in the Bronx, in the years after the Second World War, it was full of Jews who had just survived the Holocaust. When I met them, they were butchers, bakers, jewelers, tailors, cab drivers, owners of hardware and stationery stores. They were just like Ka's "most ordinary grocer"—plain Bronx Jews going to the movies and yelling at their children (who were often my classmates and friends) to do their homework. But although most of them didn't like to talk about it, many of them had been heroes of resistance movements against the Nazis only a few years before. They suffered horribly, but when they survived, they had a chance to become something like the people Ka and Ipek hope to be.

In the history of modern culture, the archetypal couple presiding over Ka's and Ipek's fantasies and hopes come from the moment of the French Revolution: they are Papageno and Papagena, from Mozart's *Magic Flute*. Ka and Ipek, two centuries later, would be a modernist variation on Mozart's theme. Their embraces will be accompanied by all the latest mass media, by movies and television, by computer hookups and hyperlinks, and by dreams of America—of *undubbed* America (Pamuk highlights this), an America in as raw and direct a form as they can imagine. Americans can feel proud to be part of their dream life and their pursuit of happiness.

Why shouldn't they have all this? In fact, it is only drastic last-minute plot intervention by the author that keeps the heroine off the train to freedom. Maybe Pamuk thought it would be a better story this way, and if he did, who knows, maybe he was right. Maybe stories of love crushed are more poignant than stories of love fulfilled. Or maybe the best story is love crushed *after* it's fulfilled: For readers, it might be a way to have the best of both worlds. Think *Romeo and Juliet*; or, closer to our time and our world, think *A Farewell to Arms*.

But there's a difference between the logic of a story and the logic of history. At the start of the twenty-first century, our history may be more open than our literature. A great many people have got out of nightmarish situations all over the globe, and America has given them space to breathe. On any Saturday or Sunday afternoon, at Herald Square, on Telegraph Avenue, in shopping malls in all sorts of American places I and Pamuk have never heard of, you can find couples that look a lot like Ipek and Ka (they are often of different colors), schlepping their babies around in ultra-modern snugglies, overflowing with new life. We could give them a super-title: *Modernist Liberalism Lives*.

This essay was first published as "Orhan Pamuk and Modernist Liberalism" in Dissent, *Spring 2009.*

Part VI

Signs in the Street

Signs in the Street:
A Response to Perry Anderson

Perry Anderson's discussion of my book, *All That Is Solid Melts into Air,* is both welcome and perplexing. He is so appreciative and generous at the beginning, so dismissive and scornful at the end—not merely toward my book, but toward contemporary life itself. What happens in the middle? I can't figure it out. There is an interesting historical analysis, building on Arno Mayer's work, of the political and social conditions that underlay the great modernist breakthroughs of 1890 to 1920. This analysis makes fascinating reading, but Anderson loads his history with far more weight than it can bear. He argues that "the intersection between a semi-aristocratic ruling order, a semi-industrialized capitalist economy, and a semi-emergent or insurgent labour movement" nourished the creative triumphs of cubism, relativity, psychoanalysis, the *Rites of Spring, Ulysses,* etc. This is perfectly plausible, though there are a number of other equally plausible ways to tell this story. (My own would place more emphasis on the experience of marginal groups like Jews and homosexuals.) Anderson then makes a bizarre leap: He seems to say that the absence of *these* conditions since the end of the Second World War must lead to the absence of *any* creative triumphs. But why shouldn't other conditions inspire other triumphs, today, tomorrow, or any other day?

This pretzel logic gets another perverse twist toward the paper's end, where Anderson claims that the current disappointment of our hopes for socialist revolution in the West means the doom of all Western spiritual and cultural life: "What marks the situation of the Western artist is . . . the closure of horizons: without an appropriable past, or an imaginable future, in an interminably recurrent present." Doesn't he realize how much human creativity grows, and always has grown, out of disappointment? Disappointment with democratic Athens led to *The Trojan Women* and Plato's *Republic*; disappointment in Jesus of Nazareth (who, remember, was supposed to bring about the end of the world) led to most of what's morally creative in Christianity—specifically, the revaluation of values that glorified suffering, lowliness, and defeat; disappointment with the French Revolution led to the creative breakthroughs of Romanticism, which nourished (and continue to nourish) a legion of new revolutions. So it goes. When people are faced with the closing of familiar horizons, we open up new horizons; when we are disappointed in some of our hopes, we discover or create new visions that inspire new hopes. That's how our species has survived so much sadness and ruin through the ages. If humanity had ever accepted *a priori* foreclosures of history, our history would have ended long ago.

Does Anderson really believe the Sex Pistols's verdict of "NO FUTURE!"? (Even Johnny Rotten, as he screamed it, was trying in his way to change it.) If Anderson's horizon really looks closed, maybe he should think of this as a problem, rather than as the human condition. Maybe his theoretical framework has pressed him into a corner, and he needs to turn around and look the other way, where there may be plenty of trouble but at least there's light and space.

All That Is Solid Melts into Air unfolds a dialectic of modernization and modernism. "To be modern," as I define it at the book's beginning and end, "is to experience personal and social life as a maelstrom, to find one's world in perpetual disintegration and renewal, trouble and anguish, ambiguity and contradiction: to be part of a universe in which all that is solid melts into air. To be a modern*ist* is to make oneself somehow at home in this maelstrom, . . . to grasp and confront the world that modernization makes, and to strive to make it our own." Modernism aims "to give modern men and women the power to change the world that is changing them, to make them the subjects as well as the objects of modernization." Anderson is willing to accept this as a vision of nineteenth-century culture and politics, but he thinks that it is irrelevant to our century, let alone to our day. When he criticizes my failure to "periodize," his point is that the liberating force of modernism is confined to an earlier period. It isn't quite clear when that period ended (the First World War? the Second?), but the main point is that it ended long ago. The hope of making ourselves at home in the maelstrom, of becoming subjects as well as objects, of making the modern world our own—these hopes have forever melted into air, at least for Anderson, and he thinks it's futile for me to try to recreate them.

I could assail Anderson's reading of modern and contemporary history in plenty of ways, but it wouldn't do anything to advance our common understanding. I want to try something different. Anderson's view of the current horizon is that it's empty, closed; mine is that it's open and crowded with creative possibilities. The best way to defend my vision might be to show what this horizon looks like, what's actually out there as I see it. For the next few pages, I want to present a few scenes from everyday life, and from an art and culture that are part of this life, as it is going on right now. These scenes do not lead logically to one another; nevertheless, they are connected, as figures in a collage. My point in introducing them is to show how modernism is still happening, both in our streets and in our souls, and how it still has the imaginative power to help us make this world our own.

Modernism has its traditions, and they are there to be used and developed. Baudelaire tells us how to see the present: "All centuries and all peoples have their beauty, so inevitably we have ours. That's the order of things . . . The life of our city is rich in poetic and marvellous subjects. The marvellous envelops and soaks us like an atmosphere, only we don't see it . . . We need only open our eyes to recognize our heroism." He wrote this in 1846, in an essay entitled, "The Heroism of Modern Life."

FACES IN THE CROWD

A CUNY (City University of New York) graduate student comes to see me about his dissertation and his life: Larry, a big, muscular redhead, usually jovial, occasionally menacing, looking a little like the Wild Man in medieval art. He comes from the steel mills near Pittsburgh. After a dreadful childhood, abandoned by alcoholic parents, brought up by a series of indifferent and impoverished relatives, he escaped to a big state university on a football scholarship. Quite by accident, as he tells it, he discovered that he loved to read, think, dream. Now he dreams vast, epic, neo-Idealist visions, communing with Fichte and Schelling and Hegel as he drives a taxi all night to make the rent. I ask him what he wants to do with his life; he says he wants to become a thinker so he can search for the ultimate truth and, if he finds it, proclaim it to the world.

I am moved by his ambition, which I shared at his age—and still do share, though I wouldn't be likely to put it as directly and honestly as he. But I tell him that part of the truth about life in Reagan's America is that it contains no job openings for independent, humanistic thought. I say that if he wants to pursue the truth, he's going to have to use all his intelligence to learn to lie, to disguise his enterprise as something else that he can get a job doing. The question then becomes, what is the best disguise? I feel like hell as I say this, but I see no way around it.

I suggest he do an ethnographic and political study of his steel town. He recoils in horror and tells me that world is crumbling. Mills are closing down; more than half the jobs in his town have recently disappeared and the others could go at any moment; men are running away or disintegrating, families are breaking up, complex social networks are ripping apart at the seams. He visits his old local bars, and men who used to taunt him for loving books and hanging out with kikes, niggers, fags, and commies in New York now envy him for having a lifeline to a world outside. Larry grew up hating this town, and the hate helped him learn who he was. Now he pities it and he's got to learn about himself all over again.

As I write this, they're playing a song on the radio that comes straight from Larry's world, "Making Thunderbirds," by Bob Seger, a hard rocker from Detroit. It has a slashing guitar attack, a driving beat, and it's sung with an intensity that doesn't come through on the radio very often these days. The narrator is a middle-aged, unemployed (or about to be unemployed) auto worker who pines for his youth. "Back in '55 we were making Thunderbirds":

> "We were making Thunderbirds, we were making Thunderbirds,
> They were long and low and sleek and fast and all you've ever
> heard. We were young and strong, we were making Thunderbirds."

The car, a splendid new model of the fifties, is a symbol of the world we have lost: when a worker could identify himself, his youth and sexual energy, with the thing he produced; when "the big line moved" and it was a thrill to be part of its momentum; when the young workers of Detroit could feel like the vanguard of America and America could feel like Number One in the world. The symbolic power rides on the music as much as the text; the beat and tempo and guitar echo the music of 1955, when Rock-and-Roll was young and the world was all before it. Thunderbirds connects especially to Chuck Berry, whose "Maybelline" defined a classic American myth—that the working man could be really manly, manlier than his social superiors, in and through his car— and tried to create a music that would be the moral equivalent of that car.

Seger takes us back to those songs and those cars, to make us feel the depths of what we have lost. For the world those workers were building, or thought they were building, is gone with the wind; no longer young or strong or proud, no longer even work-ing, they are junked, along with their old cars, along with Detroit—maybe even along with America itself. The song's text seems to say "NO FUTURE," but the music pulls against the text with desperate urgency. The narrator may well feel he's got noth-ing left; the singer-songwriter knows and shows that he's got more than he thinks. What he's got above all is the passion and depth and guts to rock and rage against the dying of the light.

It is a frozen Saturday afternoon just before Christmas. I am walking across Houston Street on Manhattan's Lower East Side, blinded by the low sun in my face. This is a poor neighborhood, full of abandoned tenements, small workshops, lumberyards, auto supply and body shops, junkyards and storage dumps. Near the East River, gathering around small bonfires, winos and junkies are almost the only people on the street; not even the kids are out, it's too cold to play. As I get further west, a few young families emerge—Hispanic, white-bohemian, inter-racial—heading across town on weekend shopping expeditions.

On a particularly desolate block, between an abandoned factory and a gas station, I walk into a jarring scene. In front of a yard full of broken furniture, old refrigerators and sinks, up against a cyclone fence, ten figures are chained in a row. Up close, I see that they are sculpted, in plaster or papier-maché, but their proportions are eerily real. The figures are covered with plastic trash bags; the bags are slit or torn in places, and rags, orange peels, old newspapers, packaging for food, drink, diapers, appliances, are beginning to leak out. Although the faces are covered up, the figures are subtly detailed and differentiated, and amazingly life-like, and it is dreadful to see them facing me just inches away, slumping over or caving in, pressing against their ropes as they rot.

What is this, anyway? It is a work of environmental art, created for this particular space and time, for this site and this neighborhood and this public, by a young sculptor named David Finn who lives a few blocks away. He will dismantle and remove it in a few days, if it has not already decomposed, or if some lover or hater of art has not removed it first. It has special resonance for this neighborhood and its people, whose fate it may symbolize. (One of its strongest undertones is a bitter meditation on the meaning of "junk.") I ask a couple of local derelicts who are hovering about what they think of it, and one shakes his head sadly and says, "Somebody's got to pay. We know it." But it has wider reverberations as well. We've met these figures before. Was it in El Salvador, or Lebanon, or . . .? This piece fulfills brilliantly one of the Left's chief aims in the Vietnam era: *Bring the War Home!* Only which war is this, so close to home? The artist doesn't tell us; we've got to work it out for ourselves. But whatever we do with it, this work of art has put us, the spectators, into the picture, implicated us a lot more deeply than we may like. The figures will disappear from our street, but they won't be so easy to evict from our minds. They'll haunt us like ghosts, at least till we recognize them as *our* ghosts and deal with them face to face.

Another student comes by: Lena, 17 years old, built like Marilyn Horne. Lena grew up in her family's Puerto Rican *bodega,* the adored only girl in an overwhelmingly male household, and in their storefront Pentecostal church, where she sang solos at an early age. She says her existence was untroubled until she entered college, when her mind came to life and her world split open; suddenly she was alive to poetry, philosophy, psychology, politics, to sexuality, romance, feminism, the peace movement, socialism. Impulses, insights, ideas, all came pouring out of her torrentially; at first her family thought she might be under a spell. Before long, however, for her ideas on abortion, sexuality, and equal rights for women, she was excommunicated from the church. After that, her family was put up against the wall by their fellow believers, who were a large portion of their customers: How long were they going to tolerate a damned soul who wore the mark of the beast in their house and in their store? Her family resisted the pressure and bravely stood by her: They would die for her—but they couldn't even begin to understand her. In the midst of this crisis, her father was shot by robbers and almost killed. The family has had to pull together closer than ever around the store, and Lena may have to go on leave from school, at least for a few months, and work there full time. She would rather die than desert her family in an emergency. But she knows that when normal life returns, if it ever does, for their sake as well as her own, she's going to have to go.

But go where? In the Hispanic immigrant working-class world that is the only world she knows and loves—a world that gave her much of the strength she has, though it turned on her as soon as she tried to use it—the only alternative to the family is the gutter. There are plenty of deviants in that world, but few rebels, and very, very few intellectual rebel girls. Moreover, she knows that in many ways she's still only a kid, far more frail and vulnerable than she looks, just beginning to figure out what she wants from life. I try to tell her that her fight for liberty and autonomy has a long and honorable history, that she can find many kindred spirits and comrades in books, and many more all over the city and the country, probably closer to home than she thinks, fighting battles like her own, creating and sustaining institutions for mutual support. She believes me but says she isn't ready to meet them yet: She's got to cross that lonesome valley by herself, got to get over, before she can join hands with anyone else.

Carolee Schneeman is a painter, sculptor, dancer, collagist, filmmaker and performance artist in New York; she has been active and innovative in many realms since the heyday of the Judson Dance Group twenty years ago. She is best known for her "body art" and performance pieces, which have shown her body, her sexuality, and her inner life in daring and fruitful ways, transforming autobiography into iconography. There was a moment, near the end of the sixties, when her sort of radical imagination was chic; she is still as free a spirit as ever, but in the Reagan era it feels lonelier and more exposed out there than it used to be. In the spring of 1982 Schneeman began a series of sexy and intimate collages that would be called "Domestic Souvenirs." The work was going along smoothly when suddenly, that June, Israel invaded Lebanon, and, as she later described it, "Lebanon invaded me."

Work she eventually did that summer and fall, and showed in New York a year later, looks radically different from anything she has done before. Within these collages, images of sexuality in an ambience of domestic tranquility and sweet communion are intercut with frightful expressionist visions of the disasters of war. Schneeman's "Lebanon" incorporates many of the images that she has been elaborating for years, but gives them darker and deeper meaning. There is plenty of naked flesh, as always, but now many of the arms, legs, breasts, etc., seem to be contorted in terror or twisted and maimed. Nakedness, once (and still) a symbol of sexual joy and energy and personal authenticity, now expresses human frailty and vulnerability—"Is man no more than this?"— as bodies sexually tense or postcoitally relaxed are mounted among bodies tensed in fright or relaxed in death. Blood, whose menstrual flow Schneeman once used to express both a woman's fertility and a self's inner depths, now suggests the blasting away of body and soul alike. Diaphanous garments, earlier images of erotic play, now evoke shreds and shrouds. A central, obsessive image is a triangular tableau of a woman rushing forward while two men move with her and hold her from behind: reproduced in many different textures and tonalities, it suggests both a romantic sexual dream and a political nightmare of wounds, terror, and hopeless flight. Throughout these works, the two modes of meaning interpenetrate and deepen each other. In the midst of our domestic bliss, their homes are being blown away. On the other hand, the maiming and murdering over there are so dreadful precisely because their victims are men and women whose bodies are made to twine around each other and whose imaginations are made for love, just like our own.

In Schneeman's "Lebanon," politics invades the most intimate spaces of the self, envelops our bodies, thrusts into our dreams. From this intercourse, a terrible beauty is born. The artist started out to talk personally, not politically; she ended up showing that the political is personal, and that is why politics matters so much. Alas, her public doesn't seem to want to see what she has to show: This show has so far attracted no reviews and made no sales. Ironically, a fairly large public (for the art public) has been happy, over the years, to look into her most private spaces; but as soon as her vision opened outward and spilled over into public space, as soon as her art penetrated a political space that everybody shared, much of this public was quick to look away. One of the perennial romances of modern times is the fusion of personal with political life. We all dream of this, at least sometimes; but when it actually happens, as it happened to Schneeman last summer, it may be too much for most people to bear, too much even to look at, like looking directly into the sun. So just when—and probably just because—she has worked harder than ever to create dialogue, she is left talking to herself. Still, the works are there, and she and we can hope the dialogue will go on.

Every year or so I go back to the part of the Bronx where I was born. It's not an easy trip to make, though it's only about five miles northeast of where I live now. The South Bronx of my youth, a ghetto with fresh air and trees for second-generation immigrants, celebrated as an ultra-modern environment in the 1920s and 1930s, was written off as obsolete by capital in the 1960s. Abandoned by the banks, the insurance underwriters, the real estate industry, the federal government, and bulldozed and blasted by a superhighway through its heart, the Bronx wasted away fast. (I talk about this in the last chapter of *All That Is Solid Melts into Air*; living through it is one of the things that led me to think about the ambiguities of modernity in the first place.) Through the 1970s, its primary industry was probably arson for profit; for a while it seemed that the very word "Bronx" had become a cultural symbol for urban blight and death. Every time I heard or read about the destruction of a building I had known, or saw it burn on the local news, it felt like a piece of my flesh was being ripped away.

I've always turned the old corner with dread: What if, when I reach the apartment house where I grew up, there's nothing there? It wouldn't be surprising: so many of the buildings in these parts have been sealed up or torn down; streets that were busy and noisy and too narrow for the crowds twenty years ago are as open and empty as deserts today. But it hasn't happened, at least not yet; the building looks surprisingly good, a little Art Deco jewel in the midst of devastation. A heroic superintendent and organized tenants have held it together; and its present landlord appears to have some interest in keeping it up rather than tearing it down. I feel a sense of metaphysical relief. As I explore further, I see that some of the buildings that were burnt-out hulks a few years ago have been, or are being, very nicely rehabbed today. It's very, very slow and fragile; under the Carter administration there was little money for rehabilitation, under Reagan there's even less, and private capital wrote off the Bronx more than twenty years ago. But it's happening, a little here, a little there, the beat and pulse of life beginning again.

I climb the steep hill on East 170th Street, our old shopping center. The quarter-mile stretch alongside our block is utterly lifeless, but the next quarter-mile has been kept up and partially rehabbed, and although dirty and gritty, is bursting with life. The street is jammed with black and Hispanic families—and now some oriental ones as well (Where do they come from? When did they get here? Who can I ask?)—loading themselves up with food, clothes, appliances, fabrics, toys, and everything else they can carry away from the post-Christmas sales.

I board a bus heading south toward Manhattan. Just behind me, a massive black woman gets on, bent under numerous parcels; I give her my seat. Just behind her, her fifteen-or-so-year-old daughter undulates up the aisle, radiant, stunning in the skin-tight pink pants she has just bought. The mother won't look, buries her head in her shopping bags. They continue an argument that has clearly been going on since they left the store. The daughter says that, after all, she bought this with her own money that she made working; the mother replies that if this is all she can think of to buy, she isn't grown up enough to be trusted with her own money or to be out working. "Come on, Mama," the girl says, turning herself around and turning the heads of everybody in the bus, "look at that pink, ain't it beautiful, won't it be nice for spring?" It's January, and spring is a long way off. The mother still won't look, but after awhile she lifts her eyes slowly, then shakes her head. "With that ass," she says, "you'll never get out of high school without a baby. And I ain't taking care of no more babies. You're my last baby." The girl squeezes her mother's arm: "Don't worry, Mama. We're modern. We know how to take care of ourselves." The mother sighs and addresses her packages: "Modern? Just you take care you don't bring me no modern babies." Soon I get off, feeling as happy and whole as the girl in the bus. Life is rough in the South Bronx, but the people aren't giving up: Modernity is alive and well.

THE LOSS OF A HALO

These are some of the people on my horizon. It's wider and more open than the one Perry Anderson sees, and it's crowded with human passion, intelligence, yearning, imagination, spiritual complexity, and depth. It's also crowded with oppression, misery, everyday brutality, and a threat of total annihilation. But the people in the crowd are using and stretching their vital powers, their vision and brains and guts, to face and fight the horrors; many of the things they do, just to get through the day and night, reveal what Baudelaire called "the heroism of modern life." The faces in the crowd today may be different from those in Baudelaire's age; but the forces that propel them haven't changed since modern times began.

Some of these people, in my book and in the vignettes above, are artists. They are caught up in the same chaos as the rest of us; they are special in their ability to give it expressive form, to light it up, to help us navigate and collect ourselves and find each other, so that we can survive and sometimes even thrive in the maelstrom's midst. These artists are like the poet in Baudelaire's prose poem, "The Loss of a Halo":

> My friend, you know how terrified I am of horses and vehicles? Well, just now as I was crossing the boulevard in a great hurry, splashing through the mud, in the midst of a moving chaos, with death galloping at me from every side, I made a sudden move, and my halo slipped off my head, and fell into the mire of the macadam. I was much too scared to pick it up. I thought it was better to lose my insignia than to get my bones broken. Besides, I said to myself, every cloud has a silver lining. Now I can walk around incognito, do low things, throw myself into every kind of filth, just like ordinary mortals. So here I am, just as you see me, just like yourself.

For artists and writers today, as much as for Baudelaire, this loss of a halo can be a step in the liberation of art; the reduction of the modern artist to an ordinary mortal can open up new lifelines and force fields through which both artists and their public can grow.

I am grateful to Perry Anderson for remembering *The Politics of Authenticity* and for pointing out the continuities between that work and what I'm doing now. Then as now, I've been trying to develop a theoretical vision of the unifying forces in modern life. I still believe that it's possible for modern men and women who share the desire to "be themselves" to come together, first to fight against the forms of class, sexual, and racial oppression that force everyone's identity into rigid molds and keep anyone's self from unfolding; and next, to create Marx's "association in which the free development of each is the condition for the free development of all." Nevertheless, *All That Is Solid*, and what I've written here, have a much thicker density and a richer atmosphere than my earlier work. This is because I've tried increasingly to situate my exploration of the modern self within the social contexts in which all modern selves come to be. I'm writing more about the environments and public spaces that are available to modern people, and the ones that they create, and the ways they act and interact in these spaces in the attempt to make themselves at home. I'm emphasizing those modes of modernism that seek to take over or to remake public space, to appropriate and transform it in the name of the people who are its public. This is why so much of *All That Is Solid* is taken up with public struggles and encounters, dialogues and confrontations in the streets; and why I've come to see the street and the demonstration as primary symbols of modern life.

Another reason that I've written so much about ordinary people and everyday life in the street, in the context of this controversy, is that Anderson's vision is so remote from them. He only has eyes for world-historical Revolutions in politics and world-class Masterpieces in culture; he stakes out his claim on heights of metaphysical perfection and won't deign to notice anything less. This would be all right, I guess, except that he's so clearly miserable over the lack of company up there. It might be more fruitful if, instead of demanding whether modernity can still produce masterpieces and revolutions, we were to ask whether it can generate sources and spaces of meaning, of freedom, dignity, beauty, joy, solidarity. Then we would have to confront the messy actuality in which modern men and women and children live. The air might be less pure, but the atmosphere would be a lot more nourishing; we would find, in Gertrude Stein's phrase, a lot more *there* there. Who knows—it's impossible to know in advance—we might even find some masterpieces or revolutions in the making.

This isn't Anderson's problem alone. I think it's an occupational hazard for intellectuals, regardless of their politics, to lose touch with the stuff and flow of everyday life. But this is a special problem for intellectuals on the Left, because we, among all politi-cal movements, take special pride in noticing people, respecting them, listening to their voices, caring about their needs, bringing them together, fighting for their freedom and happiness. (This is how we differ—or try to differ—from the world's assorted ruling classes and their ideologues, who treat the people they rule as animals or machines or numbers or pieces on a chessboard, or who ignore their existence completely, or who dominate them all by playing them against each other, teaching them that they can be free and happy only at each other's expense.) Intellectuals can make a special contribution to this ongoing project. If our years of study have taught us anything, we should be able to reach out further, to look and listen more closely, to see and feel beneath surfaces, to make comparisons over a wider range of space and time, to grasp hidden patterns and forces and connections, in order to show people who look and speak and think and feel differ-ently from each other—who are oblivious to each other, or fearful of each other—that they have more in common than they think. We can contribute visions and ideas that will give people a shock of recognition, recognition of themselves and each other, that will bring their lives together. That is what we can do for solidarity and class-consciousness. But we can't do it, we can't generate ideas that will bind people's lives together, if we lose contact with what those lives are like. Unless we know how to recognize people, as they look and feel and experience the world, we'll never be able to help them recognize themselves or change the world. Reading *Capital* won't help us if we don't also know how to read the signs in the street.

This essay first appeared in New Left Review, *March–April 1984.*

Underground Man

Toward the end of *Crime and Punishment*, the rake and child molester Svidrigailov pulls out a gun on a lonely Petersburg street and prepares to shoot himself. The only witness is a Jewish soldier whose face, Dostoevsky says, has "the eternal expression of resentful affliction that is etched on every Jewish face without exception." When Svidrigailov draws his gun, the guard rushes toward him, and exclaims, "This is no place for jokes!" But the old nihilist has prepared his last line: "If anybody asks," he says as he fires, "tell them I'm going to America." Thus, with a bang, the Russian novel was off to America. And the people who brought it over, and nourished it with their tears, were the descendants of that poor Jewish guard. One of the strengths of Jewish-American writing, from its beginnings a century ago, has been its capacity to recreate the turbulent spirit of Russian literature: a spirit of resentful affliction and desperate yearning, of self-reflection and self-mockery, of gallows humor and laughter through tears, of schlemiels who think they are heroes and heroes who think they are schlemiels. In the works of Bellow and Malamud, of Roth and Heller and Ozick, of Jules Feiffer and Lenny Bruce, of Woody Allen and Bob Dylan, we see how the thriving American Empire of the twentieth century, no less than the decaying Russian Empire of the nineteenth, has nurtured a species of marginal and maladjusted men and women who agonize endlessly, brilliantly, over the meaning of life.

"Spring, 1982. My comic book has been losing money hand over fist. My job has been getting on my nerves. I'm forty-two years old. I've been writing for nationally distributed publications for twenty-three years and I'm still an alienated schlep like I was when I was nineteen." It is the voice of Harvey Pekar, of Cleveland Heights, Ohio. Underneath the words we see a man, etched in the deepest black, emerging from an even blacker background, bent tensely over a table, clinging to his head as if to keep it from collapsing. Our vantage point is weird, from behind and below, as if through the eyes of someone who has collapsed already; the picture, drawn by Kevin Brown, suggests an expressionist wood-cut of Despair. We are in the midst of *American Splendor*, the adult comic book that Pekar self-publishes, whose latest number has just hit the stands. Pekar has put *American Splendor* together with a number of talented Cleveland or ex-Cleveland artists (Robert Crumb is the best known) who illustrate the stories he writes. These stories, "From off the Streets of Cleveland," reveal Pekar as one of the most brilliant and imaginative neo-Russian writers working in any country today.

Pekar's world is divided into three parts, which echo the classic zoning of the Russian novel. There is the solitary rented room—a friend, lover, or spouse may temporarily share this space, but the fundamental loneliness never lifts; there is the city street, generally crummy, in a neighborhood full of people who are down and out—decrepit and often dangerous, yet rich in human vitality for those who know how to look and listen; finally, inevitably, there is the government office. Pekar, like so many heroes of Russian fiction, works as a clerk in the lower ranks of the civil service. Like them, he is an educated proletarian, at once anchored and enchained by his job, smart and sensitive but with no power. Working in the bowels of a vast bureaucracy (he is a file clerk in a public hospital), he gets a close-up of the ways in which a social system can grind people down—but also of the ways in which subjected people schmooze, flirt, hondle, and create an abundant life between the lines. In Pekar, as in his Russian precursors, the clerk's job appears as a parable of the writer's vocation: This hero has absolutely no power—except for the power to describe and transcribe people and things precisely as they are, the power to record the truth.

Pekar's presentation of himself oscillates between two classical Russian archetypes: the Superfluous Man (first defined by

Turgenev) and the Underground Man (which goes back to Dostoevsky). The SM is exceptionally sensitive to other people and their needs, but inhibited in fighting for, or even recognizing, his own needs. On the job, he is likely to be passed over, if not laid off, or treated as a lovable eccentric who need not be taken seriously. With women, he is apt to be rejected, or exploited (he may be the odd man out in ménages à trois), or not noticed at all. He is a loyal friend, a sympathetic confidant, but his best moments tend to be vicarious; he is a marvelous observer of life who can't seem to make it as a participant. The UM defines himself as the SM's antithesis. He is determined not to be victimized. He overflows with rancor, spite, "resentful affliction," toward everything and everyone in his life—sometimes, it seems, toward life itself. His intensity is exciting; he raises the emotional temperature of any room or any human encounter close to the boiling point. But he is crippled by an inability to see other people, except as projections of his own needs. Where the SM falls idealistically in love with people, the UM is apt to say The Hell With Them. Ironically, the UM turns out to be just as stymied as the SM in his pursuit of happiness and fulfillment. He starts out to ride roughshod over everyone in his way—and yet, somehow, ends up turning most of his aggressive energy against himself, and humiliating himself more than he could ever be humiliated by anyone else. Pekar knows both, he *is* both. He has managed for years to make poetry out of the quarrel between them. And there are magical moments, when neither he nor we expect it, when he somehow manages to assimilate and transcend them both, to affirm himself and others. But the SM and UM complexes are never far away from Pekar: they are Family.

In some of these moments of transcendence, Pekar places himself directly in the Russian-Jewish tradition. "Miracle Rabbis" (#7; art by R. Crumb) reworks a short story by I.L. Peretz on which generations of Jewish children have been brought up. In Peretz's turn-of-the-century story, a skeptical intellectual laughs at the legend that the local *wunder rebbe* disappears in the dead of night and ascends to heaven to meet with God. He decides to trail the rabbi on his midnight rambles. To his amazement, the rabbi changes into the clothes of a Polish peasant, and, disguised, visits the wretched hut of a poor crippled widow, to whom he brings enough food and firewood to survive each day. The intellectual is so moved by this combination of charity and modesty that he becomes a disciple. From then on, whenever anybody speaks of the master ascending to heaven, he adds, "If not higher." In Pekar's version, the *wunder rebbe* is "Dr. Gesundheit," an old guy with a thick Polish-Yiddish accent who constantly accosts Harvey in hospital corridors, regaling him with jokes that are corny or inscrutable or (somehow) both, and clamoring to be put into his book. Here he tells a rather lame miracle-rabbi joke; Harvey rolls his eyes and looks toward the exits. At that very moment, a decrepit old patient schleps up to the doctor and thanks him for saving his life. But Dr. G. puts him off: "No, you must be mistaken sir, zat's not me . . . I can't take credit for zis." Harvey plays along with his shtick: "He hasn't saved a life in years. Actually, he isn't a doctor at all; he's a good humor man." The patient, a little slow, is totally befuddled; the crevices in his face deepen into craters; at last he shuffles away. Dr. G. picks up just where he left off, not missing a beat: "Zo anyway here's anuzzer story . . ." as he and Harvey fade away down the hall. What's happening here is that a modern miracle rabbi, confronted by a recipient of his goodness, puts the man on, even treats him cruelly, rather than take credit for what he has done. And Harvey, a modern skeptic par excellence, by playing along with the doctor and helping to protect his cover, is acknowledging his righteousness, and acting as his *hasid*—even if only for a couple of frames. This is how righteousness manifests itself in the modern world: it's mixed up with corniness, with crankiness, but it's for real. Indeed, the fact that righteousness exists in the midst of this mess is the real miracle.

American Splendor's peculiar format seems to ensure its marginality—alas, comic-book distributors have little feeling for the tragic, while dealers in "serious literature" can't see the seriousness in cartoons. But, at the same time, the format brings out its originality and depth. Once we have read Pekar's stories with these pictures, it is hard to imagine doing without them. The texts and images often play against each other and generate a dialectic of their own. For instance, on the front cover of #6, drawn by Gerry Shamray, it is a lovely spring day, and Cleveland's apartment houses as well as its foliage are ablaze with color. One of Harvey's friends, a clean-cut, outdoorsy-looking fellow, has stopped his English bike for a dialectical chat with Harvey. "It's hard enough," the fellow says, "to convince people that socialism is a good thing, without basing your argument on some abstract theory of human nature. Plato tried and failed, Fourier tried and failed, Marx tried and failed, Sartre tried and failed . . ." Harvey's hair is turning gray, his shoulders slump, he has a paunch, he is physically more decrepit than his friend; yet spiritually he is more youthful, springy, as he stretches himself and says, with a cracked grin, "Well . . . maybe I c'n learn from their mistakes."

The tension between texts and images expresses a contradiction in contemporary reality itself: Middle-aged souls can soar as bodies droop; alternately, bodies can grow lithe and supple as minds freeze. (On the back cover of #6, drawn by Greg Budgett and Gary Dumm, the equation is reversed. Harvey's body has grown strong and ruddy, but the text again belies the image: his rap reveals him sinking into depression, oblivious to the vitality his body exudes.) The cover of the latest issue (#8), also by Budgett and Dumm, shows Harvey in the hospital cafeteria where, with a wicked grin on his face, he makes a wisecrack to one of his superiors who doesn't happen to be as smart as he is, a wisecrack that makes the man look (and probably feel) even dumber than he is. However, in the bottom left corner, there is a much smaller image that criticizes—and in some sense refutes—the main one. Harvey is pushing a car in the snow, trying to get it to move. Here, instead of sophomoric complacency, we see naked desperation. He is trying to "get started"—not merely the car, but himself: His body is angled like a rocket on a launcher. He seems to want to hurtle himself—his real self, the person he is "deep down"—through the constraining frame, and into the center of the cover, where his "false" self reigns in the midst of a thoroughly alienated scene. This small picture of Harvey straining to move a car through the depths of the long Russian/Cleveland winter is a parable of his life and work: It is his myth of Sisyphus.

Pekar's picture has come to look especially grim to him in recent years, because there was a period when it seemed that his life was going to brighten up. At the end of 1979, Carola Dibbell wrote a laudatory article about him and *American Splendor* in the *Voice*. That fine piece put him on the map in front of a national and influential audience. Calls began coming in from both coasts; it must have seemed that fame and fortune were on the way. Indeed, if there were justice in the universe, Pekar would be rich and famous, fighting with agents, translators, and producers. But there isn't much justice in the universe—who can explain the mysteries of the culture market?—and his hopes went unfulfilled. Meanwhile, an apparently happy marriage, tenderly celebrated in #5 and #6, abruptly came apart. In #8, four years after his big break, Pekar is still on the street, still in Cleveland, still a file clerk, still horny and lonely, still working in *samizdat* because no one wants to publish his book. True, *samizdat* is a noble Russian tradition, but it is the nobility of the down-and-out, and after years and years of this nobility, who needs it? Instead of worrying about whether success would carry him too far from his working-class sources of inspiration—as Gorky, Lawrence, Mike Gold, Farrell, Springsteen had to worry—he has been thrown back on the sort of worries he knows only too well: as he said in #3, "Awaking to the Terror of the Same Old Day."

It is a tribute to Pekar's inner strength that he has been able to go on putting his life on the line. But upheavals like these have got to take their toll. The early issues of *American Splendor*, especially the brilliant #3, were distinguished by a delicate aesthetic and emotional balance: His books expressed a range of human emotions, hot and cool, up and down, and everything in between; but these eruptive feelings were remarkably balanced and counterbalanced in a dynamic equilibrium that made each book an integrated whole. In Pekar's last two books, all that is eruptive erupts, carrying everything else in its path, dragging us into Pekar's inner maelstrom, leaving us no way to get through or out—except to stop reading, or not to start. In #7, Pekar hit us with not one excruciating divorce, but two: he threw in the disastrous breakup of his first marriage in the early 1970s. The weight of all this unmediated pain was too much to bear—I put the book down for months, thereby missing many wonderful things in between the catastrophes. A panel in #8 (drawn by Crumb), showing Harvey surrounded by cartons of unsold #7s, suggests that many potential readers stayed away.

If the SM's sadness overpowers #7, the UM's rage threatens to run away with #8. "Assault on the Media," at the book's center, is a diatribe against *The Village Voice* (What have they done for him lately?), but also against all the other East and West Coast people who claim to love his work but so far have done nothing to put his name in lights. With such friends, he doesn't need enemies. Indeed, he says, he *prefers* enemies: With people who hate him and his work, at least he knows where he stands. In case the political implications aren't clear, Chairman Mao's motto, "Combat Liberalism," adorns the wall. In this centerfold, aided and abetted by Crumb, Harvey comes across as a raving *meshugginer*, shouting and banging the wall. I couldn't stand it (maybe—though I doubt it—if I myself weren't trying to plug-Pekar in the *Voice*, I would've got a kick out of it). I dropped the book like a hot rock and put it at the bottom of the pile.

I was very glad when I picked it up again: #8 is full of material that suggests Pekar's imaginative breadth. Sue Cavey, an artist who came on board in #7, does about a third of the artwork in #8. She gives Harvey and his world a radically new look, and generates a distinctive dialogue that encompasses Pekar, herself, and us. Cavey, the one woman Pekar has worked with so far (does this mean something?), is also the one artist whose visual style is rooted in symbolism rather than realism. Her figures are shadowy, spectral; they float and hover, melt and fade. In her frames, the boundaries between the self, other people, and the world are shifting and elusive; people's shadows, especially Harvey's, may appear as vivid and substantial as the people themselves. Cavey's work brings out a profound strangeness in Harvey's world, a strangeness that *American Splendor*'s artwork has tended to conceal. She opens up a realm of secret thoughts, desires, fears, just behind his back, over his shoulder, at his feet; she transforms streets, living rooms, delicatessens, automotive interiors into dreamscapes and forests of symbols. After several of these stories, a reader may well feel queasy and yearn for the familiar grimy Pekaresque world.

Cleveland, in all its griminess, obsesses Pekar: On one hand, it is a remote provincial outpost, squalid, unbearable in winter, close to bankruptcy; Harvey dreams of escape to New York or San Francisco the way a young Chekhovian lieutenant dreams of Moscow. On the other hand, it's home, it's mother and father, it offers warmth and solace when the great world outside betrays you. Thus, in #1, a man returns from California, where he was caught in a disastrous *ménage à trois*, to shoot baskets happily with his old Cleveland pals: here, at least, he can score. On the back cover, a grizzled old worker (wearing a "Vladic Moving and Storage" jacket) throws an egg at a Greyhound bus leaving for Hawaii (a bus for Hawaii?), and addresses the bizarre-looking crowd that is about to depart: "You fuckers can leave if you wanna, but I'm stayin' in Cleveland an' fightin'." His friend agrees: "'At's tellin' 'em, buddy. Let 'em go, Cleveland don't need their kind." In "Getting Adjusted" (#3), maybe the best story Pekar has ever done, an ex-San Francisco hippie, now a young mother, realizes, as she talks to Harvey, that in spite of herself she has come to like Cleveland: The people here are "real good, solid people. They're not far out or trippy but they do some magical things and they don't even know it." To accept Cleveland, in Pekar's scheme of things, is to grow up, to accept people as they are, the human condition, real life.

"Grub Street, U.S.A." Pekar's best story in recent years, reiterates this theme, but in a more complex and deeper way. After all that has happened in the last few years, Pekar finds it harder than ever to believe that the bluebird of happiness is right there in his own backyard. "Grub Street" begins with the tableau of desperate misery I quoted at the start of this piece. Then Harvey hears that Wallace Shawn is coming from New York to promote his film, *My Dinner with André*. He has heard that Shawn likes his work, and arranges to meet him. Harvey imagines New York life as one great artistic orgy and yearns to become part of the action: "Half th' city of New York's putting on plays, an' I'm here in Cleveland sitting with 25,000 comic books I can't sell. *Oy gevald!* the world is passing me by." Maybe the man from New York will help make him a star. As he listens to Shawn, whom he likes, he realizes that not only does the man lack magical powers, but he's in a bind surprisingly similar to Harvey's: Though his work has received critical praise, he can't raise money for new projects, his girlfriend must work as a waitress to make the rent, his Visa card may be repossessed. Shawn's lament makes Harvey realize that for this guy, New York is Cleveland—not a magical kingdom run by gods or demons, but a real place, the scene of endless, unremitting, everyday struggles.

And as Harvey grasps how New York can be Cleveland, suddenly, magically, Cleveland becomes New York: A vast horizon opens up (drawn beautifully by Kevin Brown); we see sweeping vistas of the city that Pekar has never let us see before, and Cleveland appears as a great metropolis with cloud-capped towers and a glamorous skyline all its own. For once, Harvey is too worn out to talk. But we can see what he has been through, and what he has won. We can share his sense of peace, and, with him, accept our own cities, our own limitations, our own hung-up and worn-out selves. It may not last, but it's real: It's the real American splendor.

This essay was originally published in the Village Voice Literary Supplement, *September 1983.*

Broadway, Love, and Theft:
Al Jolson's Jazz Singer

My name in electric lights—everything
                    The hero to his mother in *The Jazz Singer*

Mutual forgiveness of each vice,
Such are the gates of Paradise.
                    William Blake, "For the Sexes: The Gates of Paradise"

We used to hear about the Broadway white lights,
The very serious dazzling White-Way white lights . . .
It's getting very dark on old Broadway . . .
Real dark-town entertainers hold the stage.
You must black up to be the latest rage.
                    "It's Getting Very Dark on Old Broadway,"
                    sung by Gilda Gray in Ziegfeld Follies, 1922

I wanna be black.
                    Lou Reed, "I Wanna Be Black," 1980

One of the most stunning visions of Times Square comes at the climax of *The Jazz Singer* (1927), the first-ever sound movie, the first music video, and one of the great American *Bildungsromans*. The hero, played by Al Jolson, wants to sing to the whole world, and Times Square symbolizes that world. Here is where he breaks on through, becomes who he is, fulfills his crossover dreams, sings his heart out, and gets to have it all. His story began in the Lower East Side's gray day; it ends in Times Square's gaudy night, in brilliant

contrasts of black and white. A long shot unrolls a three-part structure of space stretching to the horizon: at ground level, a parade of
people; above them, pulsating neon and electric signs, a flood of *light;*
over all, a great expanse of open *sky* that frames and embraces the
people and the signs and fuses them into a whole. This is the great
Times Square spectacle. These few frames—they last less than a
minute—can help us see Times Square fresh, as if for the first time.
This is America's gift to the modern world, the most dynamic and
intense urban space of the twentieth century, the commercial sublime.

We see the spectacular Times Square, with the hero's name in electric lights, only at the movie's end. When we see it, it's the place
where Jakie has *arrived.* How did he get here? What did he give of
himself? What did he give up? The trajectory that leads to "my name
in electric light" is the primal arc of the twentieth-century American
life story. *The Jazz Singer* traces that arc and sings that story.

The Jazz Singer has long been recognized as a great
Bildungsroman. But it's also a synthesis of the *Bildungsroman*
with what seems like a completely different genre: the minstrel

Al Jolson in *The Jazz Singer*
(Wisconsin Center for Film and Theater Research)

show.[1] Most literate Americans know how important the *Bildungsroman*, the super-serious story of growing up, has always been in our national self-awareness. Not many people are aware of the importance of our minstrel tradition, in which the highest seriousness masks and mocks itself. Times Square is a place where these traditions converge like subway lines, where inwardness and emotional depth get saturated by neon and displayed as entertainment. It's the place where Jolson appeared not only as "the world's first cinematic voice," but maybe as "the world's first superstar."[2] When he appeared so big, he appeared in black: He was in blackface when he rocked the house with "Mammy."

Since American minstrel shows made their debut in the 1830s, all their actors have been in blackface, yet many have been white. Working in blackface doesn't entail being black, just *acting* black. A century ago, many of the most talented blackface comedians were immigrant Jews: Jolson, Sophie Tucker, Eddie Cantor. The Ziegfeld Follies cultivated a blackface partnership between Cantor and the great black comedian Bert Williams. Williams insisted blackface didn't "come naturally" to him:

---

1   In Constance Rourke's classic study *American Humor: A Study of National Character*, New York: NYRB Classics, 2002 (first pub. 1931), blackface minstrelsy is central to American humor and character. It is a subject that has generated many fascinating books. See, for instance, Robert Toll, *Blacking Up: The Minstrel Show in Nineteenth-Century America*, Oxford: OUP, 1974; Eric Lott, *Love and Theft: Black Minstrelsy and the American Working Class*, Oxford: OUP 1993; Wesley Brown, *Darktown Strutters*, New York: Cane Hill, 1994. More fine work continues to appear; see Margo Jefferson in note 3 below.
2   Jim Hoberman, "The Show Biz Messiah," in *Vulgar Modernism: Writing on Movies and Other Media*, Philadelphia, PA: Temple University Press, 1991, 64–68. Hoberman has another fine piece, "On the Jazz Singer," in *Entertaining America: Jews, Movies, and Broadcasting*, Princeton, NJ: Princeton University Press, 2003. This volume, the catalogue for a show that opened at New York's Jewish Museum in 2003, features a provocative and visually strong section on *The Jazz Singer*. It includes a splendid essay by Mark Slobin, "Putting Blackface in Its Place," and an elaborate chronology of Jolson's and *The Jazz Singer*'s many incarnations up to 1998. Hoberman occludes another strong candidate for "the world's first superstar": Charles Chaplin.

I do not believe there is such a thing as innate humor. It has to be developed by hard work and study . . . It was not until *I was able to see myself as another person* that my sense of humor developed.[3]

Eric Lott, one of blackface's most perceptive historians, sees it this way:

Acting black: a whole social world of irony, violence, negotiation and learning is contained in that phrase . . . an unstable or indeed contradictory power, linked to social and political conflicts, that issues from the weak, the uncanny, the outside. Above all, slipperiness.[4]

The most remarkable moment of *The Jazz Singer* comes about two thirds of the way through, when the hero "blacks up."

Before we can understand why this hero is blacking up, we have to ask, Who is this hero, anyway? We need to form some idea of his identity. But it may not be easy. The fact that he is working in blackface in the first place suggests a sense of identity that is, in Lott's word, "slippery," and a capacity, as Bert Williams said, to see himself as another person. His name, at this point in the movie, is "Jack Robin," but that is not the name he was born with. The name his parents gave him is "Jakie Rabinowitz." He grew up on the Lower East Side, a cantor's son. From his earliest years, he was in serious conflict with his father. His father taught him the *nigunim*, the holy melodies; he learned them well and made his father proud. But he felt that the songs and the world of the *shul* were not enough. He roamed the streets of the Lower East Side, listened to the secular music he heard there, and got a job singing in a cabaret. Before he goes on, the announcer says, "It's *Ragtime Jackie*, folks; give him a break." So we see he has taken a new name, what my parents called a "stage name"; in his life history, it is Name #2.

---

3   From an essay on humor that Williams wrote in 1918 for *American* magazine. Cited in Margo Jefferson, "Blackface Master Echoes in Hip-Hop," *The New York Times*, October 12, 2004 (italics mine).

4   Eric Lott, *Love and Theft*. As a lover of this book, I was delighted to see it become the object of a theft by Bob Dylan, in his powerful 2002 album, *Love and Theft*. More on Dylan later.

His father is tipped off, horrible things happen, and the sequence ends with the hero leaving home. He is born again into show business, anoints himself with a new name, "Jack Robin," and dedicates himself to a life on the road. In his life history, this is *another* New Name, Name #3, other-name #2. (I'm not going to go into this any further here, except to say that the great book on Jews and names—maybe "from Jacob to Bob Dylan"—is waiting to be written.) The name change does show us something important, what Bert Williams called the capacity to "see himself as another person." But that person won't come together until many years later, when he returns to Broadway at last, blacks up, and encounters his mother backstage.

Jakie's songs from the street were the first sounds, not quite in the history of film, but in the history of *commercial* film, film made to be shown on those same city streets where the sounds were made. As a matter of fact, "the street" is one of *The Jazz Singer*'s uncredited stars. Jolson was one of the masses of Jews who grew up in America's immigrant ghettos, but felt out of tune with the patriarchial "world of our fathers."[5] After World War One, in the 1920s, they helped to create a culture in which they and their most intimate audiences could feel more at home. This was the culture of "Broadway," of "show biz," of "the Jazz Age," of what Ann Douglas, in her wonderful book on the Harlem Renaissance, calls "Mongrel Manhattan." Douglas has a fine sentence fragment that suggests the breadth and depth of this culture: She alludes to "the moderns' finest achievements in popular culture, from Al Jolson's vaudeville act to the new skyscrapers of Manhattan."[6] She wants us to see how buildings of stone and

---

5   Irving Howe and Kenneth Libo, *World of Our Fathers*, New York: Harcourt Brace Jovanovich, 1976, is the classic study of the culture of the Lower East Side. The book aches with nostalgia for that lost world; but its most spirited portraits are of people who spent their lives as transgressors against it. In the sections on entertainment and popular culture, Howe's heroes—Jolson, Irving Berlin, Sophie Tucker, Eddie Cantor—turn out to be people who not only worked in blackface but felt personally close to black people, black music, and black culture. Howe and Libo note this in passing but don't explore it in depth.

6   *Terrible Honesty: Mongrel Manhattan in the 1920s*, New York: Farrar,

glass and performances by live people can grow out of the same modern desires and drives.

One of *The Jazz Singer*'s primary axes is the polarity of "The Street" versus "The House." The polarization was even sharper in the shooting script. One sequence apparently shot but cut featured the sounds of a "street piano." This instrument, also known as a "hurdy-gurdy," was supposed to be playing that perennially popular song, "The Sidewalks of New York." The camera showed a *cheder,* an after-school "Hebrew School." The script says, "The sound of a street piano comes through an open window, and the kids rush to the window." The cantor enters, he hears the street music, "a look of disgust comes over him, and he closes the door"[7] Soon he is tipped off that his own son is singing in a cabaret, as "Ragtime Jackie"; he pulls the kid off the stage, drags him through the streets, beats him with a strap at home for embracing "your lowlife music from the streets." When Jakie's mother suggests he might not want to follow his father (and four generations before him) and become a cantor, the father rears up and roars, *"What he wants means nothing!"*[8] Soon he throws Jakie out of the house and tells people his son is dead. Here, as in many other works about immigrants in many genres, there is a convergence of conflicts: conflict between immigrant fathers and American sons, and conflict between the rigid pietism of the house and the open wildness of the streets. Al Jolson was one of the creators of the culture of "Broadway," and Broadway was a street culture created by sons.

Jakie leaves home and anoints himself with his third name, "Jack Robin." Like so many great American performers, he grows up on the road; the road is his school, his college, his university. For years

---

Straus & Giroux, 1995. Douglas's "mongrel" title is a variation on a metaphor used by Dorothy Parker to describe herself, 5. For Jolson and skyscrapers, 8. This fine book, also a classic study, is also very interested in people who practiced "crossovers" between Jewish and black worlds. The Gershwin brothers play leading roles in both.

7   *The Jazz Singer,* screenplay by Alfred Cohn, edited with many appendices by Robert Carringer, Winsconsin: University of Wisconsin Film Center, 1979, 51.

8   Ibid., 62–65.

he doesn't look back. We are supposed to feel he does all right for himself. (A lot better than Mama Rose and her enslaved kids in *Gypsy*.) But he never reaches the big time—he's in the Omaha-Denver-Seattle orbit, something like class AA in minor league baseball—and his singing is pretty good, but nothing that would change anybody's life. When we first meet Jack Robin, "he is shabbily dressed and, although neat of person, it is obvious that he is down on his luck."[9] But then one day he hears a cantor sing,[10] and what he hears brings back all that's missing in the self and the life he has made. He realizes he needs more of something. But what? Is it Jewish religion? Not exactly. It's Jewish, all right, but in the sense of, first, Jewish "roots", connection to his past, and, second, Jewish soulfulness and gravity, qualities missing in the world of show biz.

Soon the jazz singer lands a job in a Broadway revue called "The April Follies." Now, at last, he has a chance to break through and get recognition as a star in his hometown. We the audience know he has immense talent. But we also know his morbid undertows. His act evokes many of the sad clowns who haunt the Western theatrical tradition: Harlequin, Pagliacci, "He Who Gets Slapped," and a whole line of great minstrels.[11] Jolson had in fact played with Lew Dockstader's minstrels as a kid. But the adult Jack Robin does not seem at home in his sadness; the planes in his

---

9   Ibid., 68.

10   Ibid., 84ff. That cantor was a real person, Josef/Yossele Rosenblatt, one of the first Jewish religious figures to not only record his voice but market it. His capacity to incarnate both religious and market values prefigures *The Jazz Singer*'s happy ending.

11   Jolson developed blackface routines in the 1900s, in his teens, while he was working as a solo performer and traveling from carnivals to burlesque houses around the country. He attracted the attention of Lew Dockstader, the head of a widely admired minstrel traveling show, worked in blackface with the company for the next five years, became increasingly prominent, and was written up in *Variety*. In 1909 he went to work for the Shubert Brothers. Within a few months, in a Shubert musical called *La Belle Paree*, he became "the first performer to perform minstrel comedy in what was then called the legitimate theatre." The best account I have found of Jolson's early career is Michael Alexander, *Jazz Age Jews*, New Jersey: Princeton University Press, 2001, especially chapters 14–17, on "Jewish minstrelsy" and "Jewish versions of blackness."

face drift off in different directions and don't connect. *The Jazz Singer*'s narrative, pacing, and tonalities are all carefully constructed to show us that the hero's story is not mainly about performance, or about success, but about the process that Keats called "soul-making" and Erik Erikson called "egoidentity."[12] Can this man pull his life together? The movie forces us to feel that nothing less than identity is at stake; and, like it or not, we all have a stake in that.

Everything is set up to prepare us for the dress rehearsal, the solemn moment when we see the hero actually construct the self he is trying to become. Jolson blacks up, and behold! For the first time in the movie, he looks like a serious and integrated person. He faces himself in the mirror. The encounter between him and his newly constructed image is staged very carefully. Will he recognize himself? How will he deal with the man he sees? As he gazes, his vision fragments kaleidoscopically into a montage—in the 1920s, that technique was still new and fresh—and propels him back into his father's synagogue, into "Jakie Rabinowitz," the kid whose spontaneity and joy he has repressed for twenty years. But at the same time, framing that youthful being is the face of a thoughtful, serious, mature man—not exactly a black man, but a man who has made blackness a *project*. There's something amazing about the black face he has constructed. It's as if this singer has transformed the minstrel "Swanee River" into an inner River Jordan that he needs to cross in order to grow up. Look into those eyes: For the first time he looks like a *mensch*. Putting on someone else's face is enabling him to recognize his own. By being someone else, he can become himself. There's some sort of magic working here. In fact, it's a very old and venerable magic, going back to the origins of the theater thousands of years ago. But it's

---

12 Erikson, one of Freud's most creative followers who developed the concept of ego-identity, had identity problems of his own. In 1975, in the *New York Times Book Review,* I reproached him for his cover-up of his Jewishness. In the language of 1970s culture, this was translated as "*outing* Erikson as a Jew." This episode is discussed skillfully by Lawrence Friedman in *Identity's Architect: A Biography of Erik H. Erikson*, Cambridge, MA: Harvard University Press, 1999.

also a very up-to-date and contemporary magic, the "Magic Realism" that is thriving on jazz-age Broadway and that defines the 1920s Times Square.

But why does he need to be black? What is the power of blackness for Jakie, for Jack? Right after this revelatory moment, another clown breaks onstage with another revelation. He is the shambling, sleazy "Yudelson, the Kibitzer from the Ghetto" (Otto Lederer) who has come to tell Jack his father is dying, and to urge him to return to the family, the ghetto, the synagogue, and God.[13] He can recognize the hero by his voice: "Yes, that's Jakie—with the cry in his voice, just like in the temple." But he is disoriented when he meets him face to face in blackface: "Jakie, this ain't you." Then he turns to his audience to comment on the metamorphosis he has just seen and the action he is part of, and he changes his mind. He recognizes that this is Jakie, after all, but a Jakie who has put himself through big changes: "It talks like Jakie," he says, "but it *looks like his shadow*."

What does a shadow look like? In fact, the shadow is a prime image in the history of reflection on the self and the other. For many modern psychologists, the shadow metaphor is about mental processes they call "projection" and "identification." These processes work within the self in radically different ways. In projection, we ascribe to other people feelings we cannot accept in ourselves. When we do this, we constrict the scope of our being and enlist in an unending state of war, not only with the people next door, but with ourselves, prime suspects in a hopeless quest for purity. (Jews and blacks have both been longtime casualties in these psychic wars.) In identification we yearn for others, want to reach out and touch them, talk to them, be close to them, merge with them. Identification helps people grow up, become more than they were, enlarge who they are, and learn to live in peace. But none of us is capable of identifying with other people until we can identify with the dark side of ourselves, until we can bring our shadows into the light and find ways to live with them.

We still haven't figured out what psychic undertows might be

---

13   *The Jazz Singer*, 119–23.

lurking in the jazz singer's shadows. There must be some emotional strength that he feels deprived of when he walks around with his Jewish face but that he gains when he puts on a black one. In 1927, when *The Jazz Singer* was made, American Jews were believed to have "arrived," to be "at home" at last; they were supposed to feel comfortable and grateful. (In those years, Hitler was still a face in the crowd.) Black people, on the other hand, although freed from slavery, were being lynched and humiliated by laws that could have been made by slaveholders. Some black people were making a mark in Northern cities, most strikingly in the development of jazz and in the cultural explosion known as the "Harlem Renaissance." But the great majority of black Americans were still, like Faulkner's characters, locked into the police states of the underdeveloped rural South. Barred from social striving, living under something close to house arrest, they were forced to preserve "the cry in their voice," the sound of unmediated human emotion. If we listen to some classic Delta Blues today—to Leadbelly, to Robert Johnson, to Bessie Smith—the idea that social imprisonment could evoke primal emotion doesn't sound far-fetched. And of course it's a great tradition, in fact a great *Jewish* tradition, born in the world of the Psalms: "How can we sing the Lord's song in a strange land."

You could say the Kibitzer's "shadow" line gives away the whole story: a twentieth-century epic where immigrant Jews identify with blacks in ways that help to develop both mass culture and multicultural liberalism. All this is true, but this isn't all. When I looked up this scene in Alfred Cohn's script, it said something startlingly different from what's on the screen. What Yudelson says in the printed version is, "It talks like Jakie, but it looks like *a nigger*."[14] So the original version was a crude racist insult. Amazing! What happened? No one seems to know. But somehow, in the process of cultural production, some obscure, unnoticed, maybe even unconscious revolution took place. Did that word call up the horrors of *Birth of a Nation?* Did the guys behind the scenes recoil and think, "Never Again"? In an instant,

---

14 Ibid., 120.

a spit in the black face turned into something close to an embrace, and the movie grew up.

Let's come back to Jack in his dressing room. There are many ways a black face can help a Jew. Michael Alexander says it well at the very start of his fine historical study, *Jazz Age Jews*. Even as Jolson's generation moved up from the ghetto into the American middle class, he says,

> Some of its members displayed a peculiar behavior that did not correspond to their social position. They acted as though they were increasingly marginalized. What is more, they identified with less fortunate individuals and groups . . . by imitating, defending, and actually participating in the group life of marginalized Americans. Outsider identification . . . is a paradox in the psychology of American Jews. *As Jews moved up, they identified down.*[15]

From the standpoint of *Bildung*, identification with blacks could open up fruitful paths. For Jewish kids who did not want to be comfortable "allrightniks," blackface enabled them to feel firmly, even righteously American without having to feel white. Over the generations, it could help them become Jerome Kern and the Gershwins, Artie Shaw and Benny Goodman, the Schiffmans and the Chesses, Phil Spector and all the brave knights of the Brill Building, Bob Dylan and Laura Nyro, Doc Pomus and Dr. John, Richard Price and Rick Rubin. Jews attuned to black music have opened up the gold mine of black experience to the whole world. They have confronted America with a *J'accuse*: Its betrayal of its black people proves its betrayal of itself. Michael Alexander has a nice term for this attitude: "romantic marginality."[16]

All this is fine, and yet any Jew who is hip enough to imagine he or she "wants to be black" will be smart enough to know there's something unkosher about the deal. This guilty unease shapes *The*

---

15   Michael Alexander, *Jazz Age Jews*, 1 (my italics).
16   Ibid., 164. Alexander calls this "a theology of exile" growing out of the basic contradiction in Jewish life, "a communal covenant with God and a communal exile" (180ff).

Jazz Singer's climax. When Yudelson asks Jack/Jakie to come back and help his father die, the sacrament he wants him to perform is called *Kol Nidre*. For many Jews, this is the most dramatic and spiritually intense moment of the year. It happens on the night that begins Yom Kippur, the Day of Atonement. Many secular Jews who wouldn't dream of going to synagogue all through the year feel they have to be there for this. The *Kol Nidre* prayer is special in that it isn't addressed to God, but to other people. We are supposed to recognize all the ways we have hurt each other all year, not just openly but in the shadows; we are supposed to seek and to offer forgiveness. There is a catalogue of sins and crimes. The idea is for all of us to confess, plead guilty to them all, and cover for each other:

> *We abuse, we betray, we are cruel . . .*

> *We destroy, we embitter, we falsify . . .*

> *We mock, we neglect, we oppress . . .*

> *We steal, we transgress, we are unkind . . .*

> *We yield to evil, we are zealots for bad causes.*[17]

Few of us have done all these things, but all of us have done some. Our leap of faith is that if we can face each other and admit what we have done, or even what we have imagined doing, then we will have the right to ask each other to forgive. And

---

17 *MAHZOR for Rosh Hashanah and Yom Kippur: A Prayer Book for the Days of Awe*, ed. Rabbi Jules Harlow, Rabbinical Assembly, 1972, 376–79. This is a Conservative prayer book, and Jack/Jakie's of course would have been Orthodox (and untranslated). The idea of a collective confessional and the basic items in it go back to Rabbinic times and are shared by Jews all over the world. But some congregations since the 1960s have added to the catalogue of sins. (Rabbi Jeremy Kalmanovsky, note, October 14, 2004).

Mutual forgiveness of each vice,
Such are the gates of Paradise.[18]

More than any other Jewish ritual, *Kol Nidre* is driven by music. The cantor's solo is the most passionate, heartrending music of the whole year. Jews believe nothing else can break down people's resistance or open up their emotional floodgates. Many people complain about spending money on a cantor's salary—but then, if the cantor is singing as he should (or, more and more, as *she* should), they leave *shul* in tears and hope to be forgiven for doubts. At *The Jazz Singer*'s climax, Jolson sings the *Kol Nidre* prayer. He leads the congregation with an amazing emotional fervor and intensity that have eluded him till now: Now, at last, he's *there*. His heroic act—returning to the ghetto, sacrificing for a father who didn't sacrifice for him, renewing his thrilling but dangerous bond with his mother—unites his adulthood with his childhood, frees unconscious energy, and taps emotional depths that he has had to repress in order to work and live for twenty years under his father's curse. Now, as his father dies, chains lift from his heart. He learns from his life what his father's religion couldn't teach him because it was too narrow, and what secular show biz couldn't teach him because it was too shallow: the universal lesson that *"music is the voice of God."*[19] In *The Jazz Singer*, mass culture stakes a claim to universal value, not only for its global reach but for its emotional power and depth.

After Jolson blacks up, when he faces himself in the mirror, he is affirming his act of theft and recognizing that he has something to answer for. He wants to be forgiven and believes he should be, on the grounds that his grand theft springs from love. This encounter with himself liberates waves of unconscious energy and sets him free to become somebody new, somebody bigger and deeper and more grown up than he has ever been.[20]

---

18   William Blake, "For the Sexes: The Gates of Paradise" (1793, 1818), in *The Portable Blake*, edited by Alfred Kazin, New York: Viking, 1946, 1968, 268.

19   *The Jazz Singer*, 99; italics mine.

20   But he would never have tolerated charges like those made by my late,

There is one more big thing that needs to be on the Jazz Singer's *Kol Nidre* list, something else that springs from love, and that is his incestuous love for his mother. The color of this love comes across most vividly in a scene called "Jack Robin Comes Home and Sings for Mother."[21] Here Jack sits at the piano and plays her some of what he is going to sing on Broadway. This is the one scene where Vitaphone Sound records lots of talk along with music and where the distinction between speech and song gets blurred. He plays and sings an up-tempo, jazzed-up arrangement of Irving Berlin's "Blue Skies," a cascade of pure joy. As he sings, he jokes and flirts with her, vows to move her to the Bronx, "a lot of nice green grass there and a lot of people you know." His patter grows both more frantic and more intimate, and now that they are alone together, we see that the incestuous love that has been only a subtext till now has become a text. He grows ever more outrageous, and pulls her close:

And I'm gonna buy you a nice black silk dress, Mama. You see Mrs. Friedman, the butcher's wife, she'll be jealous of you . . . And I'm gonna get you a nice pink dress that'll go with your brown eyes . . . What? Who is telling you? Whatta you mean, no? Yes, you'll wear pink or else. Or else you'll wear pink. And I'm gonna take you to Coney Island . . . An' you know in the Dark Mill? Ever been in the Dark Mill? Well, with me it's all right. I'll kiss you and hug you. You see if I don't.

To our surprise, she responds as if quoting some primal flirtation textbook. Her body language abruptly changes, she speeds up and

---

dear friend Mike Rogin in his book *Blackface, White Noise: Jewish Immigrants in the Hollywood Melting Pot*, Oakland: University of California Press, 1996, that not only *The Jazz Singer* but virtually all popular culture created by Jews is a giant rip-off of blacks. Rogin was one of the best minds of my generation, but this late work is over the top.

21 *The Jazz Singer*, 96–100. The screenplay, 144–45, gives intricate dialogue beyond what is in the script, and something like what is actually on the screen. Samson Raphaelson, author of the story and the play on which the movie was based, felt let down by the movie. But this mother-son encounter was the one scene he really liked.

bounces with the beat. She says "Oh, no!" in a way that suggests "Of course," and "and what else?" As he talks and plays on, the directness and ardor are amazing—and visibly mutual. The expression "Oedipus complex" hardly seems the word, the waves of love between them look so *simple*. This is a scene that takes us into emotional spaces that are thrilling but also scary, and neither American culture nor any other can tell us convincingly how to react. When the old man returns and shrieks "*Stop!*" it is a disappointment, but also a relief.

Jakie's mother (Eugenie Besserer) is a fascinating character, far more complex and original than she seems. She looks like the sentimental Mamas in a thousand novels, plays, and songs, including the 1930s jazz hit, "My Yiddishe Mama," and Gertrude Berg's mama-diva figure, Molly Goldberg. But she is more special. Although she herself is a devout person, she adamantly supports the right of her son *not* to be devout. Her husband the cantor says Jakie "has all the songs and prayers in his head." She responds with two different but related ideas: "*But it's not in his heart. He is of America.*"[22] In other words, first, Jakie has a right to a life of his own based on what is "in his heart"; second, this is the meaning of America. Later on, she visits her son in the theater, sees him in his new element, talks with his *goyishe* girlfriend May, the show's female lead, and she says, "Here he belongs" (149, 123). This woman has slow, solemn, old-fashioned body language but an ultramodern sensibility.

Jakie's mother draws on a reserve of collective feeling about mothers. When the conflict of generations boils over, the father often erupts and throws the child violently out of the house. But the mother opens up a back channel of communication with the excommunicated child and sustains a bond deeper than bad behavior. (This happens in Sholem Aleichem's story cycle, "Tevye and His Daughters," and in its descendant, *Fiddler on the Roof,* after the hero has denounced his daughter for marrying a goy. Jakie's mother leans on what Hegel called "the law of the heart" and on a feeling all her audience will know: "a mama's heart." But she is

---

22 Ibid., 59.

also inspired by something that in her world is far more unusual: a mother's *mind*. She is the most supportive parent in the history of the *Bildungsroman*. Fighting for her child's right to a life project radically different from her own, she could be the Existentialist Mother of the Year. Virginia Woolf, in *A Room of One's Own*, written just a year after *The Jazz Singer*, had a word to say about her: "When, however, one reads of a very remarkable man who had a mother, we are on the track of a lost novelist, a suppressed poet, of some mute and inglorious Jane Austen, some Emily Brontë." She has plenty of sisters.[23] She is a very important modern type of person, split between her conventional life and her sympathy for unconventional ideas—and for unconventional choices by her children. She is a patron saint, not only of the liberal Broadway audience that I grew up with—and, indeed, grew up *in*—but of every twentieth and now twenty-first-century avant-garde.

The hero's *Kol Nidre* solo lasts only a couple of minutes, but it is dynamite. It features a counterpoint between Jack/Jakie and the choir. He pulls against them, they resist him, he and they seem to fight each other, the emotional momentum gets frantic, then finally the choir gives way and they blend marvelously together. I was amazed how well these two minutes prefigure the sounds, a generation later, of the great flowering of rhythm and blues: Ray Charles, Sam Cooke, Stevie Wonder, Aretha Franklin, Curtis Mayfield, Al Green, Marvin Gaye, Mavis Staples, Patti LaBelle. But why not? After all, R&B was made largely by blacks who were participants in what historians call "The Great Migration,"

---

23   *A Room of One's Own*, New York: Harvest, 1981 (first pub. 1928), foreword by Mary Gordon, 49. One of those sisters was the mother of the great liberal philosopher Isaiah Berlin. Berlin was my supervisor at Oxford forty years ago, and I met his mother at his stepson's bar mitzvah in early 1963. She asked me and my friend Jerry Cohen what we thought of the bar mitzvah boy's *haftarah*. I said I thought he had read very well. When Jerry didn't seem to know what to say, I explained, "My friend had a very strict communist upbringing." This didn't faze her at all. She said, with a warm smile, "Yes, God had made human beings different so they could talk and argue, and so teaching and learning could go on." She spent the next few minutes developing this theme, a remarkable fusion of Molly Goldberg and John Stuart Mill.

and who, just like the Rabinowitz family, were going through a traumatic first-generation encounter with modern life in the northern cities of the USA. Their music was driven by religious fervor, yet they were also staking out a claim to a secular good life. Some of the greatest R&B songs, like "Higher and Higher," "For Your Precious Love," "A Place in the Sun," "Many Rivers to Cross," "I'll Take You There," get their depth and power from a vision of sacred love and profane love as metaphors for each other. Martin Luther King defined the politics of their project, their quest for religious ways to affirm secular modern city life.

Part of *The Jazz Singer*'s mythic power comes from its conquest of many media. Its first incarnation was a story by Samson Raphaelson, published in 1921 under the title "The Day of Atonement" in *Everybody's Magazine*. Its second, also written by Raphaelson, was a Broadway adaptation starring George Jessel, whose early biography and inner conflicts were a lot like Jolson's. The play ran from 1925 to 1927 and closed just before the movie opened across Broadway. In "The Day of Atonement," the cynical Broadway producer is angry at Jack/Jakie for leaving the show. But he follows him down into the depths of the Lower East Side and hears his solo. (The *tallis*, the traditional Jewish prayer shawl, is his disguise.) He is thrilled and phones his partner uptown:

> "Harry," said Lee, "do you want to hear the greatest ragtime singer in America in the making? A wonder, Harry, a wonder! Come down right away, it's a dirty little hole on the East Side called the Hester Street Synagogue, I'll meet you at the corner of Hester and Norfolk."[24]

In the sound era, Raphaelson became a great comic screenwriter and worked closely with Ernst Lubitsch (*The Shop Around the Corner, Trouble in Paradise*, etc.). He always used the English language with precision and finesse; the way he says things can tell us a lot. In his story, the producer is on the Lower East Side on what later generations would call a scouting trip. He calls his

---

24   Story included as appendix to screenplay, *The Jazz Singer*, 167.

partner uptown and says something great is happening down here. The singer, the synagogue he sings in, the neighborhood itself, are all something much bigger than themselves *"in the making"*; they are phases in a historical dialectic they don't understand. Forty-second Street and Broadway, terminal for the IRT subway, is also the terminal for Raphaelson's dialectic, the place where cultural history comes out.

The story and the play both end with the prodigal son's return: Jakie gives up a career on Broadway and sings for his people and God alone. In the shooting script, as in the play, that's the end. The screen fades to black. But then, an instant later, things change: In fact, we go through an instant 180-degree change, from renunciation to jubilation, and we see a jubilant ending on the screen, the ending with which this chapter began. Was this ending always part of the deal? If so, why isn't it in the script? Here is how the change is registered in "Appendix I: The Synchronized Sound Sequences": "The season passes—time heals—the show goes on."[25] Those dashes wouldn't get over in any respectable grammar book or English class. But fans of Keats's letters, and of Emily Dickinson's poems, will remember them: They push the narrative forward; they ensure that life will go on in spite of many formidable objections. As the dashes flash, the soundtrack turns jazzy. Then there is a quick cut to a spectacular panorama of Times Square and Broadway's blinding lights. This thrilling perspective is Times Square's special contribution to modernism. It defines the Square's spectacular trinity—people, lights, sky—as the new totality of being. The dashes are like the subway, an underground way to get there fast.

The grand finale brings us inside a jammed Broadway theater. (In fact, it's the Winter Garden.) The flood of light means "Broadway forgives all." The hero sings in blackface again, but it doesn't seem to carry the tragic weight it had only a few minutes ago. "Mammy," the song he sings, is addressed to a woman supposedly near death, yet he sings in a state of pure exuberance. He leaves the stage and focuses on his mother in the audience; they

25 *The Jazz Singer*, 146.

share an upclose ecstatic smile. With the wicked witch of an old man dead, the third leg of the Oedipal triangle collapsed, and the hero a star with his name in electric lights, they don't need a Dark Mill anymore. Now they can enjoy a communion that needs no *Kol Nidre*. Or so we're told. *The Jazz Singer* takes us for a ride, but it is a ride that most of us will be glad to take. This is the magic realism that is the heart of modern mass culture, where tragedy can morph instantly into comedy, incest can symbolize innocence, and the project of giving up everything can turn out to be just a chapter in the dialectics of having it all.

If my phrase "having it all" sounds disrespectful, that isn't what I meant at all. In fact, at *The Jazz Singer*'s moment in history, the word "all" marked a bitter controversy. For a whole century, the USA had had a policy of amazingly open immigration. But in the 1920s, in the aftermath of World War One, Congress passed a series of laws that pretty much closed the gates for the next forty years. America was hoping to stop its slide into being a nation of "all" and to stand fast instead as "fortress America" open only to "some."[26] Griffith's *Birth of a Nation* showed how America's ultramodern mass culture could be bent in the service of a pastoral vision of a lost Anglo-Saxon purity before it was polluted by a great stream of dark and dirty "others." Chaplin's cinema gave a spectacular new visual life to the drives and dreams of these others. His comedy came from neighborhoods like our "dirty little hole on the East Side." These places were the birthplace of movies and jazz and comics and the whole culture of "vulgar modernism" that made twentieth-century America a truly "new world." *The Jazz Singer*, more than any other work, defined that world's look and its sound.

---

26 Oscar Handlin, *The Uprooted: The Epic Story of the Great Migrations That Made the American People*, New York: Grosset & Dunlap, 1951. For more complex reflections on this theme, see John Higham, *Strangers in the Land: Patterns of American Nativism, 1860–1925*, New York: Atheneum, 1963 (first pub. 1955). For more recent treatments, see Nancy Foner, *From Ellis Island to JFK: New York's Two Great Waves of Immigration*, New Haven, CT: Russell Sage / Yale University Press, 2000, and Gary Gerstle, *American Crucible: Race and Nation in the Twentieth Century*, New Jersey: Princeton University Press, 2002.

In the middle of World War One, Randolph Bourne, a young disciple of John Dewey, wrote an essay, "Trans-National America" (1915), that may be the first theory of this world. Bourne argued that immigrants to America don't "assimilate" into a preexisting Anglo world: They mix their old cultures with new conditions to create a blended, hybrid American culture that has never existed anywhere till now. "Only the American," he said, "has a chance to become a citizen of the world." This meant "not a nationality but a trans-nationality, a weaving back and forth, with the other lands, of many threads of all sizes and colors."[27] A year later, many of the Jewish and other immigrant songwriters of Tin Pan Alley resisted the wartime pressure for "100 per cent Americanism" and argued instead on behalf of "a counter-sentiment for a nation of nations."[28]

Times Square, night view (c. 1930s, Museum of
the City of New York; the Gottscho-Schleisner Collection)

27 Reproduced in Randolph Bourne, *War and the Intellectuals: Collected Essays, 1915–1919*, ed. Carl Resek, New York: Harper Torchbooks, 1964, 107–23.
28 Michael Alexander, *Jazz Age Jews*, 161, and Chapter 17, "The Jews on Tin Pan Alley."

In America's "nation of nations," from Jolson's time to our own, Times Square has always been the capital. You can see it on the street or in the subway, any hour of the day or night. You can hear it everywhere, inside and outside. (In my youth you could hear it underground, at the great Times Square Records in the IRT subway arcade.) Today's ingredients are different from those of the Jazz Age—for one thing there are a lot more ingredients, come from a far greater range of places—but now as then it's a *mix*. A mix means more than just different people "side by side." It means integration, but also intercourse, blending and fusion that change everybody. In the Square the mix is insistently *there*, it's on the street, it's in your face. When you are in the mix, under the Square's spectacular light, ego boundaries liquefy, identities get slippery. You won't be able to avoid the question, "Who are these people?" And brushing against them will raise the collateral question, "Who are you?" You will be changing them just as they will be changing you; you know everybody will change, even if you don't know how. How Americans feel about Times Square, and about New York as a whole, often depends on how ready they are for a liquefication of their being. For Al Jolson, liquidity of being was his life. When Jolson paints himself black, he performs multicultural America's first sacrament: He metamorphoses into both the mixer and the mix.

P.S. At the end of 2004, the classic *Jazz Singer* cityscape—Times Square at night, in black and white, with its trinity of people, signs, and sky—was reincarnated on the cover of Bob Dylan's *Chronicles, Volume One*, his memoir of his early 1960s arrival and his debut in New York.[29] Some reviewers and many readers were puzzled why his cover featured Times Square rather than Greenwich Village, where Dylan first performed in public and became a star. If we use *The Jazz Singer* as our prism, it is easy to see. Dylan is presenting himself as Jack Robin's descendant, as the true Jazz Singer of our

---

29   Bob Dylan, *Chronicles, Volume One*, New York: Simon & Schuster, 2004. Disclosure: An early form of this essay appeared in *Dissent*, Summer 2002, entitled "Love and Theft: From Jack Robin to Bob Dylan."

time. Bob Dylan, Jack Robin: Isn't the connection obvious just from the names?[30] Now look at Dylan's cover. This expansive vision of the Square by night suggests a world that is all before him, a vast horizon, not just musical but imaginative, far beyond the range of the Village folk world where he began; a capacity for metamorphosis—what I called the power to be "at once the mixer and the mix"; an intimacy with electricity (see his battle of Newport, 1965)—as a medium for magnifying both the music and the self; an identification with show biz and a deep need to be an entertainer. There's one more Dylan-Jolson connection we can't leave out: "the cry in his voice, like in the temple." Both jazz singers are driven by a need to infuse profane entertainment with religious fervor and a desire for transcendence. Dylan's religious experience is far more various than Jolson's, more elusive and full of contradictions. Still, the Jewish Bible is right there in his title.

Chronicles has a great first scene. It is set amid the red-leather booths of Jack Dempsey's Restaurant, where Dylan's first producer, Lou Levy, has taken him out, to show him around and also to show him off. His encounter with Dempsey is sweet. First, the champ tells the scrawny kid to put on weight, learn to dress sharp, not be afraid to hit people hard. When Levy explains that Dylan is a songwriter, not a boxer, Dempsey doesn't skip a beat; he tells the kid he can't wait to hear his songs. Anybody old enough to remember Dempsey's place can imagine this scene. The old man loved schmoozing with people, he was patient and gracious with all kinds, terrific with kids. He synthesized in himself two vital parts of American popular culture, "the fights" and show biz. The fact that we know this anorexic kid is about to write one of

---

30   When I brought home my first Bob Dylan album forty years ago, my mother enjoyed the music, but got stuck on the name: "Hmm, Dylan, what was it before?" I got so mad! But of course she was right. For my parents' generation, this question was an ongoing joke with a critical edge. (See the Marx Brothers' "Hurrah for Captain Spalding, the African explorer.") My mother understood why Jewish boys had had to go in disguise in her time (and Jack Robin's), but not in mine. Soon Dylan was outed as "Zimmerman." He seemed to resent it at first, but, like Jack Robin, gradually learned to affirm his real Jewishness along with his wannabe universality in the course of growing up.

the all-time great American songs, "Blowin' in the Wind," makes this story a little masterpiece of dramatic irony. Dylan blends modern realism—a real street we know, a great figure who lived long, and whom some of us might even have met—with very old, mythical and folkloric forms of narration: "prophecy of the hero's success," "the old champion anoints the new."

There's just one weird thing about this lovely story. Somehow, he gets the address wrong. Dempsey's restaurant was on Broadway and 49th Street, in the Brill Building, aka "Tin Pan Alley." This is one of the great sites in the history of American culture. For decades it was full of musicians, songwriters, accompanists, record producers, music publishers, agents, publicists. I spoke earlier about the brilliant men and women working here. It was the place where so many songs that defined America after World War Two—"Lonely Avenue," "Chapel of Love," "Be My Baby," "Hound Dog," "Don't Be Cruel," "Stand by Me," "Walk On By," "We Gotta Get Out of This Place," "Society's Child"— were made. (And Dylan knew every note and every line.) Dempsey's was a perfect Times Square location, close to the old Garden,[31] center of the city's boxing scene, and right at the epicenter of its popular music industry. Dylan was there because some very important music people, like producer John Hammond, spotted his genius right away. But his book removes the scene from its central location and relocates it half a mile away to 58th Street, in the 1960s a dingy, anonymous periphery. What's going on? Wouldn't Jack Dempsey have knocked out anyone who tried to relocate him to that Desolation Row? Dylan's cover picture places him out in the open, at Times Square's center; his stage direction pulls him into the shadows. Even as he unfolds himself,

---

31 The old Madison Square Garden—which also figures in Kubrick's *Killer's Kiss*— was between 49th and 50th Streets, and between Eighth and Ninth Avenues. Dempsey's began at 50th and Eighth, right across the street. For a while he had two restaurants, the original and a "Broadway Restaurant and Bar" in the Brill Building. Then for a generation the Brill Building place reigned alone. The "Jack Dempsey's Broadway Restaurant" website displays a matchbook ad: LOVE MATCHES ARE MADE IN HEAVEN, FIGHT MATCHES ARE MADE AT JACK DEMPSEY'S.

he moves to hide to keep from being seen. He starts his book with an engaging story of his youth in Times Square, then breaks the engagement with a quick change of address that makes the Square disappear.[32] It seems he still can't bear to admit he is in show biz and always has been, still can't affirm his own life. Like so many modern men and women, Dylan/Zimmerman is still searching for a name that he can feel at home with.

This essay was first written for Marshall Berman's On the Town, *Random House, 2006. An earlier version appeared in the Summer 2002 issue of* Dissent *as "Love and Theft."*

---

32   Even if we can imagine this author's unconscious ambivalence, what's the publisher's excuse? Is there nobody old at Simon & Schuster who remembers, or nobody young who has read about all the years when Jack Dempsey was king of Times Square? (And what about the *New York Times?* Its Sunday "City" section reprinted this scene, false address and all, on March 26, 2005.)

"Justice / Just Us":
Rap And Social Justice In America

Thirty years ago, I was a graduate student here, first at Oriel College, then at St. Antony's. I worked with Isaiah Berlin, James Joll, Anthony Quinton, John Plamenatz, Iris Murdoch. I wrote a thesis on "Freedom and Individuality in the Thought of Karl Marx." Intellectually, I had a great time, a far better time than I could have had at any American graduate school. But I didn't open up to Oxford as a place, I didn't let myself enjoy it. It was the first time I had ever been more than a couple of hours away from the Bronx, and Oxford felt so utterly *other*. I know I loved the architecture, and I filled my letters home with sketches of Classic domes, Gothic towers, Romantic parks. But soon it got dark and cold, the gorgeous buildings cast long shadows, and I got lonely and paranoid. I came to feel that the place's very beauty was really there to crush the working class and the Jews and people like me. I traded stories of self-alienation with the two dearest friends I made, a boy from Montreal and a girl from Calcutta.

What made me feel most like an alien here was *people*. In the Oxford of the early 1960s, feudalism lived. The first person I saw every morning was my servant—"scout," he was called—whose job was to wake me up, lay out my clothes, bring me warm water to shave with, and remind me of my appointments for the day. I had a lot of trouble with this, and I never gave my scout a proper chance to do his job. I couldn't bear to be addressed as Sir, or treated as a "gentleman." And I couldn't stand the "gentlemen" around me, who in those days still dominated Oxford's streets and quads: languid young men who looked like extras from *Brideshead*

Revisited, who slouched around in tuxedos (which quite often looked like they'd been slept in), vegetating while their fathers owned the British Empire and the world. Or at least they *acted* like their father's owned the world. I knew how much of it really was an act: The Empire was *kaput*; the children of its ruling class were living on trust funds that were worth less every year and inheriting companies that were going broke. I knew that intellectually. So why did those silly kids, half asleep and putting on the ritz, intimidate the hell out of me? Those Evelyn Waugh extras were just as scared as I was, maybe even more, because at least I knew I was moving up in the world. (After a while, I found out some of them were even scared of me!)

Over the years I came to see that the place I couldn't bear really wasn't there. Oxford in the '60s was a Twilight Zone, an imperial capital of the mind whose empire was extinct. If I had sensed the darkness just behind the twilight, I might not have felt so out of time. But 20-year-old kids don't have much of a sense of time; historicity is one of the things we get as we grow up, and it's one of the reasons that growing up is nice. Anyway, thirty years later, Oxford seems to have found a solid place in a wider world, not imperial but multinational, and so have I.

Today I want to talk about rap music as a site of cultural conflict in American cities today. The conflict is taking place on three different planes: among rappers themselves, inside the serious rap audience, and within the large American public that doesn't know much about rap except that it is a powerful force in our cultural life. The conflict is not only about what rap is and what it should be, but about the nature of our shared *reality*, a reality in which rappers claim to be expert.

There are two themes I want you to keep in mind. The first is Antonio Gramsci's idea of an "organic intellectual," an intellectual who *belongs*. Who is he or she supposed to belong to? Both to a place and to a people—sometimes, as Gramsci puts it, to "*the* people." This idea is opposed to Karl Mannheim's idea of the intellectual as a being who is unconditioned and "free-floating." For the past twenty-five years or so, about half my life, I've been trying to become an organic intellectual of New York. New York was where I spent my childhood and where I became an intellectual, and I always loved the place without thinking. It wasn't till I left—in fact, it wasn't till I came here, to Oxford—that I saw how much acute and chronic trouble my home town was in, how tempting and easy it was for its children to forget it, and how much it needed intellectuals who loved it.

My second theme is "a shout in the street." This phrase comes from James Joyce's *Ulysses*. It emerges in a conversation between one of Joyce's heroes, the young artist Stephen Dedalus, and Mr. Deasy, the proto-fascist headmaster of the school where he teaches. Mr. Deasy is saying that history embodies the will of God.

> —History, Stephen said, is a nightmare from which I am trying to awake.
>
> From the playfield the boys raised a shout. A whirring whistle: goal. What if the nightmare gave you a back kick.
> —The ways of the Creator are not our ways, Mr. Deasy said. All history moves toward one goal, the manifestation of God.
>
> Stephen jerked his thumb toward the window, saying:
> —That is God.
>
> Hooray! ay! Whrrwhe!
> —What? Mr. Deasy asked.
> —A shout in the street.

In my book about modernity and modernism, *All That Is Solid Melts Into Air*, this is a very important line. I show how much of modernist writing and culture—from Baudelaire and Dostoevsky to Beat poetry, Pop Art and Rock and Roll—get their energy from the flow and the convulsions of the modern city streets. But I didn't produce much exciting street material from the years when I was finishing the book, the late 1970s and early '80s, and my narrative trails off at the end. However, very soon after I put the book to bed, I began to hear rap seriously. I heard it, and saw it, in two places: in the college where I teach, in Harlem—City College of New York, which is something like a London polytechnic—and in the South Bronx, where I grew up. In those days the radio wouldn't play rap, and you had to go, to be where it was happening. Rap knocked me out: I thought, All right, here it is, my shout in the street, I can hear. Rap music was a primary energy source for me throughout the Reagan decade.

My title today, "Justice/Just Us," comes from a rap called the "Beat Street Breakdown," from a mid-'80s film called *Beat Street*. *Beat Street* was a low-budget movie that was made to showcase the hip-hop subculture, where inner city kids, mostly black, created rap music, subway graffiti, and breakdance. The movie is made "on location" in the South Bronx, with nonprofessional kids who play themselves, rapping and breaking and writing as they try to survive. In the mid-'80s, South Bronx "location" meant sublime, spectacular, Piranesian ruins. (A German art critic I knew said that whenever her friends came to visit, and she offered to take them to her favorite New York scenes, Central Park, the Metropolitan Museum, the Brooklyn Bridge, her friends waved them all away, and said, instead, "Take me to the burning buildings, I want to see the ruins.") Melle Mel, the rapper here, performs the "Breakdown," with heartbreaking intensity, in memory of a friend who has just died: Ramon, a subway graffitist, was caught writing in the tunnels, chased by the Transit Police, and killed by an oncoming train. Here is the last verse:

> Search for justice, and what do you find?
> Just us on the unemployment line,
> Just us sweating from dawn to dusk,
> There's *no* justice, there's—*Huh!*—just us.

This is powerful protest writing, in the tradition of Broonzy and Guthrie, Ochs and Dylan, Springsteen, Bernice Reagon and Billy Bragg. It is also, like their best work, an essay in political theory. Its account of everyday reality is framed by an ideal aspiration: the search for justice. It contrasts this ideal with the fact that, per capita, American blacks are twice as likely as whites to hold menial jobs ("sweating") and twice as likely to be unemployed or poor. To suggest these facts of life aren't just is clearly right.

But Melle Mel's brilliant quatrain also sounds like the work of a poor man who has never been out of his neighborhood. He seems to think these things happen only to blacks: "just us." America's mass media, especially TV, would give him few clues that there are other people on that unemployment line. But an important fact of life in the late–twentieth century USA is that poverty and misery are multicultural. In reality, the great majority of the country's poor and oppressed people are white. But poverty today means isolation, so that poor people of different ethnic groups are mostly ignorant of each other's existence. Our media sustain this ignorance: Virtually the only time most Americans ever see poor whites is as part of racist mobs attacking blacks; as for poor Latins (by all statistical indices worse off than blacks), they don't appear at all. Latins are a lot closer than blacks to being "invisible men.") Maybe if the rapper could imagine other Americans who are poor and oppressed like him, even though they don't look like him, maybe the fellow-sufferers could become fellow-activists, and maybe then they might have at least a shot at justice. But so long as they don't see each other, they are bound to feel totally isolated and smashed by the whole structure of the world. Then their raps will be texts in what the historian Richard Hofstadter called "the paranoid style in American politics."

What has this to do with justice? If blacks appear to be the *only* victims of injustice ("just us"), it makes the search sound pretty futile. The searchers find themselves running with Thrasymachus (from Book One of Plato's *Republic*), who argues that justice is an empty scam, that it's impossible to criticize any ruling class for being unjust, because justice is simply whatever is in the interest of the ruling class. "Search for justice, what do you find?" You find there's nothing there—unless you have *power*, and then you can shove your brand of justice down people's throats, and make them grovel and accept it, until someone else comes along who can do the same to you. Thus all life gets resolved into a clash of *us* and *them*. If the contending parties don't develop some common idea of justice that they can share, there will be no framework in which they can recognize each other. And then they will be running with Carl Schmitt, the existentialist Nazi, who defined life as a fight to the death: it's *just us* or *just them*; no other outcomes are possible or even conceivable. We could easily be in post–Cold

War Bosnia or in any other land where ethnic cleansing is sweeping the country.

America is not Bosnia; hate here isn't quite so lethal. But the idea that "just us" are suffering is a familiar tribalist refrain of the 1980s. It's an idiom that the middle-aged folks here can remember from the "Black Power" politics of the 1960s; though, ironically, its high point in American history was the 1860s, when it served as the official language of the slave-owners of the Confederacy. In the Reagan era, a wide range of social groups learned to speak the language of militant separatism. This foreclosed the growth of broad coalitions that could fight for justice together; meanwhile, our old ruling class, expert in its own separatism, stepped over the bodies, enriched itself immensely, and increased all the gulfs between itself and everybody else: "just us" with a vengeance!

So there are problems with Melle Mel's *argument*, if it is an argument. But you know he hasn't given up searching for justice if you listen to his *voice*. If you listen, you feel like the Wedding Guest in Coleridge's "Rime of the Ancient Mariner": This guy won't let go of you; you "cannot choose but hear." You hear a man stretching the English language to tell a desperate story, and making a call that cries out for your response.

I grew up in the South Bronx, rap's cradle, in the 1940s and 1950s. My neighborhood was mostly working-class and mostly Jewish (including many Holocaust survivors); life was mostly poor and hard. In the early 1960s, just as the shades of poverty were starting to lift, Robert Moses's Cross-Bronx Expressway chopped the neighborhood in half, the job base crumbled, my family and thousands more moved out. By the mid-1970s, nearly all the Jews, Irish, Italians, Ukrainians had gone; so had the first waves of blacks and Latins who came in. Poverty was deeper and more chronic. The deindustrialization of America wiped out the blue-collar jobs that had kept generations of Bronxites alive. Drugs and arson were the biggest local industries now. The most striking visual feature, by the mid-'70s, was miles and miles of ruins. Dozens of blocks, blocks that for decades had been the densest and most crowded in the city, now were suddenly as open as deserts.

Within a decade the South Bronx lost half its population, as hundreds of thousands of people fled the fires. (Population loss then became the pretext for closing the firehouses.) This was the decade when New York nearly went bankrupt, and the *Daily News* summed up very aptly the federal government's role in the story: "Ford To City: Drop Dead."

At the very nadir of historical catastrophe, rap was born. In the beginning, it was a *musica povera*, made by kids who were too poor to afford instruments or lessons. Its primal form was a single black kid with a mike and a speaker that played a drum synthesizer track. Soon, as rappers began to play in local clubs, it expanded into a bipolar form, in which an MC (master of ceremonies) held the foreground—he spoke, chanted, called, grunted, cried, and occasionally sang—while, behind him, a DJ (disk jockey) established a background and created beats, rhythm, melody, harmony, and a total environment in which rap could take place. The DJ came equipped with two turntables, a drum track, and hundreds of records: On one turntable he would collage musical tracks, often at amazing speed, to make complex allusive melodies, while he scratched the other side to create percussion.

The invention of the digital sampler in the mid-1980s enabled DJs to create backgrounds as complex as any symphony orchestra. The best ones were even more complex: They appropriated every musical style in history: jazz, classical, folk, sacred, rock, soul, R&B, reggae, Broadway, Indian, African, along with background voices, street noises, and machines. (Sometimes the production apparatus has gotten overloaded, as it did in white rock in the years after *Sgt. Pepper.*) These spectacular backgrounds put more pressure on the MCs, who needed voices both strong and supple enough to scale the walls of sound. The tension between DJ and MC, between foreground and background, is what propels rap forward and gives it its moment-to-moment dramatic power.

But that isn't quite right. It makes rap sound too much like opera: as if we can get to love it—and in the last ten years, people all over the world have come to love it—without understanding the rapper's words. To see rap as opera misses too much. Rappers confront us the way Wordsworth said a poet addresses his audience: as "a man speaking to men." They are using "the language of men." (And this means something a lot deeper than the language of males.) We have to listen to the *words,* and hear how they're being said, and imagine what they might mean, because a rapper's words have the power of life and death.

In rap's early days, as in the early days of sound film, language was mainly comic: Words were juggled, caressed, turned inside out, twisted like snakes around the audience and the performers themselves. As a professor, I was glad to see how well these kids knew the power of words, and how they were staking their claim to the English language and using it to empower themselves. They denounced everything and everyone, including themselves, but their antic words and energy soared above it all so that none of it seemed to matter. They probably hadn't seen many Marx Brothers films, but Groucho was their godfather. What, Groucho in the ghetto? Well, after all, didn't he come from the ghetto? Where else could he have come from?

There are still great comic raps coming out: "OPP," Other People's Property, by Naughty by Nature, 1991, is one of the sexiest and funniest raps ever made. But very soon a tragic crater opened up alongside the comedy. Considering where rap was coming from, how could it not? "The Message," by Grandmaster Flash and the Furious Five, released in 1982, was rap's first international hit. It was a litany of dreadful things that could happen to a poor person in the South Bronx or someplace like it. You can imagine the details. The chorus, delivered with desperate intensity, went, "So don't push me 'cause I'm close to the edge, / trying not to lose my head. *Huh!* / It's like a jungle, sometimes it makes me wonder / how I keep from going under." In the rap's second half, the narrator's perspective shifts, and he talks to somebody who is like himself, but dead: someone who has gone over the edge, "lived so fast and died so young."

"The Message," at once a cry for help and a snarl that no one can help, became an instant classic. Suddenly a lot of people wanted to hear rap and thought it mattered. It opened up a genre that could channel the tidal flow of pain and rage that flooded American inner cities in the Reagan years of malign neglect. And, at a moment when American popular music was highly stylized and overblown, it sounded "real," directly connected to a "real life." The life that rap came from was distinctly marginal, but those early rap voices despaired of their marginality, rather than rejoicing in it (as post-mod theorists of culture told them they should). At this point rap became important not just musically but culturally—not just in our ghettos, but all over our country, because it became an arena in which Americans contended and argued over the nature of the reality we share.

After "The Message," many intellectuals started listening to rap. (A few had listened even before.) We admired its in-your-face intensity, its emotional authenticity, its unmediated desperation, but also its wit and way with words, its power to be playful in the midst of death, its hope that words could have the power to pull the self through. Intellectuals and artists knew and cared about rap for years before big record companies or Hollywood producers would touch it. They wrote criticism that celebrated it, much as the young intellectuals of the *Cahiers Du Cinéma* a generation before had celebrated low-budget *film noir*. Here's a concluding sentence from one of those critical pieces, by me: "They are saying, *We come from ruins, but we are not ruined*." Here's another: "From now on, nobody and nothing in the world is safe from rap." Some intellectuals put together noncommercial films (*Wild Style*, *Beat Street*, *Style Wars*, and many shorts) that introduced the world to hip-hop, the subculture that had created rap, artistic graffiti, and breakdance. I got to know many of these intellectuals up in the Bronx (or on the no. 2 subway line). It all reminded me of the Russian intellectuals of the 1880s, "going to the people": We would teach them how to organize, they would regenerate us through their moral purity. Of course, "purity" meant something different for us. We never thought the poor people of the Bronx were saintly; what we thought was that they were *authentic*. But authentically what? The idea oozed ambiguity. Some people thought it would be better for rappers to stay in the Bronx forever; to move into the "Downtown" world was bound to make them corrupt, like ourselves. I had the feeling that rappers loved the Bronx, but now that the Bronx had taught them to talk, they wanted to talk to the whole world, and if we cared for them like we said we did, we would help them get as far into the world as they could.

I had just brought out a big book on modernism, and rap felt like proof that modernism still lived. It seemed like a bridge between my middle age and my childhood, between the middle class I was now and the working class where I'd started out, between smart people with education (like me) and smart people with none (the rappers, my parents), between Jews and blacks, between the stacks in the library and the signs on the street. This was when Gramsci's idea of the "organic intellectual" came close to my heart; when an Italian newspaper asked me to describe myself, I said that I was trying to become an organic intellectual of New York, trying to carry the city's inner contradictions within myself. There were these three years or so in the middle of the 1980s—never before, never again—when I had this thrilling feeling that I *belonged*.

As the 1980s went by, more and more people, with a widening range of biographies, began to rap. Many came from the middle class and had a serious education. Some of them could even use words like "modernism." Here's a sample from a group called Public Enemy, from suburban Queens:

> Lazer anesthesia, maze ya, ways to blaze your
> brain and train ya
> . . . What I got, get on up, better get some,
> hustler of culture
> Snakebitten, been spit in the face but
> the rhymes keep fittin'

"Hustler of culture"; this rapper, Chuck D., knew something about modern poetry, as much as he knew about beats and rhymes. Public Enemy helped a lot to expand rap's vocabulary. They set a new standard in density and richness of sound, in lyrical brilliance, and in political seriousness and commitment. ("Fight the Power," incorporated into Spike Lee's movie, *Do The Right Thing*, and "Welcome to the Terrordome," are their greatest hits.) Their politics were always vague and sometimes seemed to be verging into mere bad attitude, but the vagueness was probably artistically more fruitful than specificity would have been. The central imperative seemed to be that rappers should *think* and *care* about politics, that they should overcome the horizon of their street and think about the world. "The ass is connected to the brain stem," rapped Chuck D. Before long, if you listened to rap radio, Machiavelli, Shakespeare and Nietzsche, Sartre and Camus began to appear in the mix, fighting for space with Reagan and Bush, Jesse James and Scarface Al Capone. More raps appeared that were not only smart but intellectual, reflective and complex.

Meanwhile, white kids began rapping, and some of them—the Beastie Boys, 3rd Bass—did it compellingly and got respect on the street. The best white rappers tended to be Jewish kids, as marginal in their own way as blacks; they simultaneously flaunted their culture and parodied it, as the Marx Brothers had done in the 1930s, and as Bob Dylan did in the 1960s. (Dylan's "Subterranean Homesick Blues" surely rates a place in rap's prehistory.)

I can remember the fall of 1989, that magic year when history seemed so wonderfully open. I was in Stockholm, rapping about rap, saying how it could create a universal language and a world culture. My Swedish audiences were a little mystified but fascinated with this idea. So why do I feel so silly if I say it now? I still love rap, my body still moves and my heart soars when I hear it in a passing car or on a boombox in the street. I still hear raps and rappers that thrill me. And I still think rap *is* an archetype of "world culture." But that culture and that world both look a lot more problematic to me now than they did in 1989.

The post–Cold War world's troubles are being acted out in the starkest way right now in ex-Yugoslavia and the ex-USSR. Both those nations for generations tried to hold together very wide ranges of people and peoples. Their communist rulers, though at odds with each other, both offered their peoples an enlarged, inclusive and cosmopolitan vision of citizenship. I don't know just why it happened at the end of the 1980s, but finally they both collapsed. (One reason has to be that the visions were routinely betrayed in everyday life; on the other hand, they weren't betrayed any more in the 1980s than in the 1950s or '60s or '70s.) Both states caved in to a wide array of centrifugal pressures, ethnic, national, and religious: They could not overcome. In much of Eastern Europe, racist demagogues have come out of the woodwork and had tremendous popular success; thousands of people have been killed since those nations fell apart, maybe even hundreds of thousands; and it looks like Eastern Europe's civil wars are going to get worse before they play themselves out. One of the saddest things is what's not there: There's no idea of an inclusive citizenship based on rule of law. What's replaced it is a bunch of exclusions, based on unstable mixtures of blood and soil and church and DNA and the gene pool and big guns, locked in a zero-sum war. Whoever wins here, humanism loses; it never even had a chance.

What happened in rap is a crude caricature of this reality. (Cf. Marx: "the first time as tragedy, the second as farce.") In the early 1990s, the overwhelming burst of energy in rap, emanating above all from L.A., has been in a form that called itself "gangsta rap." If Public Enemy was special in its layered complexity, the gangstas—like an antithesis to their thesis—specialized in gestures of brutal simplification. Here is Eazy-E, of NWA, Niggers With Attitude, in "Straight Outa Compton," the first breakthrough L.A. gangsta rap album:

> I'm the kind of nigger who's built to last.
> Fuck with me, I'll put my foot up your ass.

You could say this set the tone. Ironically, the persona that gangsta rappers most resemble—fluent in violence, free from guilt or pangs of conscience, able to rape and torture and murder and sleep well—is the cultural archetype that (in *Genealogy of Morals*) Nietzsche baptized as the Blond Beast.

Gangsta rap features stark explosive images of the rapper as predator, robber, rapist, murderer; guns and wounds are described in rich detail ("and then I smoked him," "and then I popped her," "I'm gonna wet'cha"—you learn exactly where and with what); the MTV clips show you both the streets and the guns, which the rappers wave with flamboyant pride. Attitude ranges from surly defiance to willed stupidity to self-mockery and gallows humor. Both the narratives and sounds of gangster rap show plenty of brains at work, but the genre calls for smart people to stupefy themselves. (This is nothing new in popular culture: think of early Marlon Brando, say, or the Rolling Stones. But they took pride in their theatricality, their ability to create *personae*: they never claimed authenticity.)

In virtually every gangsta rap, some act of explosive violence takes place. There are maybe four primal scenes:

1. Shoot-out between rival gangs, *à la West Side Story*; the fight is decided by who has the better guns; the rap features detailed description of the guns and emotional distancing from loved ones who die.

2. Shoot-out between two gangsters, same emotional complex as above; the survivor gets to tell the story.

3. Sexual encounter, which starts out with rape and gets worse: "rape," because it is a convention of the genre that this is what women want; "worse," because rape doesn't give the narrator satisfaction, so he gets more frenzied and nastier. For anybody who loves rap, brutality toward women is the most disgusting thing in it, the hardest thing to listen to without turning off. "Misogyny" is a word often used, but it doesn't convey the paradox of a man's desperate need for, and total psychological dependence on, the person who is the object of his rage.

4. Here is the Mother of all primal scenes: Cops stop the rapper on the highway. They strip-search him, beat and humiliate him *à la* Rodney King, but then somehow he gets a gun, and even as they scream for mercy he kills them all. Sometimes, while he is shooting, the narrator explains that he is doing this to avenge all black people (this theme has grown less easy as more black cops appear; they have to be shot separately). The primal road scene offers acid commentary on the American (and especially Californian) romance of mobility: These stories show how wheels

don't make you free when you're black. Some versions add a slightly different spin: No one wants to stop you because no one cares, you're on a road to nowhere when you're poor, nobody knows you when you're down and out.

The visual flamboyance of the gangsta rappers' style gave Hollywood ideas for a new visual form, the Gangsta Rap Movie. *New Jack City* was the first, in 1990; it featured Ice-T, an eminent gangsta rapper, playing the part of a nihilistic cop. These movies have created a new range of styles in youth culture, black and white. They have also created a new range of market tie-ins and have helped to unify the film, video, and music divisions of the few media conglomerates which, after a decade of frenetic mergers and acquisitions—remember, the history of rap is the history of Reaganism—now own it all.

Thanks to the market tie-ins, a few rappers have grown immensely rich while still in their early twenties, sometimes even in their teens. More striking, they have accumulated an immense *moral authority* among black youth today, which far surpasses any feelings their parents had for Stevie Wonder, Aretha Franklin, or Sly Stone, let alone for Coltrane or Monk or Bird. When gangster rappers talk to the press, they are often very grave and solemn, as if they really believe in their moral authority, even when their raps themselves suggest they believe in nothing but the will to power. Teachers and other elders are dismayed, but we shouldn't be surprised, because our kids are Americans, and Americans have always treated spectacular wealth as a source of moral authority. (And some of those great jazz musicians died without ever getting rich at all.)

This creates some strange situations. KRS-1, one of the smartest and most volatile rappers, defends gangster rap by saying, "Anything that terrifies whites, that makes them shake in their beds, is good for us." Ice Cube says "You [whites] need us [blacks] to look like rapists and murderers." Well, there is plenty of classic literature (Faulkner) and social science (John Dollard) that shows how whites can project their own unspeakable desires onto blacks, and we have all seen the lynching photos (Rodney King's is only the latest) that show how they can act when they act those desires out. But given what rappers know about white racism, isn't it crazy to actively encourage it?

Not that any of this will hurt the stars. Today rap stars live in mansions in Beverly Hills and East Hampton, consult with public relations men and semioticians on the care and feeding of their images, and—like very rich people all over America—keep up their own private security forces. But at a time when black teenagers are dying of homicide at a rate something like *nine times* higher than American youth as a whole, it shouldn't be hard to imagine how gangster rap can make it easier and sexier for fourteen-year-olds to do what "The Message" said a decade ago: "You lived too fast and died too young."

There's something to this moralism, but less than people in the media and in Congress think. Last fall the Reverend Calvin Butts, pastor of the Abyssinian Baptist Church in Harlem (Adam Clayton Powell's old church), ran over hundreds of rap tapes with a steamroller, in order, so he said, to destroy the destroyer of black youth. This was an impressive media event, as chilling as any gangster rap on MTV. (And here, too, the outcome was decided by superior hardware.) But those of us who know something about the history of culture should be skeptical of the idea that culture causes human behavior. We should think back to the *Iliad*, the *Mahabarata*, the bloody "Song of Deborah" (probably the oldest thing in the Bible), and what must be the most highly publicized and sensationalized act of violence in history, the crucifixion of Jesus. We should remember that dramatic images of violence, more horrific than anything in rap, are at the roots of our most respectable and venerable traditions; and we should lighten up.

Of course, American culture is exceptionally rich in dramatic images of violence. Since our Second Amendment, which placed guns at the very center of our political culture, images of violence have been among our prime exports to the world: our genocidal Indian warfare, our Indian fighters as murderous as any brave, Daniel Boone, Davy Crockett (first democratic politician to hire a publicist), the Alamo, Kit Carson, Custerism and its vocabulary of "extermination to the last man," gunfights in the streets, the O.K. Corral, Billy the Kid, Jesse James and Buffalo Bill, Teddy Roosevelt's Rough Riders, the Klan, *Birth of a Nation*, lynch mobs—praised by Georges Sorel as the archetype of revolutionary justice—and, in the twentieth century, our Depression bank robbers and murderers, John Dillinger and Bonnie and Clyde, plus our mobs of urban immigrant urban gangs and gangsters, Public Enemy (since we're talking about rap), Scar Face Al Capone (another rap hero), Meyer Lansky and Murder Inc., *Superfly* and *Miami Vice*. Western and gangster movies and TV police shows have not only flooded the world with these images, but consciously equated them with "America," with myths about our national character, long before rap came along. Even people around the world who denounce America for its politics love us for our violent images: large crowds of leftists in Paris or Sao Paulo or Canberra get drenched in the rain for a chance to see *Gun Crazy* or *The Wild Bunch*. And even our respectably academic field of American Studies features books with titles like *Gunfighter Nation* and *Regeneration Through Violence* (both by Richard Slotkin, both fine books). So the point to make about gangster rap is not how deviant it is, but how typically American; in Rap Brown's phrase, as American as apple pie.

Gangster rap carries on the great American tradition of the gangster film. The best thing ever written about this genre is Robert Warshow's 1948 essay, "The Gangster as Tragic Hero." As against the "official optimism" of American culture, gangster films are part of "a current of opposition, seeking to express by whatever means are available to it that sense of desperation and inevitable failure which optimism itself helps to create." The gangster lives on a plane where "the quality of irrational brutality and the quality of rational enterprise become one."

> The whole meaning of the gangster's career is a drive for success: a steady upward progress, followed by a very precipitate fall. Thus brutality itself becomes at once the means to success and the content of success—a success that is defined in its most general

terms, not as accomplishment or specific gain, but simply as the unlimited possibility of aggression.

The gangster's world is structurally opposed to the world of "civil society," a sphere where people recognize each other's rights and settle conflict peacefully. But one of the subtexts of gangster film is always how much the cops are like the robbers, how thin the line is, how tenuous the claim of civil society to embody real human progress. Thus, in *New Jack City*, the first Gangster Rap film, Ice-T won fame and fortune playing a nihilistic cop who brings down a drug lord who is portrayed as *son semblable, son frère*.

The patron saint of the congresspeople who would ban rap is Plato. (Of course, Plato would ban Congress, too.) In the second book of the *Republic*, he argues that people commit crimes (incest and murder are the ones that most worry him) because they get criminal desires from culture; if it were possible to wipe out not only dramatic poetry but the whole body of Greek mythology, then people wouldn't get any more bad desires, because they'd have no place to get them from, and then they'd be good. But Plato never finished thinking, he was always contradicting himself: In Book 9, he argued that everybody had incestuous and murderous desires, that desires like these were part of the human condition, and that we could tell that we had them by paying attention to our dreams—you can see why Freud loved to quote this. He also said that the difference between good men and bad men was that good men merely dream of what bad men actually do. This is the basis of Aristotle's idea (in *Poetics*) of *catharsis*: Tragedy should bring all our worst feelings to the surface and help us work through them.

In the 1770s, Friedrich Schiller brought out a play called *The Robbers*, which put the gangster hero permanently on the map of modern culture. Riots broke out in several towns where *The Robbers* played and even severer riots in towns where it was prohibited. When revolutionary movements erupted in Germany after 1789, many solid citizens predictably blamed the play. Kant may well have been defending it in the 1780s when he argued that if people can enjoy criminal images and visions, it will relieve them of the desire to commit criminal acts. Teachers among us can see a pattern like this in our best students (and parents can see it in our law-abiding children): For a little while they imagine themselves as marauders who terrify the world, then they re-enter real life and hit the books. Middle-aged people can discern a pattern like this in ourselves, if we can remember the Mickey Spillane books and horror comics we read in the dark, and the James Dean and Marlon Brando posters we put on our walls. The violent fantasies of gangster rap serve the same essentially conservative function that violent fantasies have always served, just as they did for Athenian citizens and for the audience at Shakespeare's Globe.

In the last few years, as some rappers have got very rich and famous, some of their audience and critics have come to feel that they've betrayed their people and become inauthentic. This is pretty silly: Rap started in the neighborhoods, but it soon became what it is, a world language, and people who love it should be glad the world has found out. It shouldn't bother us that the gangster *capos* are living in mansions. What should bother us is that they've surrounded their mansions with walls and moats of bad faith. The mystique of Afrocentrism provides good bricks for those walls. Rap in the 1990s is the most creatively impure music ever made. (And a late-twentieth-century audience, attuned to the "impure" aesthetics of collage and montage, can "get" it right away.) But many rappers, the more impure their music gets, the more right-eously they profess a cult of racial separateness and purity. The more they fast-break and slam-dunk the English language, the louder they protest they're only talking "African." The more their lives entwine with those of whites—producers, critics, managers, editors, film-makers, not to mention lovers and wives, and an audience that marketing surveys say is as much as four-fifths white—the more they insist they have no connection with whites at all, and speak to blacks alone. The better they thrive in the multinational markets that have turned their old neighborhoods into ghost towns—and the Reaganite years of rap's history are years of radical social polarization, among blacks even more than whites—the more they insist they are nothing but homeboys, identical with all those they have left behind. Even as they raise rap into a universal language, they are fighting like an undertow against themselves to turn it back into a segregated men's room. Maybe it's all just schoolyard trash-talk and we should laugh. But it feels like authenticity, one of rap's deepest sources of strength, has turned into just another set of conventions and conformities, another chic new style, another big lie.

One more dread dynamic haunts gangster rap: Guys who succeed are accused of going "soft" (a typical interviewer's first question: "people say you've gone soft"), so that they feel they have to prove they're "hard." But anything they do will be undermined by critics as a mere defensive maneuver. So no victory can ever be enough, and the stakes are always getting raised. In August 1993, the rapper Snoop Doggy Dogg, of Long Beach, California, whose album had just debuted at no. 1 on the Billboard charts, went back to his old neighborhood and killed a man. True, he was only driving the jeep in a "drive-by"; his bodyguard pulled the trigger. But his act was bloody enough to win great acclaim among young people, black and white, including many of my students, who had feared he was selling out. There seems to be nothing like homicide to keep a homeboy close to the streets. At what drive will the boys stop?

Gangster rap has provided such a "high concept" and has so successfully conquered markets—record industry people say no earlier black music has made such a "crossover" to whites—that it has often felt like a real gang, sweeping through a high school gym and blowing all its opponents away. This ambiance is satirized brilliantly in the 1992 film *CB4*, where a middle-class group of gangster rappers is terrified when real gangsters move in on them, and where a special Old Age Home for Rappers becomes the last stop for young men who are decrepit while still in their twenties.

The general American public seems unaware that there are any other forms of sensibilities in rap. But in fact there are plenty. Groups like De La Soul, M.C. Lyte, Arrested Development, P.M. Dawn, Salt-n-Pepa, Basehead, the Digable Planets, the Goats, the

Disposable Heroes of Hiphoprisy, and many more, are all smart people and sophisticated musicians. They don't need to threaten their audience or each other to get attention, and they have enlarged rap's emotional repertory to include tenderness, irony, reflectiveness about the world, and questions about the subject's own identity. Their politics are various kinds of leftism, but they have managed to imagine militancies that aren't murderous.

You might think the gangster rappers, with all their wealth and power, would be able to share space, but it seems they can't. An ominous but fascinating incident last year dramatized the volatile politics of identity that pervade contemporary rap. The rapper KRS-1, who grew up in subways and South Bronx homeless shelters, considers himself the inventor of gangster rap (he may be right) and is mad that he isn't a millionaire. He is also a self-taught and serious intellectual who describes himself as "the teacher of mankind." (This enriches his creativity but complicates his image and bars him from the "high concept" easy marketability of some of the gangsta rappers from L.A.) About a third of his "teaching" is brilliant and imaginative, a third is loopy and malevolent, and a third is utterly incomprehensible. Prince Be, the MC of P.M. Dawn, is rap's greatest ironist. He is also self-consciously effete and "soft" (market label: *psychedelic*), and he likes to laugh at machismo in rap. Late in 1991, he told an interviewer: "KRS is the teacher, but the teacher of what?" The next time Prince Be played live in New York, early in 1992, KRS and his gang assaulted him, beat him up, knocked him off the stage, and announced that he, KRS, was the boss of rap. Some accounts of the episode treated it as a streetcorner brawl that KRS had won. Prince Be was shaken up, but he has refused to act like a loser. He has kept rapping and kept laughing and trying to show how rap can be a medium where the meaning of being a man can grow.

Sometime early in the 1990s, before the gangsters had taken over the gym, but at a time when rap sales were already up in the many millions, I remember a melancholy feeling coming over me. I felt: *Rap doesn't need me anymore.* I know this was a very self-dramatizing thing to feel—what, rap should need a Jewish professor? (Of

course, Chuck D. did say, back in 1988, that he wanted rap to be a
"seminar".) It was mostly a feeling about me, how my bond with
rap had made me feel like an "organic intellectual" for a while,
and how I was going to have to find new ways to feel whole. But
the melancholy wasn't just about me; it was about a process that
happens again and again in the history of modern culture. Some
of our most creative cultural movements have been passionately
promoted by small groups of intellectuals, long before any of our
culture industries could see that there was something there. What
I felt is linked to something that Harold Rosenberg and Clement
Greenberg must have felt about Abstract Expressionism sometime in the 1950s, and that Charles Lamb and William Hazlitt must
have felt about Romantic poetry in the 1800s, and that Dr. Johnson
and Diderot must have felt about the novel in the 1750s: *The movement is getting over on its own.*

How do we frame this story? At the dawn of the Reagan era,
intellectuals—mostly but not wholly white—found rap in the
ruins. It was all the way out on the margins of America, and we
helped it get its green card. Now it has made its way to the center
of American life, where big stars drive big cars, flash millions of
bucks, shove the competition off the stage, and now and then kill
people. Well, didn't we want them to get as far as they could go?
So they're in the center now, while we are still looking on from the
sides. But wasn't there a moment when rap was about *justice*, and
justice meant more than "just them"? I think there really was, and
there will be again. But rappers are going to have to reinvent it
from the inside, just as Karl Marx and his friends did, just as my
generation of the New Left did for ourselves. As they figure it out,
they'll have plenty to rap about. I hope we'll still be able to hear.

Meanwhile, my melancholy feeling made me see something
about the place of cultural critics in history, about how we fit in.
We open up new neighborhoods of feeling and expression in
scary, unfamiliar parts of the modern city. We harangue and
seduce people to go, and we swear that once they get there, their
whole being will be transformed—that's the point of the song,
"Take the A Train." At last people do go, and they love it, and
things happen just as we said they would, and we feel fulfilled. But

then more people go than we intended, and stranger things happen than we imagined, and finally the whole neighborhood looks overbuilt to us, though it feels fine to the people who went there on our word. Then we know we've got to go. We can still love it, but we've got to break our organic link. Our sadness is mixed with pride, because we know we've done our work well and helped the city grow. But now it's time to listen for new shouts in the street.

This essay is adapted from a lecture given at Oxford University on March 15, 1994. It was published in Andy Merrifield and Erik Swyngedouw's edited collection, The Urbanization of Injustice, *London: Lawrence & Wishart, 1996.*

Part VII

The Romance of Public Space

Introduction

I don't know who I am
But you know life is for learning . . .
And we've got to get ourselves
Back to the garden

Joni Mitchell,
"Woodstock," 1970

Times Square was Marshall Berman's Woodstock. He wrote its history and mapped the forces of creativity and destruction that made and continue to make it in *On the Town: One Hundred Years of Spectacle in Times Square* (Random House, 2006). And in Marshall's narrative of those one hundred years, we can see the seeds of what would have been his next book, *The Romance of Public Space*.

The privatizing of what was once public and so the site of every kind of human possibility is the specter that haunts *On the Town*. The narrative begins with a postcard of an anonymous chorus girl kicking up her heels atop the Times Tower in the winter of 1904–1905, bringing into public view what was always in the shadows, inviting us to see "downtown" as a place where people can come to figure out who they are—"and you can get there on the subway." Marshall ends the book one hundred years later with an epilogue, "Reuters and Me." It is June 2004 and a security guard threatens that Marshall will be "forcibly removed" if he lingers in front of Three Times Square, taking notes for this very book. Since refusing to "move on" rather than insisting on his right to be on the public sidewalk might mean missing our son Danny's tenth birthday party, Marshall "let it be." But, he tells his readers, if they want to live the Enlightenment idea of "the right to the city," they should not move on; they—we—must not "let it be." If we do, the city will no longer be the place where anything can happen.

The yearning and search for that sort of "place for us" appeared in much of Marshall's work and was always part of his plan for what was supposed to be the "next" book. During the 1980s he called that book *Living for the City*. What might have become chapters in that book appeared as articles in *The Village Voice* and *Dissent*; some are in this volume. But even as he was writing about a particular part of that city in *On the Town*, he was thinking about the *idea* of cities, in the course he created for CCNY's Spitzer School of Architecture, "City and Self: Ancient Athens and Jerusalem, Modern Paris and New York." This would be the core of the new "next" book, which he started calling *The Romance of Public Space*. Early in 2012 he laid out his plan:

A very persistent psychological question in modern times is the question, *Who am I?* Erik Erikson, one of Freud's most creative followers, conceptualized this question as "the problem of ego-identity." He argued that everybody in the modern world finds their identity a problem in ways that are far more pressing and urgent than they used to be. In many books, Erikson examined family, age, sex, religion, class, ethnicity, nationality, and other forces around which people try to organize their feelings about who they are. A Jewish refugee from Nazism, Erikson saw modern ethnic nationalism as a vicious pseudo-solution to real psychic problems. Coming from the Third Reich into the New Deal, he imagined an America that could be a cosmic alternative, a place that could include and embrace everybody. My parents, and my family, and the Jewish workers around us in the South Bronx, all saw Roosevelt's America this way. In 1950 Erikson's masterpiece appeared, *Childhood and Society*, a hymn to that dream of America and that romance of the self.

I got to know Erikson and his work fifteen years later, during the Vietnam War, fifty years ago. By then, along with many liberal Americans, he was having his doubts. In those Cold War years, the great world powers nearly destroyed the world. Hope for a place where the self could feel at home still survived, but there were serious doubts that that place was a national state. The modern state was more dangerous than we had thought, its spiritual rewards less deep than we had hoped. Was there something else? Some other sort of place that could nourish people's sense of identity without crushing other people's identity? My idea in this book is to explore one of the most powerful ways in which this has happened through the ages. *The way is the city.* People can become themselves, can expand and enlarge themselves, through their connection with cities. They can find open and shareable forms of identity by *identifying with the city*.

What follows are two essays from that book. The first is an overview focusing on the Greek agora and city politics, first published in *Beyond Zuccotti Park: Freedom of Assembly and the Occupation of Public Space* (New Village Press, 2012). The second is the first chapter of the Old Testament section of the book which he completed in late August 2013. He was in the midst of revising that chapter on the morning he died, just a few weeks later, on September 11, 2013.

Shellie Sclan

The Romance of Public Space

This essay both explores and enacts what I want to call the romance of public space. This is one of the primary ideas of what historians came to call the Age of Revolutions, and finds its origins in ancient Greece, particularly Athens. Before I delve into that, however, I want to distinguish public space from the many large spaces in which, as long as human societies have existed, people have been assembled. In these spaces, rulers have assembled their subordinates and given them orders about how they should act. We get a glimpse of one of these assemblies in Book Two of *The Iliad*, in a passage entitled "The Great Gathering of Armies." Thersites, "a common soldier," challenges Agamemnon: "What are you panting after now?" Haven't these warlords accumulated enough treasure, bounties, and young women to bring back with them? Odysseus responds: "Who are *you* to wrangle with kings . . . You and your ranting slander—*you're* the outrage." The climax of his tirade is to "crack the scepter across his back and shoulders." Thersites "doubled over, tears streaking his face," his blood flowing. The soldiers' "morale is low, but the men laughed now, good hearty laughter breaking over Thersites's head." Other generals now speak: "Not until you . . . raze the rugged walls of Troy" will there be even the thought of going home; any soldier who repeats Thersites' complaint" will be instantly killed. The threats, violence, and the soldiers' "hearty laughter" combine to end the assembly—and to silence the Greek common people for the next five hundred years or so. But then, from the sixth century BC till the fourth, the Athenian common people gained more and more

power, established a political form they called democracy—
"power to the people"—and asserted themselves, above all in a
giant outdoor space called the *agora*. Thersites is a textbook case
of the people intended as *objects*, defined by what is done to them.
"Public space" is something else: a stage for the people as *subjects*.

The "Old Oligarch" is a pamphlet written sometime in the fifth
century BC.[1] No one knows who the author was, but he was the
first writer to describe the Athenian agora, a space completely
different from the ones in his own city. (Which city? Some say
Thebes, but we really don't know.) The Old Oligarch is fascinated by the Athenian agora's sloppiness. Here people dress down,
social distance is minimized, one cannot even tell masters from
slaves; Athens is the only city with a law forbidding masters to
beat their slaves. The Old Oligarch is amazed that any city can
hold together without a strictly visible social hierarchy. He
concludes that informally defined spaces like Athens's agora, and
peaceable practices like shopping and related cultural activities,
can make people feel comfortable with each other and nourish
peaceable bonds between them, so that everybody learns both
how to rule and how to obey. To have the ability *both to rule and to
obey*: Sophocles, Pericles, the Old Oligarch, and various orators
and philosophers, all came to see this as the formula for democratic citizenship. Athens's agora appears as an ideal place to learn
this contradictory behavior. It makes sense for us to call this
gigantic mess the world's first democratic space.

Not everybody liked it. Sophocles's tragedy *Antigone*, first put
on in 441 BC, features Creon, a politician and "man of the
moment" who transforms the agora into an anti-democratic political theatre. Sophocles sets his story in Thebes; many of its characters are descendants of Oedipus and could be said to share his
complex. One of Antigone's brothers tries to overthrow the city
government; her other brother fights him, and the twin brothers
end up killing each other. Creon saves the city, only to destroy it
inwardly. He decrees that only the "good" brother can be buried;

---

1 See D. Kagan, *Sources in Greek Democratic Thought*, New York: Free
Press, 1966.

the "bad" brother's corpse must lie outdoors, till his corpse is picked apart and eaten up by wild animals. Creon creates an agora for terror, using public space against not only a guilty man, but also his whole family. Creon's agora is one of the earliest examples of a totally political space, a stage where families are collectively punished for individuals' bad acts. He imagines political power as the capacity to define protest as treason and to publicly destroy the traitors. Before Antigone dies, she and the chorus (and the prophet Tiresias) proclaim that stage directions like Creon's are toxic to urban democracy.

One more crucial thing we need to remember about Antigone is that she is a *woman*. It was a nineteenth-century cliché that women were excluded from the agora. Any reader of Greek comedy, or of Plato, should be able to see that women were banned from many things in Greece, but never from shopping. (In the twentieth century, archeology made it clear that Athens's agora was a giant shopping mall.) Antigone stakes out a claim to it. She says, in effect, that a totalitarian agora is a travesty of public space. She gets the point of a democratic agora better than the man who has her killed. Creon's agora is not like the one in Athens, messy but overflowing. It resembles more the design created by Hippodamus of Miletus, the first known city planner. Hippodamus' model (described at length in Aristotle's *Politics*) was grid like and functionally zoned; it seems to have existed in various forms from city to city, but they all shared the presence of rigid boundaries for people in different ethnic, economic, sexual, and political groups. There was a strong (and apparently successful) attempt to put clamps on the ultra-agaric activity of hanging out. Hippodamus lived long, and shopped his model around the Greek world for years. The planner didn't say this, but anybody who (like Aristotle) saw his model in operation over the years saw the catch: It couldn't work unless democracy was overthrown and the army took total control of everyday life. The Athenians seem to have said, no thanks. For a couple of hundred years, they preferred their chaotic model to a rigidly clean one. Athenians fought a great deal with each other, but they were at home in democratic space. They didn't want to become a militarized Miletus. They preferred a mess.

One of Athens's first self-celebrations can be found in what we call "Pericles' Funeral Oration," delivered in 431 BC at the start of the long war with Sparta, and contained in Thucydides's *The Peloponnesian Wars*. This speech is, among other things, a hymn to Athens's public space. Pericles talks about the city's openness: Its lack of walls, he says, enables anybody to see and enjoy all there is, it brings in tourists who are thrilled by the city's openness, and helps attract original people who were kicked out of the cities they grew up in. People can explore and expand their identities and fulfill themselves as a whole.

The paradox of public space in Athens was that the city couldn't seem to live with the radiance that its public space generated and bestowed on mankind. The Old Oligarch, delighted with the phenomenology of democracy, can't understand why so many Athenian citizens get so mad at each other. After they killed Socrates, many Athenians and many other Greeks kept asking, how could this smart, sophisticated city—Pericles had called it "the school of Greece"—kill its most devoted citizen? Of course, Athens was used to killing its own. It killed Pericles's son and his fellow admirals, after they won a spectacular battle against Sparta but failed to destroy the navy and kill all the enemies. In the postwar decade, it would very likely have killed Euripides, along with Socrates, if the playwright hadn't got out of town fast.

Socrates refused to go, and so provoked his enemies. He warned the city *(Apology,* 39c-d) that if they killed him, they would be afflicted with a generation of critics who, unlike him, felt no love for them. If we read Plato long enough to pick up the emotional tones, we can see what he meant. In many early dialogues, we find a sensibility that is radically critical of Athens but dearly loves it. We find similar contradictions in Socrates's arguments with Thrasymachus in the *Republic*'s first two books. But as the *Republic* unfolds, it offers us a very different mix. By the middle of the book, we find the most vicious criticism ever written against public space, and we find a critical tone devoid of love:

Whenever the populace crowds together, at any public gathering . . . and sits there clamoring its approval or disapproval, both excessive, of whatever is being said or done; booing and clapping till the rocks ring, and the whole place redoubles the noise of their applause and outcries . . . In such a scene, what will become of a young man's mind? What . . . will give him the strength to hold out against the force of such a torrent, or save him from being swept downstream, until he accepts all their notions of right and wrong, does as they do, and becomes just such a man as they are?

Most of what we know about the lower-class Socrates comes from dialogues written by the upper-class Plato. We can't say for sure where one ends and the other begins. But if we focus on these two views of the agora—a place that is defined as lethal poison, and a place that Socrates refuses to leave, despite its risks—we see the difference between being at home in public space and being radically alienated from it. Fifth-century Athens is often seen as a city that defined public space as a place where people could feel (like Socrates) "at home." This is true, but if we see it in depth, we will also see a place that could kill the man who was most at home in it; a place that could force the rest of us to feel (like Plato) radically alien. Athens's creativity is ambiguous, paradoxical; it lays out vocabularies for both.

Socrates's execution seems to have put Athens on the defensive about itself. In the 390s BC, Athens passed a series of laws that recognized its capacity to create talk. From now on, the city would not kill anybody was not guilty of a violent crime; it grew willing to listen to people who talked and who made others talk. The idea of "atonement" was not a part of the Hellenic vocabulary; but some of the post-Socratic laws do sound like an attempt to atone for what Athens had done to its public space and to itself, and to give that space a new life, to nourish it again by creating the beginnings of what modern citizens and thinkers, especially in England, America, Holland, and France, would come to call a Bill of Rights.

BEYOND ATHENS

After Athens and all other Greek cities were conquered by Alexander the Great in the 330s and the 320s BC, the very idea of democratic space faded away and didn't come back into Western (or any other) culture till modern times: the eighteenth century, the Enlightenment, the Age of Revolution. Many of the thrills and human difficulties first seen in Athens's agora have reappeared in modern times; but in the more than 2,000 years in between, Western culture has gone through plenty and become a lot more. The rest of this essay will be brief, too brief to explore this complex history. But it will open up diverse possibilities.

I'm Talking about Jerusalem

If there is one word to convey the romance of public space in both Jewish and Christian culture, that word is *Jerusalem*. Our earliest vision of Jerusalem as a special place comes in the first Book of Kings's narrative of the reign of King Solomon. In a dream, God asks Solomon what he wants and is impressed when he asks for "an understanding mind to govern the people" rather than for riches or revenge. God gives him "a wise and discerning mind" and a "largeness of vision." In the course of his reign, the Bible says, "Judah and Israel were as many as the sand by the sea, they ate and drank and were happy." The Book of Kings gives an endlessly detailed account of Solomon's building projects, a temple and a king's palace standing directly opposite each other. It also describes projects that are likely to seem much more important to us: a tremendous population shift, to be obtained by sending thousands of Jews to Lebanon ("Tyre") every year and filling Jerusalem with an equal numbers of Lebanese, especially people with construction skills. Solomon's many marriages, too, must have brought not only "foreign women" (the "pharaoh's daughter" may have been the biggest scandal), but also great crews of servants, tailors, craftspeople, priests, and—this may have been his central idea—non-Jews. Solomon seems to have worried about Israel's smallness and lack of resources, and aimed to strengthen it by opening up channels of cooperation with other, better-situated peoples. (Later, when God is preparing to destroy Israel for its unrighteousness, the prophet Amos convinces God to be merciful by saying, "But my Lord, Israel is so small.") Like Pericles,

Solomon grasped the strength of a mixed population, and sought to make Jerusalem as diverse and multicultural as he could. But Solomon's children and successors lacked his "largeness of mind"; Israel gradually split and then was "taken," first by Babylon. In post-Solomon incarnations it will be pulled to pieces. Later on, and stretching up to today, Jerusalem became a city specially consecrated as "redeemed"; but we can't understand the spiritual meanings of "redemption" without simultaneously grasping the meanings of "damnation." Jerusalem shows us that cities can be embodiments of both.

Talking about Jerusalem puts us on a distinctive wavelength, part of a spiritual drama: we imagine a city in radically contradictory ways, simultaneously as a sinkhole of depravity and a light unto the nations. But most of our accumulated talk about Jerusalem, from the fifth century BC till 1948, has been about a glorious city that has, for whatever reasons, been *lost*. Psalm 137, one of the first documents of *exile*, proclaims the duty of thinking about the city we have lost. The vow "If I forget thee, O Jerusalem" announces one of the primary forms of urban romance: the romance of *nostalgia*. Classical Christianity gives a dramatic twist to urban self-criticism. After two thousand years of Christian culture, anybody who thinks about cities inherits the twist, whether we are Christians or not (I am not). In the Gospel of Matthew (6.1–6), just after the Sermon on the Mount, Jesus disparages people who pray "in the synagogue." Unlike Saint Paul, he does not criticize them on behalf of some other public space (the early Christian church), but rather on behalf of *no* public space. He says:

> Beware of practicing your piety before men, in order to be seen by them. For then you will have no reward from your Father, who is in heaven. Thus, when you give alms, sound no trumpet before you, as the hypocrites do in the synagogues and in the streets, that they may be praised by men . . . Do not let your left hand know what your right hand is doing, so that your alms may be in secret.

What is he saying? That we should be punished for self-knowledge—for our left hand knowing what our right hand is doing—but we get spiritual credit for ignorance of ourselves?

> And when you pray . . . you must not be like the hypocrites; for they love to stand in the synagogues and in the street comers, that they may be seen by men . . . But when you pray, go into your room and shut the door, and pray to your Father who sees in secret and will reward you.

This is a remarkable passage, which has evoked little commentary. It says that any desire to be seen or praised by other men, "in the synagogue or in the streets," is poisonous; God will show respect, Jesus says, only to people who lock the door. It appears that the gesture of *locking the door* is the paradigmatic spiritual act. The desire to be with people, to be loved by them, is vicious, corrupt, inauthentic. The Jewish God required a *minyan*, a congregation of ten, to make prayer valid. This version of the Christian God demands a congregation of one, and that's all. He shrinks away from public space. He is open only to those souls who reject community with other men or women.

Now, it is impossible to live this way! Saint Paul prided himself on his celibacy, but accepted the overall legitimacy of people's need for each other. But Matthew's Jesus rejects it, at least for a while. What are we supposed to make of this? Is it an early form of nihilism? I don't think many readers have ever been willing to take Jesus's implacability as a model of how to live; yet, the idea that only aloneness is authentic has carried a long shadow even in the hearts of people who believe it's absurd. When we are in public space today, even in the sun, we are still partly in that shadow; the cloud rarely leaves us.[2]

---

2 Ironically, though, this cloud has been incorporated into secular, middle-class culture. Dr. Benjamin Spock, writing after World War Two, may have been the first child-care expert to say that all children deserved "rooms of their own" where they could elaborate their own fantasy lives, create their own worlds. Spock, a founder of peace and anti-nuclear movements, and an official criminal in the Vietnam War years, always argued that people who grew up with more private space as children would become better citizens as adults.

The Enlightenment and Modernity

If the Platonic and Christian utopias of radical alienation gave us a twist, a great deal of modern thought and culture, starting with the Enlightenment, has been a project to untwist us. Modern Romantic poets on the street like Walt Whitman, and fighters for civil rights who sat down in the midst of traffic like Martin Luther King Jr., believed it was urgent to love, to overcome, and to do it together, openly, in public, and they believed that it could help us lift our own inner shadows.

A little while ago I talked about how Athens experienced its killing of Socrates as a trauma and passed a series of laws to ensure that nobody else would get killed for talking. This was a great expansion of public space, in the city that already had the most developed public space in the world, and it was an important moment in the history of human rights. But in its earliest incarnation, its scope was limited. For the most part, Athenians didn't see these as rights for all human beings, but only for Athenians. They didn't oppose them for other cities, they just couldn't imagine that other cities would care about them.

The concept of universal human rights couldn't emerge until centuries of Stoicism and Christianity had passed, and until the beginnings of modern science. The great leap forward that we call the Enlightenment featured the idea of a world public, and a demand for human rights for everybody everywhere. This is not to say that this idea has been fulfilled anywhere. But today, in the twenty-first century, we may have reached the point where it is *imagined* everywhere.

Montesquieu's novel *The Persian Letters* (1721), maybe the first great book of the Enlightenment, shows the connection between the idea of human rights and the forms of public space that have emerged in the modern city.[3] Montesquieu sees immigration as a central feature of Paris, which thanks to immigrant diversity becomes a microcosm of the whole world. A world city takes some getting used to. Compared with the spaces the Persians have grown up in, it is a grotesque mess. But they

---

3   C. L. Montesquieu, *The Persian Letters*, Cologne: Pierre Marteau, 1721.

come to feel the immense human vitality that is overflowing and creating this mess. They walk and talk through the streets, amazed at the variety of *the crowd*; after a while they see that they themselves are part of the crowd, and they are glad. Women come over to talk to them. At first they think these women must be whores selling themselves, but the women tell them they just want to talk, and there is this new thing, invented by women but bringing both sexes together, called *conversation*.[4] Later on they learn about salons and have some terrific conversations there. By and by they are received at Versailles, and they discover that not everybody loves Paris. They learn that the French monarchy, since Louis XIV, has felt degraded and threatened by this city that is so enchanting to them. The kings are happier in their royal theme park, Versailles, and at home in their gardens full of statues, rather than in a city full of live people. Political conflict in France, both before and after the Revolution, was often imagined as "Paris versus Versailles." One of the distinctive ironies of modern times in France is that so many grand buildings and outdoor spaces, especially in Paris, were built by the monarchy to sanctify the grandeur of the state. But the monarchy was terrified by its own creations, and ordinary people found ways to make themselves more at home in those grand spaces than their kings had ever been. In what turned out to be the French Revolution, the image of the people taking over the Bastille Prison established itself immediately as a canonical vision.

The Enlightenment, however, thought big: It wasn't only about France, or about any particular place, but about the whole world. It showed a world public and a dream of world citizenship coming into being. In the years between the early Enlightenment and now, it has become clear that Paris is winning. (This is why, even if we have never been to Paris—as I had never been at age fourteen,

---

4   This is a central theme in my first book, *The Politics of Authenticity*, New York: Atheneum, 1970, also elaborated by Dena Goodman in *The Republic of Letters: A Cultural History of the French Enlightenment*, New York: Cornell University Press, 1994.

when I saw the movie *Casablanca*—we know instinctively what Humphrey Bogart means when he tells Ingrid Bergman, "We'll always have Paris.") But it will always be a struggle, even in Paris—maybe especially in Paris. Modern city life has rarely been serene. Indeed, since the middle of the eighteenth century, modern cities have been explosive and revolutionary. But the people who meet on modern streets, or who just look at each other on the streets and in the parks and on the metro, and feel they recognize total strangers, are increasingly citizens of the world, with the capacity to imagine the world, to wear blue, and to imagine themselves with an identity as big as the sky.

A century of electronic mass media has expanded and deepened this world identity. When I was a kid, there was a vast literature explaining why electronics had killed people's desire to travel. I thought, it sure hasn't killed my desire, and it's easy to see now how silly this was. Electronics hasn't killed anybody's desire to move. Tourism is the world's greatest industry, its bottom lines eclipsing even armaments. Photographs, movies, televisions, computers, and Skype give people at least a chance to see what other people's public spaces look like, and it makes them want to go. Even if we can't go, we can read and see and feel in some crucial way these distant cities as ours.

Here, then, is the romance of public space. Pericles, in ancient Athens, argued that Athens had got there first. Most of the world can imagine it now—if only we can survive to enact it! But we have moved beyond Athens in crucial ways. We have an idea of universal humanity; we can see now that the desire to live in public space is a central part of being human. We can also thank the Enlightenment for helping us imagine we can organize to make the sun rise. When we read about and see pictures of the women of Cairo, fighting to be and to stay in the streets, and shouting, "I exist! We exist!" we know they are talking to us, as well as to the priests and police holding them back and trying to push them back into their houses. We know their need: to have a place in the street, to be recognized as the people they are. We share a conversation, struggling for a public space we all can inhabit.

This chapter was first published in Beyond Zuccotti Park: Freedom of Assembly and the Occupation of Public Space, *edited by Ron Shiffman, Rick Bell, Lance Jay Brown, and Lynne Elizabeth, New York: New Village Press, 2012.*

The Bible and Public Space

This chapter is a reading of the Bible that focuses on stories that dramatize the display of public space. There is no biblical passage that conceptualizes "public space" as precisely as various Greek writings do; there is nothing as distinctively marked as the Greek agora. Nevertheless, as I unfold a series of narratives, written hundreds of years apart, it will be clear that the Bible presents a very wide range of feelings about public space, and attitudes toward it—romance, nostalgia, yearning, loathing, classic ambivalence. These contradictory feelings and attitudes within the Bible play a leading role in making Western culture what it is.

I have been a scholar for most of my life, using my own and other people's research in sometimes surprising ways, giving reasons for what I think, trying to make ideas make sense. I'm too old to stop now. But I am also a Jew, grown up with the feeling that the Bible was "my" book, that it was my job to wrestle with it, and this wrestling would be my way to be part of Israel. This chapter has more of an aura of wrestling than my writing usually does. It will feature outbursts of feeling, but I will fight to control my feelings, fight not to flood out the feelings that animate the book itself. A great vocabulary of intense feelings is central to the life of the Bible. Trying to leave them out makes it less of a book than it is, and less of a treasury of forms of public space.

The Garden of Eden is one of the oldest images in the Bible. It's at the start, though not the very start. It does not occur in Genesis's first creation story. This is a seven-day narrative that dramatizes the development of life. It features God's tremendous achievement:

creating light and darkness, earth and the heavens, day and night, plants and seas, birds, beasts and cattle. After all this, God creates human beings "in our image, after our likeness"; "male and female he created them"; he urges them to "be fruitful and multiply," to have a sexual and a family life; he gives them the right, but also the duty, to take care of the rest of the world he has made (1.26–28). This is a story of *evolution*, with human beings at the climax. God has total confidence in what he is doing. He "gives" human beings "dominion" over all the other creatures; but there is no hierarchy between people themselves. Everybody has a place in this world system. People's place is a balance of power and responsibility. The universe is "theirs," but they can't do anything they want with it. Some idea of ethics and ethical life derive from their position: They have a high place, but they have to take care of the system and all its members. Genesis 1 is a lyrical image of total harmony and an idea of a *cosmic balance*. (This idea still animates all environmental movements, even secular ones.) It enables God the creator to say his cosmic work "is good" and to feel he has earned a rest (1.31–2.3).

The Garden of Eden actually emerges in the Bible's second version of the creation story. I have a feeling that the immense sentimentality that has developed around the primal creation story mixes up a vision of the Garden with the Genesis 1 romance of cosmic balance. But if we read the actual text of the Eden story, Genesis 2.8–3.24, we will find a God who exudes anything but a sense of inner balance. This second creation story is more dramatic and compelling than the first. But it is strangely divided—perhaps chopped up—much more clotted and inwardly troubled, and it reads as if it were repeatedly rewritten. I think it is meaningful to say Genesis 2 offers a coherent vision of "public space." But the vision is embedded in a world that is full of existential difficulties.

The story starts with a cast of one. God "formed man from the dust of the earth" and "blew life into his nostrils." This first man, Adam, is created alone— different from the "male and female" in Genesis 1. He is placed in the garden of Eden, suffused by gorgeous radiance, an enormous abundance of plants, birds and beasts, "every tree that was pleasing to the sight, and good for food"

(2.9). God gives Adam the task of giving names to everything. Adam does it splendidly, in a way that suggests he grasps the whole universe. But his brilliant performance reveals the gulf between other species and himself: They are in groups; he is alone (2.19–20). We have to ask ourselves a question very different from anything in the previous story: What is God up to? What is he doing here? We can see the problem in the very syntax of the writing. In the "naming" sentence, we see "but for man no living helper was found." Do the authors want us to think that *but*, Adam's aloneness, is an accident? God's work with people has not begun well. He will have to learn to be sensitive to human needs. The God of Genesis 2 needs to read Genesis 1, "male and female he created them", sexual reproduction, need for partners. He has to get to know the people he has made, and be prepared to make big changes, if life is going to generate more books.

The Genesis story is stuck unless God rewrites his script. It does move because *he gets it*. His big mistake was making man incomplete. His big success will be to create someone with whom he will feel and will be complete. God creates woman: a new cast! He still works in strange ways. He garbles the biological sequence humans know so well, and takes *her* out of *him*: Eve is the punch line of centuries of jokes about "Adam's rib." Many readers are perplexed by this portrait of a God whose creation of the universe is confident and majestic, but who, when he is dealing with people, doesn't seem to know how to act. The process that brings Eve onstage is ridiculous. Yet once she is there, there are great new dramatic possibilities.

Now Adam has a co-star, a partner for whom he feels something like what we today call love. His hymn to intimacy, "This at last is bone of my bone, and flesh of my flesh," could be the world's first love song. The prospect of two sexes, intimate with each other, "naked and not ashamed" (2.23–25), using the powerful minds God gave them, is a great leap forward. It gives the idea of human life a surge and flow of energy. Adam and Eve are the first *primal human couple*. Aware that they are like each other and like no one else, they are also *the first public*. We don't yet know if their life together will be a vision of human happiness, or a *telenovela* of trouble, or a mix of both. Despite its dubious premises, the new script sounds dynamic and produceable.

The garden has been endlessly represented, and pictures of Eden have always highlighted its supposed *openness*. We could call Eden the Bible's first "public space"—or at least, the first suggestion or intimation of a public space. But there are at least shadows of problems. Is God, who has imagined the garden, constructed it, and pronounced it good, part of the public with them? Or does he see himself as the public, them as his temporary private guests?

God speaks to Adam before Eve exists, and places a special emphasis on "the tree of knowledge of good and evil." It sounds alluring, yet simultaneously it opens up a whole new language of threat and danger: If they eat from it, he will kill them. The sun has hardly come up, yet he seems to be looking for a fight. Will he really kill them over this? Unlike the God of Genesis 1, he seems to be saying there is a catch: Life depends on obedience to *him*. Their creator can be their destroyer. The writers of the Bible knew as well as any Greek philosopher that "All men are mortal." But death in Genesis 2 is not, as it was for Greek philosophers, or for the author of Genesis 1, part of a larger system of nature; it is a personally aggressive, hostile act. Is God expressing his rage at his primal couple, his will to knock them out?

So early in their life together, they are faced with dangerous messages they must learn to read fast. This God is not their friend; his beautiful open space is full of traps. They have to sort these ambiguous messages out; mistakes could wipe them out. The lovely garden of Eden, like Western culture's other Edenic public space, the Athenian agora, turns out to be a minefield.

Enter the snake, another of God's solitaries. (Did God not notice that "1" is a dark number? Or is he using the darkness?) He introduces a new concept, *the lie*, at once enlarging the world of interpretation and opening up a new world of uncertainty, ambiguity and anxiety. The snake tells Eve (3.4–5) that God has lied to her:

> You will not die. For God knows that when
> you eat of it your eyes will be opened, and
> you will be like God, knowing good and evil.

Is the snake himself lying (as religions have usually taught), or showing his ignorance of God? He is wrong, of course: God will kill them; it's the system; everybody dies; read *Gen* 1. But he is also right: God *is* afraid of them. There is something bizarre about this. As the prophet Amos says, "Israel is so small" (7.1–6). Why should this Lord of the universe, this spectacular personage, capable of the most immense creative feats, be afraid of anything? And why of small people like them or us? (The story of Cain and Abel, coming in the next chapter, seems to be meant as a clue. But they, too, are small.) It's easier for *us*, lucky survivors in an age of genocide and nuclear war, to see it: *We're dangerous because we're smart.* Who is it that waves the danger sign? The first smart person, and the first dangerous person, in history. (In his Flood story, *Gen* 6–7, he nearly destroys the world.) One of his great creative acts has been to "make [us] in God's image." But God knows that being "made in God's image" is an ambiguous gift. By now, so much later, we should know both this God and ourselves.

The couple's survival seems to depend on knowledge. But what are they supposed to know? What are they *not* supposed to know? "Good and evil"? But isn't God also saying that their knowledge itself is evil? How can they know what they shouldn't know if they don't already know it? Adam and Eve have a lot to work out. Can anybody help them? Probably not in any Jewish, Christian, or Islamic establishment.

There are many medieval representations of Eve. Some have the aura of evidence obtained by the prosecution, proving "she did it." In others, like the glorious Romanesque statue of Eve built for the cathedral in Autun, France (but now in a museum across the street), where Eve seems to be caressing the fruit, the feeling is more complex and ambiguous. Does she know? We'll never know.[1] People often love Eden for their idea of its openness; but if we try

---

1   The great art historian Meyer Schapiro directed our attention to this Eve, one of the most striking and beautiful works of medieval art. See his *Romanesque Art*, New York: George Braziller, 1977; also *Romanesque Sculptures, the Charles Eliot Norton Lectures*, Chicago: University of Chicago Press, 2006.

to read the story, we are more apt to be tripped by wheels within wheels and by a mix of truth and lies, unconsciousness and self–deception, as impenetrable as any Freudian dream.

Eve loves the way the fruit looks, thinks it will taste good, imagines it as a source of wisdom. She tastes it, offers it to Adam, they share. "Then," the Bible says, "the eyes of them both were opened." Opened to what? They "perceived they were naked," this was a source of embarrassment, they wanted to hide, they worked together to make each other fig–leaf "aprons" to cover their genitals (3.7–11). Here is another of those quick changes that mark Genesis 2. It was just a little while ago that they were, and saw each other, as "naked and unashamed" (2.25), and that human sexuality, the magic of our bodies together, was a source of cosmic delight. How did sex become embarrassing? This is one of those great Genesis 2 ambiguities. For various rabbis and Christian theologians through the ages, the answer was obvious: The body is inherently sinful and polluted. Still, Adam and Eve don't do anything with their bodies except make love with each other. What's the problem here? I can think of two things. One is the tremendous thrill of sexual pleasure that people can feel with each other, especially when they are with people who feel like "bone of my bone, and flesh of my flesh," what we call love. It is obvious to us, children of parents, members of a modern society, that sexual love creates an intense bond between people. But imagine a world where human relationships are just being invented. Why on earth should God have found their love a threat, and killed them? They may not understand it, but they will imagine it as something dreadful inflicted on their bodies, something for their bodies to fear. And their bodies are a force that draws them together; when they work to create the loincloths ("aprons" in some translations) that cover their genitals, they are also discovering each other's genitals, which will bind them to each other at least as intensely as they are bound to God.

Soon God appears, knowing perfectly well what has happened; their fig leaves and their embarrassment give them away. He plays with them like a policeman in a gangster film, getting them to implicate each other (and implicate the snake). Then he crushes

them with a flamboyant display of his raw power, throwing them
together into a life whose misery he decrees. We can call God's
tirade to the primal couple his "expulsion speech." You're going
to die; that's item one. Item two: no more abundance in what's left
of your life. "Cursed is the ground because of you": The land
Adam tills will be bleak, and will yield mainly "thistles and
thorns"; he will have to work "in toil" and "in the sweat of your
brow" for little food—and all the pain I'm inflicting on you, God
says, is because "you have listened to the voice of your wife" (3.17–
18), to the woman God made out of him, to help him and be "fit
for him." Eve's sexuality now becomes God's special target: Sex
will make her suffer, pregnancy will be painful and dangerous, her
desire for love will imperil her: "Your desire shall be for your
husband, and he shall rule over you" (3.16).

God seems to think that, because people now know good and
evil and have "become like us," it is a good thing for him to make
them suffer. (Is that because they have made him suffer?) Also,
he says, if they had "eaten of the tree of life, they would live
forever" (3.22); this seems to make it right for him to inflict extra
pain on them now. It is hard to unravel God's logic here. But his
emotional pathway, his primal cruelty to the last species he has
made, is clear. God's first "expulsion speech" creates a primal
form of rage and abuse that he will inflict on people again and
again. In Genesis 6 and 7, he nearly destroys the world. He stops
in time, but the communication pattern of that speech persists
throughout the Bible and threatens to destroy a very wide range
of spaces.

I can't imagine how anyone who has grown up with reverence
for God can read this without distress. I can remember when I
read it in Hebrew school, and our teacher said Yes, they diso-
beyed, so people were punished, and they are still being punished,
and they should be punished more: Man deserves to starve, woman
to scream and die. Yes. (He didn't dare to justify the Holocaust,
from which some of the children in the class and their parents
were survivors.) I asked my parents how God could create a
marvelous universe, and then act like a gangster. My father said

the only way we can read this bloody writing and feel bound to this God was for us to believe that "God learned."

I was too young, then, to think about something that feels to me now like an obvious source of God's anger—admittedly, a probably unconscious source (I've found no textual evidence that he notices this). They are *a couple*—and the Bible goes out of its way to emphasize how important being a couple is, how strong a source of mutual life. Their bodies are one of the forces that create their identity, and their dignity, as a couple. But once God kicks them out, he removes the only creatures whose minds are in his own image. Now he is as *alone* as Adam was before Eve. Only yesterday he lived among creatures whose minds he said were on his own level; today he has no neighbors because he has slammed the door. In empty Eden's lush, abundant open spaces, who will he talk to now? Who will take care of all his creatures? Eden is a space made for people, after people disappear. If Adam and Eve are losers, then at the end of *Gen* 3 God looks like an even bigger loser. The ending he gives this story gives him a place as one of the loneliest gods in theological history.

God turns vicious toward the people he made. But Eve was right (3.6): The fruit really *did* bring them wisdom. God can hurt them, starve them, even kill them, but, just as he said (3.22), they have come to know good and evil. This really has changed the ballgame. They have learned the evil of great powers, starting with God. Another thing they learned, as he hurt them and they worked to protect themselves, is how much they have in common, and how good it is to trust each other. They have gone beyond God, who trusts nobody. He hurts them, they cry out in pain (Massacio, the Renaissance painter, portrays this memorably), but *they know too much* to give him the submission he seems to want.

As Adam and Eve survive divine malice, they find themselves enlarged. There is a lot more there now than there was just a little while ago. It took centuries before people could see this inner change, this *human expansion*. It is at the heart of *Romeo and Juliet*. John Donne, too, in Shakespeare's time, wrote about the sense of discovery, the discovered glory of being *a couple*: "O my America!

My new-found-land," he said; love "makes each little room an every where."[2] John Milton created a world theology around this romance. At the end of his epic poem *Paradise Lost,* the joy of being in a human couple is worth the loss of Eden:

> . . . then wilt thou not be loath
> To leave this Paradise, but shalt possess
> A paradise within thee, happier far . . .
>
> The world was all before them . . .
> They hand and hand, with wand'ring steps and slow
> Through Eden took their solitary way.
> (XII, 585–87, 646–49)

It took till modern times to see how far we had evolved, yet the story was there all along. Adam and Eve were expelled from Eden for trying to place themselves on the level of its public authority. They were displaced from their first public space—a place whose look of openness was a lie, a cosmic and metaphysical lie. If we try to imagine the garden after the story's ending, it is hard not to pity God. Even as Adam and Eve have learned to use the minds he gave them, it seems he himself has lost touch with his own. He has left himself in a lonely place, emptied and hollowed out. But the couple not only "became like him" in their sensitivity to good and evil; they used their sensitivity to see that being together was good. Now they are victims of God, but victims together, nourished by each other, bound by love. Kicked out of Eden's phony open space, "the world was all before them"; they were forced but also enabled, "hand in hand," to create a new world that might become a real public space. The primal couple are the world's first *refugees*, but also the first bond of *solidarity*. Their *Bildungsroman*, the story of their evolution and growth, can also be read as a preface to modernity. Expulsion,

---

2   See "To His Mistris Going To Bed," "The Good-Morrow," and many other of Donne's love poems, which focus on the special human experience of being part of a couple.

God's last gift, inspires them with the desire to create a garden of their own.

The saddest part of this story is God's disability. He begins by making a magnificent universe, but his "expulsion speech" shows he can't identify with his last great work, can't embrace the people he made whose minds matched his own. This is the biggest break in the story: They grow, but he can't. They go forth together, he slams the door. Without them, Eden will be lonely. But when my father said *God learned,* he believed God, too, had a history, just as we did; that Eden marks not only our beginnings, but God's as well; that God could learn from suffering and could grow.

The amazing new thing here is the idea of a God who not only works on the world, but *works on himself.* Søren Kierkegaard, the Danish existentialist philosopher of Marx's generation, used the idea of a *"leap of faith"* to describe the process of becoming a Christian. This grand metaphor has a larger expanse than Kierkegaard realized. We can see it happening among Jews in the biblical times, among the prophets in the prophetic age. If God can transform himself, can make an imaginative leap and, without rejecting himself, can also become his hated "other," then maybe we can imagine a renewed garden of Eden that will be open, and shared, and that will really be a public work.

Marshall Berman was in the midst of revising this chapter on the morning he died, September 11, 2013. It was intended as a chapter in The Romance of Public Space, *planned as his next book.*

Part VIII

From the Ruins

Emerging from the Ruins

Spirit is a power only by looking the negative in the face and living with it. Living with it is the magic power that converts the negative into being.

Hegel, *The Phenomenology of Spirit*, 1807

My city of ruins / My city of ruins
Come on rise up! / Come on rise up!
Bruce Springsteen, "My City of Ruins" from *The Rising*, 2002

I would like to begin with a little time travel: first, back to the 1950s, '60s, and '70s—and particularly the South Bronx of the 1970s; then, back to the Bible, back to the sixth century BCE, back to the first destruction of Jerusalem, and the start of its renewal; then a final leap into a twenty-first-century Manhattan that is full of echoes of both. I'm not going to talk now about the horrors of 9/11, or of Boston, or about the vulnerability of New York Harbor. I pay homage to the people of those places. But I'm going to focus on a distinctive landscape of ruins, an amazing, dreadful landscape that came to define the South Bronx, and for many people to define New York, for the last decades of the twentieth century. Those ruins were one of New York's great negatives. I want to try to do what Hegel says: Look the negative in the face.

The ruin was a process. It began in the late 1950s and 1960s, when the center of the Bronx was blasted and bulldozed to build the Cross Bronx Expressway. But the ruin grew far beyond anything anyone could imagine. In the 1970s there were waves of fire; in a decade the Bronx lost more than 300,000 people. Life stabilized only at the century's end. The Bronx is still New York's poorest borough, but its vast empty spaces are full of people again. Its population has risen, close to its 1950 peak. We will focus on the years when it was down. I invented a word for this process: URBICIDE, the murder of a city. Did I really invent it? Once you said it, it seemed obvious enough. But how do people in a murdered city live?

In the early 1950s, we read that our neighborhood, and many other working-class immigrant neighborhoods very like it, had been chosen for destruction. People more than a few years younger than me can't imagine a world without highways; clover-leaves are built-in, as much as anything green or glass or neon. They don't know how many of the world's grandest highways were built directly through the most densely settled and populated places. The South Bronx was one of those places. Sometime in the next few years, the papers said, hundreds of buildings were going to be torn down and thousands of people were going to be pushed out, to build a new highway. Officials said exact locations weren't yet known. They also said we all should be grateful: We were being told early so we would have plenty of time to get out.

There was a big protest meeting at Taft High School, and my father took me. I said I couldn't believe "our government" would do this. My father said governments had all sorts of people inside them. The one to watch out for was Robert Moses. Moses was in charge of many city and state agencies, and he knew how to manipulate federal money. He had a great radio voice (remember, these were "radio days"), and he would routinely say things like, "You don't like it? It's a big country. Go to the Rockies! Your friends don't like it? Take them along." Many accounts of the wreck of the Bronx may have placed too much stress on Moses because he was so flamboyantly vicious. But his projects got built because they expressed a total elite consensus, both on what to build and on how. The way to build was this: draw lines from point A to point B, obliterate everything in between. Moses knew how to do that.

The man leading the fight against the highway had a name with a magic all its own: ROOSEVELT. He was F.D. Roosevelt, Jr., a congressman from the Upper East Side. I was thrilled by the name. My father took me to the big meeting at Taft. But the hero didn't show up. He was supposed to speak at 7 p.m. Then they said his car was stuck downtown, but don't worry, he'll get in a cab. Other people came on, two guys played harmonicas. Then it was eight. My father said, "We're going home. Roosevelt's dead, we're gonna have to move."

Thousands of people were forced to move. Thousands more, like us, felt they had to. In the spring of 1955 we moved to West 237th Street, still in the Bronx, but on the 1 train. It was very green; there were the remains of forests. My sister and I missed the old neighborhood, but our parents were happy in the new one. They had a room of their own—we'd all slept in one bedroom before—and they would walk in the woods hand in hand. The whole episode would have been a perfectly ordinary "move to the suburbs," at a time when millions of people were making that move—except that, six months later, my father died of a heart attack. Our family crashed and plummeted. Our life was shattered, in a place where we hardly had a life. People even had a hard time getting to our new house, to mourn with us; mostly they didn't come. I became obsessed forever with the destruction of cities.

In our old nabe, the expressway project got underway. Eventually my life also got underway. We had moved; I was going to Bronx Science, then to Columbia. But I kept going back. One big assembly point for construction was an overpass at the Grand Concourse and 174th Street. There was what was once a vest-pocket park, now a storage dump, that offered a spectacular view. It attracted many of Robert Moses's victims. They were older than me, often involuntarily retired; their homes and jobs no longer existed. "That bastard," they said, "we'll get him some-day." Over the years, more and more road was blasted out, with tremendous craters; for the first time, in this very dense city—the South Bronx was the city at its densest—you could see for miles and miles, both east and west. Enormous equipment, steam

shovels and bulldozers, huge trucks and rock-drills and pipes—
stuff we're used to today, but seemed from another planet then—
were spread out where streets used to be. The view evoked the
dazzling perspectives of Piranesi, which I was just learning to see
in my fine arts course. One of the project's ironies: It brought a
new but real beauty into the Bronx even as it tore the Bronx apart.
But this, of course, was only the first stage in the Bronx's ruin. It
left thousands of people feeling like victims, sometimes depressed,
sometimes enraged, but always more helpless than they had
thought they were. There would be more people like them down
the road.

A decade later, movements arose against Moses, especially
against his highways, and I played a small part in them. Jane
Jacobs was the star; she generated forms of community protest
that were central to the time we call "the sixties." But Moses
had decades to build on an unprecedented scale. He could access
immense amounts of federal money, move millions of bucks
from project to project and department to department, without
explaining himself or showing anybody "the books." In his
drive for total control—highways, bridges and tunnels, recreation, housing, not just the building but the planning—the question of what we needed, and when and where, was ignored.
These activities were *his*, he had to create the whole package, he
didn't want to share. He oozed contempt for people who were
"small," who only thought of themselves and their lives.
"Boardwalk businessmen and gossiping housewives" was one
of his tags. Ironically, he led people to identify with those
housewives and boardwalk businessmen. The 1960s halo around
words like "community activism," which finally stopped his
megalomaniac planning, was a *romance of the small*. It helped
many neighborhoods stay alive, but it came too late for the
South Bronx.

After college I got a fellowship for two years in Oxford. In Europe,
I continued to follow my obsession with city destruction. I got to
know people who took me through neighborhoods in London
that had been bombed by the Nazis; they talked about how people

Marshall Berman with sculpture by John Ahearn and Rizoberto Torres, City College of New York Cafeteria, 1985.

had—or hadn't—recovered. I met some of the creators of the British Labour government's welfare state and the first-ever National Health Service. I felt sick of America, but they were so passionate about how America, Roosevelt, the New Deal, the skyscrapers of New York, had inspired them. This made me think something that I can see, after a career as a teacher, is hard for a twenty-year-old to think: I thought, "My God, my parents were right." I saw where I wanted to go. I wanted to keep studying for a while, but then I wanted a job in the public sector in New York. I loved the city; I wanted to grow old here, to teach kids from neighborhoods, to bring up my own kids here. But also I wanted to work for the public and work to give people an education that was *their right*. I was lucky: Forty-six years ago I got a job here, at the City College of New York, and I haven't let go.

I knew New York and all American cities were going to need help. Since the New Deal, Democrats have worked to give cities federal money while Republicans have worked to undermine them. In the late 1960s, the beat got more brutal. By Nixon's formula, if cities were losing population—and, in the age of highways and suburbia, most of them were—they would lose money for police, fire, hospitals, mass transit, schools. The idea was to impoverish cities, while enriching the suburbs around them. This would nourish political extremes and polarize the country. I loved the late 1960s, but life got weird. Our supposedly conservative president was cultivating and proclaiming nihilism. As Patrick Buchanan, then a Nixon White House aide, put it: "If we tear the country in half, we can pick up the bigger half."

The Bronx in this period came to embody the smaller half. It *plummeted*. Here's an example: violence. Life in the 1960s, and more or less continuously till the 1990s, grew more and more violent. New York now has about 500 homicides a year, more or less the amount it had in 1930, when the police began keeping track; but in the years around 1990, it had over *2,000*. The Bronx was hit hardest. In about five years, it became the poorest borough, the most violent, the most doped up, the most afflicted with arson, the most homeless, the most undernourished, the most widely infected with a great range of diseases. Financially, by the 1970s, it was "redlined": On their maps, banks drew red lines around the areas they wouldn't lend to, so landlords could not get loans to renovate their buildings. The South Bronx was on the wrong side of the line.

In the early 1970s, arson became a spectacular growth industry. Buildings throughout the borough were burned intentionally in an effort to recoup much of their lost value. In 1976 Roger Starr, city housing commissioner, later *New York Times* urban affairs editor, proposed a plan he called "Planned Shrinkage." The city, he said, is divided into neighborhoods that were "productive" and others that were "unproductive," a drag on the tax base. We have to eliminate the unproductive. This meant to "stop the Puerto Ricans and rural blacks from living in the city." If we turn off water, electricity, sanitation, and stop making repairs when systems break, we can drive the unproductive out. In the past, the urban system took "the peasant . . . and [turned him] into an industrial worker." But now "there are no industrial jobs," and it is our task to "keep [this man] a peasant." We must "reverse the role of the city" as a world-historical force.

That year New York was pressed close to bankruptcy. Congress passed a bill to give the city a loan that would keep it solvent. President Gerald Ford, Nixon's successor, eventually signed the bill. But first he said he was going to veto it; it didn't matter to him what happened to New York, and he believed New York's fate meant nothing to "the people of America." The *Daily News*, a paper that had always supported Ford's party, dramatized the moment in one of the great headlines in the history of mass media: "FORD TO CITY: DROP DEAD."

Around this time, something happened to me that had great impact on my life as a man and a teacher: I started reading the Bible again. I've never believed in any god. But I came to believe that if I was going to grow up, I had to find ways to connect the parts of my life: myself as an adult, with education and a PhD, with myself as a child, in a now-nonexistent part of the Bronx. The stories that haunted me then and that still haunt me are about cities. Biblical cities—Jerusalem, of course, but also the pagan cities that surround it, Tyre, Babylon, Damascus—are seen as always vulnerable, their existence tenuous. They can be great, but are not solid. They are always potential ruins. Those destroyed cities seem to have looked a lot like the 1970s South Bronx.

Here is the Book of Lamentations, from Jeremiah's time, the late fifth century BCE, soon after the destruction of Jerusalem by Babylon, in 587–586 BCE:

> How lonely sits the city
>   that was full of people!
> How like a widow has she become,
>   she who was great among the nations! . . .
> She weeps bitterly in the night,
>   with tears on her cheeks;
> among all her lovers
>   she has none to comfort her . . .
> The roads to Zion mourn,

for none come to the festival;
all her gates are desolate . . .
Her foes have become the head;
   her enemies prosper . . .
All her people groan
   as they search for bread;
they trade their treasures for food
   to revive their strength . . .
"Is it nothing to you, all you who pass by?"

From ancient times to today, the experience of seeing your city in ruins is one of the dreadful primal scenes: this is urbicide.

A great source of pain is the contrast of today with yesterday. "How lonely sits the city that was full of people!" The clashes of desolation and glory that are so vivid in the Bible felt close to home. In a country with a president who said the destruction of New York meant nothing, the question "Is it nothing to you, all who pass by?" was a question in current events.

Much of my work as a writer, over the past several decades, has been about what it means to be modern. My last chapter in *All That Is Solid Melts into Air* is on the Cross Bronx Expressway. But reading the Bible, I realized there were important things that modernism often left out. When I saw the Bronx in ruins, I saw how modern life, itself full of ruins and the terror of ruins, was still biblical. I didn't think the Bible was special in offering divine solutions to human problems, but it was special in saying very clearly what the problems were. Modern rhetoric often talked as if mankind had transcended troubles that we really hadn't transcended at all, that were still there for us to face.

The early literature of urbicide is a literature of ordeal. The ancient Jews, like the Greeks, traced urbicide to their gods. But Jewish writers ask another question that is harder to find in Greek culture (Euripides's *Trojan Women* is a rare exception): Were the gods right to do such a thing? Or were they wrong? Some Jewish writers think the people are being punished; they were bad and they deserve to suffer. Others think it is an outrage, a violation of the laws of decency by "the judge of all the earth"—this is

Abraham, protesting against God's plan to destroy Sodom and Gomorrah. The prophet Amos discovers God is planning to kill all the Jews. He confronts him and says, "But Israel is so small"; he seems to make God ashamed of himself. Job protests, too, but God blows him away.

The prophets indict God but also indict the Jews, their own people. Not only do they worship pagan gods (remember that "golden idol"), they all run after money, honors, pleasure, success, and stain their hands with the people's blood. The rich lay house to house, field to field, so there is no place for the poor in what is supposed to be their own land. Meanwhile, all the poor people seem to want is to imitate the rich, to change places and enslave their enslavers. People of every rank, from high to low, oppress and ruin. They forget their covenants, not only with God, but with each other.

This is the beginning of social criticism and one of the beginnings of democratic thought. Most ancient literature on democracy comes from Athens. But the Bible is also a primary source. The prophets horrify us with visions of destroyed cities. But then they rain magical poetry down on us and make us believe we can change the world. Take a song by Second Isaiah, a song read every Yom Kippur. He is singing to people who feel imprisoned, even if they are economically doing well. He says they can do morally better: liberate the captives, open the prisons, share your clothes, feed the hungry, satisfy the desire of the afflicted. Acts of empathy will bind people together and give them the collective power to rebuild their ruins, "to raise the foundations of many generations." Till the 1970s I never noticed the urban ending of this song: "And you will be called the restorer of streets to dwell in."

Meanwhile, the demos of the Bronx was finding voices. One voice was the explosion of graffiti on our subways. I loved it! The kids who made it were thrown into a public transit system that was far more broken down than today's. They told the world, "We are not helpless; we can make this world colorful, exuberant, exciting." I was thrilled. I took my mother to the 149th Street subway stop, near where we had lived, with a good view of the trains. She was a very reserved woman, but she said, "It's a rainbow, in a place where who would expect one?"

Another voice was the musical and poetic language called rap. On the subway platform at Columbus Circle, one day in the early 1970s, I heard it for the first time. A kid of high school age, with a recorded drum track on two small speakers in the background, was shouting the story of his life. (I gave him a dollar.) The South Bronx was an early center for rap—"Old School," my older son Eli told me. I felt that seeing the burning and reading the Bible made me more receptive to it. The massive ruins, the melodic sacrifice, the no-nonsense dead seriousness of it made it real for me. More people started doing it, the background music got more melodic and was defined by what they called "samples" from earlier records. Rap developed fast. Some of its best numbers were dialogues, between the present and the past, between kids and their parents. It was exciting cultural production, coming straight out of neighborhoods that were condemned as "unproductive."

When I came to CCNY, our college had a beautiful South Campus—the old nineteenth-century convent of "Convent Avenue"—the home of "liberal arts." Where did it go? At the end of the 1970s, CCNY tore it down. But first, before the work of destruction, every Thursday, in club hours, from noon to 2 p.m., in front of our bell tower, a disc jockey would set up, scratch a million records to create a background, and there would be an open mic for people to get up and rap. Some of the rapping was male-chauvinist gross, some just silly, but some was luminous and brilliant, and it was doing just what I was trying to teach my students to do, stretching language to grasp and envelop reality. There were a few teachers who got up and rapped. I envied them; I knew I couldn't make the rhymes.

At first, the rap audience was small and local. But the sound got around. The first international hit was "The Message," by Grandmaster Flash and the Furious Five, released in the Reagan Summer of 1982.

MC Melle Mel takes us on a tour of the neighborhood: "Broken glass everywhere, people pissing in the streets like they just don't care; I can't stand the pain, can't stand the noise, got no money in my pocket so I got no choice." Myriad horrors are packed into a couple of minutes: aggressive rats, aggressive junkies, nice girls turned into addicts and whores; kids burned out before the age of ten who want to grow up to be drug dealers, who may be the only people they know who command respect; their big brothers, who grow fast from kids to unemployed to hired killers to the dead. The rapper shouts at a handsome dead boy: How could he have been so dumb? "You lived so fast and died so young." He sees the self-destructive idiocy of his homies, but also their human dignity. He asks what's wrong with them, but doesn't settle for easy answers—not even the answer that they are victims, though he makes it clear they are. Sounds of the concrete jungle erupt, sirens, everybody ordered to freeze. But even here in the Bronx, as in the Bible, surprising things can happen:

> They pushed that girl in front of the train,
> Took her to a doctor, sewed her arm on again . . .
> Stabbed that man right in his heart,
> Gave him a transplant for a brand new start.

Some people are maimed by violence, yet they get help and live. "The Message" became an instant classic, a breakthrough for the whole genre. Suddenly there were people everywhere who wanted to listen to New York's rap and create their own.

So what's the message? That social disintegration and existential desperation can be sources of life and creative energy. A generation of kids broke out of poverty and ghetto isolation and became sophisticated New Yorkers. Some of them, like some writers of the Bible, got to a place where they could imagine not only freedom for themselves, but freedom for *everybody*: for the girl pushed in front of the train, for the man stabbed through the heart. Not only had their suffering not destroyed their idealism; in some mysterious way, it had *created* idealism. They could tell the world, *we come from ruins, but we are not ruined*. Their capacity for soul-making in the midst of horror gave the city a new aura, a new tincture of bright lights. They succeeded in the task Hegel defined two hundred years ago: If we can "look the negative in the face and live with it," we can achieve a "magical power" and "convert the negative into being." They, and New York with them, in the midst of falling apart, found ways to rise. A rainbow, where who would expect one?

New York is so different today. The stream of fire has stopped. The Fire Department is still busy, but arson isn't the source of profit that it was for years. The Left had always insisted that the landlords were setting the fires, or letting their buildings burn, in exchange for insurance money. John Lindsay established the Mayor's Task Force Against Arson, which issued pamphlets about "fire accelerants," a word I'd never heard, and "the ecology of fire": an apartment is on fire; if engines come in ten minutes, the fire won't spread; if there is no help for half an hour, the whole block can go. The Left found a surprising ally: the insurance industry. At the start of the 1980s, the insurance companies said they had strong evidence of "human participation" in tenement fires, and they weren't going to pay them off anymore. Then something that looked like magic happened. Magic formula: *No Payments, No Fires.*

In the last year of payment, the Bronx lost something like 1,200 buildings; in the first year of nonpayment, it lost something like ten. It was a thrill to be able to think about fire as a human problem and to stop feeling that the Bronx was caught up in a process of cosmic disintegration.

The next big difference was the decline in violence. The explosion of violence that began in the 1960s and that went on until the 1990s was reversed. I spoke of this earlier on. In the early 1990s, the death count was five times what it is today, close to 2,500. The rise seemed endless and inexorable; people felt helpless. Then, in cities all over America, a downward curve opened up, and life got safer. Every politician in office, all over the country, took personal credit. In New York, since the administration of David Dinkins, whoever has been mayor, life has got safer. There are at least two generations who didn't do something big that their fathers and their big brothers had done. Do you remember the 1960s phrase, "Picking up the gun"? Well, we've had two generations who didn't pick up the gun, who didn't start shooting. And thousands of live people, young and not so young anymore, who at '60s to '90s death rates would be dead. Does this story have a hero? Yes, those kids: They chose life. How? Why? Can anybody say? It's a mystery, but for once a benign mystery. Kids still get hurt, but now they get to live. Something has happened that neither I nor anyone I knew imagined—something we need to celebrate: a metropolitan life with a level of dread that's subsiding.

I began by talking about the destruction of cities. Now we've moved into what Jay-Z has called the "Empire State of Mind." So I will end with one of the Bible's Empire States of Mind, the story of King Solomon and his Jerusalem. The story is basically told in the first book of Kings, chapters 4 to 11. And it is told in a fascinating voice, important in the history of narratology, the voice of a narrator who feels in awe of Solomon yet is easily scandalized by him and his various policies. The dualism of this voice, surprising in the Bible, prefigures the dualistic voice of the *Great Gatsby*'s Nick Carraway. Here again, the biblical and the modern converge.

Solomon, the first known Jewish intellectual, is famous for what the Bible calls his "largeness of mind." He lectures on the nature of plants, birds, and beasts, creatures of the field; he creates hundreds of proverbs and songs; he attracts a new kind of audience, for both his songs and his ideas. Many of his ideas are about the city. He works to create a city that will be multicultural and cosmopolitan. He wants the Jews to be at home there, by learning to enlarge themselves. His city fills up with diverse people, and those people are meant to interact. The Bible highlights the sexuality of his vision: He loves many women, especially "loves many foreign women." He marries some, takes others as girlfriends, and insists on bringing them all, along with their entourages and dressers and gods, into Jerusalem. He enters an intimate alliance with the glamorous Queen of Sheba; He "answers all her questions" and fathers her child. He gets close to Israel's ex-enemy Egypt, makes many deals with the Pharaoh, and marries his daughter. Sexual awakening is one of the ways this city rises, and he grasps the way sexual feeling can be a cosmopolitan force. Solomon's "largeness of mind" connects him with King Hiram of Tyre

(Lebanon). They create a labor army, where thousands of Jews go to Tyre every year to learn construction skills, and thousands of Lebanese come to Jerusalem. In the new city, Jews and foreigners are at ease with each other. The Jews have traveled and been around; there are foreign men with construction skills, sexy foreign women, enormous building projects, and an abundance of gods. The king builds a great and gorgeous temple for Yahweh, with cedars from Lebanon, but he also builds temples for "those women."

The storyline of Kings is so overcrowded, it's hard to keep track. The narrator complains, there's so much going on, Solomon can't love God "wholeheartedly." This is a crucial word. The new Jerusalem opens up a whole new layer of human problems. We are in a fluid world, full of lush possibilities. Religions, jobs, marriages, all forms of life feel like open questions. In this atmosphere, can anybody be "wholehearted" about anything? Cosmopolitan culture, when it thrives, is scary. But it is also thrilling, and the people love it: "Judah and Israel prospered, as many as the sand on the sea; they ate and drank and were happy." The Bible takes place in an age of monarchy; happiness depends on the ruler. If his successors are petty crooks, as Solomon's are, the whole country falls apart.

Modern times are different in our feeling for democracy, our prejudice in its favor, our belief that it is a source of collective strength. Some of this is prefigured in the Bible. Here is Jeremiah, on the "New Covenant." God tells him, "I will put my law within them, and write it on their hearts." This is a new course for God: to *promote the people*. But it can't happen unless the people understand it, unless they know they are political subjects now. Education is one way to show them. See this grand building, this terrific room, all built from the bedrock they dug up when they dug the New York subways? CCNY is here so people can *come up*, so they can grow up smart as well as handsome, so they can learn to make new covenants and do new things. We're here for them, but also for our whole cosmopolitan city. We want their learning to be *collective learning*. Our students have the right to this, but really our whole city has the right to it. It has the right, whether it knows it or not; it has the right, whether it wants it or not.

New York has a tradition of great dreams. Its urbicidal ruins felt like a cosmic mockery of them all. And yet, by the end of the twentieth century, our city of ruins turned out to be a place where people coming from everywhere were working together. Even as New York fell apart, it rose. People looked into each other's eyes, learned to know each other face to face. If they could get that far, what else can they build?

This essay is adapted from Marshall Berman's last public lecture, the Annual Lewis Mumford Lecture on Urbanism, delivered at the City College of New York on May 2, 2013. It was published in Dissent, *Winter 2014.*

Index